HOPKINS
SPEECH

SPAN - NOV 7
VIDEO   showed
         LBJ Hopkins
         speech

audio   UCSantaBarbara
         Presidency.USb.edu

Summer

GEOPOLITICS (27)

FRANCO-SIAMESE AGREEMENT (27)
MEKONG COMMITTEE (67)
REGIONALISM AS ALTERNATIVE TO
COMMUNISM

1965. MEKONG PROJECT AS 4TH SOLUTION (100)
       & PART OF LBJ PEACE OFFENSIVE

       MEKONG LIMITED TO RVN TO WIN
       HEARTS AND MINDS & LBJ'S
                OTHER WAR

       MEKONG DELTA an essential war
       Plant (55-60% of RVN
                 population)

APRIL 7, 1965: JOHNS HOPKINS SPEECH =
                JOHNSON DOCTRINE

           1968 TET OFFENSIVE upset
                 "JOHNSON" (MARSHALL) PLANS
                 water and economic
                          development

THEME! Water politics
        can be as deadly as
        any other kind of politics

THE MEKONG RIVER AND THE STRUGGLE FOR INDOCHINA

Water, War, and Peace

NGUYEN THI DIEU

PRAEGER

Westport, Connecticut
London

Library of Congress Cataloging-in-Publication Data

Nguyen, Thi Dieu, 1951–
    The Mekong River and the struggle for Indochina ; water, war and
peace / Nguyen Thi Dieu.
      p. cm.
    Includes bibliographical references.
    ISBN 0–275–96137–0 (alk. paper)
    1. Water resources development—Mekong River Valley. 2. Water-
supply—Political aspects—Mekong River Valley. 3. Mekong River
Valley—History. 4. Indochina—History. I. Title.
HD1698.M4N44 1999
333.91′009597—dc21   97–49488

British Library Cataloguing in Publication Data is available.

Library of Congress Catalog Card Number: 97–49488
ISBN: 0–275–96137–0

First published in 1999

Praeger Publishers, 88 Post Road West, Westport, CT 06881
An imprint of Greenwood Publishing Group, Inc.

Printed in the United States of America

The paper used in this book complies with the
Permanent Paper Standard issued by the National
Information Standards Organization (Z39.48–1984).

10 9 8 7 6 5 4 3 2

Uống nước nhớ nguồn,

Ăn quả nhớ kẻ trồng cây.

When we drink from a river,

Let us not forget whence it springs.

When we pick fruit from a tree,

Let us think of the one who planted it.

(Vietnamese proverb)

To Fathers and Mothers on both sides of the Ocean

Contents

Illustrations   ix
Acknowledgments   xi
Introduction   xiii

PART I   *Water*

1.   The Mekong River in Pre-Colonial and Colonial History   3

PART II   *War*

2.   The Mekong River in the Indochina Wars   49
3.   President Johnson's Mekong Enterprise   97
4.   From War to Peace   147

PART III   *And Peace*

5.   The Greater Mekong Region   199

Epilogue   237
Selected Bibliography   243
Index   249

Illustrations

Maps

1.1	The lower Mekong basin: A physical map	4
1.2	Main canals in the Mekong delta	30
1.3	Main canals in Cochinchina	32
4.1	The Mekong Project	173
5.1	The Greater Mekong region	222

Photographs

On the Vinh-te Canal	19
Commercial activities on the Mekong River	198

Acknowledgments

The journey accomplished by this study was a long one that spanned several continents and cultures. It was made possible thanks to the support and advice of family, faithful friends and sage mentors, readers, and critics. To name but a few: Professor Charles Fourniau, who kept me from wandering into unrelated matters and has shown with his own scholarship that the inquiry of the mind never stops and that the object of study must be pursued and reached no matter how long it takes; friends and colleagues in the Association d'Amitié Franco-Vietnamienne, who have never wavered in their love for Vietnam. On this side of the continent, Professor George McT. Kahin was the first to read the early French version of this work and, by his encouraging words, provided inspiration in times of doubt. Professors William J. Duiker, Richard H. Immerman, and William S. Turley patiently read, remarked, and pointed to new directions. My friends and colleagues at Temple University, Professors Philip Evanson, Patricia Jenkins, Wilbert Jenkins (no relation), Arthur Schmidt, and Teshale Tibebu have warmed my world with their friendship and intellectual discourse. I also want to take this opportunity to thank the Lyndon B. Johnson Foundation for its Moody grant and Temple University for its grants and fellowships that have made the preparation of this book possible throughout successive summers among the libraries in France, Vietnam, and the United States; also the Kroch Library of Cornell University and the Lyndon Baines Johnson Library of the University of Texas at Austin, which stand out as immense depositories of documents that are at the same time of easy and pleasant access with helpful and knowledgeable librarians; my families on both sides, who patiently awaited the day when they could see the fruit of my long "gestation"; and, last but not least, my husband, constant companion of my tribulations, a "river man" himself, historian Mark W. McLeod. The maps are the result of Gerard Krieg's painstaking work. To him goes my grateful acknowledgment.

Introduction

The twenty-first century has been referred to as the "Century of Water," since
water will likely become a precious and increasingly scarce commodity for the
teeming populations of the future. Water, whether brought by rain, carried by
rivers, lapping up shores from sea to sea, has already become one of the main
governmental concerns throughout the world. Concurrently, in the last decade,
colossal projects have been launched in Asia to harness the potential of rivers for
power production, irrigation, flood control, and so forth. The control of and access to a river's resources has led to fierce struggles between nation-states that
share the rivers. "Water politics" or "riverine politics" can be a source of contention as devastating as any. The knowledge of history and an understanding of the
varied driving forces can lead to solutions to river-related problems. This is essentially true when dealing with Southeast Asia, a region that has been and continues to be at the heart of war, deadly contentions, and bloody struggles. Three
great conflicts have been fought in these lands during the twentieth century; although peace has returned, it remains fragile, as the Cambodian coup of 1997 reveals. Hence, any element that can contribute to the building and strengthening
of that peace, however tangential, should be nurtured and protected. In this context, the Mekong River, which has recently inspired so many hopes for economic
prosperity, is one such element.

One of the most majestic rivers in Asia, the Mekong River journeys from its
sources in the Tibetan plateau to its mouth in the South China Sea; it also travels
through space and time, through barren lands, across fertile regions that were
transformed by the action of the peoples in their migration into the lower Mekong basin, and in the upheavals of history, into states whose emergence depended in part on their harnessing of water and rivers.

During pre-colonial times, the river's journey into its lower basin did not oc-
cur unheeded by the people who had settled along its banks or those of its tributaries as they adapted themselves to its rhythms and made the river an integral

part of their lives, living with it, from it, and on it. However, there does not seem to have been any attempt at directly harnessing its might for use, since the need was probably never felt and the necessary technological level not yet reached. Before the modern period, harnessing the Mekong's resources was a concept whose time had not come for the riparians of the basin, although they knew of hydraulics, and one of its peoples, the Khmers, perfected hydraulic monuments that formed the basis of the Angkor empire.

As kingdoms and empires succeeded one another, Vietnam, a political entity east of the Mekong, which had millennially absorbed Chinese influence while fighting China's sway, rose to prominence. Its multitudes spilled out of its cradle, the Red River delta, and commenced their march south, crushing Champa and overtaking land that had been part of the Khmer empire. As they reached the Mekong delta, the Vietnamese brought with them in their settlement of the southern land their own approach to water management and to the Mekong River and its resources. Among the many differences that separate the Indianized kingdoms west of the Annamitic Cordillera from Vietnam, the Sinicized state, their divergent approaches to water and to the Mekong River and its resources, dictated both by historical circumstances and by environment, are but one aspect.

As the nineteenth century opened in Asia and Western imperialism provided it with a different, excentered framework, colonial forces, principally the French, began to focus on the Mekong River as the waterway leading into unknown riches and countless numbers of consumers still unreachable deep in the mysterious hinterland of China. The Mekong River and its potential soon acquired an almost mythical status in the milieu of explorers, empire-builders, and politicians. Concurrently, during the colonial era, the river and its lower basin became the focal point of rival interests: France and Great Britain. As territorial boundaries of colonial empires were drawn, set, and sealed by treaties, as the "pacification" phase ended in the crushing of traditional resistance, ushering in stability and control, French authorities turned to the task of colonial exploitation. Using its technology and experience in exploiting indigenous resources and peoples, France launched the first modern efforts to harness the river on a basinwide scale.

The bountiful, fertile, and untapped Mekong delta became the crown jewel of French Indochina. The French, in turn, introduced their own conception of water and river management. The first steps carried out within the framework of the Union Indochinoise were the transformation of the lower Mekong basin's ecology, in particular around the Mekong delta, referred to by the French as Cochinchina, and the way the river was conceived and used as territorial boundary, politico-legal delimitation, and water artery that linked its colonies. The French were to have barely a century in Cochinchina to attempt to harness the river before the First Indochina War put an end to this ambitious and lucrative adventure into a "frontier" region. The harnessing of the Mekong River, a Western concept introduced along with French colonialism, had to await more powerful forces for it truly to begin. Meanwhile, factors of change were at work throughout Southeast Asia, which were to attract a new player to the region.

One would think that the Mekong River, a majestic waterway in the Indochinese peninsula, and the United States of America, the twentieth century's most powerful nation, had nothing in common and were not destined to play any role in each other's realm. Yet, at some point, these two planes intersected and influenced each other in an intricate context that called upon fundamental values and forces. At the end of the Second World War, with the collapse of colonial empires in Asia, when communism seemed to be gaining ground in the struggle opposing the French colonial power to the nationalist movements of Indochina, the United States, perceiving a threat to its sphere of influence, gradually but inescapably intervened in Asia. The two planes—the physical and geographical planes in the case of the Mekong River, and the political and economic planes for the United States—would intertwine, leading to the invasion of the first plane by the second.

As the cold war began to engulf different regions of the world, countries that had become newly independent after long years of war and devastation emerged from the struggle weary, scarred, and in need of rebuilding their economies and societies. Their needs and expectations, combined with the political urgency of the cold war, led to the formation of international organizations and regional committees whose task was to guide these nations toward such goals. They were responsible for conceiving and implementing development projects that were to contribute to the "taking-off" of the newly emerging nations' economies. Among the proposals developed were some emphasizing an intensive and multipurpose utilization of the hydraulic resources of the river basins. In Southeast Asia, the Mekong River and its lower basin were selected as offering the best conditions for such development.

For the first time in the history of the riparian countries, a multipurpose effort was launched to develop the river's resources through a coordinated action among riparian countries, international aid organizations, financial institutions, and contributing nations from outside the region. The Mekong Project, as it came to be known, concerned the riparian nations of Thailand and Laos, as well as Cambodia and Vietnam, which happened to be the main protagonists of the Second Indochina War (indirectly in the case of Thailand). It represented, in the eyes of countries of the lower Mekong basin and of governments outside the region, a possible catalyst for a better economic future and a solution to disruptive social upheavals. As such, the project could not escape being drawn into the war. In fact, it became an important element in U.S. strategy at certain vital turning points of the conflict. Since the most preponderant and tangible manifestation— given its destructiveness—of American intervention in the Vietnam War was military in nature, the United States sought to counter this negative perception with a palliative in the form of economic and financial aid. Within this rationale, the Mekong River and the taming of its resources were to serve a purpose.

This study focuses principally on the period of the Johnson administration and peripherally on that of the Nixon administration, during which the Mekong Project's progress was to reach a decisive pace closely linked to American intervention in Indochina. For Lyndon B. Johnson, a Texan to whom the essentiality of water was self-evident, the Mekong River as well as the project on which it was based offered his embattled administration constructive potentialities reminiscent of the success of the Tennessee Valley Authority (TVA) decades earlier.

Later, as the pendulum swung in the opposite direction with a progressive American disengagement—military and economic—from the region, ending in the momentous events of 1975, the Mekong Project became a peripheral factor in the Nixon strategy in this part of the world. Its progress was adversely affected by the Vietnamization of the war, its potential reduced to a mere bargaining chip in the Paris Peace negotiations. With the ending of the Second Indochina War, the Mekong riparians found themselves at last alone, brothers but enemies, free to decide for themselves their own future, but opting for a Third Indochina War that was to put the Mekong Project in limbo for a time.

The study concludes by assessing the Mekong Project and the river, forty years after the formation of the Mekong Committee, with the echoes of war still faintly rumbling, as the riparian peoples and their governments, with so many needs and so few resources, are attempting to rebuild their lands. They, in turn, are casting a hopeful look at the project, expecting much from it at a time when, because of accumulated knowledge about river damming and its negative impact on the peoples and their environment, mounting opposition to its full harnessing may once again impede the fruition of the Mekong Project as it was first conceived.

In this text, the Mekong River is viewed as an entity of its own that, akin to a physical and temporal ribbon, flows from immemorial times to the present era, mute witness to and immutable presence in the rise and fall of kingdoms, empires, and nation-states. The time frame adopted will be that of the *longue durée* within which the study of the Mekong River's evolution in terms of perception, uses, and management will span Funan to French Indochina to the end of the Indochina Wars. The study will show how, over time, the Mekong River journeyed far, from being an ill-known river, acknowledged only locally as "the Mother of Rivers" or the "Great River," to being embodied in a project that envisions the harnessing of its resources, to perhaps becoming the defining and unifying element of a region increasingly referred to as "the Greater Mekong Subregion"—a river that binds together from north to south, China to Vietnam, and from west to east, Myanmar to Thailand to Laos, Cambodia, and again Vietnam.

PART I

Water

1

The Mekong River in Pre-Colonial and Colonial History

For thousands of years—beginning as early as c. 3500 B.C.E.—the peoples of the lower Mekong basin had founded their societies on rice cultivation, particularly on the cultivation of irrigated or "wet" rice.[1] Two natural elements are most necessary for such cultivation: soil and water. Brought by the monsoons, carried by rivers, water is abundant, but its uneven distribution can lead to drought or to disastrous floods over entire regions of the Mekong basin. The abundance or scarcity of water led to the early existence of flood control, drainage, and irrigation works and their organization into structured practices in some of the societies of the lower Mekong basin.[2] As the Mekong in its southern course flows through present-day Laos, Thailand, Cambodia, and Vietnam, it thus participates in their histories, its importance varying according to the country that it traverses and the use that was made of it.

THE RIVER AND ITS PEOPLES

The Mekong River is the seventh longest river in Asia (4,350 kilometers of which 2,395 kilometers flow through the lower basin); its average annual discharge is 475,000 million cubic meters. Its minimum flow of 1,700 cubic meters per second puts the Mekong in third place, in terms of volume, after the Yangzi and the Ganges-Brahmaputra. The Mekong flows from the Tibetan plateau, southward through the Chinese provinces of Xinjiang and Yunnan, and enters its lower basin as it forms a border between Myanmar, Thailand, and Laos.[3] The lower Mekong basin as defined by the Economic Commission for Asia and the Far East begins near the Burmese town of Chiang Saen and has a drainage area of 620,000 square kilometers (see Map 1.1).[4] It includes nearly all of Laos (207,400 square kilometers), the northern and northeastern regions of Thailand (190,500 square kilometers), nine-tenths of Cambodia (157,800 square kilometers), and one-fifth of Vietnam in the central plateaus and southern delta (64,300

Map 1.1 The lower Mekong basin: A physical map

square kilometers).[5] The Mekong (*Me Kong* or "Mother of Rivers") courses for more than 1,600 kilometers through Laos, of which 920 kilometers form the Thai-Lao border. From the Burmese border to Luang Prabang, the old royal capital, the river weaves its way between narrow gorges and high mountains, interspersed with narrow flood plains and steep drops from rapids to rapids. On its right bank, as it forms the boundary between Laos and Thailand, the Mekong drains the Khorat plateau, which is a "large saucer-shaped basin tilted toward the southeast and surrounded by hills and mountains."[6] Its relative flatness facilitates its crossing from the Lao side into the northeastern region of Thailand. From Vientiane to Savannakhet, as the river flows into a wider and flat plain, there are effectively no insurmountable physical obstacles to the circulation of small boats that link the two cities. In its upper and middle reaches, navigation on the Mekong River cannot be done without numerous transshipments, in particular, between Savannakhet and Kratie, because of the myriad of waterfalls and rapids, of which Khemmarat, Khone, and Sambor are the most important.[7] Some waterfalls, for example, the Sambor or the Khone, stretch for more than ten kilometers. Sandbars, rocky outcrops, and forested islands obstruct the river's course along this stretch.[8] During the rainy season, the river floods its narrow banks and plains, and lacking any outlets for its waters, it has created natural levees behind which can be found rice fields and habitations on stilts.

The Mekong (*Tonle Thom* or "Great River") traverses Cambodia for 480 kilometers, entering a plain that transversally has the shape of a basin, at the bottom of which is the *Tonle Sap* or "Great Lake." During the dry season (November to June), the Tonle Sap, with a surface of 2,700 square kilometers, flows southeast into the Mekong. With the wet season (June to October), monsoon rains cause the river to reverse its course, rising slowly and regularly to pour its overflow northward into the lake, which then expands almost fivefold, to 10,000 square kilometers. The Tonle Sap can absorb 19 percent of the flood volume. The flooded surrounding forests provide rich nutrients for the ichthyologic population that seasonally migrates to the lake to spawn.[9] The lake has brought Cambodians bountiful catches as well as fertile rice fields along its shore.

As it reaches the lowland plains of the delta, the Mekong (*Song Cuu Long* or "Nine Dragons River") placidly meanders for more than 200 kilometers through islands, mangroves, swamps, and alluvial land to finally flow out into the South China Sea. The Mekong delta, strictly speaking, is delimited in the northeast by the two Vamco Rivers; in the northwest, it extends to the confluence of the Mekong and the Tonle Sap, at the Quatre-Bras; in the south, it includes the Ca-mau peninsula.[10] As the river flows out it carries a moderate silt load that contributes to extending the delta southeasterly into the South China Sea. Some of the silt is picked up by a littoral current that also builds up the southwestern coast, which expands into the Gulf of Thailand at the rate of sixty to eighty meters a year.[11] As the Mekong River leaves the Great Lake and veers southeast through the Plain of Reeds (*Dong-thap*), which, in conjunction with the lake, partially absorbs the floodwaters, it divides itself into two parts: the easterly and main branch (*Tien-giang* or Mekong proper), which flows into the South China Sea through six mouths, and the westerly tributary (*Hau-giang* or Bassac), which reaches the sea through three mouths.[12] Small, sandy islands overgrown with mangroves dot the horizon at the river's mouths. The delta has a weak slope of 1 percent and is less than five meters above sea level.[13] As a result, there are strong tidal currents that lap upstream to the shores of Phnom-Penh. The existence of strong tides and of the floods facilitates navigation in the delta all year round.[14] During the rainy season, from May to September and October, the delta from Dong-thap to the Dong-nai River, and to the Gulf of Thailand in the west, is flooded over a vast area of more than one million hectares. Floodwaters rise slowly and, in most years, are not a threat to the riparians and their properties as they are absorbed by the Tonle Sap, the two Vamco Rivers, the Mekong, and the Bassac as well as by the natural arroyos and artificial canals.[15] But in years of heavy snowfalls (in Tibet) and rainfalls, the Mekong floods can be devastating.

In terms of climatic influence, the lower Mekong basin is influenced by the monsoon climate. The winter monsoon, which blows from the northeast, from November to March, travels south across the center of Vietnam, along the southern coast, across Cambodia and Laos, bringing dry air with rare rainfalls averaging less than eight millimeters a month. After a transition period from April to May, the summer monsoon from the southwest brings to the area abundant rains averaging 299 millimeters a month during the period from May to September.[16] Within this monsoon context, the river may be divided into two parts. The upstream region from the river's source in the Tibetan plateau to Kratie in Cambodia is the catchment basin for the river through its numerous tributaries and the monsoon rains in the summer. From its source in Tibet to its lower plains, the Mekong drains numerous tributaries (e.g., Nam Tha, Nam Beng, Nam Ou, Nam Ngum, Nam Theun) east and west, flowing down from the Annamitic chain and from the Khorat plateau. These tributaries create small and large alluvial plains that support a dense farming population.

Flood waters discharge downstream below Kratie, submerging the banks and the delta.[17] The monsoon rains and the Mekong River, including its many tributaries, are the main sources of abundant water for the region, however unevenly distributed. The most watered part of the lower Mekong basin is located in the southwest, on the slopes of the Annamitic chain. The most arid regions are the Khorat plateau and the Mekong plain, especially the Great Lake area where the rainfall level is below 1,000 millimeters a year, (the necessary minimum for wet-rice cultivation is 1,500 millimeters annually); additionally, its "irregularity, poor seasonal distribution and high evaporation are just as important obstacles to successful agriculture as low rainfall."[18] The insufficiency or even lack of rainfall can be disastrous when such a shortage occurs during the one or two months preceding rice cultivation but the more so during the time of the rice plant's highest need, that is, while it reaches maturity. Conversely, the concentration of rainfall at a particular moment of the year can lead to severe flooding, a phenomenon that riparians have lived with since time immemorial. The floods destroy crops and cause great damage to property.

FROM FUNAN TO ANGKOR

Water management or water control has been part of Asian civilizations for a long time, in particular, in China, India, Sri-Lanka, and Myanmar, where water-works up to a thousand years old endure and are still in use. Monarchs of Southeast Asia, driven by religious as well as socioeconomic forces, ordered the construction of vast irrigation networks, water tanks, dams, and sluices as recorded in innumerable bas-reliefs, temple inscriptions, and steles. At the same time, indispensable but often unrecorded and unacknowledged, villagers perfected water-management skills to levels that could sometimes give rise to whole hierarchical institutions overseeing the apportioning and pricing of water or the maintaining of the waterworks. These works made the most of an environment where water was insufficient, irregular ("the Dry Zone"), or too abundant by capturing, retaining, providing, or draining it away at the most critical times for the cultivation. What is striking, however, is that although small rivers were harnessed, earthen dams built, dikes and sluices erected to protect fields and habitations, in almost all cases, these were built in side-valleys because the pre-modern technical level had not yet made possible the harnessing of great rivers like the Ganges, the Brahmaputra, the Irrawaddy, or the Yangzi. Almost all, if not all, of these waterworks made use of the topography, exploited the gravitational pull of valley slopes, and diverted small rivers or tributaries, but no dams ever straddled the big rivers of Asia before modern times.[19] Even the Chinese civilization that had developed a millennial knowledge of water control never dared to directly harness its two giants, the Yellow River and the Yangzi (until the advent of the twentieth century and the Three Gorges Dam).[20] What then of the Mekong River and its riverine peoples?

The lower Mekong basin has witnessed the formation of numerous polities that succeeded one another, some lasting centuries and stretching over the entire lower basin, such as Funan, Chen La, and the splendid Angkor empire; others, more compact but existing still, such as Vietnam or Thailand, the latter of relatively recent formation and eager to challenge the political sway of declining empires.[21] All of these polities were heavily influenced by India, with the exception of Vietnam, which drew upon China's experience. Chinese and Indian influences were manifested in various aspects, for example, government, social structures, economy, and the arts. Naturally, the assimilation of knowledge from afar did not mean that it was absorbed wholesale, unalloyed and unchanged, permeating every aspect of the newly emerging polities. On the contrary, the peoples of the lower Mekong basin, sometimes at the state level, sometimes at the village level, interpreted, adapted, and syncretized Indian and Chinese contributions with pre-existing native elements, be they cultural such as religious beliefs, or material factors such as topography, climate, or hydrology. Artifacts scattered throughout the basin bear testimony to such processes of assimilation and adaptation. Prominent among these are remnants of hydraulic works that show that the peoples of the lower Mekong had a long familiarity with water management—for domestic consumption, flood control, drainage, and irrigation. Archaeologist Janice Stargardt has shown that irrigation had been in practice in ancient Burma, in the Irrawaddy valley, even before the advent of India in the region and that Pyu cities had evolved "from irrigated villages to irrigated towns and cities, long before the appearance of Indian cultural influences."[22]

Laos is a mountainous land without any direct access to the sea except through its neighbor to the east, Vietnam (China Sea), or its neighbor to the west, Thailand (Gulf of Thailand). It is delimited in the east by the Annamitic chain and in the west by the Mekong River, which forms a political border—imposed by the French—with Thailand. After leaving Myanmar, the river enters upper Laos, which is divided transversely by deep valleys formed by tributaries flowing from the Annamitic chain, such as the Nam Tha, Nam Beng, or Nam Ou, which form alluvial plains large enough for wet-rice cultivation. In its upper and middle reaches, the Mekong links north and south Laos as a waterway, as it courses along narrow, rocky corridors, down tumultuous cascades and over vast stretches of sandbar, making any journey difficult and arduous. The river flows through a broken relief that mirrors the related ethnic fragmentation. The opposition between highlands and plains is evidenced in human terms by the differences between peoples of the plains and those of the mountains, between ethnic Lao and nonethnic Lao groups.

The mountaintops are sparsely populated with Tibeto-Burman ethnic groups collectively known as *Lao Soung* or Lao of the mountain peaks, who lived by means of slash-and-burn cultivation of corn, rice, and opium, as well as by gathering and hunting.[23] This slash-and-burn practice is partially responsible for the gradual disappearance of forests, as is most visible in the region of Phong Saly in northern Laos.[24] The Mon-Khmer-speaking *Lao Theung* or Lao of the mountainsides were cultivators of dry rice, corn, tobacco, and cotton within an economy of self-subsistence and commercial exchanges with the lowland merchants.[25] Lower in the plains and valleys, along the narrow but fertile banks of the Mekong, population density increases in settlements of Tai-Lao ethnic groups (the *Lao Loum* or Lao of the plains) that became sedentarized and formed a civilization of villages whose livelihood depended on wet rice cultivation, fishing, and trade along riverbanks.[26]

The difference between plain and mountain ethnic groups is reflected, among many aspects, in the use of rivers. Mountain ethnic groups seldom use the full hydraulic power of rivers and streams in rice cultivation, since they practice mostly dry rice cultivation. When they do divert a stream, as in the case of the Man or the Hmong, it is only on a small scale: Waterfalls and streams are diverted by bamboo tubes to power rudimentary corn or rice mills.[27] One Tai group, the Tai Dam of the Lao Loum, practice irrigation for their wet-rice terraced fields along mountainsides.[28] As one descends, irrigation techniques become more sophisticated. Flooding of the narrow plains by the Mekong River and its tributaries contributes to the fertilization of the fields through silt deposits, but it was mainly the practice of irrigation that allowed year-round wet-rice cultivation, which resulted in a permanent settlement pattern. In Laos, the premodern development of irrigation practices was confined to the village level and did not have the state-controlled, centralized character of the great Angkorean irrigation works. Agricultural hydraulics remained at the village level and never entered Laotian history as an element contributing to the formation of a Lao political entity.

Yet the kingdom of Lan Xang (Kingdom of the Million Elephants), founded in 1353 by Fa Ngum, a Laotian prince who was raised at the Cambodian court, probably knew of hydraulics, since it was influenced by its southerly neighbor, the Khmer empire—of the late Angkor period—with the introduction of Theravada Buddhism and Khmer arts, as well as the attempt to superimpose an urban model over the pre-existing village communities of the valleys and plains.[29] The birth of the kingdom of Lan Xang in the fourteenth century, with its center at Luang Prabang, began with the conquest by the Lan Xang king, the *Cao Sivit* (Lord of Life), of the myriad Tai principalities that had existed prior to its formation.[30] The kingdom of Lan Xang, spoken of in glowing terms by Western missionaries and travelers, shone for more than three centuries, despite internal weaknesses and external aggression from its neighbors, east and west. However, in the Laotian context, from mountains to valleys to narrow plains, in a mosaic of ethnic groups and small rival princedoms, Lan Xang was condemned by the very nature of its political structures—diffuse authority and lack of centrally appointed bureaucracy—to fragmentation.[31] Only one other king in the seventeenth century, Souligna Vongsa, was capable of restoring the magnificence of Lan Xang with its capital at Vientiane.[32] At his death in 1694, Lan Xang began to dissolve back into a number of smaller Laotian political entities albeit still under the nominal control of a Lao suzerain. This political fragmentation became its fate for the centuries to come until the twentieth century.[33] The lack of permanent centralizing structures may have impeded the formation and organization by the state of agricultural hydraulic systems on the scale of the Angkorean ones. Unlike Vietnam or Thailand, which had risen from fertile, large, and populous deltas, Laos had only scarcely populated narrow plains and high mountains to contend with, physical obstacles that may have precluded the development of a centralized state and a centralized hydraulic apparatus.[34]

According to Lao historian Keo Mannivanna, in pre-colonial Laos water control may have existed only at the village level where "the most important activity was irrigated rice cultivation. It was essential to coordinate the period when water was available with the period when rice plants needed water. For this purpose, an ingenious system of canals drained water away from the fields and controlled its inflow."[35] These village economies also lived on fishing, hunting, handicrafts, and, when agricultural activities permitted, trade along the Mekong

River and its tributaries and even beyond, with Cambodia, for such products as musk, benzoin, and gold.[36] No large-scale hydraulic works such as weirs, artificial reservoirs, or water drainage systems for agricultural purposes had been built by the state, although the existence of canals in Vientiane (an ancient Khmer stronghold from the eleventh to the thirteenth century that became the capital of Lan Xang in the sixteenth century) was mentioned by a Catholic priest, Father de Marini, in a travel account that was published (in French) in 1666 and entitled *New and Curious Story of the Kingdoms of Tunquing and Laos.*[37]

In general, the main concern of the Laotian kings of Lan Xang was the defensive possibilities offered by the Mekong rather than the thought of its economic potential; the fear of invaders may have been stronger than the will to enrich themselves. A Laotian monarch, aware of the natural protection provided by rivers and mountains, rejected suggestions made by a Jesuit priest to erect sluices along the Mekong River to facilitate the crossing of waterfalls as "it would amount to giving the key of his Kingdom to his enemies, and by this means, the door that was always shut in by these precipices would be opened to them as often as they wished; and without their encountering any resistance."[38] Nonetheless, throughout centuries, while the Mekong River always posed innumerable and almost insurmountable obstacles to foreign invasion, it was used by the riparians in all seasons in varying degrees of difficulty, from north to south, from Ban Huei Sai to the Khone Falls, and was traveled by Laotian merchants transporting on boats or rafts products that they exchanged with the people of the high plains.[39] The Mekong and its many tributaries in Laos formed a link between different valleys and between rural, dispersed communities separated by physical obstacles. Thus, Luang Prabang (formerly Xieng Thong), at the confluence of the Mekong and of several of its tributaries in eastern upper Laos, constituted the heartland of Laos until the sixteenth century.

In contrast to Laos, Thailand has only a part of its territory in the Mekong basin, the Northeast, also known as the Khorat plateau. Most of the people of the Khorat plateau are different linguistically and culturally from the Thai of the Central Plain and are nearer to the Lao on the left bank of the Mekong. The Northeast and its predominantly Lao population were referred to by the Pali-Sanskrit name of *Isan*, while the people of the Northeast referred to themselves as *Khon Isan* or *Phu Isan* (the Isan people).[40] Over the centuries, the Khorat plateau has witnessed the rise and fall of kingdoms as shown by findings that speak of ancient settlements (at Ban Chieng and Non Nok Tha) going back to the Neolithic period.[41] It is even postulated to have been a transit region between the Chao Phraya and the Mekong for travelers going to and from India and China. During the time of the Chen La and Angkor empires, the Northeast was populated by the Khmers and Khmer-influenced city-states.[42] Later, the formation of the Sukhotai kingdom in the thirteenth century and then of the Ayuthaya kingdom in the fourteenth century led to the strengthening of the Tai presence and, conversely, to the weakening of the Angkor empire in the east. With the political realignment of kingdoms and territories along the Mekong River, the Northeast region of Thailand became a fluctuating stake of and a battlefield between two rival powers in the successive wars. The Lao kingdom of Lan Xang conflicted with that of Ayuthaya, and Fa Ngum, the Laotian prince, in his victorious ascent along the Mekong valley, took over the lands of the Khorat plateau. He ordered the resettlement of some 20,000 Laotian families north of the plateau and in the vicinity of Vientiane in order to affirm the Laotian presence. Laotian influence spread along both banks of the Mekong. It was only later that the Siamese thrust eastward started and became ever more insistent.

The Khorat plateau has thus belonged, at various times, to different Indian-ized states. This Indianized influence may be reflected in the existence of hy-draulic works, although modern interpretations of their usage (agricultural versus domestic) differ. Its saucer-shaped basin and the monsoon-arresting influence of the Dangkrek mountains in the southeast make it one of the driest regions of the lower Mekong basin. Artifacts found in the valleys of two Mekong main tribu-taries in the Northeast, the Mun and Chi, show the adaptability of the people to their environment. Although no center of empire arose in the Northeast of Thai-land, the tradition of water management existed there, albeit perhaps not as a state-managed institution but as practiced individually by the farmer or by agri-cultural communities.[43] It was founded on the construction of canals and large round moats that stored water for domestic consumption during the dry season. Farmers used the canals and moats for transportation and drew sustenance from them (fishing, aquatic vegetables, fruit trees along the banks). W. J. Van Liere, a hydraulic engineer, argues that these constructions were not used for irrigation and hence did not serve the goal of agricultural production, since in the early centuries, farmers mostly practiced the cultivation of flood rice—in an environ-ment of floodplains—that does not require irrigation but has only to be broad-casted during the inundation.[44]

Artifacts of the same nature as those found in the Mun and Chi basins have been excavated in relation to the nearby—although not within the confines of the Mekong valley—thirteenth-century kingdom of Sukhotai, north of the Chao Phraya basin. Sukhotai's environment was somewhat similar to that of the Mun-Chi basins: drained by a number of rivers (Ping, Yom, and Nan) but nevertheless rather arid and infertile because of infrequent rainfall and its upland location.[45] According to Srisakra Vallibhotama, the city of Sukhotai "was no doubt heavily influenced by the Khmer-type settlements of the northeast" and, as such, was equipped with moats, a large-scale irrigation network, and ponds.[46] The author's point—that "its intricate irrigation network was not built for agriculture but mainly for trapping and storing water for consumption throughout the year"—seems to parallel Van Liere's argument about the Mun and Chi artifacts.[47] Never-theless, we may conclude at this point that, whether the irrigation network and the moats were destined to serve agricultural production or domestic water con-sumption, they are the embodiments of a relative mastery of water control.

Until the seventeenth century, the Northeast was able to escape the ascen-dancy of the Ayuthaya kingdom as it continued to receive the influence of the

Laotian culture brought by successive migratory waves. However, from the seventeenth century on, this independent development away from the influence of the Central Plain and of Bangkok ended as the result of several factors. The disintegration of Lan Xang's unity into rival Laotian principalities (Champassak, Vientiane, Xieng Khouang, and Luang Prabang) in the eighteenth century signaled a growing inability to defend itself against Burmese and Siamese invasions and annexations, at the end of which these vassal-kingdoms were transformed into mere Siamese provinces in the nineteenth century.[48] The advent of the colonial powers in the nineteenth century made it possible for Siam (under the Chakri dynasty) to free itself from the Burmese threat on its western border and to devote itself entirely to the consolidation of its territory. These external upheavals were accompanied by an internal change in the attitude of Bangkok vis-à-vis its peripheral provinces. A series of reforms were instituted by the Chakri dynasty, in particular by Chulalongkorn (Rama V), the most important of which was the administrative reform that fundamentally modified the relations between, on one hand, the capital with its Thai-educated governmental elite and, on the other hand, the peripheral regions with its various ethnic groups. The administrative centralization led to the shift of power from the provinces to Bangkok and to the replacement of local leaders, the *chao muong*, by bureaucrats from and of the capital.

In the twentieth century, the loss of the decision-making power and autonomy by the peripheral provinces was further accentuated by two concomitant factors: the construction of a large communication network that ended the geographical isolation of the regions, and the propagation of public education, which allowed the diffusion among different ethnic groups of the concept of nationhood and of loyalty to the sovereign. As the result of its administrative integration, the Northeast was forced to align itself along Bangkok's guidelines and no longer had a voice in the decision-making process concerning its future. Yet, it did not benefit from this integration, since its interests were not taken into account by the government in its economic developmental efforts, and its Isan leaders were looked upon with contempt by the Bangkok hierarchy. This neglect by Bangkok of the distant and impoverished Northeast resulted in the rise of a Communist-influenced insurgency during the cold war period.

After leaving Laos and Thailand's Northeast, the Mekong River enters a country with an almost flat relief. Unlike in Laos, water in Cambodia, in the form of irregular rainfall, seasonal floods of the Mekong and its tributaries, or flooding of the central plain by the lakes, has always been foremost in the country's life. Necessary for cultivation—particularly of rice—for the renewal of fields by silt deposits, and for fishing—the other main economic activity of the peasants—water is an integral part of Cambodia's history. Its insufficiency is acutely felt the longer the dry season lasts. Under its god-kings and thanks to the labor of thousands, Cambodia, over centuries, made agricultural hydraulics the basis of its economic prosperity and political power. It was hydraulics that inspired the great Khmer works, to which the splendid vestiges of Angkor bear witness. Water control has a long tradition in the history of Cambodia and is a reflection of the capacity of the people of the lower basin to adapt to their environment as the centers of empire shifted. Already manifested in the pre-Angkorean period, at the time of the polity referred to in Chinese records as Fu Nan (Kingdom of the Mountain) from the first through the sixth centuries, located in the flat alluvial plains of the Mekong delta, agricultural hydraulic techniques were extremely sophisticated and were proof of an unquestionable mastery of the waters.[49] Funan was a prosperous commercial power (or powers) with an agricultural foundation based on the cultivation of a delta often flooded in the summer and invaded by salt water. There were canal networks for draining swamps and salt water and for irrigating fields; these networks made possible the development of a region that would otherwise have been infertile and conquered by swamps and salt water mangroves.[50] These canals also served as waterways that linked the Gulf of Thailand to the South China Sea, bypassing the Ca-mau point and thus shortening the journey for merchants and pilgrims who traveled between India and China.[51] When the kingdom of Chen La—or rather the collection of small principalities that were referred to by the Chinese under the all-inclusive, monolithic name of "Chen La"—arose in the sixth through the eighth centuries, the center of empire shifted to higher ground, to the drier, more arid plains of northern Cambodia and to the upper reaches of the Mekong River.[52] The problem of flooding and saline intrusion was no longer relevant but gave way to that of securing year-round water availability for agricultural needs as well as domestic consumption. Consequently, colossal moats used as water reservoirs for the long dry season were built close to the Mekong tributaries—such as the Stung Sen or the Se Mun—to fulfill such needs.[53]

The Cambodian climate with its uneven yearly and geographic distribution of water—torrents of water during four months and almost total drought the rest of the year—has shaped the country's economic life for centuries. Its history was founded on agricultural hydraulics raised to the level of a cult exemplified by the Angkor civilization that dominated the Mekong basin for several centuries.[54] In the ninth century, Yaçovarman I, the founder of the first city of Angkor (the City), which was then known as Yaçodharapura, laid the foundations of this Angkorean hydraulic system by building more than 800 fountains in the city. In addition, there was also a huge network of canals and reservoirs that crisscrossed the region of the Siem Reap River, and, for instance, the Eastern Baray (Yaçodharatatâka), an artificial lake of seven kilometers in length and over two kilometers in width, with a capacity of forty million cubic meters that made possible a regular irrigation of the neighboring rice fields.[55] Van Liere theorizes that these were theocratic hydraulics, ordained by *deva-raja* as symbolical offerings to the gods and as reflections of the king's power and munificence.[56] With the rise of the Angkor empire and the spread of the Khmer culture, agricultural hydraulics became more sophisticated as farmers learned to build earthen works to "retain, retard, spread or deflect water during the rainy season."[57] They also adapted to the topography, to water availability, and to soil fertility by resorting to different techniques of cultivation (e.g., field-bunding), to multiple rice varieties, and so forth.

Under the reign of Udhayatiya-Varman II (1050–1066), who was the founder of the second Angkor, another Baray, the Western Baray of eight kilometers by two and a half kilometers, was built west of the city for religious and economic reasons.[58] According to French historian Achille Dauphin-Meunier:

Until the fifteenth century, the Khmer monarchs had always ordered the construction of immense ornamental lakes or *sras*, in general, near large villages or caravan halts in order to regulate the irrigation system of rice fields and to provide bathing spots for elephants and buffaloes used as means of transport during the dry season, when ponds and streams were dried up. Therefore, the population had its main means of subsistence insured and trade was not hindered.[59]

Successors to Yaçovarman I continued his work and carried it further by enlarging, adapting, and juxtaposing successive networks all around the different Angkor groups and by building other monumental barays northeast and southwest of the capital.[60] However, it was under Jayavarman VII (end of the twelfth, beginning of the thirteenth century) that this agricultural and urban hydraulic system reached its zenith. Angkor Thom was crisscrossed by internal canals separated by sluices and temporary dams. According to a sixteenth-century Portuguese chronicler, Diego Da Couto, boats from the heartland carrying supplies traveled along these waterways.[61] Water from the reservoirs was brought either by the monsoons or by rivers such as the Siem Reap or the Mekong. These hydraulic works, which extended from the heart of Angkor Thom and spread far around in the surrounding countryside, had several purposes: They brought potable water to the city and carried away its sewage, and they facilitated traffic inside and outside the Angkorean city and protected it from annual flooding by the lakes and the Mekong River. They made possible an intensive cultivation of the rich silt lands that sprawled on more than 5,000 hectares of the Angkorean plain.[62] Bernard Philippe Groslier thus described the region: "The entire region of Angkor was meticulously divided into square rice-fields . . . that were irrigated by the always visible network . . . of collectors and sub-collectors that brought water from rivers and barays to the tiniest plots. Thanks to this organization, the Angkor region was abundantly wealthy."[63]

A thirteenth-century Chinese traveler to Cambodia, Chou Ta-kuan, who sailed down the coast of Vietnam, up the Mekong, into the Great Lake and arrived at Angkor in 1296 in the wake of a Chinese mission, mentioned that it was generally possible to have three to four harvests per year![64] This pattern of hydraulic organization repeated itself from Angkor to distant regions of Cambodia, even into Laos and the Khorat plateau. Everywhere, the Khmer people's foremost concern was to build reservoirs in order to ensure fertile rice fields as illustrated by countless inscriptions on stele, such as the following: "Concerned by the welfare of the people, he built . . . a drainage ditch, a dike and a basin for the prosperity of the region."[65] A certain level of prosperity was brought to city-dwellers and to peasants, made possible the development of vast territories, anchored temples and villages, and contributed thus to the expansion of the kingdom.[66] This agricultural wealth formed the basis of Khmer economy and power and permitted the civilization of Angkor to reach such levels of brilliance.

However, this "hydraulic civilization" carried within itself the seeds of its own destruction as it relied almost entirely on a regularly maintained hydraulic system, at both the state and village level. Canals and barays (artificial lakes or reservoirs) had to be regularly dredged to prevent their silting, and earth dams and dikes had to be continually reinforced. A combination of human factors and natural catastrophes resulted in a deadly crisis that led to the decline and then to the extinction of the Angkor empire toward the middle of the fourteenth century. Concurrently with repeated invasions from the east—the Cham sacking of Angkor in 1177–1178—and from the west—the Siamese attacks from Ayuthaya between 1350 and 1430—that destroyed villages and temples as well as water works, successive Mekong floods seriously damaged artificial lakes, reservoirs, and canals whose maintenance had been neglected. These floods, which took place under Jayavarman IX, remained in people's memories as the "Angkorean floods." Barays and canals became obstructed, and the practice of multiple cropping every year, made possible by permanent irrigation, slowly gave way to one crop, and then culture by irrigation became dry culture.[67] B. P. Groslier notes that, in addition to invasions and floods, the Khmer irrigation system was threatened by siltation as it relied almost exclusively on rivers that carry a heavy silt volume and flow through slightly sloped plains. After a number of years, the silted river was bound to shift its bed, ineluctably condemning to obsolescence any hydraulic system, and any city that depended on it. Groslier even argues that the fall of Angkor was partly brought on by an imbalance in the ecosystem that was caused by the extension of irrigated rice fields and hydraulic cities into formerly forested land in Cambodia as well as by the ravages caused by malaria, which must have been rampant along the banks of stagnant canals.[68]

The Angkor site near the Tonle Sap presumably had been chosen because of the proximity of potable water, of easy land settlement, and of mineral ores (iron in particular) as well as abundant fish catches from the lake.[69] Angkor's kings may equally have gauged the importance of the Mekong and its tributaries as possible communication arteries between the regions and, particularly, between Champa and the heart of the Khmer empire, fluvial roads that could bring invading armies and devastation to the city. They chose, hence, to build Angkor not on the banks of the Mekong or on the shores of the Great Lake, despite its bountifulness, but slightly inland, away from water-borne invasions, near the Siem Reap River.[70] Eventually, however, this precaution did not save Angkor from being sacked by the Cham invaders who sailed up "the Mekong, the Great Lake, and the Siem Reap River, taking the city of Yaçodharapura by surprise."[71] Its inhabitants may have fled Angkor in the wake of incessant Siamese attacks that cumulated in the final abandonment of the "City" in 1444; the center of empire may have shifted to the south, but the Great Lake's shores had continuously nourished its riparians by bringing abundant halieutic as well as rice harvests. In response to the particularities of the lake, the farmers developed a sophisticated "flood retardation" system that allowed them to cultivate lotus and rice in an environment of widespread flooding during the rainy season.[72] In fact, Angkor retained a fascination for its people, and it was briefly reoccupied in the sixteenth century by King Satha (in 1550), during whose reign the irrigation system was restored.

Thanks to the hydraulic policy of its kings, a policy that stretched over many centuries, Cambodia was able to enjoy great prosperity. Khmer hydraulic policies took into account the short length of the rainy season and the long dry months by organizing reservoirs, basins, dikes, and rice fields under the authority of the god-kings, dispensers of water and hence of life.[73] But the moment that the Angkorean hydraulic system was forsaken and fell prey to sand and vegetation, rice fields that had previously spread over millions of hectares turned into dusty and infertile land, and Angkor, once the center of empire, was deserted by its population. With the hydraulic and economic decline came the end of the Angkorean power and the end of a brilliant—and unique—period in Cambodian history, a time placed under the signs of water and of agricultural hydraulics. Anthropologist Francesca Bray concludes that kingdoms of Southeast Asia, and particularly the Angkor empire, which so heavily relied on irrigation networks and waterworks, used techniques and skills that had been existent at the local level and "were able to increase the scale of such works, but did not develop new technologies which would have enabled them to adapt to more challenging environments."[74] The striking fact concerning the water control works of Angkor or of the Mun or Chi cultures of the Northeast of Thailand is that they dealt with tributaries, small-scale rivers, and streams but none directly harnessed great, powerful rivers like the Mekong or the Chao Phraya. Bray asserts that "it was not until the colonial era that attempts to master the great rivers of Southeast Asia and to drain their deltas became feasible."[75]

Moving downstream, we enter the Mekong delta, whose ancient history belongs to what archeologist Louis Malleret calls the "Oc-Eo civilization," that is, a civilization belonging to a maritime Funan of the second to the seventh centuries. Based on his excavations, Malleret theorizes that Oc-Eo, located in the Transbassac, near the present town of Rach-gia, was a prosperous city and harbor that was part of a great maritime trade current between the Indian Ocean and the Mediterranean Sea.[76] Mention was also made of a vast network of canals for navigation and irrigation or drainage that crisscrossed the city.[77] An ethnically eclectic population of Malayo-Polynesian and Mon-Khmer descents (Jarai, Ede, Churu, etc.) had settled the land long before the Khmer and the Vietnamese's successive arrivals.[78] Some ethnic groups had assimilated into the Indianized polities of Funan and Chen La; others had remained independent.[79] As the Khmer migrated away from Angkor to the proximity of Phnom-Penh, some moved farther southeast to the Mekong delta. With the focusing of the center farther south and farther east—first at Louvek, then at Udong—the Mekong delta had come under closer Khmer scrutiny, though not perhaps under tighter Khmer administrative control.

Meanwhile, in the north, toward the end of the sixteenth century, as civil war raged in the Vietnamese lands causing death and severe damage to the dikes and irrigation systems of the Red River delta, peasants began to leave the confines of their overpopulated villages to seek better opportunities in the distant south, that is, in Central Vietnam, a territory that the Vietnamese had conquered from Champa.[80] Traveling mostly by sea in small junks hugging the coastline, or on foot from valleys to plains, these settlers moved first into the coastal land of Central Vietnam. There were those who made it farther into the Dong-nai delta, settling down in Ba-ria (or Mo-xoai) in the eastern delta, or slightly farther inland, in Bien-hoa, leaving the higher regions to the earlier ethnic groups. The Vietnamese migration of the sixteenth to seventeenth centuries to the south operated on the levels of individuals, extended families, and villages, all of whom were allowed to move as they pleased by the Nguyen authorities, who held the south but had not yet begun to sponsor or organize migration to the region.[81] Even with the strengthening of the Nguyen lords' control over central and southern Vietnam in the later centuries, Vietnamese settlers could still put down their roots at will, having only to notify the authorities that a certain piece of land had been brought under cultivation.[82] The overall movement of migration, conquest, and settlement of southward lands out of the Red River delta, which ended west of the Mekong delta, is termed the *Nam Tien* or Southern Expansion.

The peoples that composed the ethnic fabric of the Mekong delta were the former inhabitants of the south along with the Cham, the Khmer, and the newly arrived Vietnamese and Chinese, the latter fleeing in the aftermath of the collapse of the Ming dynasty in the seventeenth century. It is not known whether or to what degrees these populations mingled and interacted during the early years of their occupation of the delta. It is clear, however, that, very quickly, each ethnic group formed a separate settlement under a separate legal and administrative authority. Moving into territories that had been Khmer, the Vietnamese were initially in no position to seize control over the land. Diplomatic relations between the Khmer kingdom of Udong and the rising house of Nguyen, located in Thuanhoa, Central Vietnam, had been of mutual dependency, each too weak to defeat the other. One of the first mentions made by Khmer sources of official Khmer-Vietnamese contacts concerning the delta relates the fact that in 1618, the king of Cambodia, Prea Cheychesda, married a Vietnamese princess.[83] The newly elevated king, in order to balance Siamese pressure, sought and obtained Vietnamese support. In exchange, the Nguyen prince, Nguyen Phuc Nguyen (1613–1635), requested permission in 1623 to set up trading and customs posts in the Khmer provinces of Prei Kor and Kas Krobey, in the southern delta, the revenues of which would finance the Vietnamese settlement.[84]

During the Nam Tien, as they slowly moved south, battling the Tonkin-based Trinh lords and suffering many reversals, the Nguyen princes began to use prisoners of war to clear the land as their armies strengthened their hold in Central

Vietnam.[85] The *Dai Nam Thuc Luc* (Veritable records of Dai Nam), the Nguyen dynasty's official chronicle, mentioned, for instance, that in 1648, the Nguyen ruler, Nguyen Phuc Lan, remarked that "if we put the captured soldiers on this land, give them oxen and farm implements, provide them with food to eat, and let them clear the land, then in several years they could produce enough for their own needs."[86] These prisoners of war were among the first Vietnamese to be put to use by the government to clear the new land and set up villages. In 1698, a Nguyen prince named Nguyen Phuc Chu (1691–1725) ordered a high official named Nguyen Huu Kinh (or Canh) to take charge of the colonization of the south, thus establishing the prefecture of Gia-dinh. To facilitate the migration, "the Nguyen ruler began to recruit wealthy people from Quang Nam, Dien Ban, Quang Ngai and Quy Nhon to move to the Gia-dinh area. They cut down the trees, cleared and leveled the land, and rendered it fertile for planting. The government let the people occupy the land freely, to plant betel nut trees and build their own houses."[87] The *Gia Dinh Thanh Thong Chi* (History of the Gia Dinh region) noted that the Nguyen government, in order to attract settlers, was easy, generous, and uncomplicated administratively toward those who wanted to open up new fields, found villages, and own land as long as they paid their taxes, which were lighter than in the other regions.[88]

In the course of their wars against the rival Trinh house and against the rebel Tay-son, the Nguyen shifted troops from regional divisions (*dinh*) like Phu-yen and Khanh-hoa in Central Vietnam to the southern *dinh* of Dong-nai—Gia-dinh. Given the high numbers of Nguyen troops in the south and the necessity of procuring food for them, the Nguyen lords began ordering soldiers to clear land for cultivation with a view toward obtaining self-sufficiency in foodstuffs.[89] In 1711, at a time when the Khmer kingdom was rapidly declining and no longer in a position to defend its territory, the Nguyen prince ordered individual settlers "to settle down in the military divisions of Tran Bien Dinh (Bien-hoa area) and Phan Tran Dinh (Gia-dinh area). He gave them land, let them set up villages, and exempted them for three years from taxes, corvée, rent, and military duties."[90] Later, as they battled the Tay-son, the Nguyen princes systematically put settlers to work, forming *don dien*, military colonies set up by peasant-soldiers aimed at extending Vietnamese influence by cultivation and defense of new lands that were to stretch beyond the Dong-nai and Gia-dinh, into the Mekong delta properly speaking, in the southwest, that is, into Khmer territory.[91] Thus, this *don dien* policy was reinforced in 1790 when Nguyen Anh, after taking over Gia-dinh, decreed that it be mandated to ensure food supply for his troops. This *Nam Tien*, which was spearheaded by individuals, families, and now by the authorities, reached its end toward the middle of the eighteenth century in the Transbassac region, dangerously close to the Khmer kingdom. From that point onward, the Vietnamese pressure to take over the land from the other ethnic groups and, in particular, from the Khmer, mounted. From 1802 onward, it was supported by the Nguyen family in its new status as dynastic rulers of a united Vietnam.[92]

On the Vinh-te Canal

Upon founding the new Nguyen dynasty in 1802, Gia-long (as Nguyen Anh was henceforth known) set about to exploit the resources of this new frontier land. His successors followed in his steps. Minh-mang, in particular, enforced an aggressive policy of conquest to the detriment of Vietnam's westerly neighbor, the kingdom of Udong, conquering it and attempting to Vietnamize it during ten years of rule. The Nguyen government dispatched such officials as Nguyen Van Thoai (also known as Thoai Ngoc Hau) to help ensure the implantation of the Nguyen power in the west, in the region of Chau-doc province. Thoai Ngoc Hau led a number of families to settle along the Vinh-te canal that was dug during the time of Gia-long, using thousands of Vietnamese and Khmer laborers.[93] New canals were constructed, for example: the Thoai Ha canal, which links Long-xuyen to Rach-gia (1818); the Vinh-te canal, which links Chau-doc to Ha-tien (1819–1824); and the An Thong, Bo Bo, and Vinh An canals. Most of these canals were used primarily as arteries of communication and transportation rather than as drainage or irrigation canals.[94] According to the American John White, who visited Sai-gon in the 1820s, the construction of these canals cost thousands of lives. One of the canals, he wrote, was "twelve feet deep throughout; about eighty feet wide, and was cut through immense forests and morasses, in the short space of six weeks. Twenty-six thousand men were employed, night and day, by turns, in this stupendous undertaking, and seven thousand lives sacrificed by fatigue, and consequent disease."[95] The Nguyen-sponsored canal policy was complemented by the efforts of farmers who created their own hydraulic networks as need arose.

However, the extreme fertility of the delta land, the regularity of the river and its floods, and, above all, the low population density explain why the need for an agricultural hydraulic system was less pressing than in Cambodia. Most of the cultivation depended on rainwater and the rainy season. The varieties that were cultivated (e.g., floating rice) were selected largely on the basis of their adaptability to the seasonal flood conditions, brackish waters, and swampy terrain.[96]

POLITICO-MILITARY RIVALRY
OVER MEKONG TERRITORY

Preceding the intervention of the French and British colonial powers in the nineteenth century, which changed the political configuration of the countries of the peninsula, the territories on both banks of the Mekong had been coveted by the two main powers of the Indochinese peninsula, Siam and Vietnam. These two kingdoms fought for suzerainty over the diminished Lao principalities of Xieng Khouang, Luang Prabang, and Vientiane, and over *muong* along the Mekong valley, all of which had belonged to the defunct kingdom of Lan Xang. The latter had known a surge of splendor under King Souligna Vongsa (The Sun-king) in the seventeenth century, as it controlled land and peoples beyond the right bank of the river to the north and northeast of present-day Thailand. After his death, the kingdom began an agonizing decline, torn apart by succession disputes between the different royal bloodlines vying for the throne and by attempts made by Luang Prabang, Vientiane, and Champassak to overtake each other while bearing the brunt of invasions launched by Burma, Siam, and Vietnam. In one of their last sweeping invasions of the left bank of the Mekong in the 1820s to 1830s, Bangkok's armies (under Rama III), to teach the vassals a lesson, ransacked Vientiane and depopulated the region by taking more than six thousand Lao families back with them and by applying a systematic policy of Lao town removal to the Northeast that left the Mekong valley almost empty of population—save for the hill and mountain tribes.[97] Hence, the arid and feebly populated Northeast benefited from this fresh injection of resettled Lao communities, in the words of historian David K. Wyatt, while "Vientian and Champassak . . . were eliminated or reduced in size."[98] By the nineteenth century, Siam's supremacy over the Mekong valley was unequaled; its suzerainty over the Mekong principalities was firmly entrenched; it manifested itself in the tradition of selection of Lao royal heirs and high officials by Bangkok, in the regular tribute missions that each polity had to send it, in the stationing of Siamese officials at the court of these *muong*, and in the annual taxes paid by them.[99] On the other side of the Annamitic chain, the empire of Annam had equally been encroaching into Laos, playing kingmakers to Lao polities and successfully placing Xieng Khouang and Khammouane at one time or another under its tutelage. Caught between the Siamese elephant and the Vietnamese dragon, the frail Luang Prabang kingdom barely survived, having to pay tribute to both. The upper and middle Mekong valley became a buffer zone between the two ambitious empires.

Enemy armies crossed the Mekong River, and populations were deported from one bank to another, but never in pre-colonial history had the Mekong been used as a definite political boundary as it would later become with the advent of European colonization. The peoples of the two banks were "of the same side," from the same "Lao entity," united by cultural and linguistic bonds and sharing a common history.[100] These bonds united them probably more to each other than to their Thai cousins of the Central Plain. Historian Georges Coedès explains that the Mekong "is in no way a natural frontier. On the contrary, it is not only primarily a link, despite its poor navigability, between the North and the South, but also between the territories on either side of it, which in the past have always formed part of a single civilization."[101]

In its capacities as a source of water and food and as a means of communication, the Mekong has played an integral role in the histories of the lower Mekong basin. The lower Mekong riparians had long known how to put to use, albeit on an extremely modest scale, its hydraulic potential for navigation and the cultivation and irrigation of rice fields in the dry, arid zones as well as in the low, flooded plains. Its floods had from time immemorial punctuated the lives of the riparian peoples, bringing at once both benefits and destruction. The importance of the river and its influence vary according to the historical and physical context of each country, but it was used separately by each of the political entities that preceded the four nation-states, and its potential was left largely untapped. During the pre-colonial period, the river remained a relatively unknown element, untamed and shrouded in mystery to the extent that no indigenous person or intrepid explorer had apparently succeeded in reconnoitering the river in its entirety or even in significant parts. The riparians of each country traversed by the river had only a fragmented view of the Mekong, limited in terms of time and space and conditioned by the local demands of war, agriculture, or trade. All this was to change with the advent of the West.

THE FRANCO-BRITISH STRUGGLE
FOR THE MEKONG BANKS

As Siam and Vietnam battled each other for hegemony over Cambodia and Laos, the West began its own trajectory into the lower Mekong basin. Western colonial expansion in the region during c. 1860–1890 altered the role played by the Mekong. At first, the river was considered to be the penetration route into China at a time when the conquest of the China market was a determining factor in the strategies of Western powers in the Far East. Then, as kingdoms and territories were vanquished, taken over, or ceded, the Mekong was transformed into a demarcation line between the two spheres of influence, British and French. The British started from Burma in 1825, quickly taking over the Irrawaddy River

delta, journeying up the Irrawaddy River to complete their conquest of upper
Burma by 1885 through the 1890s. The French began in Cochinchina, annexed
during 1862–1867, and expanded into Cambodia and Laos by the turn of the
century.

At the initial stage of the European conquest, little was known of the Mekong
River, its sources, the territories through which it flowed, and the riparian peoples and their wealth. Apart from the few accounts of Portuguese missionaries
such as Father Gaspar Da Cruz, who traveled up part of its mainstream in 1555–
1556, or the account left by a Dutch merchant named Gerrit van Wuysthoff, who
in 1641–1642 journeyed on the river from Phnom Penh to Vientiane, the most
fantastic hypotheses were conceived concerning the origins of the Mekong (and
also about Asia's other great rivers such as the Chao Phraya in Thailand or the
Salween in Burma).[102] Francis Garnier, one of the leading officers of the Mekong exploration mission sent under official French colonial auspices from Sai-
gon in 1866, mentioned in his account the ancient local belief that these rivers
stemmed from an inland sea located in China![103] Although some Westerners—
Portuguese, Spanish, and Dutch, in the early centuries, and, later, British and
French—journeyed as far as Angkor, sailing up "le fleuve Cambodge" and into
the Great Lake, very few had gone beyond and written about it. In the nineteenth
century, one of the most detailed descriptions of the land and peoples upstream
of the Mekong was by the French naturalist Henri Mouhot, who had made four
trips to Thailand, Cambodia, and Laos beginning in 1858.

His fourth journey, from mid-October 1860 to November 1861, took him into
the Khorat plateau and northward to Luang Prabang. He leaves us the following
description of the Tonle Sap and the Mekong River in Cambodia: "On descend-
ing the great arm of the Mekong . . . I was astonished at seeing the current running from south to north instead of following the course of the river into which it
falls. . . . During more than five months of the year, the great lake of Cambodia,
Touli-Sap, covers an immense space of ground; after that period there is a diminution in depth owing to the great evaporation."[104]

As he journeyed beyond the Great Lake, Mouhot remarked on the "less gay"
aspect of the Mekong (compared with the Chao Phraya) and on the increasing
difficulties of going upstream: "The farther north we went the more rapidly the
stream ran; so that when the waters are high, two miles a day is the usual rate of
progress. . . . About 25 or 30 leagues north of Ko-Sutin, on the confines of Laos,
commence the rapids and cataracts: it is then necessary to leave the boats and
take to pirogues, which as well as the luggage, have often to be carried on men's
backs."[105] Enduring much hardship, Mouhot arrived in Laos in the summer of
1861, eventually reaching Luang Prabang, where he died in November. The first
Westerner to attempt to map the region, he was deeply moved by the Mekong's
power as it "forces its way between the lofty mountains with a noise resembling
the roaring of the sea and the impetuosity of a torrent, seeming scarcely able to
keep within its bed. There are many rapids between Paklaie and Louang Pra-

bang."[106] His accounts were published in 1863 in the French periodical *Tour du Monde*. Other French explorers soon followed in his footsteps.

The French and English dreamed of this water artery, of this royal road for their trade, and were determined to obtain access to it. Reports from French consuls in Calcutta in May 1861 revealed that "only Cochinchina, [with] its great river Cambodia [i.e., the Mekong], will seriously hinder these golden projects of our neighbors, if we have the fortune to solidly establish ourselves there."[107] These accounts also reported how intense English competition was in Hong Kong and suggested that, in order to counter their advance, a French mission should explore the Mekong, which then appeared to be the ideal commercial route to South China. When the initial benefits of conquest of the Mekong delta area by France during 1859–1862 proved disappointing, partisans for colonization in France argued that it was necessary to justify the cost of the French settlement in Cochinchina, a cost that had begun to weigh heavily on the metropolitan budget.[108] Although its poverty and sparse population had seriously disappointed some French colonial interests and had inspired the project for the retrocession of the Western provinces of 1864, Cochinchina, in the eyes of many supporters of its retention, had to be shown to contain promising possibilities as the bridgehead for a more serious French penetration into the hinterland. A small French group, the "Cochin Chinese," formed in the metropolis, as well as in Indochina, and began to urge a permanent French presence in the peninsula. Their most ardent advocates were officers of the navy, who argued that the possession of Sai-gon, a maritime harbor, had multiple advantages, of which the most important was to allow France to cease relying on the harbors controlled by the English.[109]

Cinnamon and pepper, products of Cambodia, began to appear downstream in Sai-gon, brought back by French merchants to be processed in the first plants to be set up in the city. In the early 1860s, Sai-gon was perceived by some as the advanced post of a vast hinterland of which almost nothing was known. A report to Vice-Admiral Charner, in charge of the French expeditionary forces in Vietnam, dated September 27, 1860, underlined the fact that "Sai-gon seemed to be destined to become a great warehouse, an important exchange market for all the products from Cambodia, Laos and riparian countries of the South China Sea."[110] Apart from Cambodia, where France was already represented by Doudart de Lagrée, the territories in the middle and upper reaches of the Mekong were entities the allegiance of which was still unclear. There was only a rather incomplete map that stopped at the eighteenth parallel, drawn up in 1838 by the apostolic vicar of Cochinchina, Monsignor Taberd, and entitled *La Tabula Geographica Imperii Annamitici*.[111] The sole navigable route through these regions leading to China seemed to be this river, the Mekong, also called *le Cambodge* by some, and *le Saigon* by others:

There is no doubt that trade will take place on the Saigon river and that Saigon will then become, not only the center of a prosperous colony but also one of the main world warehouses, destined to supply more than fifty millions of inhabitants. . . . Hence, it will be necessary to appoint a study committee that will examine, with certainty, the navigability of the Saigon river up to the meeting point with the Western provinces of China.[112]

In September 1862, Admiral Bonard, who had replaced Charner as head of the French forces the previous year, ordered a preliminary hydrographic exploration of the "grand fleuve du Cambodge" by sending a mission to venture up the lower stream of the river to the farthest limits of navigability, that is, to the Sambor Falls. In a report of January 1863, the admiral emphasized the fundamental role that the river would play: "These are only the stepping stones that will make it possible [for us] to estimate the tremendous importance of this river for the future of Cochinchina. . . . There is much left to do concerning the region explored for the first time as well as the region from the waterfalls to Tibet."[113]

A strong impetus in favor of the Mekong exploration emerged in the metropolis as well as in Cochinchina. High hopes were put on the fabulous possibilities of this river, hopes of lucrative trade with, first of all, the unknown hinterland of Laos: "We all agree that the Cambodge course [i.e., the Mekong] will, one day, be free of all obstacles, and the products of its immense basin will have to pass through our colony of lower Cochinchina, which will make it one of the most prosperous European settlements."[114] In a speech of November 5, 1863, Napoleon III reaffirmed the principle of French permanency by assigning to it a precise task in Cochinchina: "The Cochinchinese enterprise must allow, through commerce, the civilizing of the hinterland."[115] Added to this thirst for commercial exploitation of seemingly vast and rich resources was the desire to conquer the Chinese market to compete with the English. It was believed that the river led directly to the doors of the southern provinces of China. An article by a former officer of the navy, published in the *Journal des Economistes* of December 1861, summarized the question: "Could the Mekong be the way through which we can penetrate into the remotest provinces of China and Tibet, and link economically with hundreds of millions of producers and consumers, economic links the importance of which it is still impossible to estimate?"[116]

The French authorities were preoccupied by the Siamese presence that held sway over the territories on the Mekong's left bank, exerting a tight control over its population. This ominous presence, behind which could be felt England's influence, was all the more threatening since the official demarcations of the Siamese sphere of influence were ill-defined and the French fully intended to lay claims to all of Laos. Chasseloup-Laubat, minister of the navy and of the colonies, who had always believed in the long-term profitability of colonization, expressed his fear in a letter to the Ministry of Foreign Affairs: "Siam is a threat to everything West of the mountains, boundary to the Kingdom of Annam, where the Mekong flows . . . and which will, one day, open new routes to European trade."[117] In another letter late in 1865: "Thus, it is particularly in the North of French Cochinchina, on the great river, that Siam will maneuver to appropriate all the upper regions on the right and the left banks, and will thus succeed in barring forever the exploration of the Mekong River. This we cannot allow."[118]

In November 1864, Chasseloup-Laubat received a project conceived by Admiral Bonard for the exploration of the Mekong, entitled *Report on the urgency of the exploration of the Mekong River to create in French Cochin China, at Saigon, a commercial warehouse with Tibet and the Western provinces of China.* Likewise, a French naval officer, Francis Garnier, in a booklet published in 1864 demanded

the honor of being the first to penetrate Central Indochina [which is the region] . . . of the most interest for the development of our power in the China [S]eas because of its immense resources, the unexpected communications which it can offer to our activities. . . . How precious it would be to know with certainty about the complete navigability of this great river, which will bring to Sai-gon products from Laos and from Central China.[119]

Eventually, the idea of a mission for the exploration of the Mekong received the official approval of the French government, which appointed Commander Doudart de Lagrée to head the mission, assisted by Garnier and other naval officers. The Ministry of the Navy assigned the following tasks to the mission: "The Mission must reconnoiter the navigability of the Mekong, search and probe its waterfalls, draw up the map of its basin, and collect all information pertaining to its sources, study the history, the ethnography, and the customs of its riparian populations, and in particular, those of Laos, who live along the route to China."[120]

In sum, the mission was to prepare future arguments for the time when there would be Franco-Siamese territorial disputes. On June 5, 1866, the mission departed from Sai-gon; it would not return until June 29, 1868, after having journeyed more than 10,000 kilometers, more than 4,000 of them on foot. Among its invaluable scientific findings were "the precise determination of the river basin to the Twenty-second parallel, the survey of completely unknown regions between the Twelfth and the Twenty-fifth parallels, the drawing up for these regions of a map to complete those by the Jesuit Fathers."[121]

The immediate impression formed by the explorers, however, was how difficult the river seemed to be. Early in the journey, when the expedition was just departing from Cambodia, Garnier remarked that "the future of these easy commercial relations on this immense river, natural road from China to Sai-gon, that only yesterday I had pleasantly dreamed of, appeared to me, at this moment, seriously compromised."[122] However, as they progressed upstream, the direct and immediate consequence of the exploration of the Mekong's middle reaches and of the territories on both sides of the river was to focus the attention of colonial empires on the entire lower Mekong valley. Through the reports of the expedition's members, French authorities began to grasp the extent of Siamese influence in Laos. In a letter of January 1867 to the French consul in Bangkok, Doudart de Lagrée wrote: "We now know more or less everything about inner Laos. . . . Siamese domination extends itself firmly on both sides of the river, and in the east reaches the great chain of Cochin China."[123] The expedition also revealed the vigor of English trade, which had introduced to the remotest and—it had been believed—the most inaccessible corners of the land and to all the village marketplaces—thanks to Burmese traders—products of British industries such as fabrics and small ironware articles.[124] Concurrently, the expedition also revealed to the inhabitants on both banks of the Mekong the existence of a rival power to Siam and Britain—France—and presented to the Lao princes the enticing possibility of counterbalancing Siamese tutelage with that of a more powerful patron. The expedition eventually arrived in Yunnan, where Lagrée died in 1868. The mission, which was prevented from reaching the Mekong's sources because of a Muslim revolt in Tali, in the Chinese province of Yunnan, had shown that the Mekong was not the royal route that it had been believed to be, one that would allow navigation from the Mekong delta to China. In his account, Garnier explained the difficulties of traveling along the river:

> The river . . . formed among the rocks, a number of small lakes, without any opening, or which opened to each other only through small, impassable falls. Thus, our boats, which often were lost, had at each moment, to go back to find the narrow and deep bed of the main break; but there, the current was quite strong, and in order to go around the bend of this winding route, we had to use ropes. At the narrowest points, water surged through the channel with such speed that it became necessary to completely unload the boats to pull them upstream. The luggage was carried by men from one rock to another, over rapids, where again they were reloaded.[125]

 The dream of the Mekong as a commercial highway to China was thus never to be realized. But this failure prompted the members of the mission to consider another route, which led to the discovery and the exploration of the upper stream of the Red River that flows from Yunnan to Tonkin. Garnier, writing about "the Tong-king river" (*song Coi*) affirmed: "There is here a very promising commercial question that needs to be studied, one that concerns the French exclusively, as the Tong-king River is directly under our political influence as the result of the Treaties that link us to the Hue Court."[126] In his report of January 6, 1868, Garnier observed that "the acknowledgment of this route will, undoubtedly, be one of the most useful results of this journey."[127] Thus began the "Tonkin Affair," which was to have tremendous political and military repercussions on the relations between France and Vietnam, resulting ultimately in the extension of France's protectorate over northern and central Vietnam (Tonkin and Annam, respectively) by the turn of the century.

The disappointment that resulted from the collapse of the grandiose dreams swirling around the Mekong River was short-lived; its exploration prepared the ground for a progressive French control over Lao territories. Several decades later, with the appointment of Auguste Pavie to the position of vice-consul of Luang Prabang in 1885, and thanks to his energetic and adroit participation in the political events of the region of the Mekong valley, France was able to augment its colonial possessions to the detriment of Siamese domination. By 1895, Pavie and his men had undertaken three successive missions (1887–1889; 1889–1891; 1892–1895), covering an area of approximately 700,000 square kilometers; they explored the Mekong River upstream to the borders with Burma and China and crisscrossed the river valley from east to west. They had brought back a wealth of information recorded in a dozen volumes as well as a complete and detailed atlas of the region, making it possible for the French authorities to understand to a certain extent the subtlety of local alliances.[128] But it was mainly Pavie's diplomatic persistence in the Sipsong Chu Tai (The Twelve Cantons) region, and particularly with the Luang Prabang king, Oune Kham, that established French Laos by means of the French-Siamese Treaty of October 1893.[129]

Thus, the upper and middle Mekong valleys became a prime geopolitical stake in the Franco-British rivalry during the years 1892 to 1896. In its middle reach, the Mekong River flows through lands then occupied by the Lao kingdoms of Vientiane and Luang Prabang under Siamese suzerainty and, in its upper course, through the Shan states of Burma. Thus, it was through Siam and Burma for Britain, and through Vietnam for France, that the two powers confronted each other over the question of the delimitation of their colonial empires. The aggressive French westward thrust toward the Mekong's banks resulted in a Franco-British rivalry that turned on the question of the possession of the Mekong's banks in its upper and middle stream, leading, for the first time, to the formulation of the concept of spheres of influence between France and Britain in August 1892.[130] Border incidents between French and Siamese troops (backed by Britain) on the left bank of the river multiplied to the point that fear of an imminent war between Siam and France, which could have resulted in the disappearance of the former as an independent state and its integration into the latter's empire, became widespread.[131]

Eventually, the Franco-Siamese Agreement of October 3, 1893, conceded to France the left bank of the middle Mekong, chosen as the line of demarcation; it created a "no-man's land" of twenty-five kilometers on the right bank of the river for free circulation for French representatives and acknowledged the French occupation of the Chantaboun harbor.[132] The agreement effectively divided the Lao population on both banks into two groups and momentarily solved the question of borders on the right bank of the river. It did not, however, put an end to Franco-British rivalry, which continued in the upper stream of the river, in the Shan state of Kiang Cheng (Muong Sing), leading to the creation of a buffer state.[133] For France, the possession of the banks of the Mekong River was vital, since the river was to become the link between France's colony of Cochinchina and its protectorates of Laos and Cambodia. The river would, thus, trace in the north and in the west, the unity and cohesion of a great French empire in Southeast Asia. After long months of bargaining, the negotiators on both sides unofficially came to the conclusion that the valley of the Mekong River was to France in Indochina what the Irrawaddy valley was to Britain in Burma. In consequence, it was agreed in the 1896 London treaty between France and Britain that in exchange for the recognition of the French tutelage on the Mekong River, from the Cambodian frontier almost to the Chinese border, France would acknowledge the territorial independence and integrity of the Menam watershed basin.[134]

Through this protocol, Siam became a buffer state between the British and the French empires. Siam was thus permitted to maintain its independence at a time when the neighboring kingdoms had succumbed to Western imperialism. The price it paid was the loss of vassal territories upstream and downstream. In 1907, for instance, Siam had to cede to France the Cambodian provinces of Battambang, Siem Reap, and Sisophon.[135]

The discovery of the Mekong River as the hypothetical commercial route to the southern provinces of China, a key element in the French attraction to Indochina, indirectly contributed to the opening of riparian kingdoms to colonial penetration and to France's lasting presence in the lower Mekong basin. With the founding of the British and French empires on both sides of the river and with Siam established as the buffer state between them, the rivalry between these two powers transformed the Mekong into a territorial boundary for the first time in the history of the lower Mekong basin, increasingly referred to as the Indochinese peninsula. It would remain as such, definitely dividing people of the same ethnic group, who happened to live on opposite banks, into two so that the ambitious fiction of a riparian empire could exist.

People who represented French colonial interests in Indochina persisted in believing that the Mekong could be used as a means of transportation of commercial products—at least as far as Laos, if no longer all the way to China—despite the innumerable waterfalls, sandbars, and other difficulties that were strewn along its stream. The dream of millions of consumers and producers had even spurred the formation of the Syndicat Lao with a capital of 100,000 francs, financed by Parisian shareholders. The syndicate bought tons of products and set up a number of trading posts along the river but failed after two years of activity.[136] The dream of developing Laos's economic potential and its main waterway, the Mekong, would be evoked again and again in official speeches and in governmental or private projects. But a readjustment of colonial priorities and interests soon took place: First centered on Laos and its potential wealth, the focus shifted to Cochinchina and Tonkin, which were more readily accessible and easily exploitable.

THE BEGINNING OF MODERN EXPLOITATION

The Franco-British rivalry for the possession of the middle Mekong banks revealed a particular French attitude of possessive pride toward the river, which was, by then, referred to as *le Fleuve* (The River) or *Notre Fleuve* (Our River) comparable to no other. It was believed to have in store enormous resources as yet undiscovered and unexploited. The exploitation of colonial lands following economic and financial dictates began with the establishment of the colonial power in Indochina. As a colonial power, France brought a broader view and new dimensions to the exploitation of the river, thanks to its economic and financial means, to the use of Western technology, and to the fusion of political borders enforced by the colonial administration. The combination of these elements established, for the first time, the premises for the development of the Mekong's potential on a regional scale.

Prior to the French colonization of lower Cochinchina, the Mekong plain was partly cultivated, but the area of the plain that was called *Mien Tây* or Trans-Bassac in the west was mostly swampy forests and insalubrious lands with a total population of barely a million. The whole plain is slightly below sea level with a weak slope, but thanks to coastal bars that impede to a certain degree the advance of the sea, it is not completely invaded by tidal flood. However, because of the presence of such obstacles, floodwaters from rainfall and the Mekong cannot easily drain out to the sea. Traveling had been done mainly on waterways, using the Rach-gia, Vinh-an, and Ha-tien canals, which were of mainly strategic interest for the Nguyen.[137] Large-scale agricultural exploitation of the western delta would require canals that could evacuate excess water while supplying water, where and when it was required, for irrigation.[138] The eastern delta, which included the Sai-gon River, was, on the other hand, much better known to foreign travelers (e.g., priests, merchants) who had been visiting this region as far back as the sixteenth to the seventeenth centuries. In 1821–1822, long before the French penetration in 1858, a British surgeon detached to the British mission to visit Siam and Hue to ascertain the possibilities of trade had remarked upon his arrival that the delta generally "presented the appearance of extreme fertility: the banks were covered with areca and cocoa-nut trees, plantains. . . . Numerous navigable canals intersect the country in every direction, offering every facility for the increase of commercial industry." He also noted that there was an intense fluvial traffic up and down the river (see Map 1.2).[139]

The more intensive development of Cochinchina actually began with the installation of the colonial structures. There were two stages in this development. During the experimental stage, starting in 1866, the colonial administration under the admirals, for security and commercial reasons, put the old canals back into use by utilizing mechanical dredges and then, because of their ineffectiveness in the swampy terrain, by employing local labor under the *corvée* system. The impossibility of putting into use regularly flooded, swampy lands soon led to the formulation of the first integral plans for extensive dredging work in 1894.[140] The colonial power understood the usefulness of canals for the intensive development of the delta, for they permitted the draining of long-submerged lands and the transportation of agricultural and commercial products to the harbors for exportation.[141] These canals linked the Mekong tributaries to one another and to the Vamco and Dong-nai Rivers in the northeast.

The second stage, started in 1900, was that of construction and continuation of agricultural hydraulic works that were increasing in volume and importance: extension of the main and secondary canal network for drainage and irrigation and construction of dikes along the Mekong River and its tributaries for flood protection. This network included main canals for a total length of more than 1,375 kilometers and a width of twenty-two meters (in 1930) and a depth of more than two meters; as well as secondary canals of a total length of more than

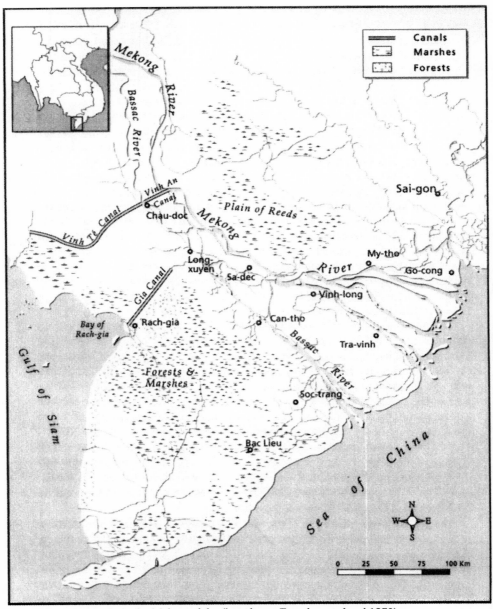

Map 1.2 Main canals in the Mekong delta (based on a French map dated 1870)

1,000 kilometers, of varying width and depth. The main canal linked the Vamco River to the Sai-gon River near Thu Dau Mot; another went from Rach-gia to Ha-tien; another ran northeast and southwest across Ca-mau (see Map 1.3). This network permitted the flushing out of floodwater and thus diminished—although insufficiently—the extent of flooding and regulated water levels according to agricultural needs.[142]

Dredging work in the Mekong delta made possible the transformation of un-cultivated and reed-covered lands into rice fields. From 1880 to 1930, the rice field area increased more than sixfold, from 350,000 hectares in 1880 to 2,400,000 hectares in 1930.[143] Along with this increase in the acreage of culti-vated lands, dredging work allowed the settlement of population, and wherever it went, "one could literally see people settling along the canals while the dredge that had dug them was advancing inland."[144] Later, these dredging and construc-tion works followed five- to six-year plans and were financed by public auction-ing of land, increased land taxes and rice taxes, and private investments.[145] These investments were aimed at developing a commercial rice agriculture for exporta-tion. Canal construction was followed by road building parallel to the canals.[146]

Before the 1929 crisis negatively affected the economy of Cochinchina, rice exportations increased regularly by 20,000 tons a year. Thanks to rice, Cochin-china from 1915 to 1924 was second in the world (1,200,000 tons) among rice export producers, after Burma (1,800,000 tons) and ahead of Thailand (800,000 tons).[147] The canals played another important role as waterways. Man-made ca-nals, rivers, and natural arroyos formed an extremely dense navigation network, heavily used for the transportation of the main agricultural products, particularly of rice and corn from Cambodia and Cochinchina to Cho-lon for processing, and then to the Sai-gon harbor for export. For six to eight months following the har-vest, vessels of all sizes crisscrossed the canals day and night.[148] In 1913, the yearly tonnage on the My-tho River, a tributary of the Mekong, was 13,500,000 tons; on the Duperré canal (between the Mekong and the Vamco Rivers) 5,000,000 tons; on the Rach-gia canal (between the Mekong and the Gulf of Siam) 1,300,000 tons of products. These canals were the "essential organ of life and wealth of the country."[149]

In addition to its water management works in the delta, the colonial admini-stration had not given up its intent of making the Mekong River the waterway that would link its empire from north to south. Within the context of great colo-nial works commenced at the turn of the century, it launched a number of con-structions to facilitate upstream navigation: the modernization of the sea harbor of Phnom Penh (yearly volume of 300,000 tons from 1925 to 1926), the clearing of sections of the river encumbered by rocks, and the dredging of the river bed.[150] For Cambodia and Laos, the Mekong River became the main commercial route through which flowed export products for the Sai-gon maritime harbor. Sea vessels of 5,000 tons starting from one of the Mekong's mouths (Cua Tieu) navigated 320 kilometers upstream to Phnom Penh in all seasons and with little

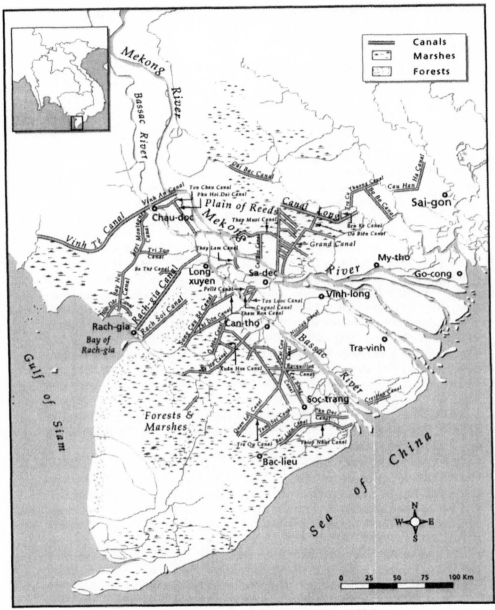

Map 1.3 Main canals in Cochinchina (based on a French map dated 1934)

difficulty. The volume of the fluvial traffic using the Mekong and its tributaries was 500,000 tons a year, mostly of export products.[151] From Phnom Penh to Kompong Cham, traffic was still dense with such export products as kapok, corn, and rubber. However, starting from Kratie, the river became less navigable, necessitating transshipment of goods to smaller crafts. Between Kratie and Khone, the fluvial navigation was greatly slowed by the Sambor Falls, and upstream of the Khone Falls, where the upper Mekong starts, the presence of numerous reaches required many costly transshipments that hampered traffic in both directions and increased transportation costs.

Although the Mekong River is the main artery linking Laos from north to south, commercial navigation was rather thin because of countless physical obstacles presented by the river and by an economic development still in its infancy. Apart from teak that was floated down the river, the traffic volume was insignificant: 6,000 tons a year. In 1900, the colonial administration began work on the reaches upstream and downstream of Khone, following a general program of development of the Mekong River, with a cost of 1,550,000 piasters, that was to increase the volume of traffic from 6,000 to 12,000 tons.[152] A complementary program of works was prepared by the Public Works Service to remedy the river's low navigability. It had envisioned expenses of 2 million piasters and an execution time of nine years, starting in 1926. However, despite these expenditures, the works completed were insufficient to facilitate a noticeable increase in the river's navigability and a reduction of its high cost of transport.[153]

In addition to the conveyance of merchandise, there was a regular fluvial service that linked the main cities of Indochina. In Cochinchina, the Cochinchinese Shipping Company, which later became the Sai-gonese Navigation and Transportation Company, subsidized by the Government General of Indochina, connected Sai-gon, Phnom Penh, Battambang, and Luang Prabang by launch boat and engine vessel, although countless transshipments to bypass obstacles were required. The Sai-gon to Luang Prabang trip was extremely long in 1937: thirty-seven days upriver and twenty-seven days downriver. The company also operated in the canals and arroyos of the Mekong delta.

To ensure the complete navigability of the Mekong, free of the natural obstacles that had prevented it from being the great north-south artery dreamed of by the first explorers, considerable work needed to be done. Many believed that the Mekong works could bring economic as well as political advantages:

Rivers are not only practical commercial waterways, these "walking roads" are also the best means of penetration, the surest road for the introduction of civilization as well as of commercial products, and to establish influence over the populations. The peoples who know how to use them and are not deterred by the momentary expenses required to make feasible a free circulation on the rivers will very rapidly reap the rewards for their sacrifices through the extension of their political and commercial influence.[154]

However, it seems that the policy of the colonial power toward its territorial possessions varied according to the importance given to each of its colonial possessions. It was rather timid concerning Laos and Cambodia, while showing more commitment to Cochinchina. In regard to Cambodia, historian Alain Forest remarks that the colonial regime's

effort was very limited concerning the development of these waterways and the support to fluvial traffic. The Mekong, the Tonle Sap, and the Great Lake were marked out, but there was only one dredge for the whole country. . . . Dredging carried out elsewhere . . . [was] sporadic and insufficient. The smallest project, even if of essential interest, and even if its realization was announced as imminent, would take several years of gestation before being realized because of a lack of money and equipment.[155]

Colonial effort was concentrated in the Mekong delta, on the mouths of the river, centering maritime commerce in the region of the Sai-gon harbor, which developed in consequence. In fact, Sai-gon became "the true economic capital of the whole Union."[156] The same partiality could be found in the question of the development of land through agricultural hydraulics. The colonial administration allotted very little of the general or the local budget to agricultural hydraulics planning in the protectorates of Cambodia and Laos. There were plans, for instance, to bypass the Mekong River at the Khone Falls level, for the irrigation of northern Cambodia, and some small irrigation projects for these two countries were carried out, but the amount spent was infinitesimal compared with the amounts spent on Cochinchina, Tonkin, or Annam.[157]

Only in Cochinchina, where the reshaping of the physical, economic, and social landscape had been carried out on an extensive scale, almost without any hindrance thanks to its relatively recent settlement and low population density, were the agricultural hydraulic works so highly efficient and productive for the colonial government. Although these works were accomplished in an empirical rather than a truly scientific manner, and although they never came close to maximizing the productivity of these fertile lands, it may be said that the economic progress achieved during these thirty-five years was the result of the development of the Mekong delta through agricultural hydraulic works.

During the pre-colonial period, the Mekong River had been considered part of the territory of each country concerned. During the French colonial period (1862–1949), although flowing through several countries, the river was no longer delimited nationally but was under the authority of the Government General of Indochina and then of the Indochinese Union. Thus, until 1949, when internal autonomy was granted to the three states of French Indochina, there had been no international agreement concerning the use of the river between the riparian countries. Agreements were concluded solely between France and Siam, which had remained independent. The Friendship, Commerce and Navigation Treaty of February 14, 1925, followed by the Franco-Siamese International Convention of August 25, 1926, for the normalization of relations between Siam and Indochina, established the High Permanent Franco-Siamese Commission of the Mekong River. This commission was responsible for "initiating the formulation of all necessary regulations to insure . . . the policing of navigation, health, and security in the frontier region."[158] An agreement on the international exploitation of the Mekong River for industrial, commercial, and agricultural purposes was discussed but never concluded. A decree of July 30, 1947, created the "Mekong Consultative Committee," which led to meetings attended by French technicians as well as by delegates of the riparian countries (with the exception of Thailand): Laos, Cambodia, and Vietnam. It anticipated the future Mekong Committee, but the political instability of the time and insufficient financial means led to its demise before any concrete projects had been achieved. France could not divert even a small part of its forces and means for the realization of a grandiose waterway project, since it was then enmeshed in the First Indochina War (1946–1954).

As they acquired the status of "Associated States," Vietnam, Laos, and Cambodia signed the Convention on Fluvial and Maritime Navigation on the Mekong and on the Waterways Allowing Access to the Maritime Harbor of Sai-gon, or Pau Convention of November 29, 1949, which involved the three riparian nations and France in negotiations on questions of common interest. The convention allowed freedom of navigation on the entire length of the river (as well as free access to the Sai-gon harbor) to all the member states of the French Union. Nonmember states were also allowed free access but only on the maritime Mekong, from the Cua Tieu mouth to Phnom Penh.[159] The convention also created the Provisional Mekong Committee. Then the Paris Convention of December 29, 1954, adapting to the new political reality, involved the three countries of Cambodia, Laos, and Vietnam in discussions concerning fluvial and maritime navigation on the lower Mekong; it mentioned in its preamble that its aim was also to ensure regional economic development.[160] The Second Mekong Committee was thus created and was responsible for all aspects concerning international navigation, including improvement of navigation, sharing of taxes and maintenance costs, and navigation regulations. However, the Second Mekong Committee had only consultative competence, and, composed of representatives of the three countries, could not effectively apply the convention since Thailand, a riparian country, was not a participant.[161] Moreover, each of the countries signatory of the convention jealously protected its prerogatives and agreed to yield to the committee only in cases of interference with navigation on the river. Finally, in its application, the Paris Convention was found to be too difficult and complex to be respected by the riparian states of the Mekong River.

With the advent of colonial occupation, the exploitation of the Mekong River had reached a new stage whereby an overall concept was partially applied to the development of the river's hydraulic resources. Thus, previously uncultivated land became productive and was settled with villages scattered along the canals. The Mekong River, which, despite its multiple obstacles, had always been the main communication route for Laos, had by now become somewhat more accessible to navigation thanks to the colonial will—however incompletely realized—to make it into a great commercial river artery: a link between its protectorates and colony through which would flow the wealth destined to the metropolis.

Conclude   The Mekong, which had so attracted the attention of commercial groups and colonial governments because of its unexploited potential, inspired ambitious dreams and grandiose projects. These were only partially realized, because of an insufficient level of technology, unstable political conditions, or a lack of urgent necessity—as had been the case for the riparian countries during the pre-colonial period—or because of colonial economic imperatives that focused on productivity and favored only works with direct and immediate benefits. Inspector General of the Colonies G. Gayet, who had never doubted the enormous potential of the Mekong River, wrote in 1949:

> It is not with the means available to the French Union, even with the 27 million inhabitants of Indochina, that the Mekong will be developed . . . [and] become a new Tennessee as dreamed by some people. . . . The Mekong River will come out of its ancient slumbers only through international unions, international systems. . . . One must count in terms of decades, even of centuries, to be able to fully use the incommensurable reserves of this river. . . . Within the context of the French Union, then of the United Nations, all its economic wealth will be developed and put to the use of the Asian humanity.[162]

Colonial France did not have the means to master the enormous question of the Mekong or to exploit the limitless potential of the river's resources in its lower basin. The development of the river on a vast scale by riparian countries, with the help and cooperation of a large number of countries and organizations, would start only after the Second World War, in a completely different context.

NOTES

1. In an article on the culture of the Mekong delta and its links to Southeast Asia, historian Pham Duc Duong explains the etymology of "Mekong" or "Cuu Long" in Vietnamese, "Me Khoong" in Lao-Thai by placing it within the larger common background of Southeast Asian culture. According to him, in Lao-Thai toponomy, all great rivers are considered "mother-rivers," signaled by the prefix "me," as in "Menam" or "Mekong" or "Me Khoong." The name "Khoong," which means "river" in general, is widely used as such in Southeast Asia and even in southern China. Pham Duc Duong, "Van Hoa Dong Bang Song Cuu Long Trong Boi Canh Dong Nam A," in *May Dac Diem Van Hoa Dong Bang Song Cuu Long* (Ha-noi: Vien Van Hoa Xuat Ban, 1984), 83.

2. For a detailed discussion on the question of water control in Asia, see Francesca Bray, *The Rice Economies: Technology and Development in Asian Societies* (Berkeley and Los Angeles: University of California Press, 1994), 62–112.

3. Commission Economique pour l'Asie et l'Extrême-Orient, *Principaux cours d'eau internationaux de la région de la CEAEO*, Recueil des Ressources Hydrauliques, no. 29 (New York: United Nations, 1968), 4. According to the exploration conducted by a Franco-British team in September 1994, the source can now be pinpointed at the Rup-sa Pass in Tibet.

4. U.S. Engineer Agency for Resources Inventories, *Atlas of Physical, Economic, and Social Resources of the Lower Mekong Basin* (New York: United Nations, 1968), v.

5. Committee for the Coordination of Investigations of the Lower Mekong Basin, *Report on Indicative Basin Plan* (Bangkok: United Nations, 1972), 2.

6. Engineer Agency, *Atlas*, 1.

7. Naval Intelligence Division, *Indo-China* (Cambridge: Cambridge University Press, 1943), 442.

8. Engineer Agency, *Atlas*, 72.

9. L. Tichit, *L'Agriculture au Cambodge* (Paris: Agence de Coopération Culturelle et Technique, 1981), 16–17.

10. Naval Intelligence Division, *Indo-China,* 44. See also *Etudes Vietnamiennes*, no. 3 (1983), an edition devoted to the Mekong delta.

11. Engineer Agency, *Atlas*, 72.

12. Huynh Lua, ed., *Lich Su Khai Pha Vung Dat Nam Bo* (Thanh Pho Ho Chi Minh: Nha Xuat Ban Thanh Pho Ho Chi Minh, 1987), 24.

13. Engineer Agency, *Atlas*, 1.

14. Charles Robequain, *L'Évolution économique de l'Indochine française* (Paris: Paul Hartmann, 1939), 123.

15. Nguyen Viet Pho, "Les Ressources hydrologiques," *Etudes Vietnamiennes*, no. 3 (1983): 67.

16. Comité pour la Coordination des Etudes sur le Bassin Inférieur du Mékong, *Avant-projet de mise en valeur des ressources hydrauliques et connexes du bassin inférieur du Mekong* (Bangkok: United Nations, 1970), 6.

17. Paul Bourrières, "Les Grands Travaux du Mékong," *Revue Tiers-Monde*, no. 42–43 (1970): 555.

18. Bray, *The Rice Economies*, 69.

19. Based on her studies of ancient "irrigation societies" in Sri Lanka, Cambodia, Indonesia, and Vietnam, archaeologist Janice Stargardt theorizes that the reasons for these societies' settlement "into side valleys" rather than in the mainstream valleys or plains were many, including defensive concerns and the desire to take advantage of "the more favorable conditions of slope." Janice Stargardt, *The Ancient Pyu of Burma* (Singapore: The Institute of Southeast Asian Studies, 1990), 54.

20. See Nguyen Thi Dieu, "State versus Indigenous Peoples: The Impact of Hydraulic Projects on Indigenous Peoples of Asia," *Journal of World History* 7, no. 1 (March 1996): 101–130.

21. In recent years, it has been convincingly argued that so-called empires under the Chinese-recorded names of Funan and Chen La may, in fact, refer to not one but a number of small principalities and chiefdoms that "had banded together and called themselves a kingdom for the purposes of sending tributary goods to China . . . or of seeking Chinese help against their neighbors." David P. Chandler, *A History of Cambodia* (Boulder, CO: Westview Press, 1992), 15.

22. Stargardt, *The Ancient Pyu*, xxvi. Stargardt and others have demonstrated that pre-Indian cultures reached a sophisticated technical level long before the so-called Indian cultural colonization. Ibid., 41.

23. Martin Stuart-Fox, *Laos: Politics, Economics and Society* (London: Frances Pinter Publishers, 1986), 44–48; Arthur J. Dommen, *Laos: Keystone of Indochina* (Boulder, CO: Westview Press, 1985), 6. For an *aperçu* on the Hmong's opium culture and slash-and-burn practices, see Christian Taillard, "L'Espace social: Quelques réflexions à propos de deux exemples au Laos," *Asie du Sud-Est et du Monde Insulindien* 8, no. 2 (1977): 88.

24. Yang Dao, *Les Hmong du Laos face au développement* (Vientiane: Edition Siao-sawath, 1975), 69–71.

25. Dommen, *Laos*, 5; Stuart-Fox, *Laos*, 45. For an explanation on the classification of Lao ethnic groups into three categories, see Jan Ovesen, *Anthropological Reconnais-*

sance in Central Laos: A Survey of Local Communities in a Hydropower Project Area (Uppsala, Sweden: Uppsala University, 1993), 31–33.

26. For a Lao view on the uses of and differences between the terms "Lao" and "Thai," see Somphavan Inthavong, *Notes on Lao History* (Vientiane: Lao People's Democratic Republic, April 1994). On the present state of research on Laos in different countries, in particular, on the paucity of historical works, see Pierre-Bernard Lafont, ed., *Les Recherches en sciences humaines sur le Laos: Actes de la conférence internationale organisée à Vientiane, 1-19 décembre 1993* (Paris: Publications du Centre d'Histoire et Civilisations de la Péninsule Indochinoise, 1994).

27. Charles Robequain, *L'Indochine française* (Paris: Armand Colin, 1935), 86.

28. Stuart-Fox, *Laos*, 47.

29. Keo Mannivanna, "Aspects socio-économiques du Laos médiéval," in Centre d'Etudes et de Recherches Marxistes, ed., *Sur le mode de production asiatique* (Paris: Editions Sociales, 1974), 312.

30. Paul Le Boulanger, *Histoire du Laos français: Essai d'une étude chronologique des principautés laotiennes* (Paris: Librairie Plon, 1931), 46; David K. Wyatt, *Thailand: A Short History* (New Haven, CT: Yale University Press, 1984), 82.

31. Stuart-Fox, *Laos*, 7.

32. Wyatt, *Thailand*, 120.

33. Katay Don Sasorith, *Le Laos* (Paris: Berger-Levrault, 1953), 45.

34. Stuart-Fox, *Laos*, 8.

35. Mannivanna, "Aspects socio-économiques du Laos médiéval," 314.

36. Bernard Philippe Groslier, *Angkor et le Cambodge au XVIème siècle, d'après les sources portugaises et espagnoles* (Paris: Presses Universitaires de France, 1958), 162.

37. Paul Lévy, "Two Accounts of Travels in Laos in the 17th Century," in René de Berval, ed., *Kingdom of Laos: The Land of the Million Elephants and of the White Parasol* (Limoges, France: A. Bontemps Co., 1959), 59.

38. Ibid., 62. An English translation of Father de Marini's account is now available: *A New and Interesting Description of the Lao Kingdom (1642–1648),* translated by Walter E. J. Tips and Claudio Bertuccio (Bangkok: White Lotus Press, 1998).

39. Paul Lévy, *Histoire du Laos* (Paris: Presses Universitaires de France, 1974), 9.

40. Charles Keyes, *Isan: Regionalism in Northeastern Thailand*, Data Paper no. 65, Southeast Asia Program (Ithaca, NY: Cornell University Press, 1967), 3.

41. See Nikom Suthiragsa, "The Ban Chieng Culture," in R. B. Smith and W. Watson, eds., *Early South East Asia: Essays in Archaeology, History and Historical Geography* (New York: Oxford University Press, 1979), 42–51.

42. Georges Coedès, *Les États hindouisés d'Indochine et d'Indonésie* (Paris: Editions de Boccard, 1964), 146.

43. W. J. Van Liere, "Traditional Water Management in the Lower Mekong Basin," *World Archaeology*, no. 3 (1980): 267. Van Liere was formerly director of the Agricultural Division of the Mekong Committee.

44. Ibid.

45. Srisakra Vallibhotama, "The Ancient Settlements of Sukhotai," in Robert J. Bickner, Thomas J. Hudak, and Patcharin Peyasantiwong, eds., *Papers from a Conference on Thai Studies in Honor of William J. Gedney* (Ann Arbor: University of Michigan Press, 1986), 232.

46. Ibid.

47. Ibid., 234.

48. The term "Siam" is used to refer to the nation of Thailand before its change of name (to "Thailand") in 1939 in an attempt by Pibul Songgram to recreate the *muong*

Thai or "land of the Thai" concept. For an original analysis on the formation of the Thai "geo-body," see Thongchai Winichakul, *Siam Mapped: A History of the Geo-body of a Nation* (Honolulu: University of Hawaii Press, 1994).

49. Achille Dauphin-Meunier, *Histoire du Cambodge* (Paris: Presses Universitaires de France, 1968), 12. The notion of a "Kingdom of Funan" that could be described as "major and unified" has been disputed; it seems rather that several chiefdoms existed in its stead, coming together when the need arose. See Chandler, *A History of Cambodia*, 15, and Claude Jacques, "'Funan,' 'Zhenla': The Reality Concealed by These Chinese Views of Indochina," in Smith and Watson, eds., *Early South East Asia*, 371–379.

50. Georges Coedès, *The Making of Southeast Asia* (Berkeley and Los Angeles: University of California Press, 1972), 61.

51. Bernard Philippe Groslier, "Agriculture et religion dans l'empire angkorien," *Etudes Rurales*, no. 53–56 (January–December 1974): 93–94. The question of whether the ancient canal network was used for irrigation or for transportation or both and of when irrigation was introduced and on what scale is still unresolved. See Pierre Brocheux, *The Mekong Delta: Ecology, Economy, and Revolution, 1860–1960* (Madison: University of Wisconsin–Madison, 1995), 11.

52. Chandler, *A History of Cambodia*, 26.

53. Van Liere, "Traditional Water Management," 269; Bernard Philippe Groslier, "La Civilisation angkorienne et la maîtrise de l'eau," *Etudes Cambodgiennes*, no. 11 (1967): 23.

54. Although the main water supply and the source for Angkor's hydraulic network was situated not at the Great Lake but rather on the Siem Reap River, fifty kilometers northwest of Angkor at Phnom-Kulen. Kenneth R. Hall, "Economic History of Early Southeast Asia," in Nicholas Tarling, ed., *The Cambridge History of Southeast Asia*, 2 vols. (Singapore: Cambridge University Press, 1992), 1:231.

55. Coedès, *Les États hindouisés*, 252–254; André Migot, *Les Khmers: Des origines d'Angkor au Cambodge d'aujourd'hui* (Paris: Le Livre Contemporain, 1960), 90. Maurice Glaize has provided us with a useful guide, *Les Monuments du groupe d'Angkor* (Paris: J. Maisonneuve, 1993), which can help the reader to envision the main monuments as a group rather than as piecemeal works detached from their environment and history.

56. Contrary to the theories of most archeologists and historians concerning the meaning and goals of Angkor's hydraulic works, Van Liere argues that theocratic hydraulics had nothing to do with agricultural hydraulics, and even that the former was harmful for the latter. Van Liere, "Traditional Water Management," 274.

57. Dauphin-Meunier, *Histoire du Cambodge*, 271.

58. For a more technical and detailed description of how the barays of Angkor functioned, see Stargardt, *The Ancient Pyu*, 139–140, and B. P. Groslier's articles, in particular, "La Cité hydraulique angkorienne: Exploitation ou surexploitation du sol?" *Bulletin de l'Ecole Française d'Extrême-Orient* 66 (1979): 161–202.

59. Dauphin-Meunier, *Histoire du Cambodge*, 37.

60. Victor Goloubew, "L'Hydraulique urbaine et agricole à l'époque des rois d'Angkor," *Cahiers de l'Ecole Française d'Extrême-Orient*, no. 24 (1940): 18. The practice of building enormous water tanks was not unique to Angkor but was widespread throughout India, Sri Lanka, and Burma, for example, the Mahendratataka tank built during the Pallava dynasty of South India or those of the Pagan dynasty in Burma, which could irrigate thousands of hectares. Bray, *The Rice Economies*, 72.

61. Groslier, *Angkor et le Cambodge*, 106.

62. Stargardt demonstrates that during approximately the same period of time, and in a climatic environment akin to that of Angkor, Satingpra in southern Thailand gave rise

to a Mon civilization that built extensive irrigation networks in an arid environment and that this irrigation network allowed rice production to rise exponentially. Janice Stargardt, *Satingpra I: The Environmental and Economic Archaeology of South Thailand* (Singapore: The Institute of Southeast Asian Studies, 1983), 119.

63. Groslier, *Angkor et le Cambodge*, 111.

64. Paul Pelliot, *Mémoires sur les coutumes du Cambodge de Tcheou Ta Kouan: Version nouvelle suivie d'un commentaire inachevé* (Paris: Librairie d'Amérique et d'Orient, 1951), 24.

65. Groslier, *Angkor et le Cambodge*, 113.

66. R. B., "Le Baray Occidental," *Bulletin de la Société des Etudes Indochinoises* 24, no. 2 (1949): 28.

67. Groslier, *Angkor et le Cambodge*, 118.

68. Groslier, "La Civilisation angkorienne," 30–31; also Groslier, "La Cité hydraulique," 192–194.

69. R. B. Smith, "Mainland South East Asia in the Seventh and Eighth Centuries," in Smith and Watson, eds., *Early South East Asia*, 453.

70. Milton Osborne, *River Road to China: The Mekong River Expedition, 1866–1873* (New York: Liveright, 1975), 17. Cham war vessels were nonetheless able to sail up the Mekong and the Tonle Sap to attack Angkor and to inflict a serious defeat to the Khmer kingdom in 1177.

71. Chandler, *A History of Cambodia*, 59.

72. Van Liere, "Traditional Water Management," 273.

73. Dauphin-Meunier, *Histoire du Cambodge*, 54.

74. Bray, *The Rice Economies*, 77.

75. Ibid.

76. Louis Malleret, *L'Archéologie du delta du Mékong*, 4 vols. (Paris: Ecole Française d'Extrême-Orient, 1959–1963), 3:402–411.

77. Ibid., 1:117–124; 3:324. Malleret's research has been taken up by Vietnamese researchers after 1975 and updated in a number of publications, for instance, the work by Le Xuan Diem, Dao Linh Con, and Vo Si Khai, *Van Hoa Oc Eo, Nhung Kham Pha Moi* (Ha-noi: Nha Xuat Ban Khoa Hoc Xa Hoi, 1995).

78. Contrary to anthropologist Francesca Bray's assertion that "Cochinchina was practically uninhabited when the French arrived" (Bray, *The Rice Economies*, 95), historian Pierre Brocheux, among others, demonstrates in *The Mekong Delta* that Cochinchina, of which the Mekong delta forms the most important part, is of ancient and multiethnic settlement and that this settlement accelerated under the early Nguyen dynasty. Indeed, this prosperous and productive region was already serving as "rice basket" of the Nguyen's empire when the French invaded it in 1859.

79. Tran Van Giau, ed., *Dia Chi Van Hoa Thanh Pho Ho Chi Minh*, 2 vols. (Thanh Pho Ho Chi Minh: Nha Xuat Ban Thanh Pho Ho Chi Minh, 1987), 1:134.

80. Li Tana and Anthony Reid, eds., *Southern Vietnam under the Nguyen: Documents on the Economic History of Cochinchina* (Dang Trong), 1602–1777 (Singapore: Institute of Southeast Asian Studies, 1993), 1.

81. Huynh Lua, ed., *Lich Su Khai Pha*, 44.

82. Ibid., 60.

83. Although this royal union was mentioned in Khmer chronicles translated by French historians, Vietnamese annals of the same period failed to do so despite its tremendous import for the later history of the Nam Tien. Phan Khoang, *Viet Su: Xu Dang Trong 1558–1777*, 2 vols. (Sai-gon, 1967), 2:400.

84. J. Moura, *Le Royaume du Cambodge*, 2 vols. (Paris: Ernest Leroux, 1883), 2:58–59; Dauphin-Meunier, *Le Cambodge*, 56.

85. Keith W. Taylor paints a vibrant portrait of Nguyen Hoang, one of the Nguyen princes considered the pioneer in the Vietnamese southward movement that began c. 1558, calling him "the beginning of a southern version of being Vietnamese." Keith W. Taylor, "Nguyen Hoang and the Beginning of Vietnam's Southward Expansion," in Anthony Reid, ed., *Southeast Asia in the Early Modern Era* (Ithaca, NY: Cornell University Press, 1993), 45.

86. Truong Dang Que et al., *Dai Nam Thuc Luc Tien Bien*, translated by Li Tana, in Tana and Reid, eds., *Southern Vietnam*, 128.

87. Le Quy Don, *Phu Bien Tap Luc*, translated by Li Tana in ibid., 126.

88. Trinh Hoai Duc, *Gia Dinh Thanh Thong Chi*, translated by Nguyen Tao, 3 vols. (Sai-gon: Nha Van Hoa Phu Quoc Vu Khanh Dac Trach Van Hoa, 1972), 2:17. Hereafter, *GDTTC*.

89. Huynh Lua, ed., *Lich Su Khai Pha*, 62.

90. Que et al., *Dai Nam*, 129–130.

91. Mark W. McLeod, *The Vietnamese Response to French Intervention, 1862–1874* (New York: Praeger, 1991), 8–9.

92. The *Gia Dinh Thanh Thong Chi* details the Vietnamese encroachments on Cambodian territory starting in the seventeenth century. As the Khmer kingdom became weaker, it had to turn to the Vietnamese as counterweight against the Siamese. *GDTTC*, 2:4–25.

93. *GDTTC*, 1:89.

94. Huynh Lua, ed., *Lich Su Khai Pha*, 140.

95. John White, *A Voyage to Cochinchina*, introduced by Milton Osborne (Kuala Lumpur: Oxford University Press, 1972), 237.

96. For a discussion of the numerous rice varieties and cultivation practices in the Mekong delta, see Nguyen Cong Binh, Le Xuan Diem, and Mac Duong, eds., *Van Hoa va Cu Dan Dong Bang Song Cuu Long* (Thanh Pho Ho Chi Minh: Nha Xuat Ban Khoa Hoc Xa Hoi, 1990), 257–279.

97. Hugh Toye, *Laos: Buffer State or Battleground?* (London: Oxford University Press, 1968), 21. This was in reaction to the Chao Anu rebellion of 1827 that was defeated by the Siamese. Anu, the ruler of Vientiane, was brought back to Bangkok, where he died in 1829. Wyatt, *Thailand*, 171. See also "Siam and Laos 1767–1827," in David K. Wyatt, *Studies in Thai History: Collected Articles by David K. Wyatt* (Chiang Mai: Silkworm Books, 1994), 185–209.

98. Wyatt, *Thailand*, 172.

99. M. L. Jumsai, *A New History of Laos* (Bangkok: Chalermnit, 1971), 125.

100. Lévy, *Histoire du Laos*, 58. According to Paul Lévy, there was no Lao nation before colonial times, since the concept of Lao nationhood resulted from the French protectorate over different Lao kingdoms. However, this essentially Francocentric view of the nonexistence of *Sat Lao* (Lao nation) has been strongly contested by Lao historians such as Katay D. Sasorith, who points out that the use of such expressions as *Sua Sat Lao* (Lao origin and race), *Pathet Lao* (Lao State) or *Muong Lao* (Lao Country) dates from "oldest antiquity to the present day." Katay D. Sasorith, "Historical Aspects of Laos," in René de Berval, ed., *Kingdom of Laos*, 29.

101. Coedès, *The Making of Southeast Asia*, 8.

102. Paul Lévy, "Le Voyage de Wuysthof au Laos (1641–1642) d'après son journal," *Cahiers de l'Ecole Française d'Extrême-Orient*, 1944, 20. For an updated, annotated,

and French-translated version of Gerrit van Wuysthoff's account of his journey into Cambodia and Laos in the seventeenth century, see Jean-Claude Lejosne, *Le Journal de voyage de Gerrit van Wuysthoff et de ses assistants au Laos (1641–1642)* (Metz, France: Centre de documentation et d'information sur le Laos, 1993).

103. Francis Garnier, *Voyage d'exploration en Indochine* (Paris: Editions La Décou- verte, 1985), 108. There has been since c. 1985 a revival of interest in the Mekong River, not only regionally, where numerous conferences and workshops have been organized on the topic, but also in Europe and in the United States. French scholars, in particular, have returned to the question of the exploration of the river by French and other European ex- plorers, missionaries, and scholars, leading to an outburst of works on the subject. See, for instance, Jean Pierre Gomane, *L'Exploration du Mékong: La Mission Ernest Doudart de Lagrée-Francis Garnier (1866–1868)* (Paris: L'Harmattan, 1994); and Luc Lacroze, *Les Grands Pionniers du Mékong: Une Cinquantaine d'année d'aventures, 1884–1935* (Paris: L'Harmattan, 1996). English-language publications of explorers' journals and ac- counts have also been reissued; for instance, Francis Garnier, *Travels in Cambodia and Part of Laos: The Mekong Exploration Commission Report (1866–1868)*, translated and with an introduction by Walter E. J. Tips, 2 vols. (Bangkok: White Lotus Press, 1996).

104. Henri Mouhot, *Travels in Siam, Cambodia and Laos, 1858–1860*, 2 vols. (Sin- gapore: Oxford University Press, 1989), 1:221.

105. Ibid., 1:231.

106. Ibid., 2:135.

107. Cited by Jean Valette, "L'Expédition du Mékong à travers les témoignages de quelques uns de ses membres," *Revue Historique*, no. 502 (April–June 1972): 351.

108. Jean Valette, "Origines et enseignements de l'expédition du Mékong," *Bulletin de la Société d'Histoire Moderne*, no. 6 (1968): 8.

109. Naval officers were among the most enthusiastic advocates of this enterprise, and in the first decades of the colonization, from 1861 to 1879, the governors of Cochinchina in charge of its pacification and organization were all admirals. The first admirals to ar- rive in Sai-gon were Vice-Admiral Charner, the commander-in-chief of all French naval forces in the China seas, and Admiral Bonard (1861–1863). See Paul Isoart, *Le Phé- nomène national vietnamien* (Paris: R. Pichon et R. Durand-Augias, 1961), 126–127; Eu- gène Teston and Maurice Percheron, *L'Indochine moderne: Encyclopédie administrative, touristique, artistique et économique* (Paris: Librairie de France, 1932), 32–36.

110. Georges Taboulet, "Le Voyage d'exploration du Mékong," *Revue Française d'Histoire d'Outre-Mer* 57, no. 206 (1970): 17.

111. Ibid., 16.

112. Cited by Valette, "L'Expédition du Mékong," 351.

113. Taboulet, "Le Voyage d'exploration du Mékong," 20.

114. Valette, "L'Expédition du Mékong," 350.

115. Ibid., 349.

116. Taboulet, "Le Voyage d'exploration du Mékong," 18.

117. Cited by Valette, "Origines et enseignements," 9.

118. Cited by Valette, "L'Expédition du Mékong," 355.

119. Georges Taboulet, *La Geste française en Indochine*, 2 vols. (Paris: Adrien- Maisonneuve, 1956), 2:554–555.

120. Roger Vercel, *Francis Garnier à l'assaut des fleuves* (Paris: Albin Michel, 1952), 26.

121. Taboulet, "Le Voyage d'exploration du Mékong," 52. Upon his return, Francis

Garnier published in the French geographic and travel review *Le Tour du Monde* an account of his journey and of the mission. It can also be found in his work *Voyage d'exploration en Indochine effectué pendant les années 1866–1868*, 2 vols. (Paris: Publications Officielles, 1873); a newer edition has been published as Francis Garnier, *Voyage d'exploration en Indochine* (Paris: Editions La Découverte, 1985).

122. Garnier, *Voyage d'exploration en Indochine*, 39.

123. Valette, "L'Expédition du Mékong," 367.

124. Garnier, *Voyage d'exploration en Indochine*, 87.

125. Ibid., 81–82.

126. Ibid., 185.

127. Valette, "Origines et enseignements," 9.

128. See Auguste Pavie, *Mission Pavie Indochine, 1879–1895, géographie et voyages*, 10 vols. (Paris: E. Leroux, 1898–1919). See also Auguste Pavie, *A la conquête des coeurs* (Paris: Presses Universitaires de France, 1947).

129. Pavie established a detailed plan of action that aimed at pacifying the cantons, a plan that was recognized by the chief of staff of the Indochinese army, General Begin, in a letter of July 1888: "The monograph that you have addressed to me . . . is a geographic and political document of the highest importance. It details the region from Luang-Prabang to the Black River, which was totally unknown until now . . . as well as the roads that traverse it and can be used for our trade in a near future. . . . You have intended, through your own efforts, to bring in French influence in this region that is much coveted by a neighboring power and is occupied by the Chinese pirate bands that we have thrown out of Tonkin." Le Boulanger, *Histoire du Laos français*, 282. See also Wyatt, *Thailand*, 202–204, for a different analysis of the events more sympathetic to the Thai side.

130. Claire Hirshfield, "The Struggle for the Mekong Banks," *Journal of Southeast Asian History* 9, no. 1 (March 1968): 30.

131. Ibid., 41.

132. Stuart-Fox, *Laos*, 11.

133. Jumsai, *A New History of Laos*, 207. Lefèvre, a member of the joint Franco-British Commission that was appointed in 1895 to investigate the question of Muong Sing and its appurtenance, wrote a detailed account of the competition between the two powers as well as the incredible complexities of the region. E. Lefèvre, *Travels in Laos: The Fate of the Sip Song Pana and Muong Sing (1894–1896)*, translated and with an introduction by Walter E. J. Tips (Bangkok: White Lotus Press, 1995).

134. Hirshfield, "The Struggle for the Mekong Banks," 49. See also "Déclaration de Londres, du 15 janvier 1896, entre la France et la Grande-Bretagne au sujet du Siam," in Raoul Abor, *Conventions et traités de droit international intéressant l'Indochine* (Hanoi: Imprimerie d'Extrême-Orient, 1929), 69.

135. Wyatt, *Thailand*, 206.

136. Alfred McCoy, "French Colonialism in Laos, 1893–1945," in Nina S. Adams and A. McCoy, eds., *Laos: War and Revolution* (New York: Harper and Row, 1970), 77.

137. Teston and Percheron, *L'Indochine moderne*, 104.

138. A. A. Pouyanne, *Les Travaux publics de l'Indochine* (Hanoi: Imprimerie d'Extrême-Orient, 1926), 98–99.

139. George Finlayson, *The Mission to Siam and Hue, the Capital of Cochinchina, in the Years 1821–1822* (London: Albemarle-Street, 1826), 314.

140. P. Cordemoy, "L'Aménagement hydraulique de la Cochinchine," *Bulletin de l'Agence Economique de l'Indochine*, no. 51 (March 1932): 85.

141. Robequain, *L'Indochine française*, 139.

142. Cordemoy, "L'Aménagement hydraulique," 88.

143. Ibid., 84. "The cultivated surface in Cochinchina went from around 290,000/ 308,000 ha in 1836 to 2,303,000 ha in 1943." Pierre Brocheux and Daniel Hémery, *Indochine, la colonisation ambiguë (1858–1954)* (Paris: Editions La Découverte, 1995), 117.

144. Pouyanne, *Les Travaux publics*, 99.

145. Paul Bernard, *Le Problème économique indochinois* (Paris: Nouvelles Editions Latines, 1934), 86.

146. Brocheux, *The Mekong Delta*, 22.

147. Cordemoy, "L'Aménagement hydraulique," 88.

148. Robequain, *L'Indochine française*, 184.

149. Pouyanne, *Les Travaux publics*, 141.

150. For a detailed description of the work accomplished by the French colonial government on the Mekong River, see Lacroze, *Les Grands Pionniers du Mékong*, 153–166. The author mentions that overall planning for the work to be carried out on the river was envisaged late, and most of the effort was left to the initiative of the local administration.

151. P. Cordemoy, "Le Réseau navigable Indochinois," *Bulletin de l'Agence Economique de l'Indochine*, no. 82 (October 1934): 376.

152. Pouyanne, *Les Travaux publics*, 23.

153. Cordemoy, "Le Réseau navigable indochinois," 374.

154. Xieng-la, "Le Mékong, voie de pénétration," *Revue Indochinoise*, no. 178 (March 17, 1902): 238.

155. Alain Forest, *Le Cambodge et la colonisation française: Histoire d'une colonisation sans heurts (1897–1920)* (Paris: Editions L'Harmattan, 1980), 238.

156. Nguyen Quoc Dinh, "L'Internationalisation du Mékong," *Annuaire Français du Droit International* 8 (1962): 96.

157. However, it should be noted that the financing of these works weighed more heavily on Cochinchina than on any other territory of the Indochinese Union. Over a period of thirty-five years (1900–1935), Cochinchina contributed more than 40 percent of the General Budget's receipts. Given the total amount of public works expenditures of 404 million piasters, Cochinchina's share should have been 161 million, and yet it was only 85 million. Furthermore, of the 176 million piasters allocated by the General Budget as direct subventions to the Union members' local budgets, given its percentage of participation in the receipts, Cochinchina's share should have been 70 million instead of the 27 million that it received. Paul Bernard, *Nouveaux aspects du problème économique indochinois* (Paris: Fernand Sorlot, 1937), 53.

158. Nguyen Quoc Dinh, "L'Internationalisation du Mékong," 101. See also the Treaty of Amity, Commerce, and Navigation between France and Siam, December 7, 1939, in Roger Lévy, *French Policy in the Far East, 1936–1938* (New York: Institute of Pacific Relations, 1939), 101–109.

159. Ibid.

160. Suphasin Jayanama, "L'Aménagement du Mékong en droit international public" (Ph.D. thesis, University of Toulouse, 1965), 126–132.

161. Although the three new states had agreed to observe the Franco-Siamese International Convention of 1926, concerning the nonobstruction of navigation on the river and other clauses. Pachoom Chomchai, *The United States, the Mekong Committee and Thailand: A Study of American Multilateral and Bilateral Assistance to Northeast Thai-*

land since the 1950s (Bangkok: Institute of Asian Studies, Chulalongkorn University, 1994), 279.

162. George Gayet, "Le Mékong, voie fluviale de l'avenir," *Bulletin de la Société des Etudes Indochinoises* 24, no. 2 (1949): 95.

PART II

War

2

The Mekong River in the
Indochina Wars

The era of international and regional organizations began in the immediate post–World War II period when the ravages of war were such that piecemeal reconstruction, each country on its own, seemed impossible. The search for global equilibrium through social and economic development of different regions of the world also contributed to its rise. Furthermore, as the cold war split the globe, dividing it into two blocs led by, on one hand, the United States, and on the other, the Soviet Union, each waged a war of influence on all fronts within geographic space as well as in the arena of international organizations. Admission of a nation, budgetary appropriations, or the choice of a particular development project were so many available means of persuasion or coercion. The stakes were the alignment of Third World countries, which were in dire need of economic and technical aid as well as of capital in order to build or rebuild their economies. Within the United Nations (UN), a multitude of commissions were rapidly formed to solve the problem of reconstruction and development of member countries. It was the conjunction of these factors—the rise of international organizations and concomitant regionalism, and the globalization of the cold war—that awakened the Mekong River from its slumber by placing it at the heart of long and devastating conflicts and by rendering it the focus of an ambitious plan, the Mekong Project.

REGIONALISM

Upon request by its members and under pressure from delegates from Asia and Latin America, the UN Economic and Social Council (ECOSOC), whose task was to solve the problem of post-war regional reconstruction, had founded not only the Economic Commission for Europe (ECE) and for Latin America (ECLA) but also a commission for Asia and the Far East (ECAFE) in March 1947. These commissions were charged with supervising the economic reconstruction of nations within their geographic area. The creation of an Asian commission equal in rank to the one for Europe was greeted with dismay by European delegates, who had no desire to contribute to the emancipation of their colonies.

The region under ECAFE's supervision included all of the territories that were colonies or former colonies, such as "British North Borneo . . . Indo-Chinese Federation . . . Netherlands Indies," and ECAFE's members were colonial powers with vested interests in the region: "France . . . Netherlands . . . United Kingdom . . . United States of America."[1] Admission to ECAFE was heatedly debated, as contention raged between the colonial powers and the newly independent states, which viewed the commission as a forum where their rights as independent nations could be defended. China and the Soviet Union, through their respective allies, also participated in the debates. According to the UN's general rule, full membership to ECAFE was granted only to countries that were already UN members. Few Asian states fulfilled this requirement: China, the Philippines, India, and Thailand. The participation of France, the Netherlands, and the United Kingdom in ECAFE was justified by the fact that the region of Southeast Asia had been and was still part of their empires in the immediate post-war period. However, the United States and the Soviet Union's seating could be explained only in terms of world leadership and by the presence of their occupation forces in Asia.

The full-membership requirement excluded the participation of so-called non-autonomous regions, that is, the majority of countries in Southeast Asia under ECAFE's responsibility; as such, it was contested by the interested parties. The United States and its Asian ally Thailand put forward an amendment adopted by ECAFE, which stipulated that the request for representation could be formulated only by the metropolitan power controlling the said territory. In the event of independence, autonomy, or division, the colonial power could obtain the official recognition of a political regime favorable to it—even though such a regime might not be recognized by its people. The colonial power could also choose not to sponsor the request made by a nonautonomous territory if it were of the opinion that it could not have control over the territory's political destiny.

In November 1947, at the second meeting of ECAFE, France, which still ruled the Indochinese countries, sponsored the admission of Laos and Cambodia. However, the case of Vietnam was left unresolved on French request as Vietnam's political fate had yet to be determined.[2] Meanwhile, the Democratic Republic of Vietnam (D.R.V.), founded on September 2, 1945, in its search for international political recognition, attempted to gain representation on the commission but was thwarted by the Western powers, adamant to block Ho Chi Minh's Communist government. With the approval of the United States, the United Kingdom, and Australia, France decided, instead, to sponsor the candidacy of the newly created State of Vietnam (S.O.V.; under Bao-dai) for ECAFE in October 1949.

It was a relatively easy matter for the Western bloc to have full-membership status conferred on Laos, Cambodia, and the S.O.V. although these states were not members of the UN. After the signing of the Geneva Agreements in 1954, the newly independent republics of Laos, Cambodia, and Vietnam (with the exclusion of the D.R.V.) became full ECAFE members—Cambodia and the S.O.V. in February 1954 and Laos in March 1955. Thanks to a motion advanced by the United States and France, the three countries of Indochina were merely asked to pay a yearly membership fee as a condition of their acceptance at ECAFE.[3]

The geographic area covered by ECAFE was a particularly vulnerable one, since independence struggles and Communist-influenced movements were still active and, increasingly, attracting the attention and support of the two opposed blocs. The membership question and the determination of ECAFE's goals were used by the protagonists as opportunities for confrontation. Within the context of the cold war, ECAFE's raison d'être, aiding post-war reconstruction, was obscured by the United States–USSR conflict. Through skillful political maneuvers, the Western bloc successfully imposed its dictates in all the critical matters: choice of nations represented by anti-Communist governments, refusal to admit Communist countries as members, and so forth. ECAFE's composition reflected more the domination of Western powers within international organizations than the political realities in Asia. The People's Republic of China (P.R.C.), the Democratic People's Republic of Korea, and the D.R.V. were newly emerging nation-states, yet they were rejected from the international and regional community and were prevented from having any say in decisions that often concerned them.

Western powers and the nations of the region were at loggerheads concerning the objectives of the commission. For the former and, in particular, for the members of the ECE, an ECAFE contributing to the reconstruction of Southeast Asian countries would take away funds that could be devoted to Europe. They feared that such efforts would be of the magnitude of the Marshall Plan of 1947. The European members envisioned ECAFE's role as a passive one, an observer that would analyze economic and technical data of the region. Conversely, the Asian states had high hopes for ECAFE, envisaging it as effectively contributing to the reconstruction and long-term development of their nations through industrialization, since their economies were predominantly agrarian. However, Western powers vetoed their plans for industrialization, considering it a potential threat to their own recovering post-war economies. Bowing to the will of its Western allies, the United States stated, through its representative, that ECAFE would overreach its original goals if it were to take up an active part in the reconstruction of countries of the region.[4]

Hence, ECAFE's regulations stipulated that its mission was to identify and analyze Asia's economic problems, to encourage activities that would foster direct cooperation between and among its members, and to help them in formulating sound policies and in improving their infrastructures for the application of these policies.[5] From the onset, ECAFE focused on the question of water and its

relevant aspects (such as flood control or irrigation), organizing dozens of regional conferences on the study and planning of hydraulic resources. As most
countries of the region were afflicted by seasonal flooding, ECAFE founded the
Flood Control Bureau, later renamed the Bureau of Flood Control and Water
Resources Development in 1949.[6] Like that of its founder-organization, the bureau's only role was to study technical problems concerning flood control and
water resources development and to research and promote the multipurpose development of river basins as well as advise respective governments upon their
request.

The bureau's first task was to examine the needs of regions most affected by
flooding and to suggest preventive measures that could be taken concerning
nineteen rivers of the region.[7] In January 1951, at the Regional Technical Conference on Flood Control (New Delhi) under the auspices of the UN, several
fundamental principles were agreed upon that defined flood control as an inherent part of the development of river basins, and it was asserted that both flood
control and the use of water resources were essential to the economic development of a nation.[8] The following month, at ECAFE's seventh session held in La-
hore, it was decided to broaden the bureau's scope by including international
rivers, that is, rivers that flow through two or more countries. There were several
possibilities: the Yellow and Yangzi Rivers, the Indus, and the Mekong. China,
despite its vast hydrographic network, was not considered a favorable terrain for
study because of the Communist victory of 1949. The tension between India and
Pakistan momentarily prevented any study of the Indus River valley. Accordingly, the decision was made to focus on the lower Mekong basin with the approval of the four riparian countries. Neither China nor Burma, the other two riparian countries, was included, since China was not yet a member of the UN, and
Burma was in the throes of its independence struggle.[9]

The study, published in May 1952 with the collaboration of consultants from
Cambodia and Thailand, enthusiastically proposed irrigation of the Northeast of
Thailand by diversion of the mainstream, the possibility of power production
between Vientiane and Luang Prabang, improved navigation on the mainstream,
and so forth.[10] However, there was no immediate follow-up study because Indochina was engulfed in war. Only Thailand was able to push for the continuation
of studies on the segment of the river that forms the boundary between Thailand
and Laos, particularly focusing on the possibility of diverting the Mekong for the
irrigation of the Northeast.[11]

In its second session held in Tokyo, April 1955, ECAFE renewed its expression of interest in the development of international rivers, in particular, the Mekong, whose exploration was recommended. Since the United States—by then
increasingly involved in the region—was sending a Bureau of Reclamation team
to the region for the same purpose, the commission expressed the desire to participate in it.[12] However, the United States, whose interest in the Mekong River
was signaled by the presidential report presented to Congress in June 1955, declined to cooperate.[13] It had high hopes of reproducing the Tennessee Valley

Authority miracle and insisted on keeping exclusive control over this exploration mission, thus denying ECAFE's involvement.

The commission's proposal went against not only Washington's ambitious plan but also the UN's policy of maximum centralization. The UN headquarters was of the opinion that the field mission should be under its responsibility. The combined pressures exerted by the UN Technical Assistance Administration (TAA) and by the UN Department of Economic and Social Affairs on ECAFE to persuade it to forsake its own exploration mission reached a crescendo at the commission's twelfth session in February 1956 in Bangalore. However, the UN did not succeed in forcing the commission to change its decision. On the contrary, the riparian countries rallied around and supported ECAFE.[14]

Concurrently, Prince Sihanouk, urged by the United States to align Cambodia once and for all with the countries of the Southeast Asia Treaty Organization (SEATO), balked at the pressure, and Cambodia expressed support for ECAFE's exploration proposal as a way to manifest its noncooperation with the United States.[15] Cambodia then turned to the commission and requested that it proceed with the plan, expressing the hope of all of the other riparian members that the exploration would be carried out without delay. Despite U.S. opposition and the UN's hesitation, ECAFE launched a mission of exploration that involved French, Dutch, Indian, and Japanese scientists, who, from April to May 1956, explored the Mekong mainstream from Tonle Sap to upstream Vientiane, a distance of 1,300 kilometers. It presented its preliminary report at ECAFE's thirteenth session in March 1957.[16] Although it took up the U.S. Bureau of Reclamation's recommendations—in particular, the necessity for more thorough information— the mission did not suggest a country-by-country development of the river (as proposed by the U.S. report) but instead recommended a community of efforts of the four riparian states, which would consider the Mekong basin "as a single dynamic and organic system" and would assume that "planning for the optimum use and conservation of water resources should cover an entire river basin, including the main river and its tributaries."[17] It suggested that tributary projects located entirely within a single country be under that country's responsibility but be coordinated and compatible with the mainstream projects within the framework of the lower Mekong basin development.[18]

ECAFE's study analyzed the state of water resources development in the four riparian countries and suggested sites that were particularly suitable for exploitation. In terms of flood control, there had previously been small-scale flood-control works in Laos and Cambodia and in the Mekong delta in the Republic of Vietnam (R.V.N.). Irrigation works such as dams and reservoirs were more common and could be found in the Northeast of Thailand (built with U.S. aid), and in Cambodia. For Laos and southern Vietnam, there were only a few at the time of the study. There was a serious need for irrigation that would facilitate double-cropping and diversification (the planting of subsidiary crops such as corn, soya beans, and sweet potatoes). At the time of the report, there was no hydroelectric work in the lower basin. And yet, the need for hydroelectricity was immense, because the cost of thermal power paid in hard currency was too high for an underdeveloped region with rapidly increasing consumption. The hydro-electric potential was uneven according to each country. The report concluded that the Northeast of Thailand did not present favorable conditions for hydro-power dams because of rain scarcity and the rather flat topography. Laos, on the other hand, had a better potential, since it is a mountainous region with a rich hydrography. There were possibilities in the Cardamom and the Elephant chains in Cambodia. In terms of navigation, river traffic was important for both Cambodia and southern Vietnam, which had an important network of canals.

The report suggested five possible sites for the unified development of the river: the Pa Mong Falls between Laos and Thailand, thirty kilometers upstream from Vientiane; the Khemmarat Falls, fourteen kilometers upstream of the confluence of the Se Moune and the Mekong Rivers, which would result in the flooding of the city of Savannakhet; the Khone Falls, north of the Lao-Cambodian border; the Sambor rapids; and the Tonle Sap Lake in Cambodia. These five projects were to be studied and undertaken as an integrated whole. ECAFE's report called for international cooperation and underlined the necessity for the creation of an international organization for information exchange and for the formulation and coordination of projects. This was considered indispensable, since uniform norms must be used for construction to avoid possible adverse effects that any work undertaken by a riparian country on one or several tributaries might have on upstream or downstream neighbors.[19]

Nevertheless, the report suggested that the economic and technical feasibility stage would not be reached immediately, since the collection of information, a tremendous task, had top priority. It emphasized the necessity of a regional approach and of international aid and the fact that strong cooperation between the four riparian states was the *sine qua non* of their success. The riparian governments unanimously approved the report's conclusions and expressed the wish that studies similar to the report would be carried out jointly by the four concerned countries to analyze potential respective benefits.[20] In view of the political situation at the time, that is, in the wake of the First Indochina War, it was remarkable that these four countries were able to reach a common agreement, expressing and maintaining their support for ECAFE despite the U.S. opposition to and desire to control the project and despite the fear that this powerful ally might discontinue its bilateral aid and refuse to participate in the financing of the Mekong Project.

Several factors contributed to the unanimous support and to the rallying of the lower Mekong basin's countries around this development project. First of all, the project, with its immense potential, emphasized the interdependence of riparian countries and the need for full cooperation between them if it were to be successful. The second factor was the rivalry between France and the United States in the matter of Indochina, which had led France to actively support ECAFE and the Mekong Project. France had exerted pressure on recalcitrant Laos and Cambodia via its embassies for their cooperation in the project and had actively participated in the exploratory missions.[21]

At ECAFE's thirteenth session in March 1957, where the report was presented and unanimously approved, there was a complete change in the U.S. position. The United States announced that it was willing to provide technical and, probably, financial aid from its Fund for the Development of Asia. France, India, and Japan at once joined the official statement of aid to the Mekong Project. In May, ECAFE rapidly organized in Bangkok a meeting of experts from the riparian countries during which the necessity for coordinated, joint action was once again emphasized to provide for an integrated development of the lower Mekong basin. The meeting recommended the foundation of a coordination committee in which all four riparian states would be represented and that this committee be placed under the sponsorship of the UN. It selected several sites on the mainstream for further detailed study: Pa Mong, Sambor, Tonle Sap, and—possibly—Khone and Khemmarat.[22]

THE MEKONG COMMITTEE

Pressure exerted by the United States from the beginning prevented ECAFE from being entirely in charge of the Mekong River Project. It had, in fact, resulted in a backlash leading to tighter control of ECAFE by the UN. The UN had hoped that the committee in charge of such operation would be the true expression of the four riparians' will; that it would be autonomous, free from any major power's tutelage; that it would be efficient and effective, capable of making and enforcing decisions and not be just another discussion group. On the other hand, the committee, in order to be able to function and to have at its disposal adequate financial and technical means, needed the support of organizations such as the UN.

Very rapidly, with the help of the UN's Bureau of Legal Affairs, the representatives from the riparian countries and ECAFE formulated the status, the organization, and the composition of the future committee. In September 1957, the "Statute of the Committee for the Coordination of Investigations of the Lower Mekong Basin" was definitively adopted.[23] The structure, composition, and functioning of the Mekong Committee reflected the duality of an organization that, while answering to the member nations, must still be accountable to ECAFE and through it, to the UN and its most influential backers.

In terms of structure, the four riparian countries (Cambodia, Laos, Thailand, and the R.V.N.) were members of the Mekong Committee, which consisted of the General Assembly and two subsidiary organizations: the Executive Agent Bureau and the Advisory Board. The General Assembly involved the four nations, each of which sent a delegation led by a plenipotentiary appointed for technical as well as political skills. His task was "to promote, coordinate, supervise, and control the planning and investigation of water resources development projects in the Lower Mekong Basin."[24]

The first executive agent, C. H. Schaaf, was appointed in November 1959 by UN Secretary-General Dag Hammarsjkold. Schaaf, an American citizen, had formerly served as assistant executive secretary of ECAFE from 1949 to 1954. He was connected with the State Department, the UN, and ECAFE, a factor that facilitated the resolution of numerous difficulties in the relations between the Mekong Committee, ECAFE, the UN, and the United States. The executive agent was at the same time an agent of and responsible to the Mekong Committee as well as a functionary of the UN. There is a certain ambiguity in this dual responsibility, since the agent is answerable solely to the UN according to Article 100 of the UN Charter; at the same, as agent of the committee, he must be accountable to the committee. This ambivalence is reflected in the dual task assigned to him: He must keep in touch with the Executive Secretariat of ECAFE, whence he receives general policy guidelines; he must also advise the Mekong Committee and the member nations about administrative and technical coordination concerning the lower Mekong basin development.

The Advisory Board of the Mekong Committee included international experts from different UN organizations or from the World Bank. Its task was to advise the committee and the executive agent in a number of fields: revision of main projects, reports and studies, and field investigation. The fact that the committee's personnel were functionaries appointed by the respective riparian governments and international civil servants of the UN explains the joint management of the committee by the four riparian members and ECAFE as stipulated by Article 3, Chapter III, of the statute. The Mekong Committee met regularly three times a year in closed sessions. It was presided over in turn by the representative of one of the four members. Each member had one vote, and each decision had to be approved by a simple or absolute majority. The Mekong Committee's main goal was to encourage the extensive development of water resources to benefit the populations of the basin without distinction of nationality, religion, or politics.[25] Its function, therefore, was to coordinate, supervise, facilitate, and guide the planning of studies concerning the development of water resources. Its powers included consultation (with the member nations), preparation, proposal, recommendation of studies, and projects. In the name of the four riparian states, the committee was able to:

a) prepare and submit to participating governments plans for carrying out coordinated research, study and investigation; b) make requests on behalf of the participating governments for special financial and technical assistance and receive and administer separately such financial and technical assistance and take title to such property as may be offered under the technical assistance programs of the United Nations, specialized agencies, friendly governments or other organizations.[26]

The Mekong Committee had its own budget, but its personnel (including the executive agent) was financed by the different organizations under the UN's umbrella to ensure its economic and political objectivity.[27] It cooperated with a number of UN agencies as well as with nongovernmental organizations (NGOs) such as the Asia Foundation, Resources for the Future, Inc., and the Ford Foundation, and private companies such as Nippon Electric and Shell. UN member nations also belonged to the Mekong Committee as donors of financial and technical aid.

One of the Mekong Committee's first decisions at its opening session (October–November 1957) was to approve the launching of another exploratory mission led by retired Lieutenant-General Raymond A. Wheeler of the U.S. Army Corps of Engineers.[28] Its findings were published in a report entitled *Program of Studies and Investigations for Comprehensive Development Lower Mekong Basin*, also called the Wheeler Report. It reaffirmed the Mekong's immense potentialities and underlined the following goals:

1. The basic data presently available in the Lower Mekong River Basin are not adequate for comprehensive or definite project planning. 2. Immediate steps should be taken for its collection. . . . 5. Priority in the collection of this basic data should be given to reaches having promising sites for development, such as the three sites given in the joint request, as well as other important sites. . . . 7. Preliminary planning for important and promising reaches should begin as soon as essential data are available. 8. Studies and investigations for the preparation of a comprehensive plan of the Lower Mekong River Basin, including major tributaries, should follow with the careful coordination and integration of the various specific sites plans.[29]

It was stated that the program should stretch over five years, but within three years the preliminary planning should start for the mainstream projects, and at the end of the five years planning should be under way for the most important tributary projects. A general plan would have to be prepared then for the integrated development of the Mekong's water resources. The estimated costs of the studies for the priority projects would amount to US$ 5.7 million and for the secondary projects US$ 3.5 million, that is, a total of US$ 9.2 million over a five-year period.[30] For some, the Wheeler Report's goals appeared much too ambitious and beyond the member countries' capacity.

As it was formulated, the Wheeler program reflected two different approaches to the problems, two trends that would develop later either in opposition or in complementarity to each other. The International Cooperation Administration (ICA), the U.S. organization in charge of aid, favored a long preliminary planning stage since it was convinced that to allow the four countries to launch these projects without the indispensable information would be a financial and material waste leading to failure.[31] The organization emphasized the absolute necessity to gather data for the preparation of the lower Mekong basin's plan, which would integrate specific projects. This approach would entail an extremely long period of preparation, study, and training of a competent local staff for the gathering of data. The length of time would unavoidably delay the much-expected moment of project realization.

The second approach, which recognized the necessity of a general, integrated developmental approach and of collecting a maximum of information, equally acknowledged the riparian countries' economic needs and the fact that their enthusiasm might evaporate when faced with the slow pace. Hence, it was understood that these countries should be able to proceed within a reasonable amount of time with the Mekong River Project, which would contribute to their national development.

THE INITIAL YEARS: 1957–1965

Although it may have appeared ambitious to some, the Mekong Project from its inception never encountered financial difficulties. At its first session in Phnom Penh (October 31–November 1, 1957), C. V. Narasimhan, ECAFE's executive secretary, announced the French offer of US$ 120,000 (60 million francs) for the Mekong Project.[32] The French grant, made at a decisive moment of its existence, allowed the Mekong Committee to start setting up hydrologic and meteorological stations on the mainstream and tributaries.

At its second session in February 1958, in Bangkok, the committee unanimously decided to implement the program of studies and investigations as formulated by the Wheeler Mission for the period 1959 to 1963. It also requested through ECAFE the UN's backing for a priority status within the UN Special Projects Fund. The UN Bureau of Technical Assistance grant of US$ 200,000 allowed the committee to call on international experts for the preliminary studies.

In addition to France, New Zealand within the context of the Colombo Plan also contributed the equivalent of US$ 100,000 toward the same goal. The Soviet Union, a member of ECAFE, expressed its willingness to participate, and its representative at ECAFE's fifteenth session in March 1959, held in Australia, reportedly declared that his country could provide technical assistance for the planning and construction of projects on the Mekong River.[33] Soviet experts could be sent to help in the realization of the first hydraulic works, but the Soviet Union's offer was rejected by Thailand and the R.V.N., both fearing Communist infiltration.

Conversely, the U.S. contribution of $2 million, the largest, manifested its interest in and commitment to the project as well as its financial domination of it. Japan was also among the first interested countries and had decided to undertake one of the proposals recommended by the Wheeler Mission, which was the exploration of the main Mekong tributaries. In 1959, the Japanese exploration team, sponsored by its government, went on a two-year mission to survey the Mekong tributaries within the context of the Colombo Plan. All the participating countries, whether from within or outside of the region, were, with the exception of France, the Republic of China (Taiwan), and Iran, members of the Colombo Plan. It was thus within the context of the Colombo Plan that these countries were to make their offers and grant their aid.

The majority of the UN specialized institutions were equally represented in the Mekong Project, in particular, in the first stage of preparation, study, and exploration: The TAA volunteered a research team on mineral resources, local navigation, and market for power; the Food and Agriculture Organization (FAO) was in charge of initial studies on irrigation, soil, forests, and fisheries; the World Meteorological Organization (WMO) sent an expert to study hydrologic and meteorological questions.[34] The Special Fund was the organization that assumed a major part of the financial burden for the first stage. It financed feasibility studies of the four tributary projects originally selected as well as the planning of experimental farms, the study of mineral resources in the Northeast of Thailand, and a number of other projects. Its grant of US$ 2.5 million to the Mekong Committee allowed the latter to meet its internal management expenses.

The World Bank carefully studied the different projects according to its own criteria of economic priority and technical feasibility, pointing out the necessity of the participation of such organizations as the IDA (International Development Agency) for the granting of long-term loans or grants, because this would alleviate somewhat the financial burden that such a vast program represented for the limited resources of the member countries. Separately from the Mekong context, the World Bank conducted a survey published in 1959 on Thailand's economic prospects, in which it addressed the problem of the Northeast and the possibilities of its development. The exploitation of the Mekong River and particularly of the Pa Mong was mentioned. Noting that the Northeast was one of the poorest regions in Thailand, the report remarked that its economic growth "may become possible through the development of the Mekong."[35] The increasing aridity in the Northeast was noted by the mission, which suggested that a Pa Mong dam could alleviate it through diversion of the Mekong for irrigation.

Private contributions by the Asia Foundation (financing of travel), the Ford Foundation (socioeconomic study), and Resources for the Future, Inc. (power market study), as well as by Price Waterhouse and Shell, provided tremendous help. As the project progressed, these contributions, which were at first not counted in annual reports, became increasingly more numerous and substantial. At the end of 1958, cooperation and exploration offers and suggestions of study proposals from countries in and outside of the region were so numerous that the Mekong Committee had to specially organize them to establish work programs for the coming years.

The Mekong Committee focused on a number of priorities, which remained largely the same over several decades despite fluctuations in their relative rankings due to changing needs and particularly to changes in the political situation. First came basic data collection, which included an aerial mapping of the mainstream and tributaries, the setting up of hydrographic survey offices, and an exploration of tributaries in the entirety of the basin. For instance, Japan, which undertook a general exploration of all the main tributaries in the lower basin, presented, in 1961, a report on all thirty-four tributaries.[36] The United States hired the service of Harza Engineering, a U.S. company, to set up a hydrographic network in the basin.[37] Second, under the category of formulating a comprehensive plan for the basin's development, new information as it was collected was to be integrated and used in the formulation of the comprehensive plan. Third, study and planning of projects on the mainstream and on the tributaries was to be conducted based on the information collected through the fulfillment of the first two activities. The construction, operation, and management of hydraulic projects formed the fourth priority.

In its first decade, the Mekong Committee emphasized the importance of three projects on the mainstream, projects that involved Thailand and Laos (Pa Mong) but more particularly Cambodia (Sambor and Tonle Sap). The truly ambitious Pa Mong project, "the largest dam in the world," had attracted U.S. interest as the Bureau of Reclamation—in collaboration with the Australian team of the Snowy Mountains Hydro-Electric Authority—sent numerous missions of exploration for a preliminary study of the site. The Pa Mong project was intended to contribute to flood control from Vientiane to the sea, to irrigate one million hectares of land in the Northeast of Thailand and in Laos, to produce cheap electricity for the region of more than one million kilowatts, and to improve navigation upstream and downstream of the project thanks to the enormous capacity of its reservoir. In the early 1960s, the committee had high hopes of advancing this project to the construction stage and having it under the responsibility of the riparian nations.

The Sambor project, although located entirely in Cambodia, was to equally benefit Laos and Vietnam through submersion of waterfalls that obstructed navigation and through production of electricity and irrigation. Canadian, Filipino, and Japanese teams carried out geologic, cartographic, and feasibility studies for the project.

As for the Tonle Sap project, it envisioned through the construction of a dam in Kompong Chnang, "a gated barrage across the Tonle Sap," flood-prevention linked to the lake, and the irrigation of more than one million hectares around the Tonle Sap. Indian and French teams conducted research on halieutic activities, sedimentation in the lake, and other related aspects.[38]

Pa Mong, Sambor, and Tonle Sap were parts of an integrated five-project development on the mainstream. Their high costs still undetermined, the vast range of studies and future works, the technical difficulties, and the unknown extent of their impact at all levels on the riparian countries, upstream and downstream, were so many difficulties, which, although not insurmountable, rendered them very long term and lacking in financial appeal. However, the Mekong Committee hoped that by pushing for the realization of tributary projects, which were less costly, smaller in scale, and more limited in time and scope, it could acquire experience and demonstrate the profitability of such hydraulic works, eventually drumming up support for those of larger scale.

Once the planning and feasibility stages were completed, the tributary projects would no longer fall under the committee's responsibility and direct financing but would become fully national projects controlled by the relevant governments. With the next stage of investment and construction, the committee would still play a role by volunteering its services: preparation of feasibility reports, loan negotiations with potential lender-nations, selection of engineering firms for the tributary construction, and so forth. The tributary projects chosen were the Nam Pong and Nam Pung in the Northeast of Thailand, the Nam Ngum in Laos, and the Battambang project in Cambodia. Technical studies were completed rapidly with the technical and financial cooperation of donor countries such as Japan, which proved to be quite active in the overall Mekong Project. Japan also volunteered its services for the study of another Cambodian project, the Prek-Thnot, as well as for two others (Upper Se San and Sre Pok) in Vietnam.

Fifth in the Mekong Committee's efforts were ancillary projects: One of the most easily achievable goals was the improvement of navigation on the Mekong, which would equally contribute to the development of all four countries. However, it was also one that would require their close cooperation in order to solve all the problems inherent to inter-riverine navigation. Offers of technical aid had come from the UN Special Fund, the United Kingdom, France, New Zealand, the Netherlands, and the United States, but the interested nations bore responsibility for the majority of expenses. A host of other projects, such as the setting up of agricultural pilot-stations (funded by FAO) in the riparian countries, research projects on bilharzia (WHO), and a study of mineral prospects by France and the Special Fund, were concurrently launched. Should there be mineral deposits, new industries, in particular, that of aluminum, could be developed using hydraulic power produced by the Nam Ngum and Nam Pong projects. This would lead to the eventual economic development of impoverished regions such as the Northeast of Thailand and northern Laos. In the early years, until the end of the 1960s, the Mekong Committee focused its attention and financial means on the collection of technical data to arrive at a better understanding of all the aspects related to the lower Mekong basin and its development. It hoped "to generate international and domestic financial arrangements for the construction of a minimum of eight tributary projects; and to bring the three high-priority mainstream project investigations to the point where they can provide the basis for similar financial negotiations."[39] As a proof of their commitments, the four riparian members pledged to provide for the local expenses: the R.V.N. US$ 109,000; Thailand US$ 81,000; Laos US$ 72,000; and Cambodia US$ 61,000. In 1962, the Ford Foundation, at the committee's request, financed a mission headed by Gilbert F. White to study the possible economic, social, and administrative impacts of the development of the lower Mekong River's water resources on its population. At the conclusion of its trip to the region, the White mission submitted a report to the Mekong Committee containing a number of recommendations, the most important of which was that the committee should work in close cooperation with the World Bank and the U.S. Army Corps of Engineers to more closely investigate the socioeconomic aspects of the region.[40] Some of its recommendations were soon carried out, such as in the study on local energy markets, and world demand for products of the electro-industry.

During its initial stage, the Mekong Project did not encounter insurmountable financial difficulties. On the contrary, grants and economic aid from numerous sources poured in. At first glance, it may appear that this cooperation was free of strings, political or otherwise, since the majority of the funds came from the Colombo Plan members, and the plan itself was apparently free of political contingencies. However, the study of the complex mechanisms that controlled the financing of the two main stages in the realization of projects, and the questions that arose concerning the participation of Colombo Plan members—some among the poorest nations in the world—leads one to question the putative neutrality of this aid.

Any development project includes two related initial stages: first, preliminary and field studies to gather a maximum of information on the project, and next, the concrete aspect, that is, the construction of the project. The preliminary and field studies are in general carried out by specialized firms, international consultants acting on behalf of the interested country. Technical and feasibility reports follow, which include, among others, economic studies as well as commercial and financial reports.[41]

There are multiple possibilities concerning financing. Very seldom does the government of the project-country have to finance both stages in their entirety. In general, a development project requires an enormous amount of capital, expertise, experience, and technical means that the project-country does not have. It has to call upon international aid, which can be bilateral (transfer of capital or technology from the donor to the beneficiary) or multilateral (granted by international or regional economic and technical aid organizations). This aid includes capital or technical aid or, most often, a combination of both. Capital aid is in the form of grants (in materials or cash) or in low-interest, long-term, favorable-repayment-condition loans that the beneficiary uses to finance the project. Technical assistance involves personnel, equipment, and training of local staff, which is all covered by the donor country.

Bilateral aid generally covers all expenses for a local, national project. But when the project extends beyond one nation to a geographic area involving several nations, such as the Indus River Project between Pakistan and India or the lower Mekong River Project when it stretches through several decades, directly influencing all aspects of economic, social, and political life of riparian nations, then the success of such a project requires the joint efforts of numerous countries and aid organizations. For the lower Mekong basin, an organization like the Mekong Committee was indispensable, because it acted as facilitator between countries with a long history of conflict.

The financial aid that the committee received directly was used to finance the first stage, that is, to finance studies, which are considered pre-investments. The Mekong Committee consistently followed a policy of using grants to finance such pre-investments, using loans only for the second stage, that of construction. It states that

no dam or other water resources development installation should be constructed unless a detailed feasibility investigation has demonstrated that benefits will outweigh costs. . . . The funds required for construction of any water resources development project are customarily very much greater—sometimes 50 or 100 times greater—than the cost of pre-investment investigations and planning. Hence, grants can often be found for the lesser expenditure, while loans are necessary for the larger expenditure.[42]

Grants in the form of financial aid or technical assistance (experts, material, equipment), or in kind, could be multilateral and made to the committee, which, in the name of the four countries, managed them to their best interests. Countries like Iran, for instance, contributed to the Mekong Project by providing petroleum products for the supply of cars used for in-field studies; India provided rain-gauges, spare parts, and other equipment. One of the most important contributions, however, was from the World Food Program, which directly provided food products to the more than seven thousand workers and their families working on the sites of such projects as the Nam Pung and Nam Pong in Thailand and other projects in Laos and Cambodia.

The majority of capital for pre-investment work was provided by participating countries from outside the region. The riparian countries had to cover local spending incurred in the context of the realization of these works in the countries. When a project took place in its totality in a given country, as was the case for the French study of mineral resources in Cambodia, the Pakistani project for an irrigation network for the Nam Pong in Thailand, the experimental farm on the Vientiane Plain in Laos, or the Japanese project of the Upper Sre Pok in Vietnam, local contributions (promised or appropriated) were theoretically covered entirely by the government of the concerned country. It was possible, however, for a country with serious financial deficits to use grants rather than loans or to directly resort to funds granted by bilateral aid to meet its obligations of coverage of the local cost of programs. The four countries of the lower Mekong basin, without exception, had permanent budgetary difficulties that prevented them from fulfilling their obligations. One could assume then that bilateral aid granted mainly by the United States, France, or Japan, among other countries, indirectly solved this dilemma. For instance, the United Kingdom's contribution was made partly in equipment and assistance to navigational improvement, but part of it was also in cash to help the committee to cover the local cost of the Special Fund tributary projects.

The aid of the United States in the context of the Mekong Project is another example. As for the other projects, U.S. aid was managed and administered by the all-powerful USAID (Agency for International Development), which had replaced ICA. In the beginning, the United States and the concerned country—Thailand, Laos, Cambodia, or the R.V.N.—signed a general aid agreement stipulating the conditions and the goals of this aid. In the context of the Mekong Project, in theory, it was up to the government of the riparian country to present a precise project, which was then examined by the Mekong Committee to determine whether this particular project fitted into the overall development program before its submission to the regional bureau of USAID.[43] When the project was approved by headquarters in Washington, an agreement was concluded between the riparian country and USAID. It sometimes happened that the agreement was signed by the Mekong Committee, by the Executive Agent, and by USAID, as was the case for the Pa Mong Phase II study project. With the agreement of the concerned country and depending on the nature of the project, USAID could decide to grant the construction contract to a private organization or to a governmental organization but, in either case, could use a U.S. company. The company or the organization would then be technically responsible for the project.[44]

Once the stage of planning and feasibility studies was completed, the second stage, that of construction, began, and the modalities of financing became vital. The Mekong Committee reached the conclusion that "for certain tributary projects located entirely in one country, financing through bilateral sources might conveniently be arranged. On the other hand, projects located in certain areas bordering the Mekong, including some of the tributaries, might be more suitable for international financing, or financing through a consortium under the management of an international financial agency."[45] In the first case, financing through bilateral sources, that is, loans, would be made solely to the project government and in no way to the committee, which could, however, lend its assistance to the concerned government to find potential creditors, inside and outside of the region.

Exceptionally, when a riparian country had a balance of payment problem such that additional loans might prove ruinous, grants rather than loans to finance construction were preferred. A participating country could finance a project by using its technical assistance funds: for example, Australia, which agreed to be in charge of the technical supervision for the construction of the Prek-Thnot project in Cambodia. In order to cover the local cost of construction, riparian countries preferred to use funds directly allocated to them by cooperating countries in the context of bilateral aid. This had been the case for all the projects sponsored by the Mekong Committee in which the riparian governments participated. Some form of international financing had to be found for tributary projects that affected more than one country.

In sum, a distinction has to be made between the two stages of the Mekong Project (study and construction), particularly in terms of the different modes of financing, whether it be for the first stage (grants from nonriparian countries and private and public international organizations and matching funds promised by riparian countries to the Mekong Committee) or the second (bilateral loans from nonriparian states and local participation of the concerned riparian countries). But one must also consider whether the projects concern tributaries—hence, national responsibility—or the mainstream—international responsibility of the four countries. Basically, there are two groups of financing: the first group involved local financial participation of the beneficiary countries, that is, of the four riparian countries, and the second group included international public organizations, mainly the UN and organizations related to it, international private organizations and private enterprises, and countries of the Colombo Plan. The Colombo Plan donors played a crucial role in the financing of the Mekong Project in its first decade, a role that is necessary to consider in some detail.

The Colombo Plan

The Colombo Plan for Cooperative Economic Development in South and South East Asia was founded in September 1950 in the wake of the emergence of the P.R.C. in 1949. Countries of the region wished to counterbalance China's formidable influence by cooperating with each other in order to arrive at some economic development and political stability in non-Communist nations. Western powers fully backed this idea since both Great Britain and Australia supported the "economic stabilization and development of the new members of the Commonwealth and the region in which they were located."[46] The Colombo Plan affirmed economic development as being indispensable to the stability of the region. It was within this political context that the four riparian countries of Cambodia, Laos, the R.V.N. (1951), and Thailand (1954) became members of the plan.[47] The Philippines and Thailand were rather hesitant, fearing that American bilateral aid would diminish as a consequence, and it was only on U.S. insistence and reassurance that they adhered to the plan. In 1959, it was agreed that American technical aid to the Colombo Plan countries would be considered as being made within the plan's context.[48] Although the use of the term "plan" implied the notion of a structured organization, in reality, the Colombo Plan was far from being an integrated economic development plan. It was, in fact, a loose gathering of non-Communist countries of Asia (unlike ECAFE, which included the USSR and the P.R.C. among its members) or outside of Asia that had accepted to cooperate technically and economically, according to specifications agreed upon at the ministerial level at each yearly meeting of the Consultative Committee: "The Colombo Plan is an international program which is bilateral in operation even though it is multilateral in approach."[49]

The group of aid donors included Western powers mainly: the United States, Great Britain, Canada, Australia, New Zealand, and Japan. The beneficiaries were the region's developing nations. The latter group could also grant aid, particularly technical aid, to the less developed nations among them. Thus, among the developing nations, India had granted the most technical aid to other members of the plan. It is well known that economic aid granted by one country to another may be considered by the former as an instrument of its foreign policy vis-à-vis the latter. Economic aid often comes with strings attached. However, on the surface, aid granted in the context of the Colombo Plan seemed to be the least encumbered with obligations. Of course, it allowed donor nations to develop friendly political relations and to reinforce their friendship with non-Communist nations of the region, as well as to promote economic interests.

But within this larger context, the United States dominated, contributing 90 percent of the financial aid going to nations of the Colombo Plan region. Without the American aid, the Colombo Plan would have lost most of its monetary importance.[50] Thus, the global volume of aid received by countries of the plan at the end of the fiscal year 1958–1959 was US$ 600 million, of which US$ 566 million were provided by the United States in grants, loans, and technical aid within the Mutual Security Program, Public Law 480. Nations of the lower Mekong basin benefited tremendously from this aid (almost 50 percent) within the context of the plan.[51] We may conclude that perhaps the Colombo Plan was a way to distribute American aid in South and Southeast Asia that conferred on it a semblance of respectability and an appearance of "no strings attached."[52]

In October 1957, at the annual session of the Consultative Committee of the Colombo Plan, the general secretary of ECAFE, C. V. Narasimhan, mentioned the Mekong Project as a promising example of intergovernmental cooperation among countries of the lower Mekong basin. He emphasized the immense needs in short- and long-term calculations and the necessity for generous aid. A few months later, in 1958, President Dwight D. Eisenhower asserted in a speech at the tenth meeting of the Consultative Committee of the Colombo Plan held in Seattle that "the United States recognizes the Colombo Plan association as a major instrument for the economic advancement of this region. . . . The United States stands ready to play its full part in this great peaceful crusade to achieve continuing growth in freedom."[53]

The Mekong Project

The Mekong Project belongs to the geographic area covered by the Colombo Plan, but it was also part of an area whose political precariousness threatened regional and global security. It was imperative that this region be developed economically to reach "social and political stability," goals that were included in the Colombo Plan. Hence, at the end of the conference, the same year, technical and financial aid was granted by Japan and New Zealand (for exploration of main tributaries), and by the United States to the Mekong Project. They were followed in increasing numbers by other countries belonging to the Colombo Plan, which also contributed to the Indus Basin Development Fund. The most important aid received by the Mekong Project from 1958 to 1964 was that from the Colombo Plan, amounting to approximately US$ 9,054,893 of a total of US$ 11,398,233.

A first appraisal of the Mekong Committee's annual reports, studies, and presentations would lead one to believe that, contrary to the Colombo Plan's tradition of multilateral approach but bilateral realization after agreement signed by both donor and beneficiary, the aid granted by the Colombo Plan countries to the Mekong Project had followed a multilateral approach from beginning to end, from the time of first contact between the interested parties to the granting of funds from several countries to a regional organization, in this case the Mekong Committee. The committee seemed to be vested with full powers by the four riparian countries to decide about the appropriation of funds according to projects and needs and to take into account the respective interests of each party and of common goals of all the members of the lower Mekong basin.

This appearance of multilateralism enhanced the committee's image as a planning organization as well as its authority and representation vis-à-vis participant nations. It drew the attention of international public opinion to the existence of goodwill and the eagerness of nations from inside and outside of the region to contribute to an ambitious regional development project, worthy of encouragement. It made it possible to de-emphasize political and economic pressures connected to bilateral aid. Nevertheless, it implied the tacit adhesion of beneficiary countries to the Colombo Plan's stated goals. It also underlined the fact that despite the tension and conflicts that separated them, the riparian members were capable of working together peaceably in a common program and demonstrated that they placed enough trust in a regional organization to delegate their power and respect its decisions.

Thus, thanks to this apparently multilateral approach, ostensibly detached from political pressures, the Mekong Committee was a showcase of successful regional cooperation acting as a foil against communism. However, a more in-depth study of the financial mechanism of the Mekong Project leads to several conclusions inconsistent with this image. This multilateral aid was, in fact, more bilateral than was immediately apparent. Although the committee prepared the list of works, studies, and research to be carried out, and although the committee was in charge of looking for funds, it was eventually entirely up to the donor country to make the decision to finance either in its totality a project or several projects, or part of the pre-investment work, and to choose the part of the Mekong River in which it would work. This means that it was entirely up to the donor to decide to which country it was granting its aid.[54] The donor kept its power of financial management and, hence, control over its aid; this was true also when such aid was given within the context of institutions related to the UN or other organizations.

The fact that the United States decided to grant its aid within the context of the Colombo Plan is significant. It financed studies on the Pa Mong project, which was situated in a territory still under the control of the Royal Lao government. It conducted a hydrographic study of the Mekong within the R.V.N.'s territory, as well as an inventory of the lower Mekong basin's natural resources for reasons that had to do more with its own policy, strategy, and interests in the region.[55] France and Japan likewise had their own reasons for selecting a particular project in a specific country. The aid granted by donor countries under the mantle of the Colombo Plan was not a "blind" one. Behind this appearance of multilateralism, there was a return to the more pragmatic approach of bilateral aid that allowed the donor to choose the recipient. The Mekong Committee, although considered an aid recipient that managed funds in the name of the riparian countries, was nothing more than an intermediary between interlocutors and through which pre-investment capital did not even transit. The committee introduced two possible future partners, suggested proposals, and advised on the best possible approach but did not make any ultimate choice. Developing countries such as Pakistan, the Philippines, India, and Taiwan—even one as remotely interested as Iran—contributed to the Mekong Project. One may wonder how a country such as Pakistan with its immense economic problems and its debt burden that had made it, along with India, one of the main recipients of aid granted by developed countries of the Commonwealth and of the United States, could afford to offer its cooperation in the form of a study of irrigation of the Nam Pong Dam (Northeast of Thailand). The project's cost was US$ 100,000. Interestingly enough, Pakistan and Taiwan specified that their aid was to be granted only to projects located in Thailand and in the R.V.N. Likewise, how could the Philippines, with its multiple financial problems, afford to offer its cooperation via a cartographic study of the Mekong River of a value of US$ 235,000? Given these examples of underdeveloped countries that were contributors, the question arises about the real reason for these contributions by countries economically strapped like the Philippines or Pakistan, nations that, on one hand, had a dire need for this kind of aid for their own economies, and, on the other hand, had been loyal regional partners of the United States. The U.S. contribution, $4 million to $5 million, by far the most important, covered a wide variety of projects, from hydrologic programs, to navigation equipment, to inventory of natural resources. Some works, in particular, were located in Laos and in the R.V.N. In the reports submitted to the U.S. Congress, it was stated that the American contributions to the Mekong Project were made in the context of the Colombo Plan and should not be considered part of the bilateral aid that riparian countries continued to receive from the United States. What then was the reason for this double channeling of American aid, and what kind of advantages did the United States derive from this association with the Colombo Plan from the point of view of its regional and international policy?

A confidential document from the State Department, dated September 1958 and addressed to President Eisenhower, dealt with the question of his participation in the annual meeting with countries of the Colombo Plan to be held in Seattle in November:

Your address would contemplate a major emphasis on the importance we attach to the Colombo Plan. . . . It is an admirable instrument through which to seek some of our objectives in the area. Since the organization is composed exclusively of free world countries, antedates the communist economic offensive, is highly esteemed by the Asian people and looked upon as their own institution it should be possible to strengthen this association of Asian countries with the rest of the free world through the Colombo Plan. Although most aid officially cited under the Colombo Plan has come from the United States (about 85% or over $3 billion since 1951) recipient countries rarely relate what they obtain from the United States to the Colombo Plan. . . . Emphasizing our desire to strengthen this regional association should more firmly establish in Asian eyes our posture of partnership with them in their economic development efforts.[56]

Thanks to its participation, both direct—one of the most important financial ones—and indirect, using the secondary channel of contributions by regional allies that were also recipients of American aid (e.g., the Philippines or Pakistan), the United States actually dominated and influenced the Mekong Project throughout its existence. It was hoped that the economic development of the Mekong lower basin would build the area into a center of regional cooperation and mutual aid and into a rampart against communism, both Chinese and Soviet. As a result of its domination, the United States was able to subvert attempts at autonomy or independence manifested in the beginning by riparian members of the Mekong Committee. Its members had to yield to financial imperatives, the more so since the American presence had progressively but definitely replaced that of the former French "protector." However, at this stage of its involvement in the early 1960s, the pressure exerted by the United States on the Mekong Committee was relatively discreet, since the Mekong Project had not been considered a major, decisive factor in its policy. In order to understand why the Mekong Project would be suddenly—if briefly—propelled into the heart of U.S. policy in Southeast Asia during the Vietnam War, one must return to the immediate post–Second World War era to retrace, in historical perspective, the evolution and motivations of the United States' policy in the region.

THE UNITED STATES IN THE LOWER MEKONG BASIN

In the immediate post-war period, U.S. foreign policy vis-à-vis Southeast Asia was, at first, characterized by a prudent noninvolvement: The United States, while recognizing the strategic value of the region and the necessity to prevent its domination by a hostile power, made a distinction between regions of vital interest, such as Europe, and those of peripheral interest, such as Asia.[57] It did not attempt to project itself as the moral and political model for the peoples of Asia, and it avoided all military involvement on mainland Asia. Its security system in the Pacific included only archipelagoes such as Japan and the Philippines.[58]

However, the founding of the P.R.C. on October 1, 1949, followed by the start of the Korean War in June 1950, signaled the advent of Chinese communism as a factor of regional and global importance. These events triggered the reorientation of U.S. policy in the direction of increasing involvement in the region.[59] Another element equally contributed to this reassessment: the political and economic upheaval taking place in Southeast Asia in the aftermath of the Second World War. The former colonies' political, economic, and social structures had been ravaged by war, inflation, corruption, and a widespread black market; production and exportation had virtually collapsed. There were enormous capital needs for the construction or reconstruction of infrastructures and for the training of technical and administrative cadres; qualified local labor forces were also lacking.[60] The equilibrium in this part of the world, which used to be maintained by several colonial empires ruled by Great Britain, France, and the Netherlands, was now disrupted by nationalist movements that were sometimes influenced by Communist elements. One of these emerged to found the D.R.V. in September 1945. In January 1950, the diplomatic recognition of the D.R.V. by the P.R.C., the Soviet Union, and the other socialist republics, the massing of the famous "Mao's legions" along the Sino-Vietnamese border, as well as political meetings held between Chinese and Vietnamese leaders all signified one thing for Washington: The D.R.V. had entered the Sino-Soviet camp.

The official statement made by Secretary of State Dean Acheson asserted that "the Soviet acknowledgment of this movement should remove any illusions as to the 'nationalist' nature of Ho Chi Minh's aims and reveals Ho in his true colors as the mortal enemy of native independence in Indochina."[61]

These new factors forced a re-evaluation—which had already started in the wake of World War II—of U.S. policy in Southeast Asia in terms of military and economic aid and led to reassessment studies conducted by the State Department, the Defense Department, and particularly, the National Security Council (NSC) on the possible repercussions of the new situation on the world's political and military equilibrium. Two reports presented by the National Security Council, *NSC 48/1* and *NSC 48/2*, formulated the main tenets of American foreign policy in Asia from 1950 onward.[62] The preliminary report, *The Position of the United States with Respect to Asia* (*NSC 48/1*), was presented to President Harry S Truman in December 1949. It analyzed in detail the military, political, and strategic, as well as economic importance of Asia for the United States. It went on to articulate the essential points of U.S. policy in the region. *NSC 48/1* emphasized the potential of Asia and stressed that in matters of security, economic factors are as important as political factors: "Asia is a source of numerous raw materials, principally tin and natural rubber, which are of strategic importance to the United States."[63] In fact, the document maintained that the control of Southeast Asia's economic resources was of extreme importance in case of conflict because of its quasi–world monopoly of the three main agricultural and mineral export products: rice, rubber, and tin. Southeast Asia provides "over three-fourths of the world's, and all of Asia's, exportable surplus of rice. . . . Over 90% of the world's natural rubber supply is produced in Southeast Asia. . . . Our vital dependence upon Southeast Asia for tin is almost as great as for rubber. Over 60% of the world's, and our own, supply of tin is produced in Southeast Asia. . . . These three commodities, rice, rubber, and tin constitute the consummate prize of Southeast Asia."[64] In addition to being a source of raw materials of strategic importance, Asia was also a potential market for Western, especially American, products. The report insisted on the close interdependence of Asia and the United States, which meant that the control or domination of Asia by a hostile nation or group of nations could prove to be a serious threat to American security. Without a doubt, "Southeast Asia is the target of a coordinated offensive directed by the Kremlin. . . . If Southeast Asia also is swept by Communism we shall have suffered a major political rout the repercussion of which will be felt throughout the rest of the world, especially in the Middle East and in a then critically exposed Australia."[65]

Estimated as a first-order Asian power with increasing activities in the region, the Soviet Union was deemed as representing an immediate danger to the United States at this time.[66] In the wake of the political vacuum left by the defeated European powers, the most immediate U.S. objective was to contain, to reduce, and, whenever possible, to eliminate the power and the influence of the Soviet Union in Asia so that it could no longer threaten from this region U.S. security and the independence of its regional allies. The solutions suggested by the final report (*NSC 48/2*) and approved by President Truman on December 30, 1949, were summarized as follows: "The United States on its own initiative . . . should now . . . be prepared to help within our means to meet such threats by providing political, economic, and military assistance. . . . The United States must develop cooperative measures through multilateral or bilateral arrangements to combat Communist internal subversion."[67]

However, given the fact that these newly independent nations were extremely suspicious of any Western action that could be interpreted as interference in their internal affairs, the NSC recommended a regional approach. The United States must strongly encourage—if not "incite"—any regional initiative for the creation of an association of non-Communist countries for the collective defense of the region, yet without appearing intrusive. Such an initiative was equally advantageous from the economic point of view. Member countries must express a common will of cooperation and create mutual assistance relations in order to solve together political, economic, social, and cultural problems inherent to the region.[68] The United States, "recognizing that the non-Communist governments of Southeast Asia constitute a bulwark against Communist expansion in Asia . . . should exploit every opportunity to increase the present Western orientation of the area and to assist . . . its governments in their efforts to meet the minimum aspirations of their people and to maintain internal security."[69]

A two-pronged approach was adopted: on one hand, the defense reinforcement of these countries through military assistance, and, on the other hand, a contribution to their economic development, since "the United States has an interest in the attainment by the free people of Asia of that degree of economic recovery and development needed as a foundation for social and political stability."[70] The application of a technical assistance program (Point IV Program) for the resolution of some of these long-term economic problems and the approval of loans by the World Bank and by the Export-Import Bank to finance specific economic projects were among the main measures suggested by the report and subsequently implemented by Washington.

The Truman administration soon made public some of its new foreign policy's main aspects vis-à-vis Asia as formulated by the NSC. Secretary of State Dean Acheson, in an important speech to the National Press Club on January 19, 1950, and in another on March 15, 1950, to the Commonwealth Club of California, introduced the main lines of this new U.S. foreign policy.[71] It involved two aspects, military and economic, and relied mainly on Japan and the Philippines, two insular countries whose defense the United States guaranteed.[72] This new policy formulation affected the other countries of the south Pacific to a lesser extent, only suggesting an American aid without any responsibility, since "in the southerly part of the area [the Pacific], we are one of many nations who can do no more than help. The direct responsibility lies with the peoples concerned."[73] In April 1950, the National Security Council, in *NSC 68,* reiterated the emphasis on the centrality of Asia (along with Europe) to the United States and its vulnerability to Soviet threat.[74] The new policy was rapidly implemented in the following months but was to accelerate toward a more direct approach with the eruption of the Korean conflict in June 1950.

Following the development of the conflict, the United States introduced the strategic concept of "defensive perimeter" stretching from the Aleutian islands to include the Philippines. Very rapidly, an air and sea defense and a military response system were set up in the Pacific, with the agreement and on the request of governments of the region. In August 1951, the United States concluded a mutual defense treaty with the Philippines, and in September, two security agreements were signed, one with Japan, and the other with Australia and New Zealand (the ANZUS Pact). Then, with Truman's speech on the Korean War, the American policy of containment became more aggressive, and military supplies were sent to French forces and to the Associated States of Indochina along with a military mission to the region. A purely military defense of the "defensive perimeter" against "Soviet Communist imperialism" was not regarded as sufficient because of the existence of other problems that rendered these countries susceptible to penetration and subversion.[75] Two reports, the *Gray Report* and the *Rockefeller Report*, conducted in 1950, had called Washington's attention to the fact that the region's unsatisfied expectations might constitute a potential threat, rendering its peoples easy preys to communism.[76] It was in America's interest, therefore, to maintain political stability through an increased aid toward economic development. In Acheson's "Strategy for Freedom," "mutual assistance" went hand in hand with "collective defense," the two facets of regionalism as advocated by Washington. The founding of a system of political alliances and military defense against Communist aggression had to be reinforced by the development of economic regionalism. It was with these goals in mind that countries of Southeast Asia, in particular those in strategic positions, were to be encouraged to weave a tight network of economic and commercial ties on the regional level that would lead to the creation of a politically strong and stable regional group.

Prior to this, toward the end of 1949, a number of missions had already been sent on fact-finding tours, two of which were crucial in the conclusions reached. The first one, led by Ambassador-at-Large Philip Jessup, traveled the length of Asia to test its political waters.[77] The second, in March 1950, led by Robert Allen Griffin, deputy chief of the China Mission of the Economic Cooperation Administration, was sent to Southeast Asia to evaluate the economic and technical needs of the region, to formulate projects that would have a direct political impact, and to prepare the field for the application of the technical aid program (Point IV Program).[78] Upon its completion, the mission made several suggestions dealing mainly with U.S. economic and technical assistance and U.S. goals in the region with respect to the political situation. One of the most important statements in the Griffin report mentions the weakness of internal revenues and the problems with technical development, which was insufficient in terms of administrators, competence, and technical equipment. The report puts particular emphasis on the political situation in the three countries of Indochina (the "Associated States" of Vietnam, Laos, and Cambodia), underlining the urgency and the gravity of the situation as well as the small chances of success of France and the Bao-dai's government unless some rapid action is forthcoming.[79] The suggested solutions involve the stabilization of non-Communist national governments of Southeast Asia through an American contribution to the improvement of the economy and the living standards of the population. Such a gesture would be considered proof of the positive American interest in these countries. However, resources must also be developed in order to prove to the indigenous populations that their governments had their interests at heart, thereby eliciting their political support.

GRIFFIN REPORT

Given the importance of rural populations in Asia, U.S. aid, according to the Griffin report, should first emphasize agriculture (and rural rehabilitation) and then, in a second phase, industry (and electricity), which would liberate the enormous potential of the region.[80] The suggestions made by the report agreed with the political agenda adopted by the Truman administration, which decided to put them into application rapidly. The sum granted, US$ 60 million (out of the recommended total of US$ 66,093,000), was intentionally a modest one, for the U.S. administration, at the time, adhered to the principle according to which a weak volume of aid would serve as a catalyst to mobilize a country's resources, leading to its contributing to its own development.[81] A number of legislative measures concerning economic and technical aid were also passed by the U.S. Congress in June 1950, which were to form the foundation of future American aid programs: The Foreign Economic Assistance Act of 1950 included the Act for International Development, which established, as a national policy, the economic development of underdeveloped regions.[82] The two main arguments formulated in passing this law on international aid followed the same themes that had been used for preceding programs of aid for Western Europe in the post-war period.[83]

More specifically, concerning South and Southeast Asia, the U.S. Congress also passed the China Area Aid Act of 1950, which transferred to the region sums formerly allocated to the Republic of China and not yet utilized. Their availability made possible the immediate application of a technical and economic aid program for Southeast Asia: A small portion (US$ 750,000) of the US$ 75 millions of the funds was used in June 1950 to start the first of the many Special Programs for Technical and Economic Aid to Vietnam.

In a letter dated May 25, 1950, and addressed to the Associated States and to France, the United States announced its decision to grant bilateral economic aid to Laos, Cambodia, and Vietnam: "United States economic aid will be granted in accordance with separate bilateral agreements between each of the Associated States and the United States of America."[84] This economic aid program was influenced in great part by the Griffin mission's suggestions.[85] Then, suddenly, in June 1950, the Korean War exploded, becoming one of the first open confrontations between the two blocs, each of which had sent troops to intervene directly

KOREA

in the conflict from its inception. Very rapidly, U.S. policy reoriented itself toward an increasing priority given to Asia, particularly to Indochina with, as a direct consequence, the increase of American aid to the region.

Although Washington still considered France as the party primarily responsible for the direction and implementation of the war effort by agreeing to pay for part of its military expenses in Indochina, Washington decided to support the development of indigenous armies by the Associated States, the consolidation or the formation of anti-Communist governments stable and favorable to the West, and launched an important economic aid program. At the time, the question that complicated relations between supposed allies, that is, the Indochinese states, France, and the United States, concerned the beneficiaries of military aid and had proved a difficult balancing act for the United States, since the problem was "to extend aid, to support those [Indochinese] governments, and to prevent Communist aggression but without at the same time appearing to support the continuation of French colonialism in Indochina."[86] The economic objectives of the United States were "directed toward the support of a program of aid and technical advice which will permit the three newly formed states to establish economic stability and to thereby lessen the danger of Communism in the area."[87] In October 1950, a letter of intent was signed by the United States, Vietnam, Laos, and Cambodia; it was followed by the Economic Cooperation Agreements in September 1951. These agreements stipulated (in section two) that the concerned government "agrees to facilitate the production, transport, within its means, and the transfer to the Government of the United States of America for such period of time and upon such terms and conditions of purchase as may be agreed upon, of raw and semi-processed materials required by the United States of America as a result of actual or potential deficiencies in its own resources."[88]

The military and economic effort of the United States was not limited solely to the three countries of Indochina but was also extended to Thailand, which represented a key element in U.S. strategy, since it was assumed that the fall of Indochina to communism would be followed by that of Thailand, Burma, and Malaysia, and, inevitably, of Eastern Pakistan, Indonesia, and so forth. Furthermore, Thailand, because of its pro-Western political structures and orientations, had come to symbolize a democratic, independent, and forcefully anti-Communist country closest to American ideals.[89] In 1949, President Truman notably approved the transfer to Thailand of "almost US$ 44 million in gold, held by Japan, as payment for previously unrequited goods and services provided by the Thais during the war."[90] In February 1950, a conference of high-ranking American diplomats from the region, in which Ambassador-at-Large Philip Jessup participated, was held in Bangkok to discuss the impact of Communist China on countries of Southeast Asia and to envision measures that would foil the danger, in particular for a country like Thailand. Military and economic missions carried out repeated surveys that resulted in the signing of the Economic and Technical Cooperation Agreement between the United States and Thailand in September 1950 and the sending of another Special Technical and Economic Mission to the latter. The mission recommended an aid program based on three objectives: to increase Thailand's rice production for export, to help Thailand produce an increasing volume of strategic products, and to reinforce the Northeast region where conditions of underdevelopment were considered conducive to Communist penetration.[91] The mission paid particular attention to the problems of improvement of cultivation, harvest, and rice sales. In October 1950, the United States and Thailand, after having negotiated an economic and technical agreement the preceding month, signed a second agreement dealing with military assistance to Thailand (supply of weapons, equipment, and provision of service). Overall, the program of American economic and technical aid to Thailand seemed to be the most clearly conceived and efficiently implemented, most suited to the particular conditions of the country. In contrast, most of the projects of economic aid to the countries of Indochina appeared to be geared to fulfill military goals primarily, aiming more at "pacification" than economic development, as was the case with the proposed establishment of "pacification villages" in the Red River delta in territory claimed by the Associated State of Vietnam.[92]

The change of U.S. administrations with the victory of the Republicans and the accession to power of Dwight D. Eisenhower in 1953 became a turning point in American policy toward Asia and, in particular, vis-à-vis Indochina, which was determined in part by the necessity to fulfill promises made by the Republican Party during the presidential campaign: "We shall put an end to the policy of neglect toward the Far East, a region that Stalin for long had identified as the road leading to victory over the West. We shall let it be known clearly that we have no intention to sacrifice the Orient."[93] In Indochina, the situation had become alarming, and, given the increasingly probable event of France's withdrawal from Indochina, a State Department report addressed the possibility of the United States taking up France's mantle in that region.[94] Nineteen fifty-four was the decisive year during which the French and American policies and points of view concerning the Indochina war clashed, leading Washington to dissociate itself from its partner and to follow a line of action that, according to its strategists, would allow it to win a complete victory over the Communists.

In the space of a few years, the United States had traveled a long road from a position of noninvolvement to the decision of direct intervention in Indochina. Its stance had evolved from the opinion formulated by Franklin D. Roosevelt at the Teheran Conference of November 1943, according to which Indochina should be placed under international trusteeship for a period of twenty to thirty years, to the determination, as expressed in the memorandum by the Joint Chiefs of Staff of March 1954, to continue the struggle against the Viet Minh in Indochina.[95] In a memorandum dated March 12, 1954, the Joint Chiefs of Staff analyzed the eventuality of negotiations between France and the three countries of Indochina. Possible results were the formation of a coalition government, the partition of one of the three countries, or coalition *and* partition. Such eventualities were unacceptable, because any one would open the gate to Communist invasion of Southeast Asia and represent a serious threat to U.S. security. Furthermore, "orientation of Japan toward the West is the keystone of United States policy in the Far East. In the judgment of the Joint Chiefs of Staff, the loss of Southeast Asia to Communism would, through economic and political pressures, drive Japan into an accommodation with the Communist Bloc. The communization of Japan would be the probable ultimate result."[96]

Should Japan be "communized," its industrial capacity and the region's natural resources would allow "Red China" to build a military infrastructure that would control the entire western and southwestern Pacific, threatening South Asia and the Middle East. The report advocated American disengagement from future negotiations in order to preserve "its freedom of action to pursue directly with the governments of the Associated States and with other allies (notably the United Kingdom) ways and means of continuing the struggle against the Viet Minh in Indochina without participation of the French."[97] The result was the American refusal to be co-signatory to the Final Declaration at the Geneva Conference of July 1954. It was determined to pursue a divergent path by contributing to the development of the three anti-Communist states of Indochina and to the formation of a regional association for the collective defense of Southeast Asia against Communist aggression (SEATO), which were among the numerous manifestations of America's progressive involvement in the Indochinese problem. These actions signaled the shift of responsibility from that of a defeated colonial master to that of the greatest Western power of the twentieth century.

Shortly after the Geneva Agreements of July 1954, the NSC, taking stock of the situation, formulated the main points of the post-Geneva U.S. policy in Southeast Asia: The United States had suffered a very serious loss of prestige in the region that challenged its capacity to thwart the rise of communism in Asia, whereas the Communists had seen their political and military prestige as well as their influence in Asia increase in proportion. With Vietnam, they had acquired a base from which military and nonmilitary pressures could be exerted in the neighboring regions. The United States must by all means, secret and open, reestablish its lost prestige in Asia by encouraging, particularly at the regional level, the creation of an economic organization that would involve the free states of Asia belonging to the Colombo Plan and function with the support and participation of the United States and of Western countries. In the case of Communist subversion and at the request of the threatened government, the president of the United States, while granting all of the official and secret support possible within the realm of the executive power, should consider—given the approval of Congress—the use of military forces against the local or external sources of subversion, including Communist China if it were the origin.

In the case of Indochina, the United States should support the friendly, non-Communist governments of Cambodia, Laos, and Vietnam; foil the Communist victory in the coming general elections in Vietnam; help Cambodia, Laos, and free Vietnam "to maintain (1) military forces necessary for internal security and (2) economic conditions conducive to the maintenance and strength of non-Communist regimes and comparing favorably with those in adjacent Communist areas."[98] In short, the report advocated the sabotage of the Viet Minh's action in Vietnam and the prevention of reunification of the country by means of the general elections stipulated by the Geneva Accords. Thailand was given special consideration. The United States must "concentrate efforts on developing Thailand as a support of U.S. objectives in the area and as the focal point of United States covert and psychological operations in Southeast Asia."[99] In response to the Geneva Agreements, which were considered secretly at the governmental level as a very serious threat for American diplomacy, Washington was to intensify its efforts to strengthen its links to stable, non-Communist countries such as Thailand by increasing its military and economic aid to this country, and then to Cambodia and Laos as well as to a non-Communist southern Vietnam, which the United States had begun to reinforce through support to Ngo Dinh Diem.

A complex economic and financial network of American aid was put in place, taking shape through the joint official statement of September 29, 1954, concerning Franco-American negotiations for direct aid to each of the Associated States; Eisenhower's letter to Diem of October 23, 1954; and the State Department Statement of December 31, 1954, of financial aid to these three countries of Indochina in order to reinforce their defense against the threat of Communist subversion and aggression. American bilateral aid was accompanied by an attempt at fostering a regional approach to form the counterpart, from the economic point of view, to the collective defense organization (SEATO). Its main objective was to maintain a certain political stability as stated by Secretary of State John Foster Dulles in his presentation to Congress of the administration's proposals for the Mutual Security Program of 1956:

International Communism is pressing hard to extend its influence in Asian countries which lack the economic strength to support an adequate defense establishment and to provide the necessary foundation of political stability and steadily improving living standards. . . . We know that nations which are economically weak find it difficult to become politically strong and secure. We believe that an increase in free Asia's economic strength can be another effective resistant to Communism.[100]

After the signing of the Manila Treaty of September 1954, Washington announced its intention to finance a vast economic program in Southeast Asia of aid to countries of the "Arc of Free Asia," which was to complement its military strategy through the setting up of a special fund of US$ 200 million for regional economic development and close regional relations. Congress appropriated the entire sum to the "Presidential Fund for the Economic Development of Asia" to be used in the exclusive financing of projects or programs originating from two or more countries of the region.[101] To avoid generating any suspicion of U.S. control or domination concerning this project, the United States stipulated that it would be the Asian nations themselves that would formulate the development projects.[102]

Several nations manifested their interest in the American offer, but India was keenest of all. Influenced in this by ICA, it organized in May 1955 the Shimla

Conference in order to discuss the use of the special fund. Among the invited countries were, notably, the members of the future Mekong Committee, that is, Thailand, Laos, Cambodia, and the State of Vietnam.[103] However, the conference failed to reach its goal; the nascent concepts of regional development and regionalism were deemed premature for the area.[104] Its participating members concurred that given the present conditions of economic development in the Asian countries, and relative to the supplementary funds available, there were no advantages in the creation of an intermediary regional organization. The participants acknowledged the fact that, because they had not yet achieved economic planning for their own nations, it would be premature to initiate regional planning. There was also an undercurrent of suspicion among Asian participants concerning the former enemy, Japan, and the perception arose that "America's real objective was to develop new markets for Japan."[105] Consequently, the $200 million fund apportioned by the U.S. Congress was used for projects that were insignificant and of very little regional impact; the fund was not extended.

EARLY U.S. INTEREST IN THE MEKONG PROJECT

The Asian countries' rejection of regional cooperation along the lines proposed by the United States did not dissuade the latter from attempting to foster regionalism as an alternative to communism. It was not America's first endeavor in using the theme of regional cooperation worldwide as a response to a serious political crisis threatening a region's equilibrium. In 1955, Secretary of State Dulles similarly suggested a program of regional cooperation as an alternative to the conflict in the Middle East. Moreover, the concept of regionalism (albeit regions within a single nation-state) and its realization through the development of multipurpose water resource projects was also not new, as demonstrated by the Tennessee Valley Authority (TVA) project in the 1930s.

The TVA project covered the whole basin of the Tennessee River in the southeastern United States. A project of great ethnic, economic, and geographic diversity, it included Tennessee and six other states. It was the first of its kind in the United States and in the world to involve the construction of dams, of hydroelectric stations, of flood control, and of navigation improvement works, simultaneously combining hydraulic resources (irrigation, electricity, flood control, and navigation) that had been exploited either separately or in groups of two or three but not previously as a totality. It was the first of its kind whereby the cost of construction was, for the most part, covered by the sale of hydroelectricity to an extended area twice the size of the valley. The bill, voted in Congress in May 1933, had allowed the establishment of a governmental organization, the TVA, created specifically to supervise planning, construction, and management, with full authority over the entire basin. It had the federal government's support as well as an enormous budget for the realization of the project. At the time, the United States was suffering a serious economic crisis, and the Tennessee region was one of the poorest in the country. The TVA thus provided the Roosevelt administration with a solution, allowing it to improve regional conditions while contributing to the resolution of the larger, national economic crisis.[106]

The launching of the TVA project at a time of severe economic crisis, and its initial success—despite some major problems—had made the TVA into a symbol of successful regionalism founded on the development of a river's hydraulic resources. During the Great Depression, the TVA's success story became a dominant concept in the country. Later, studies were carried out to analyze the possibilities of reproducing this experience in other regions of the underdeveloped world.[107] The TVA project quickly came to be considered the reference for all large-scale water resources–related works. For instance, Washington in 1953 made the proposal to finance the development of the Jordan valley, a project that was to involve Israel, Jordan, and Syria.[108] It was hoped that these common projects would engender a spirit of cooperation that would then bring a certain appeasement to the region's conflicts.

To the question whether countries at war with conflicting interests would consent to work together in a development project, President Eisenhower's personal representative with ambassadorial rank, Eric Johnston, replied that it was possible as long as "the coordinating is done by some agent above reproach and beyond prejudice" and that, in his view, "the United Nations could be trusted to do a fair and effective job."[109] By instituting the UN as the main organizer in charge of such an international regional project, the United States, while maintaining a certain control, could avoid affronting the susceptibility of these nations and the concomitant accusation of excessive involvement in their domestic affairs.

Given the domestic and international impact of the TVA, the United States was tempted to export this formula to regions with geographic and economic characteristics similar to those of the Tennessee valley: regions in which there was a river flowing through several underdeveloped areas; a large, unexploited potential; and the menace of political crisis and social instability.[110] In Asia, China represented an ideal case: a poor, underdeveloped country, teeming with millions, caught in the turmoil of social upheavals, with natural resources such as the Yangzi River waiting to be developed. It was hoped that the Tennessee "miracle" could be duplicated to stem the rise of communism. Sun Yat-sen, the father of the Chinese Revolution, had forecast the possibility of the development of the river as part of the drive to foster industry. In 1944, Chiang Kai-shek's beleaguered Republic of China began planning the development of the Yangzi River with the help of the U.S. Bureau of Reclamation, which sent a team of engineers to China.[111] Starting from Chunking, the team explored the upper Yangzi with a view to evaluating its potential and to preparing a national plan for its development. The estimated initial cost was of $1 billion, and the goals included the irrigation of more than 2.5 million hectares of land, the production of ten million kilowatts of electricity, and the opening of the river to navigation from Chunking to Shanghai. However, the project's conception came too late to have any influence on the unfolding of events in China that led to the Communist victory in 1949.[112]

The Indochinese peninsula was quickly to take a paramount place in U.S. foreign policy in Southeast Asia, a policy in which regionalism was to be fostered to reinforce its military strategy. While it continued and increased its bilateral aid to reinforce the national economy of each country of Indochina, the United States also attempted to nurture as much as possible a community of strong economic and political ties among these different parties, which would serve as a rampart against the Communist danger (Chinese or Soviet). For these reasons—the example of the TVA and the concept of regionalism—the Mekong River, with its immense economic potential and its watershed that includes in its lower basin four riparian countries, appeared to be ideal, combining a number of elements favorable to the successful realization of a project apparently similar to that of the Tennessee valley. Furthermore, the Mekong River had now, again, entered a period of conflicts and become the theater of battles between different and unequal forces.

In the First Indochina War, the middle Mekong valley—Thai territory on its right bank, Lao on its left bank—had witnessed much fierce fighting between Viet Minh and French Union forces. The goal for the former was the extension of its zone of influence; for the latter, an increasingly desperate attempt to preserve its colonial territory. Beginning in 1953, the fighting became more ferocious along the Mekong River. For a time, Viet Minh troops threatened Luang Prabang but then headed toward the Mekong, taking over Thakhek on the left bank of the river, opposite the Thai town of Nakhon Phanom. In 1954, the Viet Minh launched another attack on Luang Prabang, and then, in a pincer movement, swept down on Cambodia. The river itself was used by the Viet Minh as a means of transportation of weapons, a practice that was to continue into the Second Indochina War. Thailand, which had given asylum and even financial aid to the independence movements of Laos, Cambodia, and Vietnam and allowed the settlement along the Mekong valley of a Vietnamese community known for being sympathetic to the Viet Minh, had now to alter its policy vis-à-vis the three neighbors. The result, in the words of historian Russell H. Fifield, was "Thailand's Mekong policy."[113] On the international level, Thailand had already chosen the Western camp, siding with a powerful ally, the United States, for internal political reasons, because of the situation along the Thai-Lao border, and because of the risk of internationalization of the Indochina war and the possible involvement of the P.R.C. and the USSR.

Internally, Thailand was at the time faced with the problems of the separatist movement in the Northeast, that is, the Khorat plateau bordering the Mekong, a region that was also at risk because of the Viet Minh's infiltration of Laos from Vietnam. Thailand feared that the Viet Minh's presence might fan the separatist Isan movement.[114] The Northeast was a region that lagged considerably behind in terms of economic development as compared with the Central Plain and even with the regions in the north and south. It had barely emerged from a subsistence economy and had not benefited from the country's economic boom because of Bangkok's neglect.[115] The situation had thus generated resentment among the local elite, a resentment that was at first latent but had evolved into a certain separatist will, even leading to the adoption of a insurrectionist strategy. Bangkok was troubled by the fact that some of the Isan leaders who were formally members of the "Free Thai" organization, which had fought the Japanese occupation, were in close contact with the Communist-influenced nationalist movements of the Viet Minh and Pathet Lao. The Thai government feared a secession of the Lao-speaking provinces of the Northeast, which then might form a Communist-led autonomous zone with the Pathet-Lao-controlled regions. Despite the repression launched by Bangkok against the Isan leaders, rebellions and uprisings succeeded one another, becoming increasingly radical and better organized in the 1960s. The Northeast soon acquired the reputation of being the hearth of insurrection; furthermore, the parliamentary representatives who founded the Socialist Front came from the Northeast.[116] Linking them to the Communist parties of neighboring Laos, China, and Vietnam, Bangkok perceived them as a threat to the country's security and was convinced more than ever that the "Northeast problem" urgently needed to be solved.[117]

The other internal Communist threat was apparently represented by the Chinese minority in Thailand, a minority that played a vital role in Thailand's economy but whose relations with the government had become somewhat difficult if not tense in the last decades.[118] In the 1950s, Beijing's propaganda, aimed at large segments of the population, had called on Thailand to implement neutralism and nonalignment vis-à-vis the United States and had attempted to turn the population against the Pibun government. Since the Communist victory in China, the Chinese community of Thailand, torn between the Guomindang and the Chinese Communist Party, was suspected of sheltering Communists or of being a "fifth column." There were even two Communist parties, one Thai and the other Chinese, both closely watched by Bangkok. Starting in 1952, the Pibun government, fearing subversion, intensified its anti-Chinese and anti-Communist policy. According to the French historian Pierre Fistié, "anti-Communism was now the government's doctrine."[119] Following the discovery of a supposed Communist plot against the government, numerous personalities suspected of ties with the Communist milieu were arrested, and on November 1952, an anti-Communist law, the "Law on Anti-Thai Activities of the Year 2495 of the Buddhist Era," was adopted.[120] Aimed at the Chinese in Thailand, it gave the government discretionary power to arrest anyone suspected of being a Communist, of being linked to a Communist organization, or of possessing Communist propaganda. This anti-Communist and anti-Chinese policy, launched by Pibun toward the end of 1952, had a limited domestic goal and fitted Thailand's strategy of rapprochement with the United States and other Western powers.[121]

Thailand's Northeast is contiguous with a Laos then at war, a war whose outcome was uncertain but threatened to engulf Thailand. In the Northeast, the separatist movements were increasingly entrenched among the population, gaining wider audience and support. Concurrently, in January 1953, Beijing announced the creation in the south of Yunnan at Sipsongpanna "of an autonomous

popular government of Tai nationality," which demanded autonomy and called
for the unity of all Tai-language minorities of Southeast Asia in order to quash
the "American imperialists."[122] To the alarm of Bangkok, Communist China was
exploiting a theme that had been recurrent in recent Thai history, that of the
autonomy of the Tai people. By April 1953, the Indochina war had spread to the
eastern border of Thailand with the Viet Minh's frequent incursions into Laos. A
state of emergency was proclaimed in the border provinces of the Northeast,
military reinforcements were sent to the region, and Vietnamese who had settled
in the region were moved farther inland.[123] Thailand, faced with a most alarming
regional (but also national) situation, responded by adopting a multilevel policy.

On the international level, it brought to the attention of the Security Council
of the UN the question of the Viet Minh's incursions into Laos, close to the Thai
border, which thus threatened Thai security as well as international peace. Thailand requested that a UN observation mission be sent to the region. It concurrently applied a policy of attracting to its own sphere of influence the countries
on the opposite bank of the Mekong River by promoting political, economic,
cultural, and religious ties with them and seeking to create an "entente" among
the three riparian countries. In 1954, Thailand opened banking services in Cambodia and allowed the transit through Bangkok harbor of goods flowing to and
from Cambodia and Laos without imposing any tariffs. It facilitated the entry of
citizens of these two countries into Thailand; approved the opening of an airline
between Bangkok and Vientiane; and invited the leaders of Laos and Cambodia
to pay diplomatic visits to Bangkok, invitations that were accepted.[124]

 In January 1954, the idea of the formation of a Buddhist and anti-Communist
bloc of the three Indianized countries—as opposed to Sinicized Vietnam—began
to take root. Thailand and Laos, ethnically and linguistically close, held discussions at the highest level concerning the common problem of the "Communist
threat," that is, the Pathet Lao, which had entrenched itself in the Lao northern
provinces of Phong Saly and Sam Neua. Among the possible solutions discussed, there was in particular that of sending officers of the Royal Lao Army to
Thailand for training in the skills of modern warfare. From the economic point of
view, the argument was made that an alliance with Thailand would bring to Laos
and Cambodia numerous advantages, among which were an opening to the sea
and a means of transportation. Laos and Cambodia, which used the Mekong
River and the land route to access the South China Sea, could reduce their dependence on Vietnam by turning instead to the Gulf of Thailand, which offers
trade opportunities.[125] It was also important for Thailand to reinforce its transportation and communication network in the Northeast in order to open the region; to break its geographic, economic, and political isolation; and to facilitate
the accessibility of the region to Bangkok's control and centralization efforts.
Above all, it was essential to counter regional Communist and separatist influences.[126] Economist Robert Muscat has observed that Bangkok's fear of a Communist threat led the Thai government to, on one hand, apply a policy of sup-
pression of political opposition in the Northeast while pushing, on the other

hand, for its economic integration and development. Meanwhile, U.S. aid directed toward that region increased in volume and scope, becoming more security-oriented. As the "economic development of the Northeast assumed great urgency, . . . non-military security forces in the Northeast became major recipients of assistance under AID's appropriations and administration. While the political and security objectives of AID's Northeast activities imparted a sense of urgency for quick impact, the projects included much that was developmental in character, especially investment in physical infrastructure."[127] Given these developments and projects, it is evident that the Mekong River and the necessity of its development assumed critical importance to the Thai leadership.[128] In March 1954, Thailand proposed to the other riparian countries the joint development of the river for hydroelectric, irrigation, and transportation purposes and made known its readiness to send experts in agriculture, sylviculture, and pisciculture to Laos and Cambodia at their request.[129]

Since its intrusion in the region and its indirect involvement in the First Indochina War, the United States had formulated its foreign policy in this part of the world around the anti-Communist crusade, fired by the fear that the Communist monolith would succeed in controlling the region, thus threatening the United States, its security, its prosperity, and its position of leadership in the free world. It considered itself the only power external to the region capable of thwarting the Sino-Soviet thrust in Asia. The perception by U.S. policy makers, then, was that the fate of the region depended entirely on the extent and the efficiency of the American effort to protect the non-Communist countries. It was primordial that these countries not be attracted to the Communist sphere, that they maintain their independence—for their independence was vital to U.S. security interests.

The protection of these countries' independence, their stability, and their economic and political nondependence on the Communist bloc could be achieved only through the fulfillment of their economic and social demands and a satisfactory economic development patterned after that of the West. With the cooperation of the concerned governments, the United States prepared and implemented programs that could foster a healthy economic development, a clear proof that economic growth could be reached without resorting to "Communist methods." In order to achieve this, American technical and economic assistance was needed, and such assistance had to "take into account the economic and technical assistance being provided by other Free World nations and by international institutions, coordinating with such nations and institutions where appropriate."[130] In addition to U.S. efforts, "the United Nations agencies, other Colombo Plan countries, other friendly countries [should] contribute available resources to promote the economic growth of Southeast Asia. . . . The Southeast Asian countries [should] orient their economies in the direction of the Free World and . . . rely primarily on non-Communist markets and sources of supply for trade, technicians, capital development, and atomic development."[131]

The strengthening of the economies of the nations of Southeast Asia had to be accompanied by an intensification of interstate cooperation, the creation of mutual aid systems, and "indigenous efforts to develop regional associations so long as they do not weaken SEATO or the spirit of resistance to Communism."[132] Thailand, for instance, would have to reinforce its relations with Laos on one hand, and with Cambodia on the other hand, in terms of military planning, political association, and economic cooperation. The R.V.N., Laos, and Cambodia should also follow the same path. It was from that point of view that the Mekong River and its lower basin development had to be seriously considered and strongly encouraged. It was thus under the Eisenhower administration that, for the first time, at the highest levels, the Mekong River and its development were discussed and its use viewed from the political and strategic perspective. The National Security Council, formulating the key elements of the U.S. policy in mainland Southeast Asia in its report *NSC 5612/1* of September 5, 1956, stipulated: "In order to promote increased cooperation in the area and to deny the general area of the Mekong River Basin to Communist influence or domination, assist as feasible in the development of the Mekong River Basin as a nucleus for regional cooperation and mutual aid."[133]

The report was approved by President Eisenhower, who ordered "its application by the agencies and departments of the Executive of the government of the United States." The previously mentioned recommendation concerning the Mekong River basin was repeated at each revision by the NSC regarding U.S. policy in the region, a remarkable continuity among the numerous changes that the NSC had to make to adjust to constantly fluctuating events. From the report of September 1956 (*NSC 5612/1*), in which the Mekong River and its development were first mentioned, to the April (*NSC 5809*) and July 1959 reports (*NSC 6012*), the U.S. Mekong policy was to remain unchanged in its formulation. The Executive Office of the President specified that

in order to promote the political progress, integrity and stability of free Far East countries and to promote more effective cooperation among those countries and between them and the rest of the free world, the United States should . . . encourage the growth of regional and free world cooperation through such measures as support for the Colombo Plan, ECAFE, and regional undertakings such as the Project of the Mekong Valley and the telecommunication network in Southeast Asia.[134]

The U.S. support for the Mekong Project, while aimed at creating a positive, favorable impression of the United States, was also intended to decrease tensions that might have the potential to undermine the stability of relations among the four riparian states. Cambodia was a source of particular concern:

Since real or fancied threats from neighboring Free World countries have been a major factor contributing to Cambodia's sense of insecurity and its consequent readiness to accept Sino-Soviet Bloc support, endeavor persistently and firmly to improve Cambodia's relations with these countries, particularly Thailand and Viet Nam. . . . Encourage positive cooperation between Cambodia and neighboring countries such as joint participation in the development of the Lower Mekong River Basin as a nucleus for regional cooperation and mutual aid.[135]

However, there was little to start with in terms of scientific knowledge concerning the Mekong River, its potential, and other necessary data related to the river and to its basin.[136] There was therefore a need for a more detailed study and complete update of data related to the river. The missions of exploration launched by the U.S. government in the 1950s provided the first foundation and gave the initial impetus to the conception of the project. The first American technical team, involving officers of the U.S. Engineering and Transportation Service, was sent to do field research in May–June 1954 with the secret objective of evaluating the military and economic resources available in the case of American intervention in the peninsula.[137] The exploration of the Mekong was included within the scope of the mission. The report showed the insufficiency of logistics as well as of economic and other resources in Indochina and the necessity to remedy it in the eventuality of an intervention of U.S. troops.

The following year, upon French and American joint request and still with the view that economic and technical growth of the region would contribute to the stabilization of the existing governments, and upon the advice of officials of the U.S. Operations Mission (USOM), the leaders of the riparian states addressed a common and official request to the American organization in charge of economic development, ICA, for an evaluation of the basin's potential.[138] A special project agreement was signed between the United States and each of the riparian states in November 1955, after which a team of American experts was sent by the U.S. Bureau of Reclamation in January 1956 to carry out a preliminary study of the Mekong basin.

The report, published in March 1956 and entitled *Reconnaissance Report—Lower Mekong Basin,* gave in thirty-six pages a detailed description of existing data on the region and suggested orientations and development for the future gathering of basic data: hydrographic, geologic, topographic studies on the river; economic studies on regional agriculture; and so forth.[139] It also provided summaries of national projects for the development of water resources that were being realized (the Cai San, the Tiep Nhut, and the An Truong projects in Vietnam) or studied by the governments of the riparian states (feasibility studies on the development project of the Plain of Reeds in Vietnam, studies on the mainstream, and so forth). The report made an inventory of all the possible sites of hydroelectric stations on the mainstream and tributaries; it also studied the energy market in the lower basin. It underlined the necessity of cooperation between riparian countries for the collection, storage, and communication of data. However, the proposals made by the study did not mention a joint development of the river but mentioned instead a separate hydraulic exploitation of the river, country by country.

From the time of the U.S. Bureau of Reclamation's study, which had made possible a recapitulation as well as an updating of information concerning the river and its basin, American interest in the river or, more exactly, the Mekong Project was to be part of American policy in the lower Mekong basin. In fact, it was to increase with the D.R.V.'s victory over France and the replacement of the latter by the United States in Indochina after the Geneva Agreements of 1954. The Mekong River and Project briefly seized the limelight thanks to the skillful manipulation of President Lyndon B. Johnson, who used them as symbols of peaceful development in an endeavor to project a positive image of his foreign policy in Asia in the second half of the 1960s. According to Franklin P. Huddle, who studied the question of regionalism and the Mekong Project, Lyndon Johnson was quite familiar with both the TVA and regionalism during his years in Congress.[140] Johnson's biographer, Doris Kearns, notes his interest in water resources development, which was rooted in his memory of the benefits that dam construction had brought to farmers struggling with the lack of water in the arid part of his native Texas.[141]

In 1961, Johnson, then vice-president, was sent by President John F. Kennedy on a study mission to Asia. Prior to his departure, Arthur Goldschmidt, director of Special Fund Activities and assistant secretary of the interior, had called his attention to the Mekong's "ability . . . to train representatives of four countries, with differing political views, to work effectively together even in a period otherwise characterized by a lot of fussing."[142] During his trip to Southeast Asia, Vice-President Johnson visited ECAFE's headquarters in Bangkok in May 1961 and met with its executive secretary, U Nyun, who gave him a detailed summary of the Mekong scheme. The executive secretary remarked that ECAFE's main objective was the economic development of the region, of which the Mekong Project was an outstanding example. Johnson agreed, saying that "he could think of nothing that could help Thailand, Laos, Cambodia and Vietnam more than by working together on a river since, if they could work together on a river, they could work together on anything else."[143] Vice-President Johnson even expressed impatience and wanted to know when the Mekong Project was actually to begin; he also chatted with a fellow Texan, a Mekong-UN field official, Cesar Ortiz-Tinoco, who was chief of the Information Service of ECAFE, and it was the latter who recounted the vice-president commenting to U Nyun that he was "'a river man. All my life I have been interested in rivers and their development.'"[144] So captivated was Johnson "in the Mekong Project particularly, that, despite urging from Ambassador Young, he overstayed his time and, as a result, was nearly an hour late for an appointment he had with the Prime Minister of Thailand."[145] As one of the results of the vice-president's visit, the U.S. Bureau of Reclamation launched its first reconnaissance study of the Pa Mong site near Vientiane (Laos).[146] Upon his return, Vice-President Johnson brought the Mekong Project to President Kennedy's attention and suggested that the United States act on this promising possibility.[147]

In the ensuing years, the Mekong Project continued to be mentioned in U.S. official speeches at regional conferences. For example, at ECAFE's conference in Tehran in March 1964, the U.S. delegation confirmed that "the United States is contributing a substantial amount of supplies, materials and equipment for the maintenance and development of the Mekong delta navigation system in Viet-

Nam. . . . The United States Delegation will sign a project agreement amendment relative to the Pa Mong survey with representatives of Cambodia, Laos, Thailand and Vietnam prior to the conclusion of this conference."[148] But it was above all Johnson's early contact and knowledge of the Mekong Project and his subsequent rise to presidential power that were to bring the Mekong Project into the heart of the storm. In the context of the escalation of the war in Vietnam at the beginning of 1965 and the participation of U.S. troops in active combat in an unfavorable U.S. domestic and international context, the Mekong Project—which from the end of the 1950s to the beginning of 1965 was still relatively unknown to the public—assumed sudden prominence, attracting as much if not more international public interest than the Tennessee Valley Authority Project.

The Mekong Committee was founded at a time during the post–Second World War period when there was an immense political and economic restructuring and reorganization of the world. This upheaval had led to the creation of a number of international and regional organizations and committees, of which ECAFE was one. From 1957, the year of its origin, to the beginning of 1965, the Mekong Committee and, through it, the Mekong Project had made progress in determining its goals, establishing work programs, and defining itself financially, legally, and technically. At the beginning of 1965, it had received a total of US$ 67 million in resources.

It was successful in obtaining the constant cooperation of the four states, which, although riparians all, had a long, common history of conflict. In order to emphasize how remarkable this Mekong Spirit was, an ECAFE report released by the UN mentioned that in October 1961, "when Cambodia broke relations with Thailand, the late prime minister of Thailand, Field Marshal Sarit Thanarat, expressly made an exception of the Mekong program when he severed relations with Cambodia."[149] It similarly noted that Prince Souvanna Phouma had remarked (speaking at the time in the capacity of private citizen) "that the hope of Laos was the Mekong project. Laos, he said, was poor, but in the Mekong it had a tremendous resource which, he added, was being developed under the auspices of the United Nations, with the help of many countries, in a completely nonpolitical manner."[150] As for Thailand, the Thai monarch had remarked in 1963 to Robert F. Kennedy, U.S. attorney general, "that the work which the United States Bureau of Reclamation was conducting on the Pa Mong should be speeded up. This . . . would be of greatest importance for the Northeast of Thailand."[151]

The project had obtained the participation of international organizations (including twelve UN agencies) and twenty-one countries (in addition to the four riparian members). As a result, a vast scientific knowledge concerning the river, its tributaries, and its lower basin was developed, and studies in related domains had multiplied and diversified to reach an enormous volume and a high level of complexity. The scientific knowledge rapidly led to the realization of the first projects on the tributaries and allowed the materialization—in part—of the hopes that riparian countries had founded on the Mekong Project. These were hopes for a better economic future thanks to the development of the river's formidable potential.

Meanwhile, the war went on unabated.

NOTES

1. Lalita Prasad Singh, *The Politics of Economic Cooperation in Asia: A Study of Asian International Organizations* (Columbia: University of Missouri Press, 1966), 26.

2. Ibid., 35.

3. Ibid., 29.

4. United Nations, Documents E/CNII/SR 48–49, ECAFE, 4th Session, November 1948.

5. Singh, *The Politics of Economic Cooperation*, 77.

6. David Wightman, *Toward Economic Cooperation in Asia* (New Haven, CT: Yale University Press, 1963), 172.

7. Commission Economique pour l'Asie et l'Extrême-Orient (CEAEO), *Dégâts causés par les inondations et travaux de défense projetés ou exécutés en Asie et en Extrême-Orient* (Bangkok: United Nations, 1951), 14.

8. CEAEO, *Aménagements à fins multiples des bassins fluviaux, 1ère Partie: Manuel de mise en valeur des bassins fluviaux* (New York: United Nations, 1957), 5.

9. It has been remarked that the Mekong forms a whole river system and "in assessing its natural and physical characteristics it makes neither ecological or hydrological sense to leave the Chinese section out of calculations." Peter Hinton, "Is It Possible to 'Manage' a River? Reflections from the Mekong," in Bob Stensholt, ed., *Development Dilemmas in the Mekong Subregion* (Clayton, Vic.: Monash Asia Institute, Monash University, 1996), 52.

10. Economic Commission for Asia and the Far East (ECAFE), *Preliminary Report on Technical Problems Relating to Flood Control and Water Resources Development of the Mekong: An International River* (New York: United Nations, 1952), 4.

11. Economic and Social Council (ECOSOC), *Annual Report, 2/15/1953–2/18/1954* (New York: United Nations, 1954), 11. In 1957, the World Bank sent a team to Thailand to study its economic problems and to suggest solutions that would assist the Thai government in its development endeavors. The mission thus analyzed the Mekong's growth potential in relation to the chronically poor Northeast. Rather than stressing the role of the river as a fluvial means of transportation, the mission emphasized the importance of a system of highways that would connect the main regions to each other and to Bangkok. This idea of "Asian highways" was evoked time and again in numerous confidential U.S. reports in the ensuing decades. The International Bank for Reconstruction and Development (IBRD), *A Public Development Program for Thailand* (Baltimore, MD: Johns Hopkins University Press, 1959).

12. The Bureau of Reclamation's advance team surveyed the terrain for a few weeks in January–February 1956 and issued the *Reconnaissance Report—Lower Mekong River Basin*, which surveyed the existing data and analyzed the future informational needs. C. Hart Schaaf and Russell H. Fifield, *The Lower Mekong: Challenge to Cooperation in Southeast Asia* (Princeton, NJ: Van Nostrand, 1963), 84–85.

13. See U.S. Department of State, *The President's Report to Congress on the Mutual Security Program for the 6 Months Ended June 30, 1955: A Cooperative Survey of the*

Development Potentialities on the Mekong River (Washington, DC: U.S. Government Printing Office, 1956). The International Cooperation Administration (ICA) placed the Mekong Project on its priority list. Conversely, the State Department was extremely suspicious of ECAFE and of its executive secretary, P. S. Lokanathan, because of his political standing and the nature of his decisions. Every proposal made by ECAFE was opposed by the U.S. representatives. Wightman, *Toward Economic Cooperation,* 187.

14. Ibid., 189.

15. Malcolm Caldwell and Lek Tan, *Cambodia in the Southeast Asian War* (New York: Monthly Review Press, 1973), 98.

16. Later, the final report combined the U.S. Bureau of Reclamation's findings and ECAFE's preliminary account. The result was published in October 1957 by ECAFE under the title *Development of Water Resources in the Lower Mekong Basin* (Bangkok: United Nations, 1957).

17. Ibid., 42.

18. Ibid.

19. Ibid., 64.

20. Ibid., iii.

21. Wightman, *Toward Economic Cooperation,* 314.

22. See ECAFE, *Cambodia, Laos, Thailand and Vietnam Joint Meeting on the Lower Mekong Basin, 20–23 May 1957: Conclusions and Recommendations* (Bangkok: United Nations, 1957).

23. ECAFE, *Statute of the Committee for the Coordination of Investigations of the Lower Mekong Basin Established by the Governments of Cambodia, Laos, Thailand and the Republic of Vietnam in Response to the Decision Taken by the United Nations, October 31, 1957* (Bangkok: United Nations, 1958).

24. Committee for the Coordination of Investigations of the Lower Mekong (Mekong Committee), *Annual Report 1972* (Bangkok: United Nations, 1973), 108.

25. CEAEO, *Rapport annuel 1965 du Comité pour la Coordination des Etudes sur le Bassin Inférieur du Mékong à la Commission Economique des Nations Unies pour l'Asie et l'Extrême-Orient* (Bangkok: United Nations, 1966), 1.

26. Mekong Committee, *Annual Report 1972,* 108.

27. Comité pour la Coordination des Etudes sur le Bassin Inférieur du Mékong (Comité du Mékong), *Programme de travail et plan de financement proposés pour 1964–1969* (Bangkok: United Nations, 1965), 26.

28. General Raymond A. Wheeler, the head of the mission, was a retired chief engineer of the U.S. Army Corps of Engineers and an official of the World Bank with much experience in dam construction and other public works. For example, he had been in charge of repairing the Suez Canal after the Arab-Israeli War of 1956. His participation in the mission was explained in part by Washington's change of mind from formal opposition to participation in this ECAFE-sponsored project. The other team members were G. Duval, France; Yutaka Kubota, president, Nippon Koei K.K.; J. W. McCammon, Canada; Kanwar Sain, India; H. V. Darling, U.S. Army Corps of Engineers. ECAFE, *Annual Report 29/3/1957–15/3/1958* (New York: United Nations, 1958), 17.

29. United Nations, *Program of Studies and Investigations for Comprehensive Development Lower Mekong Basin* (Bangkok: United Nations, 1958), 35.

30. Ibid., 36.

31. Wightman, *Toward Economic Cooperation,* 191.

32. ECAFE, *Annual Report, 15/2/1956–28/3/1957* (New York: United Nations, 1957), 36.

33. ECAFE, *Summary Records, May 11, 1959* (Bangkok: United Nations, 1960), 195.

34. ECAFE, *Annual Report, 16/3/1958–19/3/1959* (New York: United Nations, 1960), 13.

35. IBRD, *A Public Development,* 19.

36. Government of Japan, Mekong Reconnaissance Team, *Report on the First Phase of a Reconnaissance Survey on the Major Tributaries of the Mekong* (Tokyo, September 1961).

37. Comité du Mékong, *Projet de Rapport de la Septième Session du Comité* (Bangkok: United Nations, 1960), 8–9.

38. ECOSOC, *Annual Report of the Committee for Co-ordination of Investigations of the Lower Mekong Basin to the United Nations ECAFE,* E/CN.11/646 (E/CN.11/WRD/MKG/L.116 Rev. 1) (January 16, 1964), 19.

39. Mekong Committee, *Annual Report 1964* (Bangkok: United Nations, 1965), 132.

40. W. R. Derrick Sewell and Gilbert F. White, "The Lower Mekong: An Experiment in International River Development," *International Conciliation,* no. 558 (May 1966): 23.

41. John A. King, Jr., *Les Projets de développement économique et leur évaluation* (Paris: Dunod, 1969).

42. Mekong Committee, *Annual Report 1966* (Bangkok: United Nations, 1967), 101–102.

43. P. K. Menon, "Financing the Lower Mekong Basin Development," *Pacific Affairs,* no. 4 (Winter 1971–1972): 575–576.

44. Ibid.

45. ECAFE, *Annual Report, 21/3/1961–19/3/1962* (New York: United Nations, 1962), 50.

46. Evelyn Colbert, *Southeast Asia in International Politics, 1941–1956* (Ithaca, NY: Cornell University Press, 1977), 146.

47. The Colombo Plan for Cooperative Economic Development in South and Southeast Asia, *Report of the Commonwealth Consultative Committee, 1950* (Colombo, Sri Lanka: The Colombo Plan Bureau, 1951), 1.

48. Daniel Wolfstone, "The Colombo Plan After Ten Years," *Far Eastern Economic Review* (August 3, 1961): 221.

49. Council for Technical Cooperation in South and Southeast Asia, *Colombo Plan: Change in Asia, The Colombo Plan 1963* (Colombo, Sri Lanka: The Colombo Plan Bureau, 1963), 11.

50. Daniel Wolfstone, "Colombo Plan Issues," *Far Eastern Economic Review* (November 2, 1962): 268.

51. Creighton L. Burns, "The Colombo Plan," *The Year Book on World Affairs* 14 (1960): 183–184.

52. Aydogan Ozman, *Les Organisations régionales en Asie du Sud-est* (Ankara, Turkey: Publications de la Faculté de Droit de l'Université d'Ankara, 1970), 36.

53. "Toward a Common Goal: A Program for Economic Development, An Inaugural Address by President Eisenhower at the 10th Meeting of the Colombo Plan Consultative Committee, November 19, 1958," *The Colombo Plan* 3, no. 12 (December 1958): 4.

54. Henry Simmon Bloch, "Regional Development Financing," *International Organization,* no. 1 (Spring 1968): 192.

55. See, for instance, *Mekong Committee, Atlas of Physical, Economic, and Social Resources of the Lower Mekong Basin* (New York: Engineer Agency for Resources Inventories, 1968).

56. U.S. Department of State, "Memorandum for the President, Subject: Your Attendance at the Colombo Plan Conference in Seattle on November 1958," The Declassified Documents Reference System [hereafter, The DDRS], Retrospective Collection, no. 734 D (Washington, DC: Carrollton Press, 1976).

57. Recent scholarship has shed more light on the pivotal Second World War years and the factors that entered into the Big Powers' decision-making concerning the fate of Asia, particularly of French Indochina. See for instance, George McT. Kahin, *Intervention: How America Became Involved in Vietnam* (New York: Knopf, 1986); John E. Dreifort, *Myopic Grandeur: The Ambivalence of French Foreign Policy toward the Far East, 1919–1945* (Kent, OH: The Kent State University Press, 1991); Stein Tonnesson, *The Vietnamese Revolution of 1945: Roosevelt, Ho Chi Minh and de Gaulle in a World at War* (London: Sage Publications, 1991); and David G. Marr, *Vietnam 1945: The Quest for Power* (Berkeley and Los Angeles: University of California Press, 1995).

58. "Top Secret: Review of Current Trends: U.S. Foreign Policy, VII: Far East, Feb. 24, 1948," in U.S. Department of State, *Foreign Relations of the U.S. 1948,* 9 vols. (Washington. DC: U.S. Government Printing Office, 1976), 1:523–526.

59. Concerning U.S. foreign policy vis-à-vis Southeast Asia in the aftermath of the Second World War, see Colbert, *Southeast Asia in International Politics;* Gary R. Hess, *The United States' Emergence as a Southeast Asian Power, 1940–1950* (New York: Columbia University Press, 1987); and Andrew J. Rotter, *The Path to Vietnam: Origins of the American Commitment in Southeast Asia* (Ithaca, NY: Cornell University Press, 1987).

60. Samuel P. Hayes, *The Beginning of American Aid to Southeast Asia: The Griffin Mission of 1950* (Lexington, MA: Heath Lexington Books, 1971), 25–32.

61. *The Pentagon Papers: The Defense Department History of U.S. Decision-Making on Vietnam: The Senator Gravel Edition,* 4 vols. (Boston: Beacon Press, 1971) [hereafter, *PP* Gravel], 1:41.

62. Both Hess and Rotter underscored the importance of a Policy Planning Staff paper (PPS 51), dated March 29, 1949, which conclusions were reinforced by another one dated July 7, that suggested possible directions for U.S. policy toward Southeast Asia. Some of the suggestions were applied in part in August, in particular, that which concerned increased attention to Thailand. Rotter, *The Path to Vietnam,* 76–77; Hess, *The United States' Emergence,* 335–339.

63. "The Position of the US, NSC 48/1," in U.S. Department of Defense, *United States–Vietnam Relations, 1945–1967,* 12 vols. (Washington, DC: U.S. Government Printing Office, 1971), 8:256.

64. "Memorandum by the Assistant Secretary for Far Eastern Affairs (Dean Rusk) to the Deputy Under Secretary of State, Jan. 31, 1951: Subject: US Military Assistance Program in Southeast Asia," in U.S. Department of State, *Foreign Relations of the U.S. 1951,* 7 vols. (Washington, DC: U.S. Government Printing Office, 1977), 6:25.

65. *PP* Gravel, 1:37–38.

66. Hess, *The United States' Emergence,* 335–36.

67. "The Position of the US, NSC 48/2," in U.S. Department of Defense, *United States–Vietnam Relations, 1945–1967,* 8:267–268. Historian William J. Duiker emphasizes the hesitancy and uncertain nature of U.S. foreign policy vis-à-vis Indochina in his work *U.S. Containment Policy and the Conflict in Indochina* (Stanford, CA: Stanford University Press, 1994), 83.

68. Ibid., 267.

69. Ibid., 272.

70. "The Position of the US, NSC 48/1," 8:257.

71. Dean Acheson, "Crisis in Asia: An Examination of US Policy," *The Department of State Bulletin* [hereafter, *DSB*] 22, no. 551 (January 23, 1950): 111–118; Dean Acheson, "US Policy toward Asia," *DSB* 22, no. 560 (March 27, 1950): 467–472.

72. Acheson, "Crisis in Asia," 115–116.

73. Ibid., 116.

74. Hess, *The United States' Emergence*, 338.

75. Acheson, "Crisis in Asia," 116.

76. Charles Wolf, Jr., *Foreign Aid: Theory and Practice in Southern Asia* (Princeton, NJ: Princeton University Press, 1960), 112.

77. Rotter, *The Path to Vietnam*, 186–190.

78. Hayes, *The Beginning of American Aid*, 8–9. Point IV Program or Technical Co-operation Program was a reference to the inaugural speech given by Truman on January 20, 1949, which suggested four lines of action for the "American Plan for Peace and Liberty"; the fourth line suggested the use of scientific and industrial progress made by the United States for the development of underdeveloped regions. Wolf, *Foreign Aid*, 57.

79. Hayes, *The Beginning of American Aid*, 74–76.

80. Ibid., 87–93.

81. U.S. Congress, House of Representatives, Committee on Foreign Affairs, *Mutual Security Act Extension 1952* (Washington, DC: U.S. Government Printing Office, 1952), 13.

82. Wolf, *Foreign Aid*, 58.

83. Ibid., 59.

84. U.S. Department of State, "US Formally Announces Intent to Establish an Economic Aid Mission to the Three Associated States of Indochina," in *PP* Gravel, 1:371.

85. U.S. aid to Indochina, a problematic question, had been preceded by the relatively simpler decision to grant economic and military assistance to Indonesia. Rotter, *The Path to Vietnam*, 176.

86. Ibid., 200.

87. "Report by the Bureau of Far Eastern Affairs, Department of State on Military Assistance for Indochina, February 16, 1950," in U.S. Department of State, *Foreign Relations of the US 1950*, 7 vols. (Washington, DC: U.S. Government Printing Office, 1953), 6:736.

88. U.S. Congress, House of Representatives, Committee on Foreign Affairs, *Report of the Special Study Mission to Pakistan, India, Thailand and Indochina, May 6, 1953* (Washington, DC: U.S. Government Printing Office, 1953), 85.

89. Edwin F. Stanton, "Spotlight on Thailand," *Foreign Affairs* (October 1954): 72–85.

90. Rotter, *The Path to Vietnam*, 78.

91. Economist Robert J. Muscat deals extensively with the question of U.S. economic and military aid to Thailand over several decades, its motivations, and the forms it assumed in his work *Thailand and the United States: Development, Security, and Foreign Aid* (New York: Columbia University Press, 1990). Muscat discusses and extends the focus of an earlier study by J. Alexander Caldwell, *American Economic Aid to Thailand* (Lexington, MA: Heath/Lexington Books, 1974).

92. This project, situated fifty kilometers from Ha-noi in territory claimed by the Associated State of Vietnam, aimed at gathering some 10,000 villagers from the surrounding twenty-five villages into one immense integrated village, the "Dong Quan Pacification Village," which could be defended against the Viet Minh attacks. It was a "plan

that was developed by Governor Tri of North Vietnam, with U.S. financial help." U.S. House of Representatives, *Report of the Special Study Mission,* 54.

93. U.S. Congress, Senate, Committee on Foreign Relations, *Mutual Security Act of 1953* (Washington, DC: U.S. Government Printing Office, 1953), 2.

94. "Report by the Department of State to the NSC on Further Support for France and the Associated States, August 5, 1953" in U.S. Department of Defense, *United States–Vietnam Relations, 1945–1967,* 9:126–133.

95. "Memorandum of Conversation between Roosevelt and Marshall Joseph Stalin at the Teheran Conference," November 28, 1943, in U.S. Department of Defense, *United States–Vietnam Relations, 1945–1967,* 7:24.

96. "The Joint Chiefs of Staff, Memorandum for the Secretary of Defense, March 12, 1954," in *United States–Vietnam Relations, 1945–1967,* 7:268–269.

97. Ibid., 7:269. This is not to suggest that the ensuing decisions were made according solely to the dictates of the Joint Chiefs of Staff but rather that it was reflective of the general U.S. rationale at the time. For a more detailed discussion of the situation, see Lloyd C. Gardner, *Approaching Vietnam: From World War II Through Dienbienphu* (New York: W.W. Norton, 1988); Larry Kaplan, *Dien Bien Phu and the Crisis of Franco-American Relations 1954–1955* (Wilmington, DE: Scholarly Resource Books, 1990). For a recent work on the role of the Joint Chiefs of Staff in the U.S. involvement in Indochina, see H. R. McMaster, *Dereliction of Duty: Lyndon Johnson, Robert McNamara, the Joint Chiefs of Staff, and the Lies That Led to Vietnam* (New York: HarperCollins, 1997).

98. "Statement of Policy by the NSC on Review of US Policy in the Far East, August 20, 1954, NSC 5492/2" in U.S. Department of Defense, *United States–Vietnam Relations, 1945–1967,* 10:731–738.

99. Ibid., 738.

100. "The Mutual Security Program—An Investment in Strength: A Statement by Secretary Dulles," *DSB* 32 (May 23, 1955): 855.

101. Wolf, *Foreign Aid,* 213.

102. William Henderson, "The Development of Regionalism in Southeast Asia," *International Organization* 4 (November 1955): 472.

103. Singh, *The Politics of Economic Cooperation in Asia,* 26.

104. Washington concluded from the Shimla Conference's failure that Asia was not yet ready for multilateralism. It decided, in part because of that failure, to continue its aid on "a bilateral, project-by-project basis." Po-Wen Huang, Jr., *The Asian Development Bank: Diplomacy and Development in Asia* (New York: Vantage Press, 1975), 16.

105. Colbert, *Southeast Asia,* 333.

106. Edward A. Ackerman and Robert E. Lewry, "Organization for Water-Resources Development in the United States with Particular Reference to the TVA," in United Nations, *Proceedings of the Regional Technical Conference on Water Resources Development in Asia and the Far-East* (Bangkok: United Nations, 1956), 440–444.

107. See Herman Finer, *The TVA: Lessons for International Applications* (Montreal, Canada: International Labor Office, 1944), 216–236. The author stresses the fact that the TVA experience cannot be duplicated in other parts of the world without modifications and that long-term planning is necessary. However, such a project, he asserts, would allow the mobilization of savings and the transfer of capital from wealthy to poor countries.

108. The Jordan River valley project emphasized irrigation using 420 million meter cubes of water for an acreage of more than 405,000 hectares. Water would come from the

Jordan and the Yarkon Rivers. Hydroelectric production was a secondary consideration. However, in the case of this project, the spirit of cooperation and of mutual trust fundamental to the realization of a common development of the Jordan valley was essentially lacking. Numerous litigious questions arose between Israel and Jordan, and between Israel and Syria, resulting in the almost total failure of the American proposals. The riparian countries eventually decided on a more onerous, separate, and partial development of their hydraulic resources, a solution that was of lesser benefit for the countries' economies. See George Ernest Glos, *International Rivers: A Policy-Oriented Perspective* (Singapore: University of Malaya, 1961); more recently and specifically addressing the question of peace in the Middle East, Daniel Hillel, *Rivers of Eden: The Struggle for Water and the Quest for Peace in the Middle East* (New York: Oxford University Press, 1994).

109. "Address by the Personal Representative of the President, Eric Johnston," *DSB* (December 28, 1953): 891–893.

110. These themes are strongly presented in David E. Lilienthal, *TVA: Democracy on the March* (New York: Harper & Brothers Publishers, 1944). Lilienthal, chairman of the TVA, played a substantial role in Johnson's plan for the development of the Vietnamese Mekong delta.

111. The U.S. Bureau of Reclamation is an organization dealing with hydraulic projects, among other concerns. It was in charge of dams combining electricity and irrigation such as the Pathfinder (1909), the Buffalo Bill (1910), and the Roosevelt Dams (1911). The scale of projects increased year by year, and the possibilities of combining the different uses of hydraulic resources also became more varied. The dams on the Columbia River in the 1930s had already combined electricity production with navigation and irrigation. Then came the TVA, which represented the ultimate multipurpose development project.

112. See Shiu-Hung Luk and Joseph Whitney, eds., *Megaproject: A Case Study of China's Three Gorges Project* (Armonk, NY: M. E. Sharpe, 1993). The project of taming the Yangzi was not, however, forsaken. It was revived under Mao Zedong and its most recent embodiment is the Three Gorges Project, which is currently under construction and has generated much opposition inside and outside of China..

113. Jean Duffar, *Les Forces politiques en Thailande* (Paris: Presses Universitaires de France, 1972), 89; Russell H. Fifield, *The Diplomacy of Southeast Asia, 1945–1958* (New York: Harper & Brothers, 1958), 249.

114. *Isan* is a term used by the Thai to refer to the Northeast region, to its population, and in particular, to its dominant ethnic group. But the term *Isan* also had a political connotation specific to the region: The Isan concept advocates the notion of an Isan people, speaking the Isan language, and living in the Isan region, a concept that is the expression of an ethnic and regional consciousness. Charles F. Keyes, *Isan: Regionalism in North-Eastern Thailand*, Data Paper no. 65 (Ithaca, NY: Cornell University Southeast Asia Program, 1967), 3.

115. Muscat, *Thailand and the United States*, 149.

116. In April 1958 an ultimatum was sent to the government by the deputies from the Northeast demanding economic development programs for the region. The following month twenty-one members of parliament from twelve (out of the fifteen) provinces of the Khorat plateau publicly declared their adherence to socialism as the sole solution to the problems of the region. The Isan parliamentarians were, for the most part, opposed to Thailand's participation in SEATO, to the anti-Communist League of Asian Peoples, and to a pro-Western and pro-American policy. Keyes, *Isan: Regionalism in North-Eastern Thailand*, 49.

117. Muscat, *Thailand and the United States,* 152. For a study on an important Tai ethnic group of the Northeast, the Phu Thai, of relatively recent settlement and their adaptation into the Thai society, see Thomas A. Kirsch, "Development and Mobility among the Phu Thai of Northeast Thailand," in Robert Tilman, ed., *Man, State, and Society in Contemporary Southeast Asia* (New York: Praeger, 1969).

118. Already in 1910, King Wachirawut, who had compared the Chinese to the Jews of Europe, had launched a vast anti-Chinese campaign in which numerous measures were taken to limit the ethnic Chinese community's political and economic power. The government's hostile attitude toward the Chinese community was a constant element in Thai political life with periods of harsh repression and racist measures followed by periods of tension between Thailand and China. Donald E. Nuechterlein, *Thailand and the Struggle for Southeast Asia* (Ithaca, NY: Cornell University Press, 1965), 100.

119. Pierre Fistié, *L'Évolution de la Thailande contemporaine* (Paris: Presses de la Fondation Nationale des Sciences Politiques, 1965), 226.

120. Ibid., 230.

121. Ibid.

122. Pierre Fistié, "Resurgence du danger au Nord-Est," *France-Asie,* no. 187 (Fall 1966): 57.

123. Nuechterlein, *Thailand,* 113.

124. Fifield, *The Diplomacy of Southeast Asia,* 254.

125. The Cambodian ocean-borne trade was paralyzed for several months when the R.V.N. imposed a total blockade of the Mekong to protest Sihanouk's visit to Beijing in 1956. This move was devastating for the Cambodian economy because of its almost total dependence on Sai-gon harbor. P. C. Pradhan, *Foreign Policy of Kampuchea* (New Delhi: Radiant Publishers, 1985), 75. Also Roger M. Smith, *Cambodia's Foreign Policy* (Ithaca, NY: Cornell University Press, 1965), 158.

126. It was thanks to U.S. aid that the railway line Bangkok-Nakhon Ratchasima-Udorn Thani in the Northeast was extended to Nong Khai on the Mekong bank, opposite Vientiane. It was also American economic aid that helped bridge the two banks and build a road to Vientiane. Fifield, *The Diplomacy of Southeast Asia,* 256.

127. Muscat, *Thailand and the United States,* 153.

128. For an economic analysis of American aid to Thailand in relation to the Mekong Committee and Project, see Pachoom Chomchai, *The United States, the Mekong Committee and Thailand: A Study of American Multilateral and Bilateral Assistance to North-East Thailand since the 1950s* (Bangkok: Institute of Asian Studies, Chulalongkorn University, 1994).

129. Fifield, *The Diplomacy of Southeast Asia,* 255.

130. "Statement of Policy on US Policy in Mainland Southeast Asia, NSC 6012, July 25, 1960," in U.S. Department of Defense, *United States–Vietnam Relations, 1945–1967,* 10:1288.

131. Ibid.

132. "Statement of Policy on US Policy in Mainland Southeast Asia, NSC 5612/1, September 5, 1956," in U.S. Department of Defense, *United States–Vietnam Relations, 1945–1967,* 10:1087.

133. Ibid., 1090.

134. "Memorandum for the NSC Planning Board, Subject: Current US Policy in the Far East, June 29, 1959," in U.S. Department of Defense, *United States–Vietnam Relations, 1945–1967,* 10:1204.

135. "Statement of Policy on US Policy in Mainland Southeast Asia, NSC 5809, April

8, 1958," in U.S. Department of Defense, *United States–Vietnam Relations, 1945–1967,* 10:1127–1128.

136. There was the small, UN-sponsored study on floods and flood control published in 1951 that examined the Mekong basin from upstream Yunnan in China to the Vietnamese delta. Nations Unies, *Dégâts causés par les inondations et travaux de défense projetés ou exécutés en Asie et Extrême-Orient* (Bangkok: Commission Pour l'Asie et l'Extrême-Orient, January 1951).

137. *PP* Gravel 1:127.

138. Schaaf and Fifield, *The Lower Mekong,* 84.

139. Ibid., 84–85.

140. Franklin P. Huddle, *The Mekong Project: Opportunities and Problems of Regionalism* (Washington, DC: U.S. Government Printing Office, 1972), 30–32.

141. Doris Kearns, *Lyndon Johnson and the American Dream* (New York: Harper and Row, 1976), 267.

142. Copy Memo, Arthur Goldschmidt to the Vice-President, 5/4/61, Vietnam Country File, National Security File [hereafter, NSF], Box 202, L.B.J. Library, Austin, Texas.

143. United Nations Press Services, Office of Public Information, Press Release ECAFE/88, May 17, 1961, Vietnam Country File, NSF, Box 202, L.B.J. Library.

144. Copy Memo, Cesar Ortiz-Tinoco to unknown, undated, Vietnam Country File, NSF, Box 202, L.B.J. Library.

145. Ibid.

146. Excerpt of Statement by Assistant Secretary of State Walter P. McConaughy before Senate Foreign Relations Committee, 6/9/1961, Vietnam Country File, NSF, Box 202, L.B.J. Library.

147. Memo, McGeorge Bundy to the President, 4/12/1965, "Meeting with the Senators," Vietnam Country File, NSF, Box 200, L.B.J. Library.

148. Excerpts, Statement by U.S. Delegation Member, Henry J. Sandri, at ECAFE Tehran, March 1964, regarding the Mekong, Vietnam Country File, NSF, Box 202, L.B.J. Library.

149. United Nations Office of Public Information, Economic and Social Information Unit, *Putting the Mekong to Work—An International Undertaking* (New York: United Nations, March 1965), 10.

150. Ibid.

151. Ibid.

3

President Johnson's
Mekong Enterprise

During the 1960s, the Indochinese peninsula sank deeper into one of the major conflicts of the twentieth century, the Second Indochina War. This conflict surpassed the destructiveness and cost of even the First or French Indochina War, in which the United States played a major, if mostly indirect and late, part. From the time of his unexpected ascension to power in November 1963, President Lyndon B. Johnson and his advisers shaped a policy of massive military intervention and heavy-handed political manipulation in Vietnam. However, the Johnson administration also carried on the tradition dating back to President Harry S Truman of using economic aid as a political tool. Often, as in the case of the Mekong Project, this aid was envisioned more as an opportunistic response to the crisis of the moment than as a long-term contribution to the recipient's economic development.[1]

Among the many forms that it assumed—depending on the political effect desired—American economic aid worldwide had been channeled into hydraulic projects that focused on rivers spanning several nations at loggerheads with one another. President Dwight D. Eisenhower briefly launched the "Water for Peace" plan in the 1950s, which attempted to use the Jordan River's water resources development as a solution to the existing conflicts among the riparian members. This short-lived attempt was crushed by the historically deep-rooted hostilities and irreconcilable differences of the parties concerned. In such infertile ground, the seeds of economic aid and growth through the development of a river basin could only wither. Yet, more than a decade later, a similar plan—the Mekong Project—was attempted again in another region with equally contentious conditions.

In 1965, at the very time when the United States was on the verge of fully deploying its destructive power in Indochina, the Mekong Project intersected the trajectory of American policy. It was to become a component of a strategy and a war that were profoundly altering the regional equilibrium toward a polarization of Southeast Asian nations. The Mekong Project progressed in leaps and bounds thanks to its perceived serviceability to American policy during the Johnson period. In fact, its progress and the realization of several projects on the tributaries depended—one of the project's essential weaknesses—almost entirely on American political imperatives.

THE PREMISES

The Johnson administration as it came to power quickly escalated its intervention in the region by taking extensive and diverse measures in Vietnam and in the neighboring countries to buttress their governments against the Communist threat of China, the Soviet Union, and their ally, the Democratic Republic of Vietnam (D.R.V.). The military and political situation in the Republic of Vietnam (R.V.N.) as it appeared in CIA reports was alarming: Coups followed one another with distressing frequency, and almost every element in the society from workers to peasants to Montagnards seemed to be in rebellion against the government. One CIA report stated that "there has been a disturbing increase in anti-American sentiment at various levels of Vietnamese society. Recent demonstrations in Hue, Da Nang, Qui Nhon, and Nha Trang have had definite anti-American overtones."[2]

President Johnson's advisers, such as the Bundy brothers (William P. Bundy, assistant secretary of state for Far Eastern affairs, and McGeorge Bundy, special assistant to the president for national security affairs) and Assistant Secretary of Defense John McNaughton, were unanimous in their negative assessments of the situation.[3] Secretary of Defense Robert McNamara concurred, recounting decades later in his memoirs that both he and McGeorge Bundy presented Johnson with an "explosive" memorandum in January 1965 that gave an extremely negative appraisal of the situation in Vietnam, warning that if the current policy continued, it would "lead only to disastrous defeat."[4] Within the Army of the Republic of Vietnam (ARVN), defeats and desertion mounted, thus increasing the widespread fear that the regime was on the verge of collapse. The erosion of the situation in Vietnam and the apparent incapacity of Washington to halt it contributed to the weakening of the U.S. position vis-à-vis its allies in Asia, as William Bundy argued in a report to the president:

In key parts of the rest of Asia, notably Thailand, our present posture also appears weak. As such key parts of Asia see us, we looked strong in May and early June, weaker in later June and July, and then appeared to be taking a quite firm line in August with the Gulf of Tonkin. Since then we must have seemed to be gradually weakening. . . . With all the weaknesses that we all recognize in the Saigon political situation, the fact is that it is not an unusual or unfamiliar one to an Asian mind, and that our friends in Asia must well be asking whether we would support them if they too had internal trouble in a confrontation situation.[5]

What ensued then was the policy of sustained reprisals that combined air and naval strikes in retaliation against the "whole Viet Cong campaign of violence and terror in the South."[6] With presidential approval, bombing north of the 17th parallel, beginning rather mildly with Flaming Dart in February 1965, widened in March into Operation Rolling Thunder, targeting urban and economic centers of the D.R.V. such as Dong-hoi or Ha-tinh. The escalation was used as a means of pressure based on the assumption that, eventually, the D.R.V.'s will to fight would be broken, that the United States would be free to escalate or to de-escalate the bombing, and that the United States would dictate the rules of the game.[7] The strategy of sustained reprisals was followed by the sending, upon General William C. Westmoreland's request, of the first Marine battalions with the original aim of protecting Da-nang airbase, from which the air operations were launched. At Washington's initiative and without any official invitation from the host government, Marines stepped ashore on March 8, 1965. These two decisions marked the beginning of the United States' direct and massive troop involvement in the long and bloody conflict in Vietnam.

For the time being, bombing did not bring the expected D.R.V.'s capitulation—indeed, there was no apparent softening of its resolve or diminution of its support of the National Liberation Front (NLF). In fact, the bombings only reinforced the D.R.V.'s determination and hardened its allies' attitude concerning compromise. General Earl G. Wheeler's report to Robert McNamara, concerning the air strikes during the period of February 7–April 4, 1965, concluded that "the air strikes have not reduced in any major way the over-all military capabilities of the D.R.V. . . . Our strikes to date, while damaging, have not curtailed D.R.V. military capabilities in any major way. The same is true as regards the North Vietnamese economy. . . . The Hanoi government continues to maintain, at least publicly, stoical determination."[8]

Washington not only had arrived at meager results but also had had to face increasing criticism and protests outside the United States as international public opinion learned about the use of riot-control gas (CN-DN) and napalm in Vietnam. However, at this juncture, most criticism against U.S. policy in Vietnam did not question the legitimacy of such an intervention: Generally speaking, the Western world viewed it as a just war for peace and democracy against the threat of communism in Vietnam and against the D.R.V.'s two Communist allies, China and the USSR, questioning rather the efficacy of this form of war and wondering whether it would not have been advantageous to initiate negotiations. The escalation of the war gave rise to the fear of a possible chain reaction with the intervention of China and the USSR, which had threatened to send "volunteer armies" to take part in the conflict.[9] Pressures from all directions for negotiations began to mount. They emanated from nations that had been traditional allies of the United States, including Great Britain, France, and Canada, whose prime minister, Lester Pearson, in a speech at Temple University on April 1, 1965, suggested to President Johnson a halt in the air war to allow for diplomatic ma-

AS A BARGAINING CHIP

neuvers leading to peace negotiations; he also suggested that an emphasis on the vast Mekong River Project to help millions of people to a better life might be a way to set up political negotiations and guarantees of neutrality.[10] Neutral countries, including India, also intervened in favor of negotiations. In March 1965, in Belgrade, Yugoslavia, seventeen nonaligned nations made an appeal for peace in which leaders of these countries expressed their concerns about "the aggravation of the situation in Vietnam." They advocated "a peaceful solution through negotiations . . . without posing any preconditions."[11] The appeal was delivered to Washington, to the UN secretary-general, to both states of Vietnam, and, via Hanoi, to the NLF.[12] The seventeen-nation appeal was sent to other capitals of the world, where it was well received.

ANOTHER LOST OPPORTUNITY

For his part, UN Secretary-General U Thant worked to establish a dialogue with the concerned parties, but his public statements in favor of negotiations were not well received by the White House. In fact, in 1964, U Thant attempted to start discussions by secretly contacting the D.R.V., with the knowledge of Secretary of State Dean Rusk and Robert McNamara. According to George McT. Kahin, U Thant also contacted Ho Chi Minh, who agreed to the principle of direct and secret bilateral discussions with the United States. A secret meeting place, Rangoon, was proposed and agreed upon. The D.R.V. was "ready and willing."[13] However, President Johnson was apprised of the secretary-general's effort only in February 1965, by which time he had already made the decision to escalate bombings—the opportunity had been lost. One of many chances for peace had been quashed by Johnson's senior advisers, particularly Rusk and McNamara, who had not informed the president of this option until after he had made the decision to escalate. Given this precedent, it is understandable that Johnson's later offer of $1 billion in aid was never seriously considered by D.R.V. leaders. Meanwhile, Beijing had similarly rejected the secretary-general's offers of mediation. The repeated rejections of U Thant's goodwill efforts—and through him, of the UN—implicitly denigrated the UN's role as a global peace-keeper by demonstrating its impotence.

Domestic pressures were equally strong as U.S. senators and representatives received thousands of letters from their constituents demanding an end to the war. Public opinion polls showed that the American people in its majority was in favor of negotiations between the two parties (although a majority opposed any Communist victory).[14]

THE WATERSHED YEAR: 1965

In this contentious context, numerous suggestions were made concerning the resolution of the war. The United States could continue its military, political, and economic support to local governments, shoring up the Royal Lao Government (R.L.G.) against the Communist Pathet Lao, the R.V.N. against the NLF and the D.R.V., while strengthening Thailand, the last rampart against communism. This approach, however, achieved neither the desired stabilization nor an end to the conflict. The United States could take the war to the D.R.V. to cut off the supply lines to the NLF in southern Vietnam. At its best, such a solution would create another Korea; at its worst, it could degenerate into a global conflict with the Communist bloc's direct participation in the war. Another possible solution was the neutralization of the region via international agreements under the supervision of a multilateral force. This last possibility was unacceptable: Washington considered neutralism a dangerous and unreliable notion. Neutralization as a possible solution was, however, looked upon favorably by a number of U.S. politicians. Senator J. William Fulbright, the chairman of the Senate Committee on Foreign Relations, commissioned a study by the Center of International Studies of Princeton University in 1966. The result sent to President Johnson concluded that "at a minimum [exploratory negotiations on neutralization] would offer a chance to test existing national policies in regard to Southeast Asia. They might also have some positive effects on the attitude of other nations toward the United States."[15] Given Johnson's opposition to neutralism, this solution was doomed from the start. Examples of past attempts at neutralization of countries of the region—from the attempted neutralization of Laos by the 1962 Geneva Conference to French president Charles de Gaulle's proposal for neutralization of Vietnam and Laos in recent years—and their utter failures—led the president to conclude that such a solution was not viable given the unstable regional conditions.

The Fourth Solution

A fourth solution was beginning to emerge, formulated mostly by private citizens from diverse backgrounds, who suggested the development of the Mekong River as a positive approach to conflict resolution. Numerous articles and reports written by journalists, politicians, and development specialists presented the Mekong Project as "*the* solution." For instance, the executive secretary of the Northwest Public Power Association, Gus Norwood, urged the president "to consider the Mekong River Basin development program as the strategic solution or as a key to the ultimate solution to the impasse of Southeast Asia."[16] Gilbert F. White, the author of the Ford Foundation report on the socioeconomic aspects of the lower Mekong basin development, mentioned in an article published in December 1964 the multiple advantages of such a solution:

A peaceful and honorable resolution of the conflict in South Vietnam and Laos may be found in a bold plan for land and water development which already unites factions in four nations of Southeast Asia. For seven years, Cambodia, Laos, Thailand, and South Vietnam have been working with little publicity and without disagreement on a huge development program. . . . If the United Nations were to designate this area for international development . . . there is a strong possibility that peace could be achieved in a common pursuit of agricultural and industrial growth. . . . The Lower Mekong River may be the key to a fourth course of action, a more constructive and humane one than any of the others.[17]

In addition to being the more constructive approach, this would not, in White's opinion, prove as costly and destructive as the war that was currently being waged, since "the total U.S. contribution to Lower Mekong planning has cost less than four days of military aid in South Vietnam, now reported to exceed $1.5 million per day."[18] Although geographically the D.R.V. was not considered part of the lower Mekong watershed, the construction of mainstream projects could transform the northern cities into important markets for the electricity generated by these hydroelectric works. However, White recognized that financing for these projects would be more generous and forthcoming with the return of security in the region and suggested that UN peace-keeping forces, "the blue-helmeted watch and ward service," be used for the task.[19] Nevertheless, the Fourth Solution would require the consent of all parties involved, which would withdraw their troops and pledge to dedicate themselves to reconstruction and to the development of water resources. This should "permit the United States to withdraw gracefully," and its contributions would henceforth be used toward the more peaceful purpose of economic development.[20]

The so-called Fourth Solution attracted the attention of political pundits as well. Senator George McGovern (Democrat, South Dakota) in an analysis presented in *The Progressive* (March 1965), while criticizing the American policy of intervention in Vietnam, suggested that, given the deteriorating situation in Vietnam and the absence of any prospects for ending the war, the only reasonable decision that the United States could make was that of "negotiation and a political settlement." McGovern went on to discuss the minimum terms acceptable to both sides, among which he cited "cooperative planning to benefit North and South Vietnam from the Mekong River development," which, for the North, "could mean hydroelectric power for industry."[21] He also favored neutralization of both regions and the participation of UN peace-keepers. An old Asian affairs hand, Kenneth T. Young, the former U.S. ambassador to Thailand, who had accompanied the then Vice-President Johnson to the Mekong Committee's headquarters in Bangkok in 1961, was a fervent proponent of the Mekong solution, which, according to him, should be one of the five components in the search for a peaceful solution to the Vietnam conflict.[22] In his words, "If we assume military insulation and U.N. presence in Southeast Asia . . . the Mekong Project offers the most hopeful prospects for peace and progress in that region. . . . A TVA on the Mekong stirs our imaginations, and well it should. But releasing the tensions of men, channeling the ambitions of governments, and subduing the feud of nations could also be the gift of the mighty Mekong. . . . This is why I would make the Mekong community the center and keystone of the search for lasting peace and real progress."[23]

Prior to this increasing public awareness of the Mekong Project, the White House had already requested and received possible solutions to the conflict, many of which cited the Mekong Project approvingly.[24] In May 1964, for example, the State Department's Marshall Green made suggestions about the possible use of the Mekong Project in a memo to Bundy entitled "The Carrot and the

Stick." Green prophetically emphasized the following aspects: "If Hanoi were to stop directing and supporting aggression in Southeast Asia this would create the climate in which the long-awaited Mekong Valley project and other programs of promoting the economic advancement of Southeast Asia mainland could go forward. We might specifically propose some kind of little Marshall plan for the area . . . in which undertaking we would be prepared to be generous supporters."[25] He then went on to mention the fact that if ever implemented, the project would improve "regional unity" and "promote Titoism in North Vietnam," although he doubted that the D.R.V. "would be allowed by China to accept, but meanwhile we would have scored a few international brownie points in terms of our 'image' and would have presented a carrot to North Vietnam."[26] Furthermore, in 1964, presidential aide Douglass Cater also suggested the Mekong solution: "You may wish to consider the feasibility of swift insertion of United Nations technical personnel to begin preliminary work on the Mekong River Valley Development Project. . . . But the more important reason for speed would be two-fold: (1) to provide heartening evidence to the people of that region of a project to bring future bounty rather than bloodshed; (2) having U.N. personnel in the area might cause the Communist[s] to be more reluctant in their aggression. It would also provide world opinion a more solid reason for U.S. intervention to protect the peace."[27]

One recurrent theme in the proposals was a "Southeast Asia Development Association" scenario (laying thus, perhaps, the foundation for the creation of the Association of Southeast Asian Nations or ASEAN in 1967) that would "contribute to the creation of a common front against Communist China's expansionist ambitions."[28] One proposal, written by Rutherford Poats of the Agency for International Development (AID) and entitled "A Southeast Asia Peace and Progress Plan" (March 26, 1965), harked back to the Policy Planning Staff papers and National Security Council memos of the post–World War II period. Poats, however, suggested the membership of North and South Vietnam and the leadership of "Asian Wise men" and named in passing the Mekong River Project. A figure of $2 billion in terms of U.S. commitment was estimated necessary. Confidential consultations with UN Secretary-General U Thant and with Economic Commission for Asia and the Far East (ECAFE) Secretary U Nyun were advised. Walt W. Rostow, chairman of the Policy Planning Council, in his memo to McGeorge Bundy in response to the latter's request for a "scenario," transmitted Poats's outline, remarking that to link the UN to a Southeast Asian Development Association (SEADA) would be "proper," since "a principal advantage of attaching the organization to the UN would be to detach it from U.S. South Vietnam policy."[29] Rostow was of the opinion that an "economic carrot for North Vietnam, relevant to a settlement or immediate post-settlement circumstances, should be direct and *ad hoc*," although he was skeptical about its having any impact on Ha-noi: "We should not count on the hope of future economic assistance to Hanoi as a major factor in determining its posture over coming weeks and months in the Southeast Asia confrontation."[30]

In the following days, similar memos reinforcing the SEADA idea from other high-ranking officials such as Chester Cooper reached Bundy. These also named the Asian Highway and the Mekong Project themes as potential solutions. The latter quickly acquired centrality within the White House's strategic thinking. After all, one should not forget that ever since learning of the Mekong Project during his visit to Southeast Asia in 1961, Johnson had shown a certain fascination with the river and had had visions of its development on a scale that would surpass even the accomplishments of the Tennessee Valley Authority (TVA).[31] He thought it would be possible to reproduce the same miracle, using it as a symbol of peace superimposed on the destruction of the war. After all, as historian Lloyd C. Gardner puts it, "Johnson's whole career _was_ [italics in the text] the politics of economic development." His Mekong choice "resonated with [his] earliest political memories and ... [his] political career had been intimately entwined with the positive role of government in the economic development of 'backward' regions."[32]

Given the number of memoranda suggesting the Mekong Project as a possible solution, the White House requested that an assessment be made of its potential. In March 1965, Jack Valenti, special assistant to the president, reported that the "harnessing of the Mekong and its tributaries would cost many billions of dollars, being far larger in scope than the Tennessee Valley Authority," and that "many other urgent development requirements in the region also demand large amounts of foreign capital and local savings."[33] Because of its tremendous scale and the paramount question of security in the region, Valenti concluded that the project was unlikely to be immediately feasible and of direct relevance to the riparian countries' economic progress. On the other hand, the Mekong Project was "a focal point of non-political cooperation among the riparian nations, assisted by technicians of 20 Free World countries, 11 U.N. agencies and two foundations."[34] And it was the United States, through AID, that had, "in 1956, stimulated the start of planning for Mekong development as a symbol and focal point for regional cooperation. AID [later] contributed $3.2 million in technical services and equipment for cooperative surveys, data collection, and studies."[35]

According to Valenti's report, for the fiscal year 1966, AID intended to support several projects: an analysis of the Mekong's economic and hydrologic systems, a cartographic inventory of the physical and social resources of the basin, and the first phase of a feasibility study on the Pa Mong.[36] Concurrently, the report also pointed out that a mainstream dam the size of the Pa Mong "would not be economically justified during the next decade."[37] Tributary projects were more feasible and of portent; some were already functioning, although the situation varied depending on the country. At the time of the memorandum, two dams were being built in Thailand, but Laos lacked completed hydroelectric projects because of limited power demands and the war. In Cambodia, the expulsion of the U.S. mission had led to the removal of "two tributary projects from current AID consideration."[38] Although the United States did finance small projects in the R.V.N., such as the creation of a barge fleet as suggested by the Me-

kong Committee, the development of the delta had been suspended because of
the conflict. The report concluded that, while "the river's potential is great, . . .
in the next decade its exploitation is likely to be less significant to the economic
progress of Thailand, Laos, Vietnam and Cambodia than many other immediately promising investments."[39]

One National Security Action Memorandum, dated March 30, practically outlined the president's speech as it mentioned the role that the UN and its secretary-general, U Thant, could play in U.S. efforts, the participation of industrialized countries (including the USSR), and a request to Congress to pledge $1
billion. The memo remarked that "something similar was done by Ike in establishing the Inter-American Bank—a pledge before authorization," and that "of
course the amount is fairly arbitrary." A closing line was later to resonate
throughout the world: "We will negotiate with anyone, anywhere, anytime if
there is any substantial chance of an honorable peace."[40] The same month, President Johnson began testing the waters by hinting at a Marshall Plan for Asia. At
a cabinet meeting on March 25, 1965, Johnson read a statement later made public that was meant to emphasize constructive possibilities:

The United States looks forward to the day when the people and governments of all
South East Asia . . . will need not military support . . . but only economic and social
cooperation for progress in peace. Even now, in Vietnam and elsewhere, there are major
programs of development which have the cooperation and support of the United States.
Wider and bolder programs can be expected in the future from Asian leaders . . . and in
such programs we would want to help.[41]

Actually, the administration had never lost interest in the Mekong Project and
had closely followed its evolution as demonstrated by its conferences organized
on the Mekong theme. In June 1964, for instance, Harlan Cleveland, U.S. assistant secretary for international organizations, chaired a conference that gathered
UN and U.S. experts in Washington to discuss the Mekong Project. The general
opinion was that from the political point of view, the Mekong enterprise "should
serve as a political carrot that would reduce the appeal of communism to Southeast Asians and perhaps induce North Vietnam to seek prosperity through international economic cooperation rather than through conquest."[42] As the political
imperatives of the war became more urgent, Washington would select proposals
from the Mekong Project for financing based on their relevance to the conflict.

On April 6, 1965, on the eve of his historic speech at Johns Hopkins University in Baltimore, Maryland, President Johnson approved a National Security
Action Memorandum (NSAM 328) outlining General Harold K. Johnson's proposal of U.S. combat troops' active participation in the conflict in Vietnam.
President Johnson, in fact, had approved the concept of American troops directly
fighting "an Asian foe" with the active participation of allied forces of the region.[43] The decision to change U.S. troops' mission from defense and advisory
positions to active participation in the war—a definite step into the quagmire—
was kept secret on Johnson's strict orders so as to avoid any undue publicity.

Hence, on the eve of his speech, President Johnson had already made a decision
that would lead the United States beyond the point of no return, to the wasting of
billions of dollars and thousands of American and Vietnamese lives. As he was
pressed by all sides to start negotiations with the D.R.V., and since he had often
professed his willingness to "go anywhere at any time, and meet with anyone" in
the interest of peace, Johnson had to act quickly to show the world and the
American people his administration's goodwill and pacific intentions. With an
astute sense of timing, Johnson created a historical illusion that, though temporary, was powerful enough to generate a strong surge of hope for peace, a momentum that was never to return in the coming dark years of the conflict.[44]

The Johns Hopkins Speech   *PROJECT FOR PEACE IN SE ASIA*

On April 7, 1965, President Johnson read a speech entitled "Project for Peace
in Southeast Asia" at the Johns Hopkins University in Baltimore. It embodied
the two conflicting facets of U.S. policy in the region:

For what do the people of North Vietnam want? They want what their neighbors also
desire—food for their hungers, health for their bodies . . . and they would find all these
things far more readily in peaceful association with others than in the endless course of
battle. . . . The first step is for the countries of Southeast Asia to associate themselves in a
greatly expanded cooperative effort for development. We would hope that North Vietnam
would take its place in the common effort just as soon as peaceful cooperation is possible. . . . For our part I will ask the Congress to join in a billion dollar American investment in this effort as soon as it is underway. And I would hope that all other industrialized countries, including the Soviet Union, will join in this effort to replace despair with
hope, and terror with progress. . . . The vast Mekong River can provide food and water
and power on a scale to dwarf even our TVA.[45]

The speech was broadcast by radio and television to more than sixty million
people in the United States, communicated to the UN Security Council and to
member nations, and given all the appropriate official fanfare. More than a million leaflets with the translation of Johnson's speech were dropped over cities in
Vietnam, in both the South and the North.[46]

Johnson's purpose for the speech was threefold: "To explain our policy as
clearly as possible, to urge Hanoi once more to join us in trying to reach a peaceful settlement, and to describe what peace and cooperative effort could do for the
economic development of all of Southeast Asia."[47] These intentions were also
spurred on by the appeal made by the seventeen nonaligned nations at the Belgrade Conference, March 1965, to all interested parties in the Vietnam War for
peace negotiations without any preconditions. Secretary of State Rusk had made
reference to the appeal during a National Security Council meeting and advised
the president to give it a firm but positive response.[48] The Johns Hopkins speech,
partly prompted by the seventeen-nation appeal, contained several main points
that perfectly illustrated Johnson's "carrot and stick" policy vis-à-vis Southeast
Asia. First, the reaffirmation of American support to South Vietnam and its de-

termination to build a South Vietnam that would be "securely guaranteed . . . free from outside interference" was non-negotiable. Second, however, it also announced that it was ready "for unconditional discussions." The gesture of "goodwill" was reinforced by the offer of $1 billion to finance the social and economic development of Southeast Asia, which would presumably benefit all the countries of the region. As an important and significant gesture, the D.R.V. was invited to participate "in the common effort just as soon as peaceful cooperation is possible." The UN and its secretary-general were invited to play a determining part in this economic—and political—scheme. All the industrialized nations, the USSR included, were equally called upon by Washington to take part in this cooperation plan.[49]

Although the speech mentioned the region's overall economic, medical, and nutritional needs, and Johnson promised to "speed up a program to make available our farm surpluses to assist in feeding and clothing the needy in Asia," it specifically targeted the Mekong Project as the recipient of this offer because it was a development scheme that could satisfy a number of riparian countries' needs on an almost limitless scale.

What did the Johnson administration hope to accomplish through this speech, which marked the beginning of its peace strategy? Over the short term, the president attempted to rally domestic and international critics and to create a consensus and a well of sympathy for the "American cause."[50] The speech attempted to reassure American and international public opinion by stating that the U.S. government, in search of a pacific solution to the conflict, stood ready to negotiate; it was therefore the other side's responsibility to respond to the offer. Implicitly, any failure or refusal to engage in the proposed dialogue was the D.R.V.'s fault, and it would have to pay the price for its supposed intransigence. Johnson's speech intended to demonstrate that peace could be obtained in twenty-four hours, and that the final decision was in the hands of Ha-noi and its Communist backers.[51]

Thus, the United States would receive worldwide support and sympathy for its gesture of goodwill and be able to soften or even erase its previous image of a war-mongering nation that had obstinately refused to make peace overtures. The speech called upon the USSR but ignored the People's Republic of China.[52] This came as the result of a subtle calculation that Soviet participation, if it materialized, would likely counterbalance Chinese influence, perhaps widening the gap that separated China and the USSR and contributing to the collapse of the Communist bloc, with the concomitant weakening of aid that these countries had been providing the D.R.V.[53] Although the USSR's participation in the Mekong scheme was welcome, the Johnson administration did not make any serious, high-level effort to contact Moscow. Johnson did not even send the old Moscow hand, veteran of several administrations, W. Averell Harriman, who was more than eager to present the Johnson administration's views to Leonid Brezhnev.[54] Furthermore, this invitation to the Soviet power derived from a global policy of détente sought by Washington in its diplomatic relations with Moscow and countries of the Socialist bloc. The speech did not mention the "Vietcong," that is, the NLF, a sign of Washington's persistence in refusing to consider this political movement as a valid participant. In the first draft, there had been mention of all the combatants, and an appeal to put down weapons was made. But in the final version, this paragraph was removed.[55] It was thought that in the eventuality that the D.R.V., attracted by the tantalizing offer, would decide to start unconditional negotiations and become part of the American economic development program for Southeast Asia, a rift would be created, eroding the solidarity between "North Vietnam" and the "Vietcong" in the South. Such a development would weaken the adversary, and the United States could end the war by winning it on its own terms.

U.S. officials in post-speech interviews also pointed out that, much like President John F. Kennedy's formulation of the concept of the Alliance for Progress, Johnson's offer did not carry a specific blueprint. The intent was to mobilize the spirit and will of people of Southeast Asia to work toward economic and social development.[56] The political effects would be to alleviate Communist ideological pressures on neutralist countries and, hopefully, to pry the D.R.V. from one of its staunchest supporters, China. If all these positive developments were not to take place as expected, the United States would, nevertheless, have conveyed to the D.R.V. its determination to continue the war, and the latter, as a result, would have to endure more sufferings and heavier casualties were it to persist in its refusal. Its acceptance to negotiate would, on the other hand, open the door to an economic manna that the D.R.V. desperately needed for reconstruction and development.

The offer of an American contribution to the development of Southeast Asia and the impressive figure of $1 billion to be spent on it marked a shift in American policy. Henceforth, two starkly different visions of the conflict existed. One was of the war, of destruction linked to the military presence of American forces in Vietnam and in other countries of the Indochinese peninsula, a reality that was omnipresent and overpowering. The other, which purported to be constructive and positive, was of American economic aid destined, in particular, for the Mekong Project. This second vision was to become the object of grandiose gestures and spectacular speeches, generous offers and impressive plans that hopefully would help to drown out the clamorous images of death and destruction. This new phase in American diplomacy as it manifested itself in Asia also strove to defuse tension in an unstable region, to foster a spirit of cooperation between antagonistic riparian nations that should eventually evolve into a powerful regionalism that could counter communism's pervasive influence. To do so, the United States attempted to attract industrialized nations' contributions that were to be channeled to a development project that could be beneficial to the stability of Asia. It also attempted to make them contribute more to the region's defense. Along the same line of reasoning, the USSR's economic involvement in a development project in Southeast Asia could result in the reduction or even the termination of its military and economic aid to the D.R.V. Such an evolution would surely defuse the war.

Within this framework, the UN secretary-general was called upon to play a paramount part in this vast constructive effort. Since the speech was made partially in response to the Belgrade appeal, the UN's involvement in the economic development process would rally the dissenting voices of nonaligned countries and improve American relations with nations of Africa, the Middle East, South Asia, and Southeast Asia within this international body. These nonaligned nations would more willingly accept that the security question of the region be vested in an impartial third party that had been a long-standing peace-keeping organization. Its geographic zone of responsibility was much more encompassing than that of a geographically limited South East Asia Treaty Organization (SEATO). Moreover, the work accomplished by the UN in the field of development assistance, and the prestige that it had garnered, were undeniable and provided the United States with an important asset in its crusade to rally domestic and international public opinion. The UN with its host of specialized agencies was the ideal vessel to carry international cooperation to regions where it was most needed, that is, Southeast Asia. Finally, according to the Pentagon Papers, another factor added practically at the last minute by the president to the Johns Hopkins speech "to lend more credibility and prestige to the somewhat improbable peaceful development gambit in the midst of war" was the appointment of Eugene R. Black as special adviser to the president. Black was a person esteemed in financial milieus and specialized circles, a former president of the World Bank, respected both by the Democrats and the Republicans, and, at the time, director of Chase Manhattan Bank in New York.[57]

Reactions both in the United States and abroad were in general favorable. American newspapers considered that the president's speech had opened a door and that the peace process was started. For the *New York Times*, the president's speech was prompted by two main considerations: One was to "erase the impression that the President and his country were heartless, stubborn and unreasonable where peace was at stake"; the other was "to suggest that Hanoi could profit from a settlement while emphasizing how Hanoi would suffer largely alone, in further combat."[58] In its editorial, the *Times* said that the president had "projected an American policy on Vietnam in which the country can take pride" and had "broken new ground . . . in offering to North Vietnam American-aided regional development." As the editorial put it, "neither they [the Communist countries] nor anyone else can dispute the fact that a serious peace offer has been made, it is now clearly up to them to make a reasonable response."

While recognizing the "generous offer of peace and conciliation," the press nevertheless underlined Johnson's "carrot and stick" policy. The *Washington Post* lauded the speech as "a major offer for negotiations" and "an attempt to launch a peace offensive."[59] However, the *Post* sounded a note of caution, citing official sources that "acknowledged that the proposal is still only a concept, rather than a plan," and noting that the term used was "investment" rather than aid, which might lead one to conclude that it could "include anything from business investment to loans and grants." Overall, the American press were unanimous in recognizing that the Baltimore speech did accomplish one of its goals— to rally American public opinion, whether it was for or against the war, Democrat or Republican. The *Times* underscored that "the speech had evidently served the President's purpose." Some newspapers even acknowledged President Johnson's skill in rallying American public opinion on a topic that had been dividing it. The American press, while lauding the presidential initiative as a promising new opening, was awaiting the Communist countries' reactions. The ball was now in the enemy's court, and, certainly, Communist countries were to be criticized if they responded negatively to such a generous offer.

Reactions in Congress were partisan. All parties approved the president's vehement reaffirmation of the continuation of the war to preserve the independence of the R.V.N. In fact, the immediate impact of the speech was to help the administration to obtain the withdrawal of a military aid cut proposed by the Senate Foreign Relations Committee and the restoration of funding to its previous $1.17 billion ceiling. Opinions were divided when it came to the aid proposal of $1 billion and the call for unconditional negotiations. The Democrats felt the offer was generous although onerous; the Republicans argued that peace could not be bought with dollars and asserted that unconditional negotiations would be considered forerunners of capitulation. Democrats such as Senator Fulbright of Arkansas, chairman of the Foreign Relations Committee, and Senate majority leader Mike Mansfield of Montana welcomed the speech, saying that "the door is open to a bonafide settlement which will permit the people of Viet Nam to live in peace and freedom."[60] However, the chairman of the House Appropriations Subcommittee, who was in favor of drastically reducing foreign aid, professed to be shocked as he was confirmed in his opinion that "we are trying to buy friends with our dollars." And the Senate minority leader, Everett McKinley Dirksen of Illinois, who had been one of the president's constant supporters, questioned Johnson's offer: "Do we actually buy peace with an American aid program? Do you buy freedom for a humble people with a billion-dollar package? I doubt it, and I doubt also that we can preserve face and prestige with such an approach."[61]

Johnson's proposal for the economic development of Southeast Asia based on the Mekong Project, as well as his offer of $1 billion, led to controversies inside the administration and in Washington circles generally. According to Chester Cooper, a member of the National Security Council, Johnson surprised "experts and technicians" with his unexpected $1 billion Mekong proposal, and there were a number of people who doubted the viability of such a project, since the financial sources, the responsibilities, and the countries involved remained unclear. Would it involve North and South Vietnam, Cambodia, Laos, Thailand, Burma, and Malaysia? In what ways would the UN, ECAFE, and the Mekong Committee fit into the president's proposals?[62] Even the figure of $1 billion seemed to have been decided upon because it was "a nice, round, dramatic figure" rather than because it was related to any realistic estimates.[63]

On the international scene, in barely twenty-four hours, the Baltimore speech succeeded in reversing the negative world opinion toward U.S. policy in Indochina. The UN secretary-general, to whom the speech assigned a pivotal constructive role, rallied at once to the idea by sending a personal message to the president, qualifying the speech as "positive, forward-looking and generous."[64] The secretary-general had good reason to view the proposal favorably: After all, the presidential proposal was a timely measure allowing the UN, which had failed until then in its Indochinese initiatives, to salvage its credibility and raise hopes for possible peace negotiations, perhaps under UN auspices. The president's newly appointed special adviser, Eugene Black, and the U.S. ambassador to the UN, Adlai Stevenson, had formally consulted the secretary-general on the proposals presented in the Baltimore speech, and in particular, on the project of international cooperation for the development of Southeast Asia.[65] By so doing, the United States contributed to enhancing the UN's prestige and that of its secretary-general. Stevenson had also expressed Washington's intention to set up a concrete program of economic aid with which the UN and its secretary-general were to be closely associated.[66] Press conferences were organized by UN officials, particularly by the under-secretary general for General Assembly affairs, Chakravarti V. Narasimhan (former ECAFE executive secretary), who had contributed much to the creation and promotion of the Mekong Committee. In a press conference, Narasimhan acknowledged that it was mainly because the four riparian countries lacked resources that the Mekong Project had not been further advanced, citing "the apprehension about the political instability" as a major obstacle to project realization.[67] He emphasized the remarkable cooperation among the riparian states, a cooperation that had been maintained uninterrupted for seven years in the face of daunting challenges and the omnipresent fear of political upheavals. In the course of these conferences, it was mentioned that the D.R.V. had not been allowed to participate in ECAFE discussions despite its repeated requests and obvious need for hydroelectric power.[68] At the time, the D.R.V. was not a member of ECAFE, since it was not officially a member of the UN.

Black moved quickly to "create a climate of cooperation in Southeast Asia and to enlist the aid of Western Europe." He nevertheless cautiously emphasized the fact that patience was imperative as "the program by its very nature involves years of development."[69] Black stressed that Johnson's program should be viewed as an international effort in terms of funding, that industrialized Europe should be persuaded to participate, and, above all, that "economic development is basically a matter for Asian leadership."[70] For the moment, he asserted, the most pressing need would be to assess the priorities and the possibilities in consultation with nations of the region and of Europe.[71]

Official reactions within the European community were few although positive. In London, the Harold Wilson government greeted the proposal favorably, stating that it would provide "a framework within which it would be possible to resolve the present conflict and extend to the peoples of Vietnam the hope of progress toward peace and economic betterment."[72] Paris noted that President Johnson had simply followed the policy line advocated by de Gaulle in August 1963, of negotiations without conditions, but expressed doubts that the Baltimore proposal could succeed, since the NLF was not considered by Washington to be a viable party. French diplomats expressed doubt that the D.R.V.'s powerful ally, China, would allow it to start a process that might diminish or even terminate Chinese influence over the D.R.V. and in Asia generally. The leading French daily, *Le Monde,* pointed out that this peace offensive went hand-in-glove with American military escalation. Observers agreed that the escalation explained the swiftness and the extent of the American political action at the UN, quickly exploiting the initial success of the president's speech in non-Communist capitals. Having long been on the defensive, the American government wanted to use the opportunity to launch on the global political marketplace a "product" that apparently sold well under the double label of unconditional negotiations and economic aid.

Johnson's offer of $1 billion for the Southeast Asian development received general praise in the Western press, which commented that the "President had seized the diplomatic and psychological initiative and had put the responsibility for peace or war directly on the Communists."[73] The following days, more scrutiny was paid to other aspects of the speech, for instance, the American "insistence on South Viet-Nam's independence."[74] The Western press did not question the enormous sum but believed that the project had slim chances of success as it did not involve the NLF. In Europe, the speech was viewed in the overall context of the escalating conflict, and the colossal aid offer along with "negotiations without pre-conditions" were not really taken seriously. Hence, the proposals were analyzed as so much political maneuvering rather than as a potential turning point. Nevertheless, most agreed that the Johns Hopkins address "considerably improved the image of the United States in the context of the Viet-Nam situation," and in the words of the conservative Copenhagen *Berlingske Tidende*, it "changed the whole basis for the evaluation of world opinion of American efforts in Viet-Nam."[75]

The Soviet Union, China, and the D.R.V., the focus of the Baltimore proposal, were unanimous in their rejection of it, denouncing in violent terms President Johnson's speech, which, it was pointed out, did not mention a bombing halt or American troop withdrawal. Nevertheless, there were nuances behind the Communist rhetoric; what was left unsaid spoke more loudly than the spoken. Beijing denounced the proposal without officially rejecting it and indicated that U Thant would not be welcome in China if he were to pay a visit for purposes of mediation, since "the conflict can be settled only by nations that participated at a conference in Geneva in 1954 to divide Vietnam." (China at the time of the conference had not been admitted to the UN.)[76] Beijing Radio described Johnson's proposal as "overflowing with lies and deception."[77]

The Soviet Union was more sanguine in its statements than China or the D.R.V. Even before the speech, Soviet sources at various levels had been hinting at the USSR's willingness to help in the negotiations in order to contain Chinese influence and to prevent China from threatening the détente that the USSR was working toward with the United States. An article published in *Pravda* reflected the contradictions inherent in such a policy. On one hand, the USSR had to support the D.R.V. in words and deeds through public statements and secret shipments of weapons and ammunitions as well as economic aid in order to counterbalance China's influence on the D.R.V.[78] On the other hand, the USSR was wary of being sucked into a global war at a time when Moscow was straining to develop a détente with the United States to offset escalating Sino-Soviet hostilities. With these concerns to take into account, the USSR had to publicly support the D.R.V.'s stand by denouncing Johnson's speech. Thus, Radio Moscow asserted that there could be no reaction but a negative one "to the continued U.S. aggression" in the D.R.V.[79] Likewise, the Soviet Union continued to insist on the participation of the NLF in peace talks; it had often expressed its support of that movement and could not now renege, since such an action would damage its credibility in the eyes of the Communist world. Unofficially and discreetly, however, the Soviets were advising their ally to take a more conciliatory attitude in favor of negotiations. These maneuvers suggest that the Communist world was not united; it was, in the words of one observer, "totally at odds over Vietnam policy." Indeed, increasing this disarray had been one of President Johnson's goals in making the policy initiative.[80] At the regional level, the Soviet embassy in Vientiane, for instance, which had been holding informal talks with its U.S. counterpart, advanced "the prospect of Soviet contribution to . . . Nam Ngum Dam; and there was considerable interest in new ADB [Asian Development Bank]."[81] A potential Soviet contribution to either project would actually signal a shift in Soviet policy vis-à-vis Southeast Asia, "a sudden reasonableness of line, . . . conspicuous support for Souvanna Phouma and ostentatious ignoring of Pathet Lao."[82] The implication for the United States would be the "possibility of a tacit United States-Soviet undertaking which would guarantee the continued existence of Laos against Chicom (or DRV) encroachment."[83]

Ha-noi had given much publicity to Ho Chi Minh's statement of March 5, 1965 (published by the Japanese newspaper *Akahata*), which demanded the end of all bombing and the withdrawal of American forces, after which the Vietnamese should be allowed to determine their destiny without foreign interference.[84] The D.R.V.'s first public reaction to the Johns Hopkins speech appeared in the official organ of the Vietnam Workers Party, *Nhan Dan* (*The People*), of April 11, 1965. The editors pointed out that, barely twenty-four hours after Johnson's speech, U.S. planes bombed and strafed North Vietnam, and two U.S. Marine battalions landed in the South, acts that contradicted Johnson's words and constituted a breach of the 1954 Geneva Agreements. The articles went on to say that Johnson's offers of "unconditional talks" and of "one billion dollars" were part of the "deceitful psychological warfare tactics employed by the imperialist

United States." The commentary rejected the offer of "one billion dollars to buy fourteen million people in Southeast Asia." Southeast Asians were, the commentator asserted, "determined not to take ten dollars each to sell their countries." The commentary cited Prince Sihanouk (out of context) to the effect that "Kampuchea rejects American aid because such aid carries humiliating economic, political, and military conditions." Throughout the following year, editorials and articles in *Nhan Dan*, *Hoc Tap* (*Studies*), and *Lao Dong* (*Labor*) continued to criticize the Baltimore speech, calling it "a stinking bait" and "a hoax," proclaiming the ardent desire of Southeast Asians to resist Johnson's "honeyed words," and demanding that the United States immediately withdraw from the South, halt all bombings, respect the 1954 Geneva Agreements, and recognize the NLF as a genuine participant in negotiations. In a speech to the D.R.V.'s National Assembly (third session), Ho Chi Minh rejected Johnson's offers of negotiations and of $1 billion of economic aid but thanked socialist countries for their help and solidarity, mentioning in particular the USSR and China. Ho Chi Minh demanded that the United States "respect the Geneva Agreements, withdraw from South Vietnam! [The United States] must cease immediately its attacks on North Vietnam. *That is the only solution* [italics in the text] to the question of the conflict in Vietnam: to apply the Geneva Agreements of 1954 to protect peace in Indochina and in Southeast Asia. There is no other solution. That is the answer of our people and our government to the imperialist United States."[85]

Ho Chi Minh went on to characterize the offer of $1 billion as a sham. Other official commentators brought out the fact that the NLF was not even mentioned in Johnson's speech; the United States had thus refused to acknowledge the NLF's pivotal role in the struggle. "Unconditional negotiations" were equated to "unconditional surrender."[86] Economic aid was viewed as "an instrument of economic penetration"; as such, it had been rejected by Southeast Asian people from the Philippines to Indonesia and from Laos to Cambodia.[87] Radio Liberation (the NLF's mouthpiece) referred to the offer as "tactics using a rotten carrot and a broken stick" and, stressing the NLF's right to speak for the fourteen million people of South Vietnam, demanded a role in any future negotiations.[88] Numerous articles brought up the contradiction between "hundreds of American airplanes . . . dropping bombs every day, on hospitals, schools, busy market places" and the offer of economic aid and reconstruction. A long *Nhan Dan* article by Hoang Quoc Viet entitled "Johnson's Lure Will Definitely Fail" argued that "the people of Vietnam and of Southeast Asia, who had sacrificed all for independence and freedom and had no fear of American planes and weapons, would never want the dirty dollars of American imperialists."[89] As the American military escalation continued, a number of articles continued to point out the contradiction between the American president's promises of a better future and the harsh reality of destruction. Prime Minister Pham Van Dong, interviewed by the United Arab Republic's *Al-Akhbar* newspaper, emphasized the four-point position of the D.R.V. as a precondition to the political solution to the Vietnamese conflict.[90]

It should be noted that the Baltimore speech was not reproduced in its entirety in the D.R.V.'s press, and there was no mention made of the Mekong Project. There may be several explanations for why the project was never mentioned in any articles. Throughout the war, articles that appeared in the D.R.V.'s journals, magazines, and newspapers rarely paid any attention to the question of the lower Mekong basin's water resources and prospects for their integrated development. The D.R.V.'s state and society were so focused on fighting the war that few resources remained to be devoted to such an uncertain, costly, and remote issue as the potential future development of the Mekong.[91] Furthermore, the enterprise that was begun in the late 1950s had involved only its non-Communist southern counterpart, the R.V.N. Later on, the D.R.V. had attempted to obtain membership on the Mekong Committee but had been repeatedly refused. The exclusion left it devoid of any regional experience in the matter and excluded from the "Mekong club."

Additionally, it was an enterprise that had fostered the famous "Mekong Spirit" of cooperation, cordiality, and solidarity between states that had not distinguished themselves in the past for such amicable relations. Although the Mekong entente was occasionally somewhat tumultuous and rocky, it nevertheless had survived because of the financial, technical, and political support of Western nations. Hence, the governments that were represented at the annual sessions of the Mekong Committee were viewed by the D.R.V. as puppet governments that sided with the "imperialist United States" and were themselves embroiled in the Vietnam conflict. As such, the Mekong Project and the Mekong Spirit could not be invoked as symbols of regional or socialist solidarity and were best avoided by the press. The reluctance to broach the question of the Mekong's development may also have been due to the leadership's decision not to distract their beleaguered people's energy and focus from the war or allow them a glimmer of hope that the conflict could be solved by any means other than total victory for the revolutionary forces. Thus, the Communist protagonists to whom the speech was addressed, the D.R.V., the Soviet Union, and implicitly China, rejected— each in its own way and for its own reasons—the offer of unconditional negotiations and of economic assistance as just another stratagem in the American policy of aggression.

In the R.V.N., the press was prompt to react to Johnson's speech, which was reproduced in its entirety in some newspapers. Most articles chose to emphasize the "constructive," development-oriented aspect of the offer. Despite the overall tone of optimism, however, a note of caution was sounded in an editorial of the *Saigon Post*, which warned that "only when the Vietcong and the Hanoi regime cannot hope for a military victory, and when the power of our arms reaches wide and far into the Northern sanctuary causing there more destruction than they can ever hope to achieve in the South, only then . . . would there be a small ray of hope for the realization of the Johnsonian peace in Southeast Asia."[92] In terms of official responses, the foreign minister and vice-prime minister, Tran Van Do, stated his agreement on the general content of the Baltimore speech but cautiously emphasized that, according to his government, "unconditional discussions" meant only an exchange of ideas rather than "true negotiations," since the R.V.N. insisted on the withdrawal from the South of all "VC soldiers and cadres" before negotiations could take place.[93] Furthermore, he asserted, it was the position of his government that negotiations could not take place without the representation of the R.V.N. Overall, the response in the R.V.N. as it appeared in newspapers was positive in welcoming Johnson's offer of $1 billion to be used by Southeast Asian people in their fight against poverty and for economic development and prosperity. Prime Minister Phan Huy Quat concurred, expressing his satisfaction that the United States had reiterated its commitment to "an independent South Vietnam."[94] An R.V.N. communiqué issued on April 11, 1965, came out more forcefully, formally declaring that it insisted on preconditions: that all Communist troops and cadres be withdrawn before any peace negotiations and that it would not recognize the South Vietnamese Liberation Front as a qualified representative of the opposite side in any negotiations.[95]

In Southeast Asia, nations that had been traditional allies of the United States and members of SEATO, such as Japan, Thailand, and Australia, were unanimous in their praise of the Baltimore speech. Japan considered the president's proposals to be an opportunity for Japan to play a role that would bring it greater regional and global recognition. Washington and Tokyo were in close contact because the latter wished to be informed as soon as possible of intentions concerning the use of the promised "gold mine" of $1 billion. Prime Minister Eisaku Sato declared that Japan was ready to participate actively in the $1 billion American economic aid program for Asian countries. Indonesia also voiced its approval. Laos's neutralist government of Souvanna Phouma equally expressed approval of the speech, which was, the government stated, timely. In fact, at the twenty-first session of ECAFE held in Wellington (New Zealand), the Lao delegation emphasized the Nam Ngum project's importance for its economy in terms of water control and irrigation. The World Bank expressed its interest in the project, but its approval was conditional upon a number of factors.[96]

Regional leaders and governmental officials reacted with euphoria, taking the offer literally and hoping that it would be concretized in its totality. They hastened to present ambitious development projects and proposals for an "equitable" appropriation and a "judicious" use of the billion dollars to the presidential envoy Eugene R. Black. The Thai minister for national development, Pote Sarasin, presented to the envoy a list of thirteen priority projects that, Thailand hoped, would be financed by the future program of aid, knowing full well that Washington was searching for regional projects that would associate several countries of Indochina. Nevertheless, the Thai prime minister warned that such projects were difficult to realize and that Thailand was more interested in the ones that would directly affect its own development. The governor of the Bank of Thailand organized a meeting with his colleagues of the Bank of Malaysia to discuss appropriate measures to prepare the realization of the future aid program in Southeast Asia. He had hoped to convene the governors of national banks of the Philippines, Burma, and Cambodia for a discussion on national development projects.[97]

Despite the lack of response from the Communist countries, Washington decided to continue its campaign in order to exploit to the fullest the return of approval and support from the non-Communist nations that resulted from the generous offer formulated in the Johns Hopkins speech. While continuing its "Peace Offensive," the United States had not relented its military activity in Vietnam. It had, in fact, intensified it. To a certain extent, the focusing of public opinion on a positive aspect of American policy had deflected criticism of the U.S. role in the war in Vietnam. This political action was aimed at the non-Communist nations of Asia for which the United States had defined a clear role and position as manifested in a speech by Assistant Under-Secretary for Asian Affairs Leonard Unger:

First, that the nations of Southeast Asia, as with all other Asian states, should develop as free and independent countries according to their own views and toward increasingly democratic structures. Second, that the nations of the area should not threaten each other or outside nations. . . . Third, that no single Asian nation should either control other nations or exercise domination either for the whole area or for any major part of it. And fourth, that the nations of the Far East should maintain and increase their ties with the West in trade and culture, as a major means of knitting together a peaceful and stable world.[98]

The "Peace Offensive" to promote a tighter economic cooperation with nations of "Free Asia" included a number of measures. Soon after the Johns Hopkins speech, President Johnson, seeking to demonstrate that he was not going to wait for the conclusion of the war to fulfill his economic promises, ordered on April 9, 1965, the immediate sending of foodstuffs to the Mekong countries of Thailand, Laos, Cambodia, and the R.V.N. American agricultural surplus, valued at $500,000, were to be distributed to workers on Mekong Project sites. Johnson also ordered the organization of a mission of American experts from the Edison Electricity Institute to carry out research on the potentiality of the power market in the region of the lower Mekong basin and on the possibilities of rural electrification of Vietnam for which a crash plan was put together by AID. It is interesting to remark that, while this measure had been discussed before, the administration chose to announce it in the context of the generalized fanfare of the Baltimore speech. The choice of rural electrification was of note, since it was a decision more directly linked to the question of rural pacification and security than to the prospects and problems of economic development and cooperation for the whole of Southeast Asia.

Johnson appointed McGeorge Bundy to head the Task Force on Economic and Social Development for Southeast Asia, which was responsible for preparing projects and proposals for the president and Eugene Black to consider. The task force was to pay special attention to the UN secretary-general's initiatives. The specific objectives that the president assigned to the task force were the following: an evaluation of the most suitable regional solution for the development of Southeast Asia; the requisite conditions to render the American contribution most effective and to inspire the maximum public confidence in its effectiveness; an estimation of other industrialized nations' contributions that the United States could expect in the present circumstances or in the eventuality of a negotiated solution in Vietnam; the means that would allow the most contributions; and "the steps that can be taken to encourage additional private investments by industrialized nations in Southeast Asia."[99]

Out of the American scheme emerged several lines of action. The main emphasis was on multilateralism. The United States would use the UN channel and its secretary-general's indispensable patronage to work toward its aims. Adlai Stevenson, the head of the American delegation to the UN, met with U Thant to discuss international cooperation projects for the development of Southeast Asia. U Thant was convinced that "Johnson's Aid-to-Asia Program" should not be hastily implemented and should utilize existing structures. The secretary-general was reported to be "worried about the appointment of Eugene Black. He considers Black the type of personality who might want to move too fast."[100] One week later, Washington announced that the U.S. government was ready to finance certain projects of the Mekong Committee and to participate in a bank for the development of Southeast Asia. The United States reversed its position of opposition to the creation of a regional bank that had been envisioned some time ago by the members of ECAFE and undertook to support an Asian development bank. Washington concurrently resorted to the bilateral channel as well. Regarding the Mekong Project, the U.S. Bureau of Reclamation resumed Phase II of the program of pre-engineering studies concerning Pa Mong, the gigantic project on the mainstream. Proposals for a number of measures to reinforce the economies of riparian countries were made, although they did not include Cambodia, which had rejected American aid in 1963 and severed diplomatic relations with the United States in May 1965.[101]

The American program would be supported by an $89 million budget, supplementary to the aid program of 1966 that President Johnson had presented to Congress on June 1, 1965, to be divided as follows:

1. Approximately $19 million will provide the first installment of our contribution to the accelerated development of the Mekong River Basin. . . . This money will enable us to meet a request for half the cost of building the Nam Ngum Dam, which the international Mekong Committee has marked "Top Priority" if the Mekong River is to be put to work for the people of the region. This will be the first Mekong power project to serve two countries, promising power to small industry and lights for thousands of homes in Northeast Thailand and Laos. The funds will provide also for powerlines across the Mekong, linking Laos and Thailand; extensive studies of further hydroelectric, irrigation, and

flood control projects on the Mekong mainstream and its tributaries; [and] expansion of distribution lines in Laos.[102]

Although the request for additional funds was presented in the context of a program of aid to Southeast Asia, the major part of the funds was earmarked for the financing of South Vietnam's infrastructure and economy in order to sustain its war effort. Thus, in general, the funds requested had two well-defined objectives: (1) to implement the Baltimore offer and to demonstrate to other industrialized nations the U.S. intention to play its part, and (2) to allow the R.V.N. to increase its war effort while improving its economy. As the war intensified, the successive economic aid budget proposals presented to Congress were to give an increasing preeminence to the economic and social development of South Vietnam while the share taken up by the economies of other riparian countries would diminish in consequence.

The Role of the Asian Development Bank

The idea of a regional credit institution specializing in the accumulation of capital to be used to finance regional projects went back to 1954, when ECAFE members had seriously considered the creation of an Asian bank for development. However, the United States and the World Bank had opposed the project throughout the 1950s, fearing that the requirements imposed by such an institution for the lending of funds would not be sufficiently stringent, that the funds thus would be wasted, and the United States would not have the leading role.[103] Eugene Black was opposed to the idea of creating regional banks: "I feared that they would become political institutions which, while ostensibly charged with tasks very like those of the World Bank, would tend to undermine the kind of lending standards we were trying to get accepted and the confidence we were trying to build up in the bond markets of the world."[104]

Until March 1965, a few weeks before President Johnson's Baltimore speech, the State Department and the Treasury Department had opposed the idea of an official participation by the United States in an Asian development bank, even stating at the ECAFE meeting in Wellington that the United States would be willing to help nations of the region draft a charter for an Asian bank but would not formally and officially participate. The following excerpt from the memorandum of a conversation between Secretary of State Dean Rusk and Japanese Prime Minister Eisaku Sato on an official visit to Washington in January 1965 shows the U.S. position regarding the formation of such an institution:

The Prime Minister said that Mr. [Takeshi] WATANABE, formerly the Japanese Director at the International Bank for Reconstruction and Development (IBRD), is conducting studies on the practical aspects of formation of an Asian Development Bank, which would operate much along the lines of similar institutions for the Americas. He did not think that overt American participation would be desirable, but he asked the Secretary whether the United States might support such a plan. The Secretary welcomed the idea of an Asian Development Bank and said that the United States, to the extent possible, could play the role of a "silent partner" in such an undertaking.[105]

The Baltimore speech publicly signaled a change in the U.S. attitude toward an Asian regional bank. Almost overnight, Washington wanted nothing more than to see the regional bank quickly materialize. The administration was torn between the two Southeast Asian priorities, the Nam Ngum project and the ADB, hesitating to waste its leverage as it was attempting to convince its allies (Europeans and others) to contribute to Johnson's Southeast Asian proposal. The following memo in reference to German aid questioned the advisability of pushing in both directions: "It [the draft request] indirectly requests Lilienfeld to suggest to Erhard [chancellor of Germany] that he make a German pledge to the financing of the Nam Ngum project in Laos. . . . I would argue . . . that this letter might well disperse our leverage too much . . . [since] we are hammering at Erhard to up his contribution to the ADB for precisely the same reasons we are pushing Nam Ngum."[106] The memo concluded that the administration "must focus our pre-visit on *either* the ADB or Nam Ngum, and I think we made a choice when the president wrote Erhard on behalf of the Bank."[107]

What, then, were the reasons for this about-face regarding official support of an ADB?[108] At a time when the world's attention was focused on the Vietnam War, the creation of the Asian Development Bank, according to Averell Harriman (ambassador-at-large with responsibility for Southeast Asia), would be a demonstration of the concept of pacific development in Asia. The bank would be proof that the United States intended to look beyond the war to a future when all the resources used at present for fighting against Communist aggression would be dedicated to reconstruction and peaceful development.[109] In a speech to Congress urging American participation in the ADB and requesting Congress to approve his administration's pledge of $200 million to the bank, President Johnson argued that "joint action with these major subscribers [Japan, India, and Australia] provides another instrument of cooperation between the donors of aid. That is a long-sought goal of the United States, for it offers the most efficient use of all the free world's aid resources."[110] The ADB, thanks to American participation and with the approval of the World Bank, would be able to attract funds from industrialized nations and Asian countries that would be used for the development of the region.

During the campaign launched to drum up support for the Asian institution, the United States did not fail to underline the fact that the bank was, above all, an Asian bank founded by and for Asians, working together toward their own development with their own funds. As such, the bank should provide the best example of Asian economic cooperation and, hopefully, inspire comparable efforts in other sectors—social, cultural, and, indeed, political. Within the context of American policy, the ADB could make loans in conjunction with the United States and other donor nations for projects that were beyond the means of a single donor. The bank could also reinforce the effectiveness of American aid.

Finally, the ADB could further the economic development program for Southeast Asia launched by President Johnson by giving priority in its lending policy to regional projects. As Johnson stressed in his speech, the ADB "will reinforce existing aid programs in Asia, and thereby multiply their effectiveness. It will link its resources—financial and human—to such institutions as the Mekong Coordinating Committee, already joining the countries of the Mekong River Basin in major water resource projects."[111] Thus, this financial institution could become the main channel to which funds for the Mekong Project would be directed.

Eugene Black, who had long opposed the idea of a regional bank, became its principal advocate after Johnson entrusted him with the mission of helping to establish the institution.[112] The Consultative Committee (CC) was set up under ECAFE's leadership to discuss the charter, and several delegations from the Consultative Committee toured numerous capitals for consultations and to elicit support and funds. These delegations visited Western nations as well as Communist bloc states. Western powers reacted positively and even enthusiastically to the proposal, many promising to join in the creation of ADB. Only one nation, France, dissented from the chorus, arguing that the bank was nothing but another financial institution controlled by the United States: "In Paris French officials received [the] group cordially but during discussions stated France had no interest in participating [in the] ADB. French officials expressed [the] opinion [that the] bank was basically [a] US venture and would be US-controlled after being established."[113]

Surprisingly, nations of the Soviet bloc also reacted enthusiastically. The CC delegation was received in Moscow by the deputy minister of finance, who declared in the course of the interview that his government viewed favorably the creation of ADB, despite its concern that it was an "American Bank." The Czech government, while noting that its banking system was incompatible with a capitalist one, declared its willingness to indirectly participate in the bank through technical aid.[114] Yugoslavia's request to be a member of the bank was rejected on grounds of ineligibility. However, the United States, for numerous reasons, mostly political, strongly supported and even applied pressure in favor of the Yugoslav candidacy. Overall, the United States, via the CC's delegation, communicated its favorable attitude regarding the Soviet Union's participation and even encouraged its involvement in ADB.[115]

In Asia, reactions to the creation of an Asian bank were generally favorable. Nevertheless, some Asian nations such as Burma and Cambodia expressed their concerns that the bank could be used politically by the United States.[116] The charter of the new bank, patterned after that of the World Bank, was quickly signed in Manila in December 1965 by nineteen nations of the region and by thirteen other states. The United States and Japan each contributed 20 percent of the capital (US$ 200 million each); other significant donors were India (US$ 93 million), Australia (US$ 85 million), West Germany (US$ 34 million), the United Kingdom (US$ 30 million), and Canada (US$ 25 million). Total contributions amounted to US$ 970 million. The membership of a large number of countries of the Eastern bloc was encouraged in the hope that it would contribute to American short- and long-term political goals in the region concerning the war in Indochina. Memberships of such nations as Cambodia, Burma, and Afghanistan augured well for the bank in political terms.

During his consultations with regional governments, presidential envoy Black expressed the White House's intention not only to contribute 20 percent of the capital but also to revive the defunct Fund for the Economic Development of Asia, launched more than a decade before under the Eisenhower administration, under the new name Southeast Asia Development Fund. With the participation of other countries, the United States expressed its willingness to contribute up to $100 million to this multilateral fund, which would be managed by ADB as a Special Fund and used to finance regional projects.[117] As a telegram sent by Black from Bangkok revealed:

As for $100 million SEA Development Fund, Malaysian and Philippine delegations expressed to me their satisfaction over fund, since they [had] not [been] clear before just where they fitted into the expanded program for SEA offered in Baltimore speech. I recognize that this fund is somewhat tainted by some for its close connection with United States special interests [in] Southeast Asia and its success depends on significant contributions from non-US sources. I am satisfied though that SEA Development Fund as part of bank is one of most promising possibilities for creation of multilateral arrangement for financing regional projects with sound international administration.[118]

The American proposal for a Southeast Asian Development Fund had thus given rise to much interest and hope from those countries in the region that felt excluded from the promised manna. However, it was a short-lived proposal and was not followed by any concrete measure as the constraints of the war and its mounting expenses took precedence over all other economic imperatives.

The creation of ADB highlighted the resurgence of Japan on the international scene, backed by the United States, which considered Japan as its staunchest ally in the region. Pressure that the United States could not apply openly on rebellious or reticent capitals such as Djakarta, Phnom Penh, and Rangoon, could be conveyed by Japan thanks to its "silent diplomacy."[119] Japan played a pivotal part in the success of the development program for Southeast Asia. As the sole Asian donor-country, Japan could call upon other aid donors and Southeast Asian countries to incite them to participate in the presidential development initiative. Within the ADB, Japan was an equal partner with the United States in terms of contribution (US$ 200 million), and the bank's president, Takeshi Watanabe, was a Japanese financial expert and former president of the World Bank. In reaction to the American proposal of a Southeast Asia Development Fund of $100 million, Japan came up with its own offer of $100 million for a Special Fund for Agriculture within ADB.[120] It was understood that the bank would channel funds used to finance projects linked with the development of the lower Mekong basin. However, the orientation given from the start to ADB was based on such strict financial viability requirements and credit conditions that the Mekong Committee was forced to look elsewhere for the financing of its projects, through either grants or loans on more favorable terms.

REPERCUSSIONS FOR THE MEKONG PROJECT

In the days following the Baltimore speech, the executive agent for the Mekong Committee, C. Hart Schaaf, received numerous calls and communications from countries eager to participate in the future development program.[121] As a result of consultations between Black and the secretary-general of the UN, there was an increase of activity at ECAFE's level. U Thant instructed ECAFE, as well as the Mekong Committee, to be ready to take advantage of the American proposal. ECAFE was to devote its efforts to the Mekong Project, the Asian Highway, and ADB, and members of the Mekong Committee were to convene at a closed meeting in Bangkok for a special session on May 11 and 12, 1965. The development was closely followed by Washington, which, while influencing the course of events, gave the illusion to Mekong members, in particular Cambodia, that they were acting of their own volition. The American embassy in Bangkok summarized the situation concerning the Mekong Project in a telegram to the State Department dated April 22, 1965:

(1) The Mekong has not changed its stripes. Mekong Projects continue [to] have basic problems (A) engineering design, land surveys, etc., (B) political problems plus security of areas to be developed. Technical problems can be met in time with acceleration [of] US and Mekong Committee effort. Members despite political differences participate and work together in Mekong Committee. US will be pressed [to] commit financ[ing] for specific Mekong projects. US can find in consultation with committee [a] number [of] valid projects on which [to] press forward in all four riparian states. Believe projects should be undertaken in bilateral agreement with Mekong Committee rather than under UN Special Fund. We should look to specific Mekong Projects which serve several US purposes. Thus Pa Mong could provide urgently needed water in current US economic-security program for Northeast Thailand and back into the Mekong.[122]

The Nam Ngum Project

The purpose of the special session in Bangkok was to discuss various possibilities and priorities for the Mekong Project overall. Cambodia, which had rejected American aid in 1963 and severed its diplomatic relations with the United States in May 1965, nevertheless insisted on sending its director of external finances in addition to its permanent representative to participate in the meeting.[123] As a result, a provisional list of needs for a ten-year development program that would cost more than US$ 3 billion, as well as a list of priority projects at a cost of US$ 200 million, was suggested and promptly approved. The Nam Ngum topped the list, and the American representative promised that the United States would provide half of its costs. The list was then sent to the UN secretary-general, who officially served as the intermediary between the United States and countries that were eager to respond to the president's offer. Eventually, the Nam Ngum project became the first scheme in the action program that would see the concrete application of the Baltimore speech's promises; its realization would require US$ 19 million. It was presented as a priority project by President Johnson in his Message to Congress, which asked for a fund of $89 million supplementary to the program of foreign aid.

The reasons behind the administration's selection of the Nam Ngum project were complex. In the estimation report concerning the Mekong Project prepared for the White House in March 1965 before the Baltimore speech, the Nam Ngum project had already been designated as one of the projects ready for construction. It was therefore logical that it be chosen by the administration. In addition, one has to take into account that, since Eisenhower, the United States had always accorded Laos a high strategic value within the geopolitics of mainland Southeast Asia. Laos had always been used as a buffer state on which depended the security and the stability of the R.V.N., Cambodia, Burma, and, above all, Thailand. Former President Eisenhower, in his advice to President-elect John F. Kennedy, had insisted on the necessity to defend Laos as this country "was the key to the entire area of Southeast Asia. . . . If we permitted Laos to fall, then we would have to write off all the area; . . . one of the dangers of a Communist take-over in Laos would be to expose Thailand's border."[124]

Under the Kennedy administration, Laos was, in fact, engulfed in the Second Indochina War, which locally pitted the Pathet Lao and Vietnamese Communist forces against those of the Royal Lao government (R.L.G.) and the United States. The Mekong valley as a result held a great strategic value, since the Mekong, the river-border between Laos and Thailand, was also a natural demarcation separating the R.L.G.'s forces and those of the Pathet Lao. The R.L.G.'s forces occupied 40 percent of the Laotian territory with two-thirds of the population living mostly in the Vientiane plain and in the Mekong valley; the Pathet Lao held the mountains.

Under Presidents Kennedy and Johnson, the infiltration of the Mekong valley by the Pathet Lao was considered a serious threat to U.S. interests, as it allowed the Pathet Lao to penetrate the Northeast of Thailand, a region that was already unstable and undermined by Communist insurrections.[125] The Mekong River, as pointed out in the secretary of defense's memorandum to the president in December 1963, was used as a means of infiltration of men, weapons, ammunition, and raw materials from the D.R.V. through Laos and Cambodia and into the Mekong delta in the R.V.N.[126] On the other hand, in the context of the Vietnam War, Laos and the Northeast of Thailand constituted a springboard for launching American operations against the D.R.V. Hence the necessity to extend the R.L.G.'s influence as far north of the river's left bank as possible through sweeping military campaigns. The war effort had intensified in 1964 with American bombing of the northern region of Laos and on the ground, General Vang Pao's clandestine army, created and financed by the CIA, fought the Pathet Lao in the Plain of Jars.[127]

As always, the military aspect, which was predominant in U.S. policy, was in a small way balanced by American economic aid to the R.L.G., in particular, in favor of "rural development" as defined by AID in its different programs: for example, the Agricultural Development Organization (ADO) and the Cluster Villages.[128] The focus on rural development was an attempt to counterbalance the R.L.G.'s profound incapacity to deal with Laos's needs in terms of rural development. The Nam Ngum project was to take place within such a background. A deliberate choice was thus made to select Laos, one of the least developed of the four riparian countries, with an economy that had been virtually subsidized by U.S. aid but which had immense natural resources. President Johnson made the formal announcement of America's commitment to the Nam Ngum project at a White House press conference in March 1966, in which he reiterated his themes as formulated in the Baltimore speech of the previous year: "For the United States it is our first major commitment under our promise to expand economic and social development in Southeast Asia. The Nam Ngum project . . . represents a major accomplishment in joint cooperation in the world. . . . This is just one example of how the fruits of technology and the ingenuity of cooperation can bring new life to whole new regions of the world."[129]

This project was to give Laos for the first time a significant source of income; if it could provide its dormant economy the necessary momentum to "take off," it was thought in Washington, political stability would follow. Furthermore, it was a project that, despite its scale, was achievable within a relatively short amount of time; and it was located in the Vientiane plain, that is, in R.L.G.-controlled territory. It was to symbolize R.L.G. achievements and garner increased prestige for Vientiane, not so much with the disillusioned local population, but in the eyes of the international community and neighboring countries. The R.L.G. was aware of these elements: In a telegram sent to the UN secretary-general, the R.L.G. prime minister promised that his government would guarantee law and order in the Nam Ngum region so that technical and financial missions could be conducted safely.[130] In fact, ECAFE's executive secretary, U Nyun, remarked on "the agreement of all political factions in Laos to Nam Ngum and that all Laos quote from the King to the farmers unquote were agreed on its value."[131] The Nam Ngum project was also to benefit from the Pathet Lao's tacit acknowledgment of its great usefulness for Laos in general; it had left undisturbed the preliminary work of site reconnaissance and exploration.

From the point of view of the overall Mekong Project, the Nam Ngum project was to be the first to benefit more than one country of the lower Mekong basin (Laos and Thailand), thus conferring on it an international quality, which the Mekong Project had always tried to promote. It was to be the tangible proof of the promising possibilities of projects on the tributaries and on the mainstream. The feasibility studies had demonstrated that it was the largest of the group of tributary projects to have a favorable cost/benefits ratio. The site choice was made based on the study carried out by a Japanese team on the main Mekong tributaries early in the enterprise. The preliminary studies that followed were financed and conducted either separately or jointly by the UN, other institutions, and various cooperating countries. The feasibility reports were the work of the Japanese team and financed in part by the UN Special Fund and in part by Japan within the framework of the bilateral accord of economic and technical coopera- tion signed between Japan and Laos. The experimental farm located near the dam site was managed by a joint team as decided in the bilateral agreement be- tween the two countries.

Washington worked hard to secure financial, economic, and technical support from donor-nations and international agencies, as numerous memoranda and cables from several U.S. agencies, departments, and embassies in Southeast Asia testify.[132] The Thai prime minister promised Eugene Black during his visit in June 1965 to cooperate with Laos and, concerning this project in particular, to buy its electricity. After all, Bangkok had lobbied Washington for the realization of the Nam Ngum.[133] Very quickly, with the help of ECAFE, the UN, and the United States, all of the necessary elements were put in place. In Vientiane in August 1965, for the first time in the history of the Mekong Project, a conven- tion on electricity exchange was signed, by Thailand and Laos as well as by the downstream nations of Cambodia and the R.V.N. and by the UN as the parties directly concerned by the integrated development of the Mekong basin.[134] All the most favorable financial conditions were gathered: the World Bank's agreement to manage the funds of the Nam Ngum project and to supervise its realization and the pledge by a number of countries to cover almost all of the funds needed for the first phase.

In May 1966, the Nam Ngum Development Fund Agreement was signed by the two concerned countries, Laos and Thailand, and by the contributors: Austra- lia, Canada, Denmark, Japan, the Netherlands, New Zealand, the United States represented by US AID, and the World Bank. Seven participating countries agreed to extend grants in the amount of US$ 22.815 million, which were to be used to cover the cost of building the dam, a power station, and a power trans- mission line from the dam to Vientiane and from Vientiane to the Thai town of Udorn Thani in the Northeast of Thailand.[135] The main contributions were from the United States ($12.065 million with the obligation of purchase of American products and services), Japan (US$ 4 million), the Netherlands (US$ 3.3 mil- lion), and Canada (US$ 2 million). The U.S. pledge was "the first major com- mitment under President Johnson's program to expand economic and social development in Southeast Asia."[136] Contributions by Denmark (US$ 600,000), Australia (US$ 500,000), and New Zealand (US$ 350,000) were without pre- conditions.

Thailand and Laos also concluded agreements according to which Thailand agreed to provide Laos with the equivalent of US$ 1 million, to be used for the purchase from Thailand of cement for the construction of the Nam Ngum proj- ect. Thailand also agreed to supply Laos with electricity during the entirety of the construction via the extension of the transmission line from the Thai Nam Pong dam to the Nam Ngum dam site in Laos. In exchange, Laos would repay the funds and the power consumed by providing the equivalent in electricity produced by the dam once it became operational. Japan, following up on its promise made previously to the Mekong Committee, pledged US$ 315,000 for this project on a bilateral basis with Laos.[137] The other two riparian countries, Cambodia and the R.V.N., signed the World Bank's Protocol concerning the question of the Nam Ngum funds and expressed their satisfaction with the agreement as members of the Mekong Committee. It must be emphasized that the World Bank played an all-powerful role in this project, since the Agreement for the Nam Ngum Development Fund gave it full powers in the matter of grant administration. The bank, after consultation with Laos and Thailand, would make all the decisions concerning the disbursement of funds "in order to ensure that the monies contributed by the donor countries are not diverted to purposes other than for which the grants are made" and that it was the bank that would pay "directly to suppliers of goods or to others."[138]

The Pa Mong Project

From the beginning, the Pa Mong site had attracted the attention of engineers, technicians, and builders by its enormous possibilities, so enormous that they could have a tremendous impact on the futures of Laos and Thailand and the nations downstream and, in consequence, on the political decisions made by riparian countries. Acting on this assumption, the United States became the dominant and major contributor, focusing its effort on the Pa Mong project, taking over the responsibility of carrying out the numerous studies on the site. As mentioned before, the first reconnaissance study had been prompted by then Vice-President Johnson's visit to Southeast Asia in 1961. Following the visit, the U.S. Bureau of Reclamation published a report on Pa Mong in 1962, which proposed an eight-year study program, divided into three phases, the success of each phase conditioning the initiation of the next one. After the signing of an agreement between the Mekong Committee and AID in May 1963, Phase I was launched under the supervision of the U.S. Bureau of Reclamation. Its experts had shown more enthusiasm than those of AID in recommending the continuation of study. AID decided not to pursue the financing of Phase II and not to include it in its budget presentation to Congress for fiscal year 1966. The agency had been discouraged by the cost of Pa Mong studies, by the prospects of a long lapse before construction could begin because of the colossal dimensions of the project, the enormous investments, and other seemingly insurmountable obstacles of all natures.

At this juncture, when the situation seemed to have slowed down concerning the Pa Mong project, the Baltimore speech reignited the process. Some of the underlying motivations that led to the selection of the Pa Mong project as the other concrete project of Johnson's development program for Southeast Asia could be found in the following telegram sent by the U.S. embassy in Bangkok:

We should look to specific Mekong Projects which may serve several US purposes. Thus Pa Mong could provide urgently needed water in current US economic-security program for Northeast Thailand and back into the Mekong. . . . Burec's [U.S. Bureau of Reclamation] Mabbot here tells Embassy informally he feels project feasible and that final assessment date in order [to] estimate costs would be completed in about two years. Mabbot also feels action first on Pa Mong would not alter priorities or feasibility of other Mekong projects.[139]

Because of its location, the Pa Mong was thought to be a possible major contribution to the development of the poorest and most unstable region of Thailand, the Northeast, where the threat of insurrection had contributed to weakening the most strategic ally of the United States in this part of the basin. Hence, in the wake of the Baltimore speech, the Bureau of Reclamation (BR) was able to complete Phase I of the feasibility studies and present its report in June 1965, recommending the continuation of investigations into Phase II, the estimated cost of which was in the proximity of US$ 4.5 million for fiscal year 1966.[140] In October 1965, reversing its former reluctance, AID concluded with the Mekong Committee an agreement concerning Phase II of the project according to which the United States agreed to provide a team of thirty-eight specialists and to finance the cost and the necessary equipment to the amount of $4 million over three years. Thailand pledged to provide a supplement of US$ 7 million.[141] The final agreement was concluded between the United States and the Mekong Committee—after agreement by the three concerned riparian countries, Laos, Thailand, and Cambodia—in December 1965, and the USBR team was able to pick up its study where it had left off.[142]

The promises of Johnson's Baltimore speech accelerated the tempo of the Mekong Committee's activities. During its extraordinary session of May 1965, the committee considered the possibility that, in view of the extension of studies in all directions and into multiple fields and their increasing complexity, "its terms of reference should be expanded to reflect the widening fields with which it is concerned, and that its title should be formally altered . . . to . . . 'the Committee for Coordination of Comprehensive Development of the Lower Mekong Basin.'" It was proposed that an amendment be introduced to Chapter IV of its Statute to read as follows: "The functions of the Committee are to promote, coordinate, supervise and control the planning, *investigations*, construction and operation of water resources development projects in the Lower Mekong Basin, and other *development projects related thereto* [italics in text]."[143] However, some members expressed concern over a possible division within the committee if its functions were to be extended; consequently, the proposed amendment was not passed.

Concerning the Mekong Committee's budget, the Johns Hopkins speech led to an influx of pledges and promises of grants and loans reaching some US$ 37 million, bringing the total sum in pre-investment and construction from US$ 67.7 million in 1964 to US$ 105 million for the fiscal year 1965. Of that sum, 32 percent was contributed by the riparian countries (US$ 33.6 million) and 68 percent by the cooperating countries (US$ 71.4 million); 36 percent (US$ 37.8 million) would be used for preliminary studies, and 64 percent (US$ 67.2 million) for construction. However, this generous influx was short-lived, lasting only long enough for the cooperating countries to realize that the United States did not actually mean to implement its offer of $1 billion. The following year, contributions dropped to only US$ 4.9 million (total: US$ 110 million). Activities suffered when Washington's interest in the Mekong Project was superseded by other more pressing military matters.

In the Northeast of Thailand, two minor tributary projects, the Nam Pung and the Nam Pong, were completed in November 1965 and in March 1966, respectively. The electricity produced supplied the provinces of Khon Kaen, Khorat, Mahasarakam, Udorn Thani, and Roi-et. However, a severe flood in September on the Mekong River led to enormous losses and destroyed a demonstration farm in the Vientiane plain. Such a catastrophe was a reminder of the necessity, in the short term, for a flood alarm system, and, in the long run, for flood control works.

The Particular Case of Cambodia

Cambodia is the perfect example of the kind of problems the Mekong Project had been facing as it endeavored to forge ahead within a context of instability and warfare, not to mention the ambiguous nature of the relations between the riparian countries, the United States, and other Western nations as cooperating nations in a multilateral development program.[144] In the 1950s, Cambodia had adopted a politically neutral stance, and its head, Prince Sihanouk, struck a balance between the two cold war blocs of the United States, on one hand, and the Soviet Union and China, on the other, reaping much economic and technical aid from both sides. The USSR had been the most generous; it had built, among other projects, Phnom Penh's modern hospital, the Khmer-Soviet Lycée, and Cambodia's first important hydroelectric projects (in Kamchay).[145] Thus, Cambodia could ill-afford, given its serious economic dependence on external aid, to lose any aid donors, small or large, Communist or non-Communist.

Furthermore, agricultural hydraulics had, after all, shaped the Angkor period of Cambodian history for centuries, and, while the Mekong Project was under way, the Cambodian government had striven to marshal its own long-term program of water resource development at the local and national levels, with dams built with the help of Yugoslavia in Kirirom and of the USSR in Kamchay. It is in Cambodia that the most important mainstream dam projects were to be located, Pa Mong notwithstanding: Sambor and Tonle-Sap, which, together with Pa Mong, could form a multipurpose hydraulic complex that had been at the top of the Mekong Committee's list since its very beginning. Additionally, the Khone Falls, although on the Lao-Khmer border, could have a considerable impact on Cambodia and would, with Stung Treng, another Cambodian mainstream scheme, and the others, form an integrated system of five projects.

As far as Cambodia was concerned, these projects could signify an improved economic future for this impoverished nation that had nonetheless put aside a relatively substantial share of its budget to finance the preliminary studies. However, the waxing and waning of diplomatic relations between the United States and Cambodia considerably influenced the Mekong Project in its Cambodian part to the extent of hampering its realization—although, according to official criteria, it was considered multilateral, and hence, in theory, less susceptible to the vagaries of politics. The case of Cambodia was an example of the truism that any development project that evolved within a certain political context could not escape being hostage to greater political forces.

When the concept of the Mekong Project took shape in the 1950s, Cambodia supported it wholeheartedly, favoring an international, multilateral approach for the development of the Mekong resources, whereas the United States attempted to convince the four riparian countries to apply a principle of separate development under the supervision of the United States.[146] Thus, the confrontation between the two countries began. Cambodia was opposed to the American initiative, arguing that an American supervision of the works would unavoidably pull the riparian countries into the cold war. Cambodia succeeded in convincing Laos to choose a more neutral ECAFE support, and as Washington retreated from its former position of separate development, Thailand and the R.V.N. allowed themselves to be convinced jointly to create the Mekong Committee. The U.S. plan of separate development, which would have allowed for easier and tighter control of projects and, incidentally, of the recipient nation, failed mainly because of Phnom Penh's opposition.

During the 1960s, relations between the United States and Cambodia fluctuated between two extremes: utter distrust, if not open hostility, and the recognition of a mutual dependence imposed by the search for a balance of power in the region. This uneasiness manifested itself later in the Prek Thnot project to the point of constituting a threat to the precarious "Mekong Spirit" prevalent at the time. The Prek Thnot project was located in one of the most arid regions of Cambodia, seventy kilometers southwest of Phnom Penh, downstream from the city of Kompong Speu. It was a multipurpose project essential for the irrigation (70,000 hectares) and energy needs of Cambodia—needs that kept increasing by 13,000 kilowatts per year. Its power production could have supplied the factories in the capital after its full completion.[147] The preliminary studies were conducted relatively quickly in 1961–1962 by Israel and Japan. With American support an international consortium was created to finance the project.[148] The first stage of the Prek Thnot project in terms of total costs would amount to US$ 27 million.[149] The United States had promised to provide one-third of the foreign capital necessary for the project. Unfortunately, the rejection of American aid by Cambodia in November 1963 came at an inopportune moment, leading to the collapse of the consortium for the financing of the Prek Thnot and the cessation of all works.

Cambodia, nevertheless, decided to forge ahead by resorting to its own budget and by turning to France, the former colonial power with which it had long-standing ties. A French loan of US$ 12 million was granted to be used for the financing of the project but was eventually diverted for the construction of an oil refinery in Sihanoukville.[150]

The Johns Hopkins speech of April 1965 rekindled hope of a possible American contribution to the Prek Thnot scheme. Cambodia, whose break in diplomatic relations with the United States in May 1965 created a major stumbling block to obtaining external financing, let it be known in Mekong Project milieus that it was still interested in the continuation of the project and was willing to receive multilateral aid via the Mekong Committee. Sihanouk also proposed to move the Mekong Committee's headquarters from Bangkok to Phnom Penh. This last Cambodian initiative was negatively received by the United States, which, as a telegram from the U.S. embassy in Vientiane to Washington revealed, was not in "favor [of] transfer . . . for technical reasons . . . but also for political reasons, since . . . [the] committee would be continuously (1) bombarded by anti-US media, [and] (2) blandishments by neutral or Communist embassy personnel residing [in] Phnom Penh."[151] It was even feared that the Asian staff of the Mekong Committee "such as Indians, would conceivably lost [sic] their objectivity and hence their usefulness if they permanently headquartered in Phnom Penh."[152] Phnom Penh vehemently protested with the Mekong Committee, and Sihanouk threatened to leave it if a solution were not rapidly found to the problem. And for the first time in the contentious history of these riparian nations, while the heated dispute between Thailand and Cambodia concerning the Preah Vihar temple was still going on, and while the ARVN continued its incursions into the Cambodian territory, a solidarity movement initiated by Thailand, the R.V.N., and Laos coalesced in favor of Cambodia.[153] Their delegates at the Mekong Committee pleaded for Cambodia in the name of the Mekong Spirit, creating "a feeling in the Mekong Committee that it was necessary for the next major project to be in Cambodia since Laos and Thailand have already received major benefits from the Mekong program."[154] The committee promptly decided then to make 1966 Cambodia Year and to give it (and the R.V.N.) priority in terms of investment and construction. The riparian nations knew full well that Cambodia's participation was a *sine qua non* for the future success of the Mekong Project and of the interdependence of all riparian countries in terms of production, distribution, consumption of electricity, and irrigation when mainstream dams would become operational. After all, three of them were to be located in Cambodia.[155]

The delegates of member countries expressed to the Cambodian representative their "total support" for the Prek Thnot project and were successful in putting together a list of possible contributors (including Japan). Yet, as for the donors, enthusiasm for the Cambodian project was somewhat lackluster despite U.S. prodding. According to political scientist Roger M. Smith, who interviewed the representatives from cooperating countries participating in the annual Mekong Committee session, at no time there appeared more clearly the true motivations of donor countries concerning their contributions to a multilateral project such as the Mekong. More prosaic interests in favor of maximum bilateral relations with riparian countries were to be found lurking behind the façade of a supposed commitment to the concept of regionalism and multilateralism:

The representatives of Australia, Canada, France, Japan, the Netherlands, the United States, West Germany and others made it clear . . . that it was the bilateral nature of relations with the riparian states that interested them most. The participating nations might proclaim their commitment to the concept of regional development, but when it came down to actually making a contribution, these states were clearly more interested in how their contributions would benefit them individually.[156]

For these donors, Smith elaborated,

contributions in six or more figures would be worthwhile for they might pave the way later on for a national firm to land a multi-million dollar construction contract; or it might even be worthwhile for the industrial nation itself to put up a long-term, low-interest loan to win the contract. Such arrangements, of course, can best be made in bargaining with individual states rather than with an international body.[157]

Washington was nevertheless anxious not to push Cambodia over the brink, noting that in recent months, "progress on the Mekong River development program is being seriously impeded by the current uncertain attitude toward the program by Cambodia and the low level of Cambodia's participation in Mekong Committee activities."[158] In the matter of the Prek Thnot project, to avoid any accusations of American manipulation that could trigger rejection or refusal, the United States went out of its way to encourage its allies (e.g., Australia, Canada, France, and Germany) to support Cambodia's Prek Thnot. The U.S. ambassador to the UN in New York, Arthur Goldberg, was urged to make the following arguments to U Thant: "Persuade the French to firm up their loan commitment for . . . the Prek Thnot hydroelectric project in Cambodia. . . . If the French cannot be persuaded to finance alone, perhaps some other countries, such as Canadians [sic], might be encouraged."[159] In the case of a French refusal, the Australians would be approached as "it is logical that we ask the Australians to take the lead with the project. The Australians did the engineering design work, . . . they are active in the regional affairs . . . [and] they have shown a continued interest in the Mekong program."[160]

At the time, the United States found itself faced with a dilemma. As Walt W. Rostow (special assistant for national security affairs) pointed out to the president, "The Mekong Committee and others had counted on a U.S. contribution to this, the next natural Mekong Project after Nam Ngum." However, Rostow continued, "section 107-B of the Foreign Assistance Appropriations Act requires that you [the President] determined that it is in the security interest of the US to make a loan to a country which is trading with North Vietnam."[161] A congressional decision made at the presentation of the aid budget for fiscal year 1966–

1967 forbade loans and grants to any country that "traded with or gave economic aid to North Vietnam."[162] U.S. officials contended that Prince Sihanouk had done so and had allowed the use of Cambodian territory by Communist troops. However, U.S. aid could still be extended to the Prek Thnot Project if Prince Sihanouk were to agree to cease aid to Ha-noi, according to some administration officials who "asserted . . . that his situation could change if Prince Sihanouk stopped helping Hanoi."[163] The following year, negative congressional sentiment concerning Cambodia in general and the Prek Thnot project in particular continued unabated.[164] Although some senators (e.g., William Fulbright and Mike Mansfield) were in favor of financial support for the Prek Thnot, "in the House, attitudes are negative."[165]

The following text of an interview given by Sihanouk to the Japanese newspaper *Asahi* in 1966 shows the prince's ongoing interest in the Mekong Project:

Cambodia is in principle favorable to the Lower Mekong basin development. . . . The projects to which ECAFE devoted itself are, on the other hand, so momentous that we could not predict their conclusion in a near future. Therefore, we give the priority to those of reasonable scale that we deem to be acceptable within our present plans of development. Such projects are the Battambang project, the Prek Thnot, and eventually, the Sambor on the Mekong river.[166]

But as relations became more tense, in April 1967, Sihanouk stated via *Le Sangkum*, a periodical that he controlled, that "in fact, what the United States will never forgive Cambodia is the moral and political support we give to Vietnam, which is fighting against American invaders."[167] Phnom Penh expressed its skepticism about the "disinterested nature" of American aid in general and regarding the offer of $1 billion made by President Johnson in particular. It argued that the United States offered, on one hand, to finance the Mekong Project, but on the other hand, it refused to grant this aid to those countries that did not correspond to the American definition of "free countries." The situation reached such a point that Prince Sihanouk, in a letter to the UN secretary-general dated January 25, 1967, declared that "the Prek Thnot was not vital to our economic development [and] it was all too clear that countries which had declared themselves willing to grant us aid, were not devoid of any secret political or 'tactical' motivations in favor of the 'Free World.' Cambodia is presently too threatened not to take into account this aspect of the question."[168]

The following month, Cambodia decided not to participate in the thirty-third session of the Mekong Committee, held in Vientiane, as it was convinced that the Prek Thnot project would not receive financing. The "Cambodian question," the resolution of which had become a priority for the committee as it threatened to destroy its precarious consensus, led to interventions by both the UN secretary-general and ECAFE, which had to call upon the generosity of those countries friendly to the committee. This sparked apprehension among the donors, Japan, in particular, that they might have to devote more resources than they had promised in order to compensate for the defection of the United States.[169] Sec-

retary-General U Thant, for whom the Prek Thnot project was "a dramatic example of the United Nations effort to realize a vista of the future, a future in
which the immense potential of the Mekong River will be controlled and harnessed for the benefit of the peoples of Cambodia, Laos, Thailand and the Republic of Vietnam," made every effort to ensure that the project would come to
fruition.[170]

In April 1968, Cambodia again refused to participate in the Mekong Committee's annual meeting in Tokyo to protest the insufficiency of funds. Eventually, it had no other choice but to assume an important share of the financing of
Prek Thnot, amounting to US$ 11 million matched by contributions in the form
of grants and loans from Australia (US$ 1.3 million); Canada (US$ 2 million);
Great Britain (US$ 600,000); Japan (US$ 11 million); the Netherlands (US$ 1
million); Pakistan (US$ 150,000); India, Italy, the Philippines, and the Federal
Republic of Germany, altogether more than US$ 16 million.[171] The multilateral
agreement for the Prek Thnot project (Phase I) was signed between Cambodia
and these nations in November 1968, establishing, among other institutions, the
Société Nationale des Grands Barrages du Cambodge, which was to take charge
of the construction and operation of the Prek Thnot project. Then, in July 1969,
diplomatic relations between the United States and Cambodia were reestab-
lished, thus removing any obstacles to American contributions. Nevertheless, the
construction of the storage dam and power station was halted in 1971 at 20 percent and 50 percent of completion, respectively.[172]

The Prek Thnot project and the multiple obstacles that it had to overcome in
order to attract investments underlined the paramount role played by the United
States in the realization of any such development project. The absence of American support and financial contributions could doom any plan, whereas its participation allowed the project to advance rapidly as demonstrated by the Nam
Ngum scheme. This project did not encounter any difficulty once Washington
gave its approval, thus opening the gate to an influx of funds in the form of
grants from cooperating countries and the World Bank. The R.L.G. did not have
to have recourse to its own (almost nonexistent) budget as did the Cambodian
government for the Prek Thnot project.

The Johns Hopkins speech, followed by the wide publicity campaign and the
multiple professions of faith reiterated time and again by President Johnson and
by members of his administration in favor of regional cooperation in Southeast
Asia in general, and in favor of the Mekong Project in particular, may have been
indicative of the administration's willingness to adopt regionalism and regional
development as possible solutions to the conflict rather than escalation and
Americanization. Yet, the Prek Thnot example is a contrary proof, which leads
us to ask the following question: What were the limits of American interest in
facilitating regional cooperation in Southeast Asia? Naturally, the economic
benefits of a project, the possible stabilization of the region, and the strengthening of anti-Communist governments were powerful incentives by themselves, but

when a possible aid recipient goes against Washington's political dictates as was the case with Cambodia with its unacceptable neutralism, then these incentives apparently counted for naught in the face of military and political demands. For Cambodia, the American attitude toward the Mekong Project and its own Prek Thnot was a litmus test of its actual political priorities and commitments. According to Roger M. Smith, by facilitating projects in Laos, Thailand, and the R.V.N. and, at the same time, withdrawing its support for projects located in Cambodia, the United States reinforced client regimes and implicitly encouraged them in their attitudes of aggression toward Cambodia.[173]

The impact of President Johnson's Johns Hopkins address on the evolution of the war and the international reactions to Johnson's proposal were broached in a meeting on April 13, 1965, between the ambassador of Japan to the United States, Ryuji Takeushi, and U.S. Secretary of State Dean Rusk: "The Secretary said we hope Japan will find ways to take a strong lead in Southeast Asian economic development. Japan might be able to influence countries in the area which are reluctant to respond to U.S. stimulation. . . . The Secretary said that one purpose of the President's address had been to show that there could be peace in 24 hours if the other side wanted, that the problem of peace rests with Hanoi and Peiping."[174]

The secretary of state remarked that, according to him, there were a number of encouraging signs, such as the fact that "Prince Souphanouvong, head of the Pathet Lao, had sent a message to Prince Souvanna Phouma agreeing to the resumption in Laos of discussion among the three Lao political factions [that] might open the way for settlement."[175] Another potentially positive sign was the Soviet proposal for a conference on the question of Cambodia's territorial integrity, a proposal that might have been indicative of the other side's willingness to open negotiations. However, apart from these rather minor moves, since the announcement of unconditional negotiations and the offer of $1 billion, it seemed that Johnson's new approach of encouraging, concurrently to the war efforts, the economic development of countries of the Indochinese peninsula had not significantly influenced the evolution of the war. On the contrary, it seemed even to have had the opposite effect of increasing the distrust of Communist countries toward any suggestion made by the West in the matter of regional cooperation. The expected schism apparently did not take place between allies of the D.R.V., which still refused negotiations as suggested by Washington. The utilization by the United States of the Mekong Project for flagrantly political purposes actually added to the tension in the diplomatic relations between Washington and Phnom Penh. President Johnson's Baltimore proposals notwithstanding, in 1965 the war in Vietnam had spilled into Cambodia, threatening to shatter its neutrality.

According to Eugene Black, witness to and participant in these events, although the new strategy of regional cooperation launched by Johnson's speech in April 1965 had not significantly deflected the course of the war, it nevertheless had a tremendous, long-term impact on Southeast Asia. In a March 14, 1972,

get this

interview with Black, Franklin P. Huddle of the Congressional Research Service asked about the short- and long-term impact of Johnson's speech on the riparian countries. Black replied:

The political impact of President Johnson's offer of large-scale postwar assistance to Southeast Asia was substantial. . . . I considered the $1 billion offer to be more symbolic than mathematically precise. . . . Both an immediate and short-range political impact of our offer was its positive role as a catalyst in stimulating the interest in and moves toward regional cooperation. . . . Many of the regional organizations and groupings in Southeast Asia owed their origin or vitality to the boost for regional cooperation given by the United States in the period 1965–1969 . . . [such as] the Asian Development Bank. . . . Less recognized but no less real was the large increase in inter-regional personal contacts which occurred in Southeast Asia over these years at various levels and in varied forums.[176]

In retrospect, Black recognized that "it was as unrealistic in 1965 as it is today to believe that leaders in North Vietnam [bent] on conquest of the South would abandon their goals simply in response to offers of aid."[177] In the ensuing years, Black tirelessly carried out his task, visiting countries of the lower Mekong basin, meeting with its leaders to push for the Mekong Project but increasingly more so for the ADB, serving as Johnson's personal representative in discussions with Cambodia officials, as he did, for instance, in his November 1968 visit to that kingdom. But to no avail.[178]

When it became increasingly apparent that the Mekong Project could not directly influence the evolution of the war, the project was relegated by the Johnson administration to the same status as many other regional schemes. Already toward the end of 1965, the White House had undertaken a number of parallel (if not rival) but discreet planning efforts similar to the Mekong Project in scope but without its physical specificity. The idea of an Asian Development Task Force (ADTF) was seriously discussed and names of experts proposed. President Johnson indicated that it would "set in motion a concept looking toward an enlarged long-term Asian regional development program."[179] The task force would be interdepartmental, would establish informal contacts with the World Bank, and would "examine the . . . scale, duration . . . and external assistance required in a long-term program to bring the countries of free Asia into a position of regular self-sustained growth at . . . 2½ percent per annum per capita."[180] There was an emphasis on discretion and on the project's long-term character, and the initiative, were it to strike a responsive chord, "would best appear as an Asian, not a US, initiative."[181] However, such an effort (similar to the Alliance for Progress) was bound to be extremely expensive; estimates were of a magnitude that would have doubled the volume of American aid to Asia. Meanwhile, budgetary constraints imposed by Congress's increasing reluctance to appropriate funds for war and aid, along with the enormous expenses imposed by the war itself, dampened the Johnson administration's Mekong enthusiasms and brought further delays in action concerning the Mekong Project.

Guns not butter

Although Washington continued its strong support for the ADB—a bank is more likely to be more viable than a long-term development project in an insecure and unstable region—as well as for the construction of the Nam Ngum dam, and although it had agreed to continue the expensive Pa Mong feasibility studies, it now made the decision through AID to finance those studies that might be useful militarily or be applicable in counterinsurgency. Among these types of projects were feasibility studies in Laos and Thailand, on the possibilities of construction of harbors, landings, and transshipments on the Luang Prabang/Pakse reach, which could provide a possible communication and transportation link between Laos and the Northeast of Thailand. One should also note the supply of more than US\$ 1 million of laminated steel for the modernization of fluvial vessels in the R.V.N. In general, however, most studies dealt with geological exploration and the hydrology of the Northeast of Thailand. Nevertheless, the United States did not commit itself to other similar large-scale projects, focusing instead on smaller-sized dams, irrigation works, and water tanks in the Northeast of Thailand, a region that was within the American security perimeter and part of the United States–sponsored Accelerated Rural Development (ARD) program.[182]

From 1966 to 1968, as the war continued to escalate, and death and destruction became regular features on American news programs, official American interest concerning the Lower Mekong basin development shifted focus from the four riparian countries to the single state of the R.V.N., and to the development possibilities of its postwar economy. After all, the White House optimistically expected to see the light at the end of the tunnel shortly. Since the Mekong Project as a regional scheme had not immediately fulfilled the goals assigned to it in U.S. strategy because of its excessive cost, unmanageability, complexity, and temporal remoteness and, above all, because the political and military imperatives outweighed all else, it was accordingly reformulated. Washington's Mekong Project focus became national, that of a project bearing the promise of economic development for a single political entity, the R.V.N., with an emphasis on the Mekong delta.

This reorientation of priority was to open the phase of so-called constructive programs launched early in 1966 as part of Johnson's "Other War" in Vietnam, intended to demonstrate that the United States and his administration were capable of constructive actions, of building as well as destroying. As for President Johnson, Doris Kearns argues that he was convinced that he could shape the world of Asia, that he could mold the Vietnamese peasant in the image of the Texan farmer, and that this new Asian TVA, the Mekong Project, would one day yield green and bountiful rice fields. Like their American counterparts, the Vietnamese peasants would benefit from all the modern amenities that progress brings: "I want to leave the footprints of America in Vietnam. . . . I want them to say when the Americans come, this is what they leave—schools, not long cigars. We're going to turn the Mekong into a Tennessee Valley."[183] Even with the war in Indochina drowning out all else, Johnson's vision of progress continued to impose itself. The Mekong Project theme was thus not given up; on the contrary, it was to be tailored to the specific needs of the escalating American war in Vietnam. War and progress; progress and war—such were the two irreconcilable poles of the Johnson presidency.

NOTES

1. For an excellent analysis of Lyndon Johnson's many facets as Texan, politician, and president, see Lloyd C. Gardner, *Pay Any Price: Lyndon Johnson and the Wars for Vietnam* (Chicago: Ivan R. Dee, 1995).

2. Central Intelligence Agency (CIA), "The Situation in South Vietnam, October 1, 1964," in Gareth Porter, ed., *Vietnam: The Definitive Documentation of Human Decisions*, 2 vols. (Stanfordville, NY: Earl M. Coleman, 1979), 2:323.

3. *The Pentagon Papers: The Defense Department History of U.S. Decision-Making on Vietnam: The Senator Gravel Edition*, 4 vols. (Boston: Beacon Press, 1971) [hereafter, *PP* Gravel], 3:293–294. For an analysis of the evolving roles of Johnson's advisers from 1965 to 1968, see David M. Barrett, *Uncertain Warriors: Lyndon Johnson and His Vietnam Advisers* (Lawrence: University Press of Kansas, 1993).

4. Robert S. McNamara, *In Retrospect: The Tragedy and Lessons of Vietnam* (New York: Random House, 1995), 167. However, McNamara's denial of personal responsibility in terms of decision making has been strongly challenged by, among others, H. R. McMaster, *Dereliction of Duty: Lyndon Johnson, Robert McNamara, the Joint Chiefs of Staff, and the Lies That Led to Vietnam* (New York: HarperCollins, 1997).

5. "Memorandum for the Secretary Rusk from William Bundy, Subject: Notes on the South Vietnam Situation and Alternatives, Jan. 6, 1965," *PP* Gravel, 3:684–686.

6. "Memorandum for the President from McGeorge Bundy, Feb. 7, 1965," in Porter, ed., *Vietnam*, 2:354.

7. Wallace J. Thies, *When Governments Collide: Coercion and Diplomacy in the Vietnam Conflict, 1964–1968* (Berkeley and Los Angeles: University of California Press, 1980), 20.

8. Larry Berman, *Planning a Tragedy: The Americanization of the War in Vietnam* (New York: W. W. Norton, 1982), 52.

9. McMaster argues against the view held by, for instance, Brian VanDeMark, *Into the Quagmire: Lyndon Johnson and the Escalation of the Vietnam War* (New York: Oxford University Press, 1991), that the "Americanization of the war was inevitable," brought on by the "cold war mentality." Instead, McMaster finds that it was the human follies of a cluster of men at the highest level in Washington that brought about the U.S. involvement in Vietnam and that those most competent to advise the president on military decisions, the Chiefs of Staff, were shunned by Johnson and his advisers.

10. *New York Times* [hereafter, *NYT*], 4/9/65.

11. "The 17-Nation Appeal," *The Department of State Bulletin* [hereafter, *DSB*] (April 26, 1965): 612.

12. *NYT*, 4/2/65.

13. George McT. Kahin, *Intervention: How America Became Involved in Vietnam* (New York: Knopf, 1986), 242–243.

14. *NYT*, 3/26/65.

15. U.S. Senate, Committee on Foreign Relations, *Neutralization in Southeast Asia: Problems and Prospects* (Washington, DC: U.S. Government Printing Office, 1966), iv.

16. Gus Norwood to the President, 2/23/1965, FO–31, International Waterways, WHCF, Box 21, L.B.J. Library. Norwood even suggested Dave Lilienthal as "best am-

bassador." Indeed, Lilienthal was to play a leading role in the later part of Johnson's Mekong enterprise.

17. Gilbert F. White, "Vietnam: The Fourth Course," *Bulletin of Atomic Scientists* (December 1964): 6.

18. Ibid., 7.

19. Ibid., 9.

20. Ibid., 10.

21. George S. McGovern, "Affirmative Alternative in Vietnam," *The Progressive* (March 1965): 13.

22. Kenneth Todd Young, *The Southeast Asia Crisis: Background Papers and Proceedings* (New York: Dobbs Ferry, 1966), 122–125.

23. Ibid., 152.

24. Gardner offers an interesting interpretation of Johnson's understanding of the conflict in Vietnam, arguing that, for the president, "the conflict in Vietnam and the War on Poverty were indeed joined together symbiotically," and that this "economic development-war" parallel was reinforced by some of his advisers, including Walt W. Rostow, Chester Bowles, and Robert Komer. Gardner, *Pay Any Price*, 122.

25. Memo, Marshall Green to Mr. Bundy, 5/30/64, Vietnam Country File, NSF, Box 52–53, L.B.J. Library. See also Green's previous memo dated 5/29/64, which introduced the Mekong idea as a forward-looking step "to help overcome the backlash features of our actions." Ibid.

26. Ibid.

27. Memo, Douglass Cater to the President, 6/9/64, Vietnam Country File, Box 52–53, NSF, L.B.J. Library.

28. Draft outline, Rutherford Poats, AID/FE, 3/26/1965, "A Southeast Asia Peace and Progress Plan," Vietnam Country File, NSF, Box 200, L.B.J. Library.

29. Memo, W. W. Rostow to McGeorge Bundy, 3/30/1965, "Southeast Asian Development Scenario," Vietnam Country File, NSF, Box 200, L.B.J. Library.

30. Ibid.

31. For an aperçu on Johnson's 1961 trip to Southeast Asia and his brief encounter with the Mekong topic, see Gardner, *Pay Any Price*, 52–53.

32. Ibid., 193–194.

33. Memorandum for the Honorable Jack Valenti, Special Assistant to the President, The White House, Subject: "Lower Mekong Basin Development Scheme, March 26, 1965" by Rutherford Poats, Assistant Administrator, Far East, The Declassified Documents Reference System [hereafter, The DDRS] (Washington, DC: Carrolton Press, 1979), 225 A.

34. Ibid.

35. Ibid.

36. U.S. Engineer Agency for Resources Inventories, *Atlas of Physical, Economic, and Social Resources of the Lower Mekong Basin* (New York: United Nations, 1968).

37. "Lower Mekong Basin Development Scheme," The DDRS, 225 A.

38. Ibid.

39. Ibid.

40. Memorandum to the President, 3/30/64, National Security Action memo, NSF, Box 17, L.B.J. Library.

41. *NYT*, 3/26/1965.

42. *Washington Post* [hereafter, *WP*], 4/10/65.

43. Herbert Y. Schandler, *The Unmaking of a President: Lyndon Johnson and Vietnam* (Princeton, NJ: Princeton University Press, 1977), 21.

44. Gardner, who analyzes Johnson's personal rationale as well as those of his close advisers behind the decision to make the Mekong Project the focus of the Baltimore speech, attributes its main ideas to his speech writer, Richard Goodwin, the author of the Great Society speech. Goodwin drafted the Baltimore address for the president with its $1 billion offer, to which Johnson brought his personal input. Gardner, *Pay Any Price*, 191–200.

45. "Pattern for Peace in Southeast Asia," Address by President Johnson made at Johns Hopkins University, Baltimore, MD., on April 7, *DSB* (April 26, 1965): 606–610. According to Rostow, some of the ideas that appeared in the Baltimore speech were suggested by Rostow in a memo dated January 9, 1965; in particular, Rostow claims the concepts of regionalism and regional organizations as important peace-contributing factors in Southeast Asia. Walt Whitman Rostow, *The Diffusion of Power: An Essay in Recent History* (New York: Macmillan, 1972), 508.

46. *Chinh Luan* [hereafter, *CL*], 4/11–12/1965.

47. Lyndon B. Johnson, *The Vantage Point: Perspectives of the Presidency, 1963–1969* (New York: Holt, Rinehart and Winston, 1971), 132.

48. Ibid.

49. As one author has pointed out, President Johnson's initiative bore some resemblance to an Eisenhower initiative of a decade earlier: the $200 million Presidential Fund for Asian Economic Development. However, this time, the stakes were much higher, and Asian states were more responsive. Po-Wen Huang, Jr., *The Asian Development Bank: Diplomacy and Development in Asia* (New York: Vantage Press, 1975), 52.

50. Carl Sulzberger, "Generous Peace—or Just War?" *NYT,* 4/ 9/65.

51. U.S. Department of State, Memorandum of Conversation, April 13, 1965, Subject: "President's Johns Hopkins Address," The DDRS, Retrospective Collection, 645 A.

52. VanDeMark notes how the fear of Chinese expansionism weighed on Johnson and his advisers, leading them to consider the P.R.C. as the most important threat to Asia. VanDeMark, *Into the Quagmire*, 121–122.

53. Ilya V. Gaiduk, *The Soviet Union and the Vietnam War* (Chicago: Ivan R. Dee, 1996), 42; see also Franklin P. Huddle, *The Mekong Project: Opportunities and Problems of Regionalism* (Washington, DC: U.S. Government Printing Office, 1972), 5. For updated versions by Huddle, see U.S. Congress, House of Representatives, Committee on International Relations, *Science, Technology, and Diplomacy in the Age of Interdependence* (Washington, DC: U.S. Government Printing Office, 1976); and Committee on International Relations, *Science, Technology, and American Diplomacy* (Washington, DC: U.S. Government Printing Office, 1977).

54. Rudy Abramson, *Spanning the Century: The Life of W. Averell Harriman, 1891–1986* (New York: William Morrow, 1992), 638.

55. *Le Monde*, 4/11–12/65.

56. *WP*, 4/9/65.

57. *PP* Gravel, 3:355. Apparently, it took a lot of persuasion to induce Black to head the efforts proposed by Johnson. It was only the day after the Baltimore speech, on April 8, that Black began to discuss the economic development plan. Huang, *The Asian Development Bank*, 54–55.

58. *NYT*, 4/8/65.

59. *WP*, 4/8/65.

60. Ibid.

61. *NYT*, 4/9/65.

62. Chester L. Cooper, *The Lost Crusade: America in Vietnam* (New York: Dodd, Mead, 1970), 273.

63. Cooper states that in the original reference, the figure was c. $500 million. Ibid.

64. *NYT*, 4/9/65.

65. On April 14, 1965, President Johnson announced at a press conference the formal appointment of Eugene Black as "Special Advisor on South East Asian Economic and Social Development," and the U.S. participation in the Nam Ngum Dam and the Delta Development Project. It was UN officials who had suggested both "the Nam Ngum Dam in Laos, part of the Mekong Valley development program, and, second, the Asian Development Bank." Huang, *The Asian Development Bank*, 57–58.

66. *Le Monde*, 4/11–12/65.

67. *NYT*, 4/9/65.

68. *Le Monde*, 4/10/65.

69. *Saigon Post* [hereafter, *SP*], 4/17/65.

70. Ibid., 4/21/65.

71. Ibid.

72. *NYT*, 4/9/65.

73. Research Report, Foreign Reaction to President Johnson's Johns Hopkins Speech on Viet-Nam, SP 3–72, WHCF, Box 168, L.B.J. Library.

74. Ibid.

75. Ibid.

76. *SP*, 4/13/65.

77. *WP*, 4/9/65.

78. Russian historian Ilya V. Gaiduk cites the figure of "more than $1.5 billion" in socialist aid to the D.R.V., of which Moscow's share was 36.8 percent. Gaiduk notes that "while Soviet leaders were trying to create an image of seeking the earliest peaceful settlement of the conflict, [the presence of] Soviet advisers in Vietnam . . . might be perceived as an escalation of commitment." Gaiduk, *The Soviet Union*, 58, 62.

79. *WP,* 4/9/65.

80. *SP,* 4/14/65.

81. Embassy telegram (Embtel) 1899 (Vientiane) Sullivan to DOS [Department of State], 11/3/1965, Laos Country File, NSF, Box 270, L.B.J. Library.

82. Embtel 0041 (Vientiane) Sullivan to DOS, 11/1/1965, Laos Country File, NSF, Box 270, L.B.J. Library.

83. Ibid.

84. On April 8, 1965, a four-point proposal was presented by Prime Minister Pham Van Dong to the National Assembly of the D.R.V. After adoption by the National Assembly, the four points became the basis of the political solution formulated by Ha-noi concerning negotiations with Washington. They included: "1. Recognition of the basic national rights of the Vietnamese people—peace, independence, sovereignty, unity, and territorial integrity. . . . 2. Pending the peaceful reunification of Vietnam, while Vietnam is still temporarily divided into two zones the military provisions of the 1954 Geneva Agreements on Vietnam must be strictly respected. . . . 3. The internal affairs of South Vietnam must be settled by the South Vietnamese people themselves in accordance with the program of the South Vietnam National Liberation Front, without any foreign interference. 4. The peaceful reunification of Vietnam is to be settled by the Vietnamese people in both zones, without any foreign interference." Joint Publication Research Service, "The Only Correct Stand on the Settlement of the Vietnam Problem," *Hoc Tap* 4 (1966): 1–2.

85. *Nhan Dan* [hereafter, *ND*], 4/13/65.

86. Ibid., 4/14/65.

87. Ibid., 4/15/65.

88. Radio Liberation Broadcast, 4/15/65.

89. *ND*, 4/21/65.

90. *ND*, 10/6/65.

91. The Red River delta in North Vietnam is not part of the Mekong watershed. The river's devastating floods wrought havoc to the D.R.V.'s economy year after year, adding to the hardships created by the war's devastation.

92. *SP*, 4/11/65.

93. *Thoi Luan*, 4/11/65.

94. *CL*, 4/10/65.

95. *SP*, 4/12/65.

96. Communiqué Divers, Lao Presse, 4/21/65.

97. Department of State, Telegram from E. R. Black, American Embassy in Bangkok, June 30, 1965, The DDRS, Retrospective Collection, 320 B.

98. Leonard Unger, "Present Objectives and Future Possibilities in Southeast Asia," *DSB* (May 10, 1965): 712.

99. The White House, April 9, 1965, National Security Action Memorandum No. 329 to Secretary of State, Treasury, Agriculture, Commerce, AID, Export-Import Bank, Subject: "Task Force on Southeast Asian Economic and Social Development," signed L. B. Johnson. The DDRS, 1980:371 A. The Task Force was formally terminated in November 1967.

100. Cable, Central Intelligence Agency, 4/22/1965, "U Thant's Views on President Johnson's Aid-to-Asia Program," United Nations/Mekong Development Country File, NSF, Box 293, L.B.J. Library.

101. Huddle, *The Mekong Project,* 36.

102. L. B. Johnson, "Southeast Asia Aid Program," *DSB* (June 28, 1965): 1055–1056.

103. Concerning Japan's much more aggressive role in the creation of the bank and a history of the ADB's formation, see Huang, *The Asian Development Bank*. Japan had been pursuing the idea of such an organization since the 1950s but had received negative responses from Asian nations wary of Japan's motivations.

104. Eugene R. Black, *Alternative in Southeast Asia* (London: Pall Mall Press, 1969), 96–97.

105. Department of State, Memorandum of Conversation, date: Jan. 13, 1965, Secretary Rusk Luncheon for Prime Minister Sato, Subject: "US-Japan Relations and Related World Problems," The DDRS, Retrospective Collection, 642 F. Japan apparently attempted to involve the United States in the creation of the bank to alleviate regional concerns about Japanese hegemony. Huang, *The Asian Development Bank*, 19.

106. Memo, Hamilton to McGeorge Bundy, 12/6/1965, Laos Country File, NSF, Box 270, L.B.J. Library.

107. Ibid.

108. However, this change of mind was incomplete and hardly unanimous throughout U.S. agencies and departments. For example, a memo from Under Secretary of the Treasury Joseph W. Barr to the president expressed some reserve about—even opposition to— American participation in the Asian Development Bank because of the perception that the United States was "carrying a disproportionate share of the aid efforts in the world." Memo, Joseph W. Barr to the President, 11/18/1965, Vietnam Country File, NSF, Box 200, L.B.J. Library. Barr disagreed with Black, although, ironically, the two men were later to work in tandem, representing the United States at the signing of the agreement establishing the ADB.

109. "Statement by W. Averell Harriman, Ambassador-at-large, made on February 2 before the Subcommittee on International Finance of the House Committee on Banking and Currency," *DSB* (March 7, 1966): 379.

110. "President Urges Participation in Asian Development Bank," *DSB* (February 14, 1966): 256–257.

111. Ibid., 256.

112. Black, *Alternative in Southeast Asia*, 98. Black states that President Johnson ordered him to get in touch with U Thant to ask for suggestions for concrete measures that would reflect the American interest in promoting regional cooperation. It was the UN Secretary General who suggested the Asian Development Bank.

113. Telegram from American Embassy in Bangkok to Department of State, August 8, 1965, Subject: "ADB Consultative Committee," The DDRS, Retrospective Collection, 320 D. The telegram also reveals that the French business community was concerned that the French government's hostile attitude toward ADB would result in the exclusion of French business interests from Asia.

114. Ibid.

115. Telegram from Eugene R. Black in American Embassy in Bangkok to Department of State, June 30, 1965, The DDRS, Retrospective Collection, 320 B.

116. "ADB Consultative Committee," The DDRS, Retrospective Collection, 320 D.

117. "Mr. Black Reports on Southeast Asia Economic Development," *DSB* (August 2, 1965): 215.

118. Telegram from Eugene Black, June 30, 1965, The DDRS, Retrospective Collection, 320 B.

119. "US-Japan Relations and Related World Problems," The DDRS, Retrospective Collection, 642 F.

120. In addition to its capital, the Asian Development Bank has at its disposal a number of Special Funds to which member nations voluntarily contribute. These funds are used for long-term, low-interest loans to finance agricultural projects, technical aid, and multiple-purpose projects.

121. W. R. Derrick Sewell and Gilbert F. White, "The Lower Mekong: An Experiment in International River Development," *International Conciliation*, no. 558 (May 1966): 63.

122. Telegram from American Embassy in Bangkok to Department of State, April 22, 1965, The DDRS, Retrospective Collection, 734 E,

123. Sewel and White, *The Lower Mekong*, 63.

124. Memorandum from Clark Clifford to President, of Conference on Jan. 19, 1961, between President Eisenhower and President-elect Kennedy on the subject of Laos, dated Sept. 29, 1967, in U.S. Department of Defense, *United States-Vietnam Relations, 1945–1967*, 12 vols. (Washington, DC: U.S. Government Printing Office, 1971), 10:1360–1364. Historians Immerman and Greenstein have demonstrated that there were differing perceptions among those present about what Eisenhower actually advised Kennedy to do concerning the Indochina conflict. See Fred I. Greenstein and Richard H. Immerman, "What Did Eisenhower Tell Kennedy about Indochina? The Politics of Misperception," *Journal of American History* 79, no. 2 (September 1992): 568–588.

125. The memory of the Korean War, in particular the events of 1950, when movements of American troops in the direction of the Yalu River led to the involvement of the Chinese People's Liberation Army, was vivid enough to incite the American military to caution. Laos has a common border with China, and there was a serious risk that Amer-

ican involvement in Laos would provoke an armed Chinese response. Berman, *Planning a Tragedy*, 18.

126. Memorandum for the President from the Secretary of Defense, Subject: "Vietnam Situation, December 21, 1963," *PP* Gravel, 3:495.

127. For years, a secret war was waged by the United States in Laos against the Pathet Lao. It involved the training of Hmong forces (e.g., "General" Vang Pao and his army) and of the Royal Lao Army and Air Force, secret bombing missions along the Mekong valley, and other overt and covert activities. See Timothy N. Castle, *At War in the Shadow of Vietnam: U.S. Military Aid to the Royal Lao Government, 1955–1975* (New York: Columbia University Press, 1993); Kenneth J. Conboy with James Morrison, *Shadow War: The CIA's Secret War in Laos* (Boulder, CO: Paladin Press, 1995); and Roger Warner, *Backfire: The CIA's Secret War in Laos and Its Links to the War in Vietnam* (New York: Simon·& Schuster, 1995).

128. Jean-Pierre Barbier, "Objectifs et résultats de l'aide économique au Laos, une évaluation difficile," *Revue Tiers-Monde* (April–June 1975): 344.

129. "United States to Cooperate in Economic and Social Development in Asia," Remarks by President Johnson, *DSB* (April 4, 1966): 522.

130. P. K. Menon, "Financing the Lower Mekong River Basin Development," *Pacific Affairs* (Winter 1971–1972): 578.

131. Embtel 20258 (New York) USUN to DOS, 7/28/1965, "Southeast Asia Development: Requirements for Mekong Basin Development," United Nations/Mekong Development Country File, NSF, Box 293, L.B.J. Library.

132. See, for instance, Telegram, USUN New York to Department of State, 6/24/1965, "Southeast Asian Development," United Nations/Mekong Development Country File, NSF, Box 293, L.B.J. Library.

133. Embtel 1899 (Vientiane) Sullivan to Secretary of State, 8/7/1965, Laos Country File, NSF, Box 270, L.B.J. Library.

134. Chalerm Dhanit, "Progress Report," *Far Eastern Economic Review* [hereafter, *FEER*] (September 2, 1965): 419.

135. U.S. Congress, Senate, Committee on Foreign Relations, *Foreign Assistance Act, 1966* (Washington, DC: U.S. Government Printing Office, 1966), 281.

136. "Announcement of Pledges to Mekong River Project," White House press release dated March 16, *DSB* (April 4, 1966): 522.

137. Ibid., 523.

138. Menon, "Financing the Lower Mekong," 573–574.

139. Telegram from American Embassy in Bangkok to Department of State, April 22, 1965, The DDRS, Retrospective Collection, 734 E: 2.

140. Statement by Secretary Rusk made before the Senate Committee on Foreign Relations on June 3, *DSB* (June 28, 1965): 1058–1059.

141. Chalerm Dhanit, "More for Mekong," *FEER* (October 7, 1965): 11.

142. Economic Commission for Asia and the Far East, *Annual Report 1966* (New York: United Nations, 1966), 55.

143. The proposed amendment would have extended the functions of the Mekong Committee to involve the construction and administration stage; originally, the committee had concerned itself only with the preliminary phase of pre-investment studies. Committee for Coordination of Investigations of the Lower Mekong Basin, *Annual Report 1965* (New York: United Nations, 1965), 76–78.

144. See, for instance, Willard A. Hanna, *The Mekong Project, Part III: The Agency and the Rationale*, Southeast Asia series, vol. 16, no. 12 (New York: American Universities Field Staff Studies, 1968), 6.

145. Memo, Bill Moyers to the President, 11/10/1965, Office Files of Bill Moyers, Cambodia, Box 81(1392), L.B.J. Library.

146. Roger M. Smith, *Some Remarks on Cambodia's Attitude toward U.S. Foreign Policy in Southeast Asia and the American Role in the Development of the Lower Mekong Basin*, SEADAG Paper No. 28 (Washington, DC: Southeast Asia Development Advisory Group, 1968), 3.

147. "The Prek Thnot Dam and Power Station," *Indian Journal of Power & River Valley Development*, The Mekong Project Number, 1966, 98.

148. Smith, *Some Remarks on Cambodia's Attitude*, 4.

149. United Nations Press Services, Office of Public Information, Press Release Dev/307/Rev. 1, Nov. 13, 1968.

150. F. T. Mits, "Cambodia's Neutralist Flair," *FEER* (May 13, 1965): 322.

151. Embtel 1000 (Vientiane) Sullivan to Secretary of State, 5/22/1965, Laos Country File, NSF, Box 270. L.B.J. Library.

152. Ibid.

153. The Preah Vihar temple, situated in Cambodia near its northern border to Thailand, had been an object of contention between the two countries since the early 1960s. P. C. Pradhan, *Foreign Policy of Kampuchea* (New Delhi: Radiant Publishers, 1985), 111.

154. Memo, The White House, 7/13/1966, "Prek Thnot Dam in Cambodia," Cambodia Country File, NSF, Box 237, L.B.J. Library.

155. Smith, *Some Remarks on Cambodia's Attitude*, 6.

156. Ibid., 7.

157. Ibid.

158. Memo, The White House, "Prek Thnot Dam in Cambodia."

159. Telegram, Department of State to USUN, 9/4/1965, "Ambassador Goldberg's and Eugene Black's lunch with U Thant, Tuesday September 7," UN/Mekong Development Country File, NSF, Box 293, L.B.J. Library.

160. Memo, The White House, "Prek Thnot Dam in Cambodia."

161. Telegram, Walt Rostow to the President, 11/11/1966, Cambodia Country File, NSF, Box 237, L.B.J. Library. The administration attempted to find a way around it by using a "national security waiver" to persuade Congress to relent but was apparently unsuccessful.

162. *NYT*, 3/2/67.

163. Ibid.

164. Numerous suggestions had been made to remedy the problem of "the use of Cambodia by Viet Cong and North Vietnamese troops as a sanctuary and source of supply." One suggestion advocated closing "the Mekong River to all Cambodia-bound ships in order to apply economic pressure on the Cambodian Government to live up to its self-proclaimed policy of strict neutrality." Letter, Congress of the U.S., House of Representatives, Charles E. Chamberlain to the President, 12/8/1967, FO 3–1, International Waterways, WHCF, Box 21, L.B.J. Library.

165. Memo, William J. Jorden for Rostow, 3/25/1967, "Congressional Sentiment on Prek Thnot," Cambodia Country File, NSF, Box 237, L.B.J. Library.

166. "Samdech Sahachivin répond aux questions posées par le journal *ASAHI*, MM. Nishimura et Maeda," *Le Sangkum* (January 1966): 20.

167. "Le Désintéressement de l'aide américaine au Comité du Mékong," *Le Sangkum* (April 1967): 4–5.

168. "Echanges de messages entre U Thant et Samdech, Réponse de Samdech Norodom Sihanouk," *Le Sangkum* (February 1967): 9.

169. David Jenkins, "The Lower Mekong Scheme," *Asian Survey* (June 1968): 460.

170. United Nations, Press Release, Nov. 13, 1968.

171. ECAFE, *Annual Report 1968* (New York: United Nations), 158.

172. Comité pour la Coordination des Etudes sur le Bassin Inférieur du Mékong, *Rapport Annuel 1975* (New York: United Nations), 76.

173. Smith, *Some Remarks on Cambodia's Attitude,* 3.

174. U.S. Department of State, Memorandum of Conversation, April 13, 1965, Subject: "President's Johns Hopkins Address," The DDRS, Retrospective Collection, 645 A.

175. Ibid.

176. "Comments by Eugene R. Black on Topics Related to This Study, March 14, 1972," in Huddle, *The Mekong Project*, Appendix, 69.

177. Ibid.

178. Memo, Rostow to the President, 9/16/1968, "Gene Black's trip to Cambodia," Cambodia Country File, NSF, Box 237, L.B.J. Library.

179. Memo, Dean Rusk to the President, 3/2/1966, "Asian Development Task Force," C.F. FG600, WHCF, Box 35, L.B.J. Library.

180. Ibid.

181. Memo, Komer to the President, 3/5/1966, C.F. FG600, WHCF, Box 35, L.B.J. Library.

182. The Accelerated Rural Development program was a Thai effort at rural development that was insurgency-oriented and geared toward the at-risk northeastern provinces. With U.S. contributions, it became "the largest single development activity in the history of the Thai aid program." Robert Muscat, *Thailand and the United States: Development, Security, and Foreign Aid* (New York: Columbia University Press, 1990), 160.

183. Doris Kearns, *Lyndon Johnson and the American Dream* (New York: Harper and Row, 1976), 267.

4

From War to Peace

From the point of view of the United States and its allies, the military and diplomatic situation in the lower Mekong basin continued to deteriorate during late 1965 and early 1966. The war had spread to Cambodia even as Prince Sihanouk continued to play a dangerous balancing act for the country's survival. Laos did not seem to fare better as it too was drawn deeper into the conflict. Thailand's Northeast was threatened by Communist-influenced insurgency. In Vietnam, the Nguyen Cao Ky and Nguyen Van Thieu regime was assailed by protests from all segments of the population, in particular, the Buddhists. Victory was not in sight, despite the introduction of U.S. combat troops, which were further increased on July 28, 1965, when President Lyndon B. Johnson announced his decision to bring up the number of U.S. troops in Vietnam from 75,000 to 125,000, with more to come if necessary. The United States had moved definitively to deepen its involvement in the Indochina conflict. The domestic political situation was turning increasingly negative as the balance of payment deficit and racial tensions worsened along with the erosion in Johnson's popularity. More than ever, President Johnson needed "to point out to the American public and to the world that the United States was doing a great deal in the midst of war to build a new Vietnam."[1] It was imperative that attention be focused on constructive American activities in Vietnam that were not directly linked to the war to counterbalance the image of destruction and death associated with the American presence on Vietnamese soil. It was equally imperative, given the increased public pressure to lift the heavy burden that had been shouldered by the United States, that America's allies now do their share.

Thus emerged the Johnson Doctrine for Asia, an attempt to articulate a cogent and coherent U.S. policy toward the region that would combat the negative image of the United States and build up the region against communism without the cost in U.S. human lives and balance of payment deficits that had been the pattern in the past. In sharp contrast to the Baltimore speech of April 7, 1965, which offered generous aid to Southeast Asia to the scale of $1 billion, the Johnson Doctrine for Asia proposed that America's allies be self-sufficient. Within the Doctrine, the Mekong Project still played a role—albeit much diminished and with a more geographically and politically limited focus, the Mekong delta of the R.V.N. Then came the 1968 Tet Offensive, shattering all illusions and ending Johnson's dreams. The ensuing administration, led by Richard M. Nixon, formulated its own Doctrine for Asia, which, although surprisingly similar to its predecessor in terms of rhetoric and goals, sought to achieve its goals through a wholly different strategy, one not of involvement but of disengagement. In this new context, the Mekong Project found itself reduced to an image, a symbol, a "carrot" in contrast to a "stick" that kept raining blows.

THE JOHNSON DOCTRINE IN ASIA

In his memoirs, Lyndon Johnson mentions a particularly interesting proposal that was submitted to him at the end of 1965 by Secretary of State Dean Rusk and entitled "Interdependence": "No nation, including the United States, can guarantee its security, its prosperity, or its tranquillity by pursuing narrow policies of nationalism. Our task is to find ways of working together which respect the dignity and the abiding national interest of each nation, while respecting also the inescapable interdependence of us all in a world of modern weapons, communications, and close economic linkages."[2] This notion was to form the premise of the Johnson Doctrine for Asia, which, while reiterating the grandiose vision of the "Great Society" that he had conceived and applied to his domestic policy, mainly emphasized the many facets of regionalism (association of nations, regional organizations, and cooperation) in "developing continents": "Thus, the concept of regionalism in areas outside Europe emerged as one of my administration's most serious commitments in its efforts to build a stable world order."[3]

One of the main "areas outside Europe" was, of course, Asia. Whereas previous presidents had been preoccupied with Europe, Johnson wanted to leave his historical footprint in Asia (and Latin America), for "Asia is now the crucial arena of man's striving for independence and order, and for life itself."[4] The essence of his Doctrine for Asia was conveyed in his July 12, 1966, speech, addressed to the American Alumni Council and broadcast on radio and television, entitled "Four Essentials for Peace in Asia": "First is the determination of the United States to meet our obligations in Asia as a Pacific power. . . . The second essential for peace in Asia is . . . to prove to aggressive nations that the use of force to conquer others is a losing game. . . . The third essential is the building of political and economic strength among the nations of free Asia. . . . [The fourth essential is that] a peaceful mainland China is central to a peaceful Asia."[5]

The Johnson Doctrine underlined the obligation of developing countries to help themselves: "We serve notice here and now from this day on that our foreign assistance will go to those nations and only those nations who are willing and ready to help themselves."[6] It aggressively asserted that American aid would not be allowed to "become an international dole" and that it would be given only to meritorious and industrious nations that "will put it to the best use."[7] Since American aid as the main impetus to development was de-emphasized, it became necessary then to call on other nations to help make up for the possible decrease in aid. Consequently, the other element in the Johnson doctrine was multilateralism. President Johnson proposed that the United States "increase its contributions to multilateral lending institutions, particularly the International Development Association [and] the United Nations development program."[8] Crucial collateral aspects of this emphasis on multilateralism were regionalism and regional cooperation, which, given the context of the Vietnam War, played an essential part in the administration's two-front—military and economic—strategy. According to Secretary of State Rusk: "I think it is important that these works of peace continue even while the military struggle continues. . . . The need for closer regional cooperation is particularly great in Southeast Asia."[9] As such, the Mekong Project once again was the ideal implement for carrying out America's dual purpose: to allow it to continue the war on the military front while attempting to win "hearts and minds" on the politico-economic front by satisfying basic economic needs.

Given the escalating cost of military involvement and the burden it placed on the budget, the second aim was best pursued by calling for the participation of other nations. In this way, American financial resources would not be stretched too thinly, and in congressional debates over budgetary demands, images of the destruction caused by the war in Indochina could be countered by images of constructive involvement by the United States and other cooperating countries in the Mekong Project. Concurrently, by emphasizing multilateralism, regionalism, and the contribution of international agencies, Washington could channel American aid through apparently impartial organizations, thus reducing the beneficiaries' skepticism about its actual purposes, while still fulfilling its aim of consolidating non-Communist governments and societies. President Johnson wanted "the American people and the world to lift their eyes, for a time at least, from concentration on the war in Vietnam to the larger problems and possibilities of the new and vital Asia—the Asia I felt was being born, in part at last as a result of our commitment to its security."[10]

With this formulation of the Johnson Doctrine early in 1966, increased regional activities with an apparently peaceful content became highly visible concurrently with the deepening of American involvement in the war in Vietnam. These activities included, for instance, Washington's encouragement of diplomatic initiatives taken by leaders of allied states in Southeast Asia, such as the Philippines, South Korea, and Thailand (all loyal U.S. allies), in favor of regionalism. It also involved the creation of regional organizations such as the Southeast Asian Ministers of Education Council late in 1965; the Asian and Pacific Council (ASPAC), dedicated to the preservation of "solidarity against external interference and threats and to cooperation in working for the peace, freedom, progress, and prosperity of its members and of the regions as a whole"; the Association of Southeast Asian Nations (ASEAN), founded in Bangkok, August 1967, whose members included Indonesia, the Philippines, Malaysia, Singapore, and Thailand; Operation Rice Bowl, sponsored by SEATO "to raise food production in Southeast Asia"; and many others.[11] All of these activities and organizations had one fundamental purpose: the formation of a cohesive regional bloc, reinforced by regional exchanges, that demonstrated support for American policy in Vietnam and in the other countries of the Indochinese peninsula.

MEKONG DELTA PLANNING

From December 1965 to January 1966, in yet another futile attempt to demonstrate to the world his intentions to negotiate for a peaceful end to the war, Johnson launched a worldwide, high-visibility diplomatic maelstrom, sending special emissaries W. Averell Harriman to Eastern Europe and U.S. Ambassador to the United Nations Arthur Goldberg to call upon heads of states and governments, including Pope Paul VI, French president Charles de Gaulle, and British prime minister Harold Wilson.[12] Vice-President Hubert Humphrey was sent to Asia, Assistant Secretary of State Mennen Williams to Third World countries, and McGeorge Bundy to Canada to confer with Prime Minister Lester Pearson. This flurry of activity was viewed in certain diplomatic milieus as "counterproductive showboating." Ho Chi Minh denounced the peace offensive as a fraud.[13] In a joint telegram from the State Department and U.S. Information Agency dated October 4, 1965, the following instructions were given to the American Mission in Sai-gon: "There is continuing concern at the highest levels here regarding need to emphasize our non-military programs in Vietnam and give them maximum possible public exposure both in U.S. and abroad. . . . We recognize that the Mission is fully cognizant of this problem and already has underway measures to broaden public knowledge and understanding of non-military activities. . . . We are also conscious of difficulties involved in enlisting greater press interest in these developments when it finds military actions more dramatic and newsworthy. Nevertheless, we hope we will continue to give non-military programs increasing priority."[14]

Thus took shape President Johnson's "other war," "the war for the loyalty of the Vietnamese people," which involved ultimately unsuccessful efforts to bring economic development and social change to the Republic of Vietnam (R.V.N.), while generating positive press reviews.[15] In Johnson's "other war," the Mekong delta was to provide another chance, a second "Mekong opportunity" for the president "to have a war that will build as well as destroy."[16] In the past, the Mekong delta had often been the object of countless planning efforts, one of the earliest ones being the "Delta Plan" undertaken in November 1961 by Sir Robert Thompson, the British architect of the successful counterinsurgency campaign in Malaya.[17] These "rural development" schemes were closely linked to and even inseparable from the deadly pacification campaigns advocated by Robert W.

Komer, William Colby, and Henry Cabot Lodge.[18] Posted a second time as the U.S. ambassador in Sai-gon in August 1965, Lodge had always been an ardent advocate of the concept of pacification, "the heart of the question" in the war; in Lodge's view, the primary target of pacification programs should be "the area around Saigon and south of Saigon (all of the Delta) [which] must be pacified. This area includes about 55 to 60% of the population of Vietnam. . . . In brief, a pacified area is economically, socially, and politically, a part of the RVN."[19] Military and intelligence reports had been calling attention to the increasing use of the Mekong River as a means of transportation for ammunition and weapons and to the use of the Mekong-Bassac region, particularly in Cambodian territory, for sanctuary by the National Liberation Front/People's Army of Vietnam (NLF/PAVN). One report observed that "the network of waterways leading east and west from the Mekong and the Bassac along the border and across it into South Vietnam offers excellent routes for use by the VC/NVA for movement and distribution of such supplies."[20] Consequently, much effort had to be focused on the Mekong delta, one of the essential war fronts but also one that was limited enough that it should easily lend itself to the application of economic measures that would bear fruit within a relatively short length of time.[21] As the realization that the Johns Hopkins offer of $1 billion for economic aid for the regional development of Southeast Asia with the accent on the Mekong Project had failed to influence the D.R.V. in any way, the offer of economic aid to the region was reformulated to concentrate mostly on the Mekong delta of the R.V.N.

Given the deteriorating military situation, Washington needed to win over the local population in the R.V.N. One of the ways to do this, it thought, was by instilling a hope for a better life, a brighter economic future at the end of the war through American economic aid and delta development projects. At the time, the government of Vice-Marshall Ky, prime minister since June 1965, was the target of virulent criticisms domestically and internationally because of its corruption as well as its repression of Buddhist elements.[22] The criticisms reflected on its ally and protector, the United States. From the Johnson administration's point of view, Ky's government was in urgent need of remaking its image more in conformity with American demands and expectations. Acting on U.S. advice (in particular, that of the much seasoned Major General Edward Lansdale, aide to Henry Cabot Lodge), Ky began to express concern for the people's welfare and to emphasize his government's determination to address the economic and social problems gripping the country. Concurrently, the Sai-gon political elite was pressing for a deeper, "permanent" American involvement alongside the R.V.N., to be manifested, for example, through American investment in infrastructure projects for the R.V.N. economy.

The confluence of these factors led to the Honolulu Conference of February 6–8, 1966. Convoked by President Johnson, it assembled the main representatives of the R.V.N. and of the United States. The political context was highly charged: The United States had renewed bombing of the Democratic Republic of Vietnam (D.R.V.) on January 30, 1966, after a reprieve of thirty-seven days;

American ground troops had already reached 200,000; and it was evident that the war was not going to be brought to a conclusive end. Hence, in accordance with Johnson's wishes that the Honolulu Conference be the counterpoint to the all-pervasive image of destruction, heavy publicity was centered on economic development, social progress, rural reconstruction, and electoral reforms in the R.V.N. Consequently, Ky's speech for the occasion followed Johnson's lead concerning the "economic and social revolution," using concepts and key words tailored for U.S. public opinion: "We must bring about a true social revolution and construct a modern society in which every man can know that he has a future; . . . that he has the opportunity to live in an environment where not all is disappointment, despair and dejection."[23] The two governments agreed on numerous points concerning economic aid and rural reconstruction, that is, pacification, economic and financial measures, the question of refugees, and so forth. In October, a follow-up conference was organized in Manila, where the same themes and advice were broached again by Johnson in his discussion with Ky and Thieu: "Ky should try to reflect [in his speech] the new emerging Asia . . . beginning to build institutions like the Asian Development Bank, the Mekong Committee. . . . Ky, going back to an earlier suggestion of the President's, said he would love to talk in a speech about the future of Asia."[24] What was being envisaged then was a program that looked toward a postwar future for the R.V.N. After all, in 1966, the "light at the end of the tunnel" was still brightly shining for U.S. strategists, despite signs to the contrary. Victory was estimated to be shortly in view, and there seemed to be a perceived need (at least rhetorically) for some postwar planning.

It was thus in the midst of wartime decisions, of bombing escalation and increased military engagements and casualties, that a number of high-level memos began to lay the groundwork for peace by calling for studies of the possibilities of postwar reconstruction and development: "The study should plan in advance for the efficient and economical use of US and Vietnamese resources in the transition from wartime to postwar reconstruction and development."[25] Such an effort would "display the constructive side of U.S. and R.V.N. plans for the future of Vietnam and the durability of the U.S. commitment to that country."[26] The study would focus on the postwar period and select "constructive programs to be undertaken as soon as possible, whether the situation in Vietnam can be strictly labeled 'postwar' or not."[27] One such memo to Robert Komer (special assistant to the president) suggested that the R.V.N. prime minister initiate the call for a "Postwar Reconstruction and Development" study to be carried out by "US specialists, led by a prestigious individual, and working jointly with a Vietnamese team designated by the GVN."[28] The choice of Prime Minister Ky as the initiator of this idea was made so as to "buy goodwill from the Vietnamese, who are always grousing about unilateral initiatives by us." It would also boost Ky's image of being his own man, not a puppet whose strings were pulled by a foreign master.[29] In the following days, letters went out to a number of potential consultants who would be in charge of the study. By the end of the year, David Lilienthal was formally appointed.

Publicly, the first step was taken on December 16, 1966, when, on Ky's official request, a joint planning program concerning the long-term development of the R.V.N. was launched under the double sponsorship of the U.S. government and the R.V.N. On the same day, David Lilienthal on the American side and Vu Quoc Thuc as his Vietnamese counterpart were named to co-head the Joint Development Group.[30] The choice of Lilienthal was dictated by an acute sense of publicity. Lilienthal, a former chairman of the Atomic Energy Commission, was known mainly as the architect of the celebrated Tennessee Valley Authority (TVA) project, which had had a considerable influence on the poverty-stricken southern region of the United States during the New Deal.[31] Johnson hoped that this man would be able to reproduce the TVA miracle by tackling the problem—albeit dissimilar—of the exploitation of the Mekong delta:

For a good long time I have been wanting Mr. Lilienthal to spend some time in Viet-Nam in connection with our "other war" out there. From the early stage of the TVA I have looked forward to and admired the novel, constructive, and far-reaching thoughts and programs which he has inaugurated. . . . He has given us his help. I think it will have far-reaching results and effects. It is going to be essential to our success in that area. This goes back to what was said in Baltimore in April of 1965.[32]

Lilienthal's Postwar Reconstruction and Development Program

In his memoirs, Lilienthal recounts a telephone conversation with Walt W. Rostow, presidential adviser for national security and chairman of the influential Policy Planning Council. Rostow was a strong advocate of regionalism as a complement to American global security policy. His ideas paralleled Johnson's: He had made numerous suggestions pertaining to potential U.S. regional initiatives in Asia, including the joint economic development of the Mekong, the taking charge by Asians of their own destiny, and the thaw with China, all of which formed components of the Johnson Doctrine. From 1966 to 1968, he worked closely with Eugene Black, the presidential adviser for Southeast Asia.[33] Rostow explained to Lilienthal the administration's motivations for appointing him to this postwar planning project: "We're now going through a long process out there, but you can see the balance shifting from chewing away at their military strength bit by bit to a whole set of constructive moves. . . . A critical part is giving these people a sense that they not only have a future, but what shape it might have. This means a postwar plan. . . . I regard this as having great political importance. More than that, it has short-range operational importance."[34]

Once again, the same intentions could be found in this new U.S. effort at economic planning. Domestically, the initiative was to rally critics of the administration by providing a positive image of U.S. accomplishments not so much in the vast lower Mekong basin but in the narrower region of the Mekong delta of the R.V.N. Within the Democratic Party, for example, Senator Robert Kennedy had recently demanded in a Senate speech that the United States apply new social and economic programs in Vietnam.[35] And Arthur Schlesinger, Jr., former assistant to Presidents Kennedy and Johnson, argued the merits of possible solutions for the Vietnam crisis, among them "a neutralization program . . . for Cambodia, Laos, North and South Vietnam." He went on to say that "if these states could work out forms of economic collaboration, as in the development of the Mekong valley, the guarantors should make economic and technical assistance available to them."[36] In the R.V.N., U.S. goals were to stimulate the urban and rural middle-classes, to inspire confidence within the peasant masses, to perhaps sway the NLF, and even to catch Ha-noi's attention.[37] The postwar planning effort also provided President Johnson with the opportunity to return to his vision of the "Great Society," of social reforms and of an economic development founded on great dams, irrigation, and power works that he had not been able to achieve with the Mekong Project but hoped to be able to bring to fruition quickly with the Mekong delta planning and development.[38] After all, as David Lilienthal enthusiastically explained to the president, the Baltimore speech with its "picture of the future" founded on the development of the Mekong valley, "should be known even more widely than the Marshall Plan, as the Johnson Plan."[39]

Lilienthal's Development and Resources Corporation was then contracted by the Agency for International Development (AID) for three years to conduct research on long-term planning, and to "restore the Mekong River delta as one of the world's great rice producing areas."[40] The Joint Development Group, which had a budget of $1.5 million contributed both by the United States and the R.V.N. (in fact, indirectly by American aid for the latter), functioned, at least in theory, independently from American and Vietnamese governmental organizations. It was to review over three years (1967–1970) the problems and obstacles that the R.V.N. would likely face in the postwar era and to initiate strategies of development to help restore the economy and allow the country to become economically independent in the shortest possible time.[41] Assuming that the end of the war was imminent, bringing a context of restored peace and stability, the planned postwar development should take at least a decade to achieve.

However, the Tet Offensive of 1968 upset these finely laid plans, hastening the timetable for their application, which could not be postponed until the return of peace. It had to take place immediately, for, in Lilienthal's words, "it would be nothing less than a disaster if economic development by the Vietnamese were to await a conclusion of the war—disaster because inflation would take over, disaster because the needs of the country are great and the opportunities are great."[42] After his first mission, Lilienthal, in a White House press conference, waxed lyrical about Vietnam's resources, among them "the Delta of the Mekong River . . . which is producing enormous amounts of rice. . . . This river has water resources that are almost unmanageable. I thought I knew rivers, but I have never seen a river with such fertile land stretching out as far as the eye can see."[43] According to Lilienthal, the Mekong delta was one of the main assets—economic but also strategic—of Vietnam. At the time, the official opinion was that the delta was a region where rapid results could be obtained, seen, and (hopefully) recorded by the press.[44] The voluminous report presented in March 1969 to the American and Vietnamese governments estimated the necessary investments at US$ 5 billion, half of which would be provided by external sources.[45] It put forward strategies for the economic development of Vietnam, such as increases in exports, import substitution, and monetary and fiscal policy to fight inflation, that would allow the R.V.N. to escape its dependence on foreign aid.[46] Agriculture would play a fundamental role. The Mekong delta was designated as the region with the best potential for rapid growth, since development of water resources would allow an enormous increase in the production of rice as well as other crops.

Nevertheless, the report pointed out that the development of the Mekong delta would be an enormous endeavor that could not be fully accomplished for several decades. For the moment, the initial stage would require expenditures of more than US$ 400 million. If carried out, the R.V.N. could become the granary of the entire peninsula through the use of a variety of miracle-rice strains and water-control works. If integrated within the overall lower Mekong River basin development, it could offer tremendous possibilities: "Such development would mean the creation of a hinterland market without which much of the war-born investment in that country, particularly the investment in harbors and airfields, will simply have to be written off."[47]

The interest generated by the Mekong delta led Washington to concurrently commission Lilienthal's Development and Resources Corporation to carry out another special study on the region, entitled *Mekong Delta Development Program, Preliminary Appraisal Report*, which detailed a system of water control for a large-scale development of the delta. The preliminary studies started in November 1968 on what was to be the largest agricultural scheme in history.[48] The Mekong Committee cooperated in this endeavor, which used the Mekong delta Mathematical Model prepared by the French firm SOGREAH for the Mekong Committee.[49] If the scheme were to be realized as planned, the construction of water-control works would start in 1970, and the R.V.N. would become the first of the four riparian countries to use the Mekong mainstream for such purposes. According to the study, projected Pa Mong and Stung Treng dams on the mainstream could totally control the river's flood in Cambodia and in a large portion of the delta provided that the dams reached a maximum capacity of 100 billion to 160 billion cubic meters. However, dams of such size could not be built for at least decades, and a calculation comparing the respective costs of construction of either of these dams with the building of a network of levees and canals for flood protection indicated that the second solution would be less costly.[50]

The problem of water drainage and salinity intrusion, it was argued, should be solved locally without waiting for the construction of upstream reservoirs. On the other hand, irrigation during the dry season should use water stored in one of

the two upstream reservoirs.[51] A hydraulic system combining all four functions (flood control, drainage, salinity control, and irrigation) would include main works (dikes and levees, irrigation and drainage canals, pumping stations, and navigation locks) that would come under the responsibility of a Mekong Delta Development Authority; secondary works (secondary and tertiary canals of drainage and irrigation and small pumping stations) would fall under the authority of local development associations of farmers. The report gives a detailed description of this network of dikes parallel to the Mekong and to the Bassac, and of a flood by-pass from the Bassac flowing out into the Gulf of Thailand.[52] These constructions would be under a politically and financially independent Mekong Delta Development Authority. There were high hopes for this body, which had received favorable reports in the press and among the Mekong Committee officials. It would serve as a positive conduit and establish good working relationships between the R.V.N. and Cambodia, which had been hostile neighbors for years.[53] Given the context of tensions between the R.V.N. and the United States, on one hand, and Cambodia, on the other hand, regarding the question of sanctuary provided in Cambodian territory to the NLF/PAVN forces, it was essential to foster friendship between the two riparian nations. Through this Mekong Delta Authority, it was hoped that Cambodia and the R.V.N. could join together to work toward the first hydraulic system on the mainstream that would consider the river as a unit, instead of, as previously, dividing it into tributary projects conceived separately to satisfy each of the four riparian nations, particularly Thailand and Laos. The latter approach had been criticized by David Lilienthal as "the old Rivers and Harbors pork barrel approach."[54] This study, like earlier reports, argued that the construction of upstream dams was the *sine qua non* for an integrated development of the Mekong delta's water resources.

At the time, numerous studies of all kinds were carried out or commissioned by AID focusing mainly on the R.V.N.'s postwar economy: preliminary reports on a strategy for the future urban development of the R.V.N. and studies on national transportation, electricity, and telecommunication networks for the postwar period. AID also cooperated with U.S. military authorities in reviewing military equipment and installations that might become surpluses that could be used in the postwar economic development of the R.V.N.[55] More directly related to the war, a study requested by the Defense Department, entitled *Accelerated Development of the Plain of Reeds*, was carried out. Its objectives were to "investigate and report on the agricultural potential of the Plain of Reeds, the problems that would be involved in reclaiming it for agriculture at an earlier date than it would be by the Mekong Development Project (MDP), and the advantages which may accrue to the Republic of Vietnam and its allies through thus doing."[56] The study was also to determine "the military, political, and social benefits which would be derived."[57]

The Plain of Reeds is a natural reservoir for the Mekong, reducing the effects of its flooding. The report underlined the fact that the Plain of Reeds, while an integral part of the delta, was, in fact, economically isolated from the rest of the region. An insalubrious and sparsely populated area of acidic soil, it had traditionally served as a sanctuary for "dissident elements." The report assigned the region's economic stagnation to "unsettled political conditions of the past 25 years or more."[58] Its development could bring military, political, and economic benefits. The study estimated that with total water control, the utilization of new rice strains, and the cultivation of one-half million hectares, the Plain of Reeds would yield "five rice crops in 24 months, with the yearly value of rice production alone worth more than 130 million dollars in constant price."[59] Population increases would constitute a stabilizing force, creating more security and generally working to the advantage of the forces of order. Improvement in the means of transportation would allow increased troop mobility, giving the forces of order the advantage over insurgents. Concurrently, improvement of canals would also facilitate troop mobility, while construction of main canals would form an obstacle to the enemy. From the political point of view, the provision of health, education, and farming services would reinforce the population's support for the government. From the economic point of view, the development of the Plain of Reeds would increase agricultural production, expand trade, and improve exploitation of fishing resources. The system advocated in this study included canals and levees that would lead to poldering with irrigation and drainage carried out polder by polder.

The Baltimore speech, which had inaugurated an era of thunderous statements and ambitious projects pertaining to the economic development of Southeast Asia, highlighted the Mekong River and touted its development as an alternative to the war. Countries of the Indochinese peninsula, in particular the D.R.V., were presented with the promise of $1 billion for the region's development. Later, the Johnson administration shifted its focus to the Thuc-Lilienthal plan for the R.V.N.'s postwar economic growth, which emphasized the development of the Mekong delta's water resources. It was a project feasible only with enormous American investments, which were rendered impossible because of the war—investments that were, moreover, opposed by Congress. Faced with colossal military expenditures caused by the war in Vietnam—in 1968, they amounted annually to $22 billion—Congress had no intention of continuing to finance a project that had already cost several million dollars just in paperwork without any concrete result other than studies and reports.

The war was everywhere, taking precedence over all long-term and nonmilitary planning. What counted most was the search for a "magic wand" or quick-fix measure that would permit rapid resolution of the successive crises in American policy in the Indochinese peninsula and, in particular, in Vietnam. Therefore, it is understandable that the Thuc-Lilienthal project could not long hold the attention of American policy makers. No firm, long-term action or financial commitments in a concrete, precise, constructive project were possible in the face of exigencies of the war.[60] Writing in 1968, David Lilienthal had these words concerning the Mekong Project:

The Mekong River is the most important single economic and symbolic factor in the long-term development of Vietnam, and of Southeast Asia as part of that development. I have found that so far there has not been a practical overall look at the river, to get some order of priorities. The UN Mekong Committee has been working out there in Bangkok for ten years and has spent $115,000,000—mostly on a whole series of investigations and surveys. . . . A quick, crisp look at the whole river system hasn't been done. What has been going on more nearly resembles the old Rivers and Harbors pork barrel approach, a tributary dam for each of the Southeast Asian countries, to keep each one happy.[61]

What was taking place was a concentration of all efforts on the military aspect of U.S. involvement in the war. There were aggressive, large-scale campaigns of publicity on television and radio to reassure the American public regarding military developments.[62] Thus, in November 1967, General William C. Westmoreland predicted that the Communist forces in Vietnam would be diminished to the point where there could be a partial withdrawal of American troops: "With 1968," he affirmed, "a new phase is now starting. We have reached an important point when the end begins to come into view."[63] Then, as if to prove him wrong, the Tet Offensive of 1968 exploded, dramatically changing the course of the conflict.

Launched in late January and early February, the Tet Offensive targeted cities, particularly Sai-gon and Hue, drawing American and ARVN forces to urban centers and destroying the meager results of the latter's pacification campaigns in the rural areas.[64] In the United States, the intensity, scope, and impact of the offensive coming after the optimistic statements of late 1967 and early 1968 led to a drastic drop in President Johnson's credibility rating in the public opinion polls. It forced American policy makers to fundamentally revise their view of the war. Generals Westmoreland and Earle G. Wheeler estimated that, in addition to the 500,000 U.S. soldiers already in the field, the United States needed 206,000 troops to bolster "strategic reserves." Finally, it was decided that 10,500 more soldiers would be sent to Vietnam and that a complete re-evaluation of the American military policy would be necessary. American policy makers began to realize that the end of the war was nowhere in sight, and the prospects for an American victory were, to say the least, hardly promising. Increasing attention began to be paid to the question of disengagement—the search for an "honorable" means to extricate the United States from the quagmire. Clark Clifford, who had replaced Robert McNamara (who went on to become president of the World Bank) at the head of the Defense Department in January 1968, chaired a task force in charge of presenting to the president answers to several questions: Should the United States plan to engage in continued war or seek a negotiated peace? Should U.S. forces be increased or maintained at an acceptable minimum? As a result of this consultation, Johnson announced in a televised speech on March 31, 1968:

Tonight, I renew the offer I made last August—to stop the bombardment of North Vietnam. We ask that talks begin promptly, that they be serious talks on the substance of peace. . . . Tonight I have ordered our aircraft and our naval vessels to make no attacks on

North Vietnam, except in the area north of the demilitarized zone where the continuing enemy build-up directly threatens allied forward positions and where the movements of their troops and supplies are clearly related to that threat. . . . Our presence there has always rested on this basic belief: the main burden of preserving their freedom must be carried out by them—by the South Vietnamese themselves. [65]

It was decided that the burden of the war from now on would be shouldered by the Vietnamese allies. Thus began the "Vietnamization" of the war, a term that would not enter official discourse until introduced by Secretary of Defense Melvin Laird, during the Nixon administration. On June 19, President Thieu decreed general conscription and stated that the R.V.N. intended to assume full responsibility in the war. On October 31, Johnson announced that the United States would cease all air, sea, and artillery attacks on the D.R.V. starting on November 1, 1968. Meanwhile, on May 13, 1968, the long and drawn-out official negotiations between the D.R.V. and the United States had begun, negotiations that were to be punctuated with the renewal of bombings, with ruptures, and even secret parallel discussions.

The administration's decision for a progressive military disengagement in Vietnam had its corollary in terms of economic aid. During the Johnson administration's main phase, that is, during 1964–1965, economic aid was essentially bilateral from the American donor to the lower Mekong basin recipients. Like its military counterpart, American economic aid was massive and had high visibility because of the presence of American aid experts in the beneficiary countries. Projects that had been selected received much publicity, were dictated by political exigencies of the particular moment, and were conceived and controlled (mostly) by Washington through AID. These projects suffered therefore from the fluctuations of American foreign policy and were often resented by the beneficiary countries as attempts to interfere in their domestic affairs.

However, during the Johnson administration's last years, when it began to transfer military responsibility to its main Indochinese allies, it also decided that American participation in development projects would be less direct and visible. In the future, a multilateral approach through international aid organizations would be preferred. Henceforth, the beneficiary countries would have to take the initiative and invest more heavily in projects that concerned them. They would be encouraged to increase their cooperation with neighboring countries. The Mekong Project, or rather American interest in the project, followed the same evolution. The United States wished that other countries besides itself and other organizations besides AID take up the burden of financing studies on the Mekong River. Among these organizations, the Asian Development Bank (ADB) was foremost. Secretary of the Treasury Henry H. Fowler, during a conversation with the ADB's chairman, Takeshi Watanabe, expressed Washington's desire that the Mekong Project become the central element in the bank's program. Given the American refusal to underwrite the R.V.N. permanently, and given the fact that the Mekong River was a regional concern, it was argued that this should be the bank's priority as a regional and international organization. [66]

This reorientation was reflected in speeches given by President Johnson, who had always demonstrated a particular fascination for this project. Johnson referred to it again during the last months of his presidency as an alternative to the war, the future solution that was awaiting the D.R.V. if only it would agree to negotiate. For instance, in his speech of March 31, 1968, when he announced the partial halt of bombing and his decision not to seek re-election, Johnson returned to his proposal concerning the Mekong Project:

At Johns Hopkins University, about three years ago, I announced that the United States would take part in the great work of developing Southeast Asia, including the Mekong Valley, for all the people of that region. Our determination to help build a better land . . . for men on both sides of the present conflict . . . has not diminished in the least. . . . So, I repeat on behalf of the United States again tonight what I said at Johns Hopkins that North Vietnam could take its place in this common effort just as soon as peace comes.[67]

In his meetings with regional allies—leaders of nations that had participated in the war through the sending of troops to the R.V.N.—Johnson never ceased to stress the paramount importance of the project. Thus, Thai Prime Minister Thanom Kittikachorn's official visit to the United States in May 1968 was the occasion for President Johnson to emphasize how important the project was for regional cooperation and the development of regionalism:

Referring to his speech at Johns Hopkins in April 1965, the President cited our support for Southeast Asian regional development as clear evidence of the United States' continuing concern for and commitment to the nations of this region. In particular, the Prime Minister reported to the President discussions held in New York with a US team headed by Mr. Eugene R. Black concerning the favorable outlook for the Pa Mong dam on the mainstream of the Mekong River. The President and the Prime Minister agreed on the importance of this project and the desirability of accelerating present project feasibility studies under the Mekong Committee.[68]

On another occasion, during President Johnson's visit to the Korean consulate in Honolulu in April 1968, he restated the importance of regionalism and cooperation among allies to American strategy in Southeast Asia:

We wish to see Asia—like Europe—take an increasing responsibility for shaping its own destiny. And we intend and we mean to help it do so. We look—eagerly, even impatiently—to the day when the real battle of Asia can be joined with all of our resources: . . . to exploit to the hilt the fantastic possibilities for developing the Mekong Valley, and all the other great conservation works of this continent. . . . And in their benefits and in their development all the nations of Southeast Asia should participate—not just our present allies—but North Vietnam and all human beings in that great region who long for freedom and dignity and liberty.[69]

The Johnson period profoundly shaped the Mekong Project. And, to a certain extent, the project left its imprint by contributing, along with projects such as the Indus scheme, to an era dedicated, at least rhetorically, to the theme of "Water for Peace." War and economic development were the two themes and facets of the Johnson policy in Southeast Asia, an ambivalent policy that, seeking to reverse the negative view of the war and to erase the image of the United States as bearer of death and destruction, focused its effort and economic power on development projects. These projects were tremendous in scale; indeed, it seems that, to the Johnson administration, the larger and more grandiose the project, the stronger its impact on public opinion, on pressure groups, and on political blocs.

The Mekong Project benefited from this calculation of American policy. Important tributary projects, in particular, that of the Nam Ngum, which was the first Mekong development scheme to call on international cooperation, came to fruition thanks to American support. These projects opened the way to what was believed to be the most important phase in the whole scheme of integrated development of the river and its resources. In the aftermath of Johnson's promises, the riparian countries even came to believe that the time of dam construction had come for projects on the mainstream: Pa Mong, Sambor, Stung Treng, and Tonle Sap. However, the evolution of the Mekong Project was fraught with one fundamental weakness: its dependence on and close correlation with politics. This weakness was fundamental, because, within the context of a long and costly military conflict, the aid policy conducted by the United States was necessarily short-term. Only short-term and *ad hoc* solutions were considered, even if, as was often the case, they were incompatible with economic development projects that required a long-term vision and continuity in terms of goals, research, financing, and construction.

Consequently, as the war deepened, the interest manifested by the United States in the Mekong Project began to shift when the project did not at once bear fruit. American interest took different forms and was channeled to other projects such as the postwar economic development of the Mekong delta that was hoped to have more direct bearing on the evolution of the war in Vietnam. But in the last instance also, as we shall see, the imperatives of the war turned official American attention away from a development project lacking in immediate relevance to the military situation. Yet, at the end of the Johnson period, the Mekong enterprise had acquired a sum of experience that should have allowed it to progress were it not for this dependence on the U.S. presence. The Johnson administration was succeeded by another that would bear the mark of an entirely different personality, that of President Richard M. Nixon, and the application to Asia of his own doctrine—a doctrine and a policy in which the Mekong Project would still find its place, albeit a much diminished one.

FROM JOHNSON TO NIXON

In the 1970s, under the pressure of a public that had become wary of the war and of the budgetary deficit, in the battle that pitted the legislative against the executive branch, Congress acted to put an end to the massive American troop presence in Southeast Asia.[70] It was determined to reduce the budget allocated to military and economic aid spending to countries of Indochina, to restrict the executive war power, and end all U.S. armed intervention in Indochina. Consequently, numerous bills to that effect were made into legislation, including a ban on the introduction of American ground combat troops in Laos and Thailand (PL 91-171, December 1969, the first Cooper-Church Amendment) and in Cambodia (PL 91-652, January 1971, the second Cooper-Church Amendment), and repeal of the Tonkin Gulf Resolution (PL 91-672, January 1971).[71] By passing further bills in January and December 1971 (PL 91-668 and 92-204) and again in October 1972 (PL 92-570), Congress reiterated its refusal to grant funds for the financing of U.S. ground troops in Laos and Thailand. Defense Secretary Melvin Laird emphasized the practical consequences of such budgetary measures in a memorandum for the president after his inspection trip in Vietnam in February 1970: "The major constraint on US involvement was now economic, . . . the actual and prospective diminished US funds available for national security are consistently narrowing our operational latitude in Southeast Asia [and] . . . the key factor, if we are to (a) operate within the resources available and (b) sustain the support of the American people, is to continue shifting the burden of military combat to the South Vietnamese."[72]

The Nixon Doctrine was a cost-conscious policy that rendered possible the preservation of American hegemony while decreasing expenses in terms of dollars and American lives thanks to "Asian regionalism," "Vietnamization," and progressive partial transfer of military and economic responsibility to regional allies. Asian regionalism would allow the great powers to avoid direct confrontation with each other thanks to regional defense agreements through which the signatory nations would attempt to contain aggression by their own means. The United States would play "a low-profile role" while supporting its partners and allies. There was an economic corollary to this aspect.

In September 1969, Nixon commissioned the Task Force on International Development, headed by the president of the Bank of America, Rudolph A. Peterson, to formulate the new directions for American economic assistance. The conclusions of the Peterson Report, which concurred with the main lines of the Nixon Doctrine, were adopted almost totally. The report argued that given the changed international context, the United States could not continue to take center stage as in the 1960s or persist in believing that, thanks to economic aid, it could obtain "short-term foreign policy gains from . . . participation in international development. Neither can it assume that development will necessarily bring political stability" to recipient countries.[73] From now on, the United States must adopt a less visible stance and reformulate its policy in such a way that the developing countries must be the ones to establish "their own priorities in receiving assistance in relation to the efforts they are making on their own behalf."[74] The Peterson Report underlined the fact that "a predominantly bilateral US program is no longer politically tenable in our relations with many developing countries."[75]

In its stead, multilateral aid should take center stage within the framework of international development organizations and financial institutions. The reorientation from bilateral to multilateral was advantageous to American interests, since it called on the participation and contribution of other industrialized countries in development projects that could be of strategic, political, or economic benefit to the United States. Naturally, the Peterson Commission's recommendations of emphasis on multilateral aid and international lending institutions were diversely received by members of Congress. Senator J. William Fulbright, chairman of the Senate Foreign Relations Committee, as well as Senator Jacob K. Javits, commented favorably on it, finding it to be a timely solution to the perceived failure of bilateral aid. On the other hand, Congressman Otto E. Passman, chairman of the powerful House Appropriations Subcommittee, which yearly examines the foreign aid budget, was adamantly opposed to it, stating that "with a bilateral aid program, we can look at it and interrogate it and contain it. Imagine what would happen if we turned these vast sums over to an international organization where we would have no right to make a detailed inquiry."[76] Concurrently, it could help American capital and entrepreneurial interests to establish themselves in developing regions while minimizing an otherwise blatant American military presence. This shifting of economic aid from bilateral to multilateral avenues and a less visible role for the United States were manifested in different fund-channeling economic assistance programs under the Nixon administration, which were critical components of the Nixon Doctrine for Asia.

Nixon's views of Asia and the war in Indochina coalesced during his tour of the region in 1953 as Eisenhower's vice-president, after which he made a radio and television address, "Meeting the People of Asia."[77] In this address, he explained his opinion concerning the Indochinese conflict—remarkably unchanged more than a decade later—according to which, within the framework of the domino theory, this was essentially a war for all of Asia: "If Indochina falls, Thailand is put in an almost impossible position. The same is true of Malaya with its rubber and tin. The same is true of Indonesia. If this whole part of Southeast Asia goes under Communist domination or Communist influence, Japan, who trades and must trade with this area in order to exist, must inevitably be oriented toward the Communist regime."[78] In the years that followed, Nixon had the opportunity to revisit Asia, and his discussions with Asian leaders seemed to have solidified his earlier convictions concerning the region and the threat of communism. What came to be known later on as the Nixon Doctrine for Asia was essentially formulated in an article published in *Foreign Affairs*, October 1967, entitled "Asia after Vietnam," in which he extolled Asian regionalism:

The developing coherence of Asian regional thinking is reflected in a disposition to consider problems and loyalties in regional terms, and to evolve regional approaches to development needs and to the evolution of a new world order . . . a recognition that Asia can become a counterbalance to the West, and an increasing disposition to seek Asian solutions to Asian problems through cooperative action.[79]

When Nixon became president, his views concerning Asian regionalism remained constant. His plan for Asia was officially presented during a press conference in Guam in July 1969 and was elaborated on and refined in the President's Annual Reports to Congress on U.S. Foreign Policy for the 1970s.[80] For instance, in his Second Annual Report to the Congress on U.S. Foreign Policy, presented on February 25, 1971, President Nixon stated, "Asian regionalism has an essential role to play in the future structure of Asia. It is already a source of growing strength to the individual Asian nations. Through joint action, their potential influence on the future of the region far exceeds that which they can exert acting individually."[81]

The Johnson and Nixon Doctrines were both defined by the imperatives of "containment" of communism, of "protection" of Asian countries against this threat by the signing of treaties between the United States and the nations of the region and the building-up of their armed forces.[82] However, whereas the Johnson Doctrine largely understood Asia's defense as necessarily leading to a massive build-up of American troops and direct intervention, costly in American lives and dollars, Nixon advocated Asia's defense to be undertaken by Asians and underwritten by the nations of the region.[83]

In contrast to Johnson, who used American military power directly in the Vietnam War, Nixon argued for the "Vietnamization" of the conflict and made the withdrawal of U.S. troops his public message. Although Nixon did not hesitate to strike militarily at Communist forces whenever he deemed it necessary (for instance, resumed bombing of the D.R.V. and mining of its harbors), his administration, as promised, had, by May 1971, "brought home more than 265,000 Americans, almost half of the troops in Vietnam."[84] The U.S. troop withdrawal policy was also applied to other countries of Southeast Asia, thus ending the era of massive U.S. presence in this part of the world.

In terms of ideology, the Nixon Doctrine for Asia did not differ greatly from that of Johnson.[85] Both emphasized the "greatness" of the United States and its role in Asia, the importance of the region in the global American strategy and the necessity of maintaining it in its sphere of influence. From the economic point of view, both doctrines stressed the importance of regionalism, regional agreements, and regional cooperation between and among countries of the region. Under the Johnson administration, AID thus defined the contribution of regional projects in the following terms: "These regional projects are more than just desirable activities which will bring some physical results in the form of more food, better health, and more educated people. Effective regional projects and institutions can build a sense of mutual commitment among the countries of Southeast Asia . . . [and] out of this can come a new era, after the war in Vietnam, which offers a prospect of both accelerated development and a stronger political basis for peace in this area."[86]

The emphasis given by the Nixon Doctrine to regionalism was made in the hope that the creation of common institutions and the multiplication of exchanges between neighboring countries or of the same region could foster a mutual entente, a communality of spirit that, if "correctly" channeled, could become a political force that would obstruct communism. [87] In the context of the lower Mekong basin and of the omnipresent Vietnam War, regionalism represented for Washington a possibility—though fragile—to re-establish equilibrium, to attenuate age-old antagonisms, and to provide an alternative to the "Communist-leaning" nationalism of countries such as Laos, Cambodia, and Vietnam: "A central purpose of the new partnership we are building with Asian states is to nurture a growing sense of regional identity and self-confidence. Without it, a vital impetus for cooperation would be lost; . . . [by] working together, however, smaller powers can gain the influence needed to mold their own futures, while their efforts provide a natural focus for assistance and cooperation from others."[88]

The two doctrines conceived of American economic aid as an extension of U.S. foreign policy and used it as an instrument to reinforce regionalism. They differed only in the form they took. Under the Johnson administration, economic aid had a greater visibility, a more direct and bilateral approach; under Nixon, as a result of Congress's tightening control, American economic aid assumed less visibility and an indirect, multilateral approach.[89] The Johnson Doctrine called upon a massive American financial participation in regional projects of prestige where the American presence dominated the very secondary cooperation between and among countries of the region. Nixon's Asian regionalism, in particular concerning the four countries of the lower Mekong basin, emphasized regional development projects that featured internation cooperation with a lower U.S. profile and participation. Hence, the Mekong Project, being central to all four countries of the peninsula, was to prove useful to the Nixon administration and its rhetoric—useful by justifying continued, though diminished, funding to the Mekong Project and the Mekong Committee.[90]

The Johnson administration understood American economic aid to developing countries of Southeast Asia as direct, bilateral financing of large projects in which the United States assumed the greatest share of the cost but also held a large percentage of invested capital and, in consequence, control of projects. According to the Nixon Doctrine's formulation, the economic aid burden should be divided between the industrialized countries in such a way as to reduce American spending. Hence, American economic assistance under Nixon was mostly multilateral through an increased American participation in multilateral development lending organizations such as the World Bank or through regional development banks such as the ADB. Under the Nixon administration, the latter occupied an influential position in Asia and more actively involved itself in the Mekong Project.

THE MEKONG PROJECT DURING THE NIXON ERA

The New Rationale for the Mekong Project

In 1969, Johnson's former special adviser for the economic and social development of Southeast Asia, Eugene R. Black, published a work entitled *Alterna-*

tive in Southeast Asia in which he suggested peaceful solutions to restore regional equilibrium and to fill the vacuum left by the American withdrawal from
Southeast Asia. These included, for instance, regional cooperation and a stronger
role for Japan and the ADB, precisely aspects that were to define the Nixon Doctrine for Asia.[91] According to Black, the Mekong Project appeared to be the solution that American diplomacy must consider vis-à-vis the four riparian countries if it were to replace a destructive military presence with a constructive civilian one. Black cited the examples of such "Great Rivers for Peace" as the Zam-
bezi between Zambia and Zimbabwe, with its great Kariba Dam, and the Indus
between Pakistan and India, with the Mangla Dam, rivers that flow or that form a
boundary between hostile nations. The construction and operation of dams between antagonistic nations seemed to supersede the surrounding hostility, providing a threshold before which wars and rivalries cease. These two projects, in
which the World Bank had participated (as well as the Aswan Dam in Egypt,
from which the United States had withdrawn, to be replaced by the Soviet Union), are, according to Black, examples of "investments for Peace." Although
their existence did not constitute a sufficient deterrent to the war that exploded
between Egypt and Israel, between Zambia and Rhodesia, and between India and
Pakistan and did not lead to any peace negotiations, such a "Rivers for Peace
project," Black asserted, "does inhibit extreme violence."[92] Their presence constituted one of the rare common grounds that constrained the parties from wreaking total havoc.

Thus, according to Black, "those nations interested in stability and security in
Southeast Asia now have in the lower Mekong basin another opportunity to
make a river work for peace."[93] If international resources and goodwill were to
be invested in this project through the construction of dams, irrigation networks,
and ancillary projects, then violence and warfare could be neutralized in this
dangerous corner of the world. Thus it was imperative

to reconcile with the short-term needs and demands of the riparian countries the long-
range interest that the rest of the world has in restoring peace and stability in this area.
Mekong development offers the opportunity to protect this interest by building inhibi-
tions in the form of development projects among fragmented countries that are likely to
find themselves beset with turmoil and threats for some to time to come. Mekong development is an invitation to North Vietnam to join in a vast program of regional cooperation. It is just the sort of commitment needed to counteract the ill-effects of the Vietnam war.[94]

If the United States were to make the Mekong development the heart of its
diplomacy in Southeast Asia, it would engender hope and trust that would benefit the riparian peoples as well as the United States. By working with and through
regional and international organizations, it could replace "the costly, dangerous,
and highly uncertain business of American involvement in counterinsurgent warfare with American involvement in an internationally sponsored Mekong development program."[95] The United States could also use its influence to convince
other governments, for example, Japan, to take a larger share in this development

effort and thus avoid accusations of seeking hegemony. Ultimately, Black concluded, as the cases of the Kariba and of the Indus Dams demonstrated, the decision to go ahead and build is essentially a political decision.

The various elements outlined by Black in *Alternative in Southeast Asia* were echoed in President Nixon's public speeches, especially to the Congress. Throughout his reports to Congress, Nixon used the Mekong theme formerly advanced by Johnson to proffer the olive branch to the D.R.V. In 1970, for instance, Nixon declared that "when the war in Vietnam is ended, reconstruction can be carried out in a regional context. We look forward to continued cooperation with a regional effort to harness the power of the Mekong River."[96] The following year, he developed that theme in his annual presentation of U.S. foreign policy to Congress:

Political differences notwithstanding, the effort continues to develop within a regional framework, Southeast Asia's single major resource—the Lower Mekong Basin. This project has an almost immeasurable potential for the well-being of the countries of the Basin: Thailand, Laos, Cambodia, and Vietnam. Along with a large number of other non-Asian states, we continue to participate actively in this massive scheme to harness the hydro-electric, irrigation, and transportation potential of one of Asia's greatest rivers. Its promise for transforming the life of the area is at least equal to the impact of TVA in our own country.[97]

The Mekong Project in the 1970s

The Nixon administration's strategy of keeping "alive" the Mekong theme (despite Nixon's expressed skepticism concerning the efficacy of aid in stemming communism) was reflected in the U.S. aid policy toward the Mekong Project as it evolved in the 1970s. In one of AID's yearly presentations of its budget to Congress, the goals of American assistance to the regional projects were explained in the following manner: "A.I.D. support for regional programs in Southeast Asia is designed to improve the prospects for peace and stability by assisting in development activities involving several countries working together on common problems. Regional programs and projects not only provide social and economic benefits to the people of the area but also encourage regional cooperation, understanding, and interdependence."[98]

While contributing to the reinforcement of Southeast Asia as a region, the support of regionalism allowed for cost reductions and for technical and financial resource sharing with other donors. Consequently, the United States continued to participate in the Mekong Project at two levels: (1) that of regional activities in coordination with the Mekong Committee, with the United Nations Development Program (UNDP) and other UN-related organizations, and with the World Bank and the ADB, and (2) on a country-by-country basis for Mekong-related projects (again with the ADB's cooperation).

Starting in 1973, in order to escape Congress's scrutiny and budgetary cuts, the U.S. military and economic aid that was granted previously to Indochinese countries for the war effort was now disbursed under the Indochina Postwar Reconstruction Program under various headings. For example, the Commodity Import Program, which had allowed the R.V.N., Royal Lao, and Khmer Republic to maintain high levels of governmental spending, was continued under a new program called Food Aid; military budgets were placed under the rubric of Humanitarian Aid to Refugees. Within the Postwar Reconstruction Program, regional development proposals took center stage, with the Mekong Project being touted as "the most important natural resource of Southeast Asia with the potential for becoming one of the largest producers of food and energy in the world."[99] Concurrently, during the 1970s, in the field of development, most economic assistance programs were oriented toward helping developing countries achieve food self-sufficiency along with economic growth. Agriculture was given priority with the introduction of innovative techniques for cultivation and new high-yield varieties. These new techniques required local experimentation to find the varieties that would be most efficient and most attractive to farmers. Experimental farms and pioneer projects thus sprang up everywhere throughout the predominantly agricultural countries of Southeast Asia; in particular, the launching of miracle-rice strains (for instance, IR-8 or TN-20 and TN-5) by the International Rice Research Institute in Los Banos, the Philippines, fundamentally changed traditional methods of cultivation.

The Mekong Project followed the same orientation, particularly since the increasing precariousness in the lower Mekong basin had prevented the integrated development of tributary projects, let alone the mainstream ones. Emphasis was placed on the Agricultural Pioneer Projects Program, which seemed to be the ideal provisional solution for the riparian nations while they prepared for the return of peace. The American contribution was second (US$ 500,000) to that of the UN (US$ 1 million) for a feasibility study fund for Mekong pioneer projects, a fund to which other industrialized countries were encouraged to contribute. American experts were of the opinion that "this project will be big enough to make a real impact on agricultural technology throughout the basin, with particular attention given to the control of water."[100]

However, once the feasibility studies were carried out and the time came to move on to the next stage of implementation, the World Bank, which had suggested the establishment of another fund of US$ 20 million for the construction and operation of the first ten pioneer projects, encountered scant enthusiasm from aid donors, who were not eager to invest in schemes in countries on the brink of total devastation. The proposal and the multilateral approach had to be forsaken in favor of the bilateral, donor-by-donor policy for each of the pioneer projects. The Nixon administration in its presentation to Congress for the fiscal year of 1975, for instance, claimed that it intended to devote a sum of $1.7 million to $2 million to the "construction, repair, and agricultural experimentation" of pioneer projects in the R.V.N. (Go-cong), Laos (Tha Ngone and Casier Sud), and the Northeast of Thailand (Nong Wai).[101]

At the level of the Mekong Committee, the United States contributed to the financing of several Mekong-related projects, such as construction on the Mekong of port and cargo handling installations in Laos and in Thailand, delta soils management and flood control studies, and fishery projects in the R.V.N. While financing some of the Mekong Committee's projects, the United States also continued to fund tributary projects in each country within a bilateral framework. In response to the question about whether the United States would derive more benefit from financing small-scale, non-Communist regional projects rather than spending enormous sums in a particular country, for example, Thailand, an AID representative explained to the House of Representatives Committee on Appropriations:

It is difficult to compare the return from a dollar spent supporting Thai efforts to deal with a Communist insurgency and a dollar spent toward the international development of the Mekong River Basin. We help the Thais because it is important to us to see an end to the insurgency as quickly as possible. On the other hand, we have funded extensive Mekong studies so that the Mekong basin can be developed. In effect, each aid program in East Asia has a specific objective and we are allocating the available funds according to the priorities as we see them.[102]

But a comparison between the Nixon administration's pronouncements and the reality of its actions during the Second Indochina War shows that its Mekong strategy, like that of the Johnson administration, was dictated by the evolution of the politico-military situation in the region. Its Mekong priorities focused on Laos and to a smaller measure on the R.V.N., followed by Cambodia and Thailand, where the United States had its strategic bases. Grants or funds provided by the United States to Mekong tributary projects went mainly to Laos (the Nam Ngum) or to Laos-related (the Pa Mong) studies. For the R.V.N., a U.S. loan of US$ 4.5 million was in the works to increase the production capacity of the Drayling hydropower station (from 0.5 megawatts to 12 megawatts), located on the Upper Sre-Pok, a Mekong tributary in the central highlands. Its increased production was meant to supply the power needs of the central highlands and eventually those of Cambodia. But the instability of the region as well as the worsening of the war prevented the realization of the project.[103]

In Laos, the Johnson administration had pledged, for the Nam Ngum Phase I (under the World Bank's responsibility) to finance half of the costs, which had amounted by then to US$ 24.150 million. For the 1966 fiscal year, American contributions of US$ 12.065 million came from the Emergency Fund for Southeast Asia. But when the decision was made to increase the Nam Ngum hydroelectric capacity from twenty to thirty megawatts, the actual costs (US$ 31.130 million) far exceeded the estimations; the United States then agreed to provide a supplemental contribution of US$ 3.5 million of which US$ 2.705 million (fiscal year 1969) was provided by the same Emergency Fund. The remaining sum of US$ 795,000 was allotted from the Supporting Assistance Funds generally used for countries that the United States sought to maintain politically and economically, in situations where American interests considered vital were threatened. This form of aid was used for only three countries: Laos, Thailand, and the R.V.N.

It was only with American support that Nam Ngum Phase I was able to quickly gather the necessary funds, which came in the form of grants, a considerable relief for Laos, given its almost nonexistent foreign currency reserve. Later, when a World Bank feasibility study carried out in 1973 concluded in favor of Nam Ngum Phase II (construction of two supplementary forty megawatts generators and an additional 115-kilovolt transmission line from the dam to Vientiane and to Nongkhai), the U.S. government offered to provide part of the financing with a $5 million loan to Electricité Générale du Laos.[104] Equally, following American advice, the Royal Lao government asked the ADB to take up the responsibilities of promoter, coordinator, and fund administrator previously assumed by the World Bank, a request to which the bank acceded. In June 1974, the Second Nam Ngum Development Fund was formally established. Again, the backing provided by the United States for the Nam Ngum Phase II project made it possible to attract foreign donors. Nine countries pledged to cover the costs estimated at $24 million to $25 million in the form of either loans or grants.[105]

One may wonder about the reasons behind the U.S. decision to finance the construction of the Nam Ngum Dam by providing more than half of the advanced capital. Successive American administrations had always expressed geostrategic concerns for Laos. Under the Nixon administration, perceptions of Laos had not greatly changed, and the domino theory was still relevant. From a general point of view, the administration believed that if Laos were to fall to the Pathet Lao and "North Vietnamese," it would mean the fall not only of Cambodia and the R.V.N. but, more seriously, of Thailand, bastion of anticommunism and faithful ally of the West. Thailand, threatened in the Northeast by insurrections, might succumb to the "Communist onslaught." The Northeast of Thailand, where the Thai Communist Party was active, is linked to the Vientiane Plain by the Mekong River, and the Mekong banks were deemed a strategic region that should be strengthened by a tight governmental control and an increased economic and military assistance. During the war, U.S. AID's rural development projects for Thailand were for the most part to be found in the Northeast.[106] While American bombings as well as the fighting in the Plain of Jars between the Pathet Lao and the Royal Lao Army accelerated, the United States continued its financing of the Nam Ngum project and of studies on the colossal Pa Mong mainstream project, both located in the same strategic Mekong valley.[107] U.S. aid officials had readily acknowledged that the "American aid program in Laos was an appendage to a war and not something to be considered primarily development-oriented."[108] Joel Halpern, an anthropologist specializing in Laos, in one of his interviews of Mekong-related officials and nonofficials, mentioned a Thai minister's remark that the Pa Mong Project "should proceed at top speed, for it would raise the standard of living of the poor peasants in the Thai Northeast and make them more resistant to Communist appeals."[109]

In December 1971, the King of Laos, Savang Vatthana, inaugurated the completion of Phase I of the Nam Ngum project. For the first time, the Royal Lao government could boast of a concrete economic achievement to counterbalance a record marked by years of corruption, wasteful spending of aid money, and indifference toward the people's plight during the war. The Nam Ngum Dam was not only one of the government's few accomplishments in terms of rural development but also one of its main foreign currency earners because of the sale of electricity to Thailand.[110] An agreement stipulating the sale to Thailand of electricity produced by the Nam Ngum was also concluded, according to which Laos was to provide the dam-generated electricity to Thailand for a ten-year period at the rate of US$ 0.45/kilowatt-hour. It was stipulated that its production would be transmitted by a 115 kilovolt power line from the Nam Ngum Dam, via Vientiane to Udorn Thani in Thailand, and on to the Nam Pong Dam in the Thai province of Ubol Rattana.

Udorn Thani was the site of the Royal Thai Air Force base, where the following installations were based: the 7/13 U.S. Air Force headquarters, "the most important operational military nerve center in Thailand"; the CIA local station that trained and sent Thai and Lao "irregulars" into Laos; the 56th Special Operations Wing that trained Royal Lao Air Force pilots; and Air America and Continental Air, the two American airlines that flew military and civilian supplies into Laos.[111] The existence in the Northeast of Thailand of this base (along with a number of large U.S. bases at Ubol, Korat, and Takhli), a major U.S. operational headquarters for the war in Indochina with its enormous power consumption, could partially explain the American willingness to finance the construction of a hydroelectric power station of sufficient capacity and its subsequent enlargement.[112] Its construction took barely five years, from 1966 to 1971, a remarkably short lapse of time given the fact that the Nam Ngum Dam was located in an insecure region controlled by the Pathet Lao. As for the latter, although it had attacked the U.S. AID office and the military barracks, it had left intact and unharmed both the dam and the Japanese, Canadians, and other workers, who were relatively free to move about. The Pathet Lao did influence a number of neighboring villagers, who refused to be resettled by the government and went over to the Pathet Lao instead.[113]

As for the Mekong Committee, a major undertaking came to fruition in 1971: the Indicative Basin Plan (1970–2000).[114] The 600-page document was a massive plan that analyzed water and water-related resources development in a comprehensive fashion. Based on data collected over more than a decade, the plan estimated that by 2000 the energy demand in the lower Mekong basin would reach 22,772 megawatts in peaking capacity; the irrigated area essential for agricultural production was evaluated to be 1,868,000 hectares (double cropping).[115] Flood control, salt-water intrusion prevention, and other ancillary activities were also analyzed. As the needs were predicted to increase, and given the fact that the riparian economies were among the poorest and the least developed (with the partial exception of Thailand) in the world, the plan recommended the comprehensive multipurpose development of the Mekong River. To that end, it suggested sixteen possible mainstream dams, a delta development project, and 180 tributary projects in the four member countries; it also analyzed their cumulative and reciprocal impact over a thirty-year period. The projects were divided into two groups: The short-range (1971–1980) group comprised single and multipurpose tributary projects focusing on hydropower, flood control, and pioneer agricultural stations that each nation could implement independently from the others and which should not have any detrimental effect on the mainstream.[116] The second group involved a number of projects that, because of the enormous scale of their construction and possible far-ranging repercussions, were to be implemented over a longer period (1981–2000) with costs estimated in the billions of dollars. It included fifteen mainstream multipurpose projects and one flood-control project on the Tonle Sap (see Map 4.1). In addition to these sixteen mainstream projects that could be permuted in different combinations (the central one included a cascade of seven mainstream dams, of which the Pa Mong was key), there was also a group of ten minor hydropower projects in the Vietnamese central highlands to provide Cambodia and Vietnam with power during 1980–1985.[117] The plan emphasized the priority of Pa Mong, Stung Treng, Sambor, and the delta development projects. Outside of these projects, the plan saw the need for the undertaking of a number of ancillary activities such as social policy, domestic water supply, and industrial, mineral, and agricultural development.

From the point of view of Washington's political analysts, the continuation of the Mekong Project could represent for nations that had a long, antagonistic history the possibility to develop, if only briefly, relationships of cooperation and entente. Such a development might allow the riparians to put behind them the burdens of war and hatred, develop a better cooperation, and generate a regionalism that would overcome overheated nationalisms. However, the stark realities of the war overshadowed these hopes, and under the Nixon administration, as under its predecessor, the Mekong Project was destined to serve as bait and pawn during negotiations with the D.R.V.

Postwar Reconstruction: The Promise and the Project

The question of economic aid weighed heavily during the negotiations leading to the signing of the Paris Agreement, which brought an end to the U.S. involvement in the Vietnam War. The Nixon administration adopted Johnson's April 1965 Baltimore approach to the Indochina War and to the peace negotiations, namely, the offer of aid for postwar reconstruction in exchange for the D.R.V.'s cessation of hostilities. Through his national security adviser, Henry Kissinger, one of the main architects of the Paris negotiations, Nixon, like Johnson before him, made higher and higher offers to the other side to entice it to

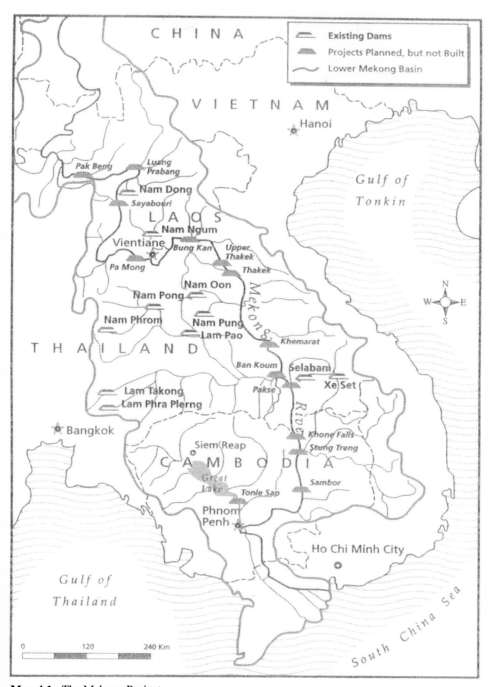

Map 4.1 The Mekong Project

come to the negotiating table and in public speeches professed his willingness to contribute to Vietnam's postwar reconstruction. On September 18, 1969, in an address to the UN General Assembly, Nixon stated that "when the war ends, the United States will stand ready to help the people of Vietnam—all of them—in their tasks of renewal and reconstruction."[118] In his First and Second Annual Report to the Congress on U.S. foreign policy in 1970 and 1971, Nixon mentioned the "Lower Mekong Basin" effort as a component of Asian regionalism and of the postwar reconstruction plan for Vietnam in which the United States would cooperate. In his Third Annual Foreign Policy Report of 1972, Nixon restated his administration's intention to include the D.R.V. in its reconstruction program for Indochina—on the condition that the D.R.V. cease all aggression: "We are prepared to undertake a massive 7½ billion dollar five-year reconstruction program in conjunction with an overall agreement, in which North Vietnam could share up to two and a half billion dollars."[119] This offer was repeated in different forms throughout the press and reaffirmed in a number of statements by members of his administration, including Secretary of State William P. Rogers, AID Administrator John A. Hannah, and Ambassador William J. Porter of the U.S. delegation to the Paris peace negotiations.

They voiced the American commitment to "a massive reconstruction program in Indochina" (Rogers), to "rehabilitation and reconstruction in Viet Nam, Laos, and Cambodia" (Hannah), and to "the rebuilding and to the healing tasks" (Porter).[120] Kissinger, in a January 26, 1972, press conference, affirmed that "there would be no reparations for North Vietnam, but there would be 'voluntary undertaking' for all of Indochina, including North Vietnam, to the extent of several billion dollars."[121] To reassure Congress and domestic public opinion, Kissinger emphasized that it was not a question of "reparations" to the D.R.V. but rather of "contributions," and that the aid offer was conditional upon the D.R.V.'s ceasing its aggression against the R.V.N. Then, as negotiations progressed, the offer became conditional upon the D.R.V.'s respecting the cease-fire in Vietnam, Laos, and Cambodia. An additional condition would soon be added: The offer had to meet congressional approval before the Nixon administration could make a commitment.

During the lengthy negotiations, the POW-MIA problem (along with other aspects) became inextricably linked to the question of U.S. aid for reconstruction/reparation.[122] According to the U.S. Senate's 1993 investigation of the POW-MIA question, the U.S. transcript of Kissinger–Le Duc Tho negotiations in September 1972 seemed to indicate that "the North Vietnamese continued to link POW/MIA provisions with a commitment for U.S. aid."[123] Both Nixon and Kissinger were well aware of the resistance and even hostility in Congress concerning the continuation of funding to the countries of Indochina, to any financing of the war, and, above all, to any postwar assistance for the "enemy." Consequently, they were careful to appease Congress, and on the eve of the signing of the Paris Peace Agreement, during an information session held by Nixon and Kissinger for the House and the Senate, both men presented the economic reconstruction assistance to the D.R.V. as "an incentive to keep the peace": "the best investment that we could make to turn them to their own problems and to provide something that they want from us in future years," while affirming that there were no secret deals (Nixon) or commitments to the other side (Kissinger).[124] In his memoirs, recalling the Paris Agreement and in particular the question of economic aid, Nixon remarks:

> There was also a provision embodying the principle of American economic aid to North Vietnam, *which I considered to be potentially the most significant part of the entire agreement* [emphasis added]. The Communists tried to claim that this money would be reparations for the war they charged we had unleashed upon them; but . . . taking money from the United States represented a collapse of Communist principle. More important, our aid would inevitably give us increasing leverage with Hanoi as the North Vietnamese people began to taste the fruits of peace for the first time in twenty-five years.[125]

During postwar congressional investigations concerning the fate of POWs-MIAs, Kissinger contended that "he repeatedly informed the D.R.V. that any reconstruction assistance would have to be approved by the U.S. Congress and could not be guaranteed by the Executive Branch acting alone."[126] Neither side agreed about the prisoners of war question, and as the 1993 Senate report aptly put it: "It was the U.S. position that the prisoners must be released whether or not aid was forthcoming. The D.R.V.'s preferred position was that aid be forthcoming whether or not prisoners were released."[127] Each side's position was the mirror image of the other.

The Paris Agreement on ending the war and restoring peace in Vietnam was signed on January 27, 1973, by Secretary of State William P. Rogers for the United States and by the minister of foreign affairs for the D.R.V., Nguyen Duy Trinh, ending in principle the war and the military, as well as the political, presence of the United States in Vietnam. It established a cease-fire and called for free elections over the entire territory. Among the clauses agreed to by the United States regarding the D.R.V., postwar economic reconstruction was clearly stipulated by Article 21 of the agreement, which also referred to the possibility that the Mekong Project would be part of the postwar economic reconstruction.

During the discussions, the American delegation suggested that the Mekong Project, with its technical experience and financial ties with the World Bank and the Asian Development Bank, could be of possible interest to the D.R.V. The World Bank, chaired at the time by former Defense Secretary Robert McNamara, could act as executive agent for the D.R.V., and through it could transit American contributions for reconstruction. The International Development Association, a World Bank affiliate specializing in "soft loans," could also be of help, as could the Asian Development Bank, which had the advantage of being "on the spot" and had contributed to numerous projects in the Indochinese countries. A proposal entitled *Postwar Mekong Development Activities of Possible Interest to Hanoi* was used by the American delegation during its discussions with its Vietnamese counterpart and was among the documents that Kissinger provided to the House of Representatives Subcommittee on Asian and Pacific Affairs during the hearings it conducted on the question of aid to the D.R.V. Projects cited as being of maximal benefit to the D.R.V. included the Nam Theun complex of tributary hydroelectric projects, which was to be situated in Laos close to the Vietnamese border. This series of projects could be quickly completed and promised to provide the D.R.V. with cheap electricity for its industrialization. The Pa Mong project, also in Laos but over which the United States had some sort of exclusivity because of the numerous advanced and sophisticated studies carried out by the Bureau of Reclamation, was also cited. With a potential production capacity of 10,200 megawatts, located some 220 kilometers from the D.R.V. at the center of the Indochinese peninsula, the colossal Pa Mong Project "could supply large blocks of power to all four Indochina states as well as Thailand."[128] These projects were presented as most likely to contribute to the D.R.V.'s economic recovery. In addition, the Mekong Committee, operative for more than a decade, had acquired a vast sum of experience in the field of hydraulics as well as "a large fund of information regarding improved agricultural practices . . . and other matters related to water resources development" that could be put to work toward that goal.[129]

The day after the signature of the Paris Agreement, that is, on January 28, 1973, in answer to Senator Mike J. Mansfield's questions, Kissinger reiterated that there were no negotiations or agreements concerning the possibility of aid to the D.R.V., promising that "before anything about this is done, Congress will be consulted."[130] Yet, Article 21 of the Paris Agreement states: "The United States anticipates that this Agreement will usher in an era of reconciliation with the Democratic Republic of Vietnam as with all the peoples of Indochina. In pursuance of its traditional policy, the United States will contribute to healing the wounds of war and to postwar reconstruction of the Democratic Republic of Viet-Nam and throughout Indochina."[131]

Despite Nixon and Kissinger's protests to the contrary and unbeknownst to Congress and the public, there had been secret promises made to the D.R.V. during the talks.[132] In the final sessions in January 1973, economic assistance for postwar reconstruction was at the center of acrimonious negotiations between the two parties. Le Duc Tho demanded that more concrete and detailed terms be added to Article 21 in a presidential letter, a demand that Kissinger knew he could not refuse if he wanted the agreement to be rapidly signed. The existence of such correspondence was long denied by the Nixon and subsequent administrations, and it was only in connection with congressional investigations of the POW-MIA matter that Nixon's letter of promise finally surfaced in May 1977. As the result of the investigation conducted by Lester L. Wolf, chairman of the House Subcommittee on Asian and Pacific Affairs, the State Department was forced to release the Nixon letter along with documents provided by Kissinger that had been used during the negotiations. The letter, dated February 1, 1973, and addressed to D.R.V. Prime Minister Pham Van Dong, states:

(1) The Government of the United States of America will contribute to postwar reconstruction in North Vietnam *without any political conditions* [emphasis added]. (2) Preliminary U.S. studies indicate that the appropriate programs for the U.S. contribution to postwar reconstruction will fall in the range of $3.25 billion of grant aid over 5 years. . . . (3) The United States will propose to the Democratic Republic of Vietnam the establishment of a United States-North Vietnamese Joint Economic Commission [JEC] within 30 days from the date of this message. (4) The function of this Commission will be to develop programs for the U.S. contribution to reconstruction of North Vietnam.[133]

An apparently later, separate addendum states that "the recommendations of the JEC mentioned in the President's note to the Prime Minister will be implemented by each member in accordance with its own constitutional provisions." A second addendum mentions other forms of aid in the range of $1 billion to $1.5 billion. Prior to his February 1973 visit to Ha-noi to discuss the concrete aspect of this reconstruction aid (as well as other issues) with Pham Van Dong, Kissinger was directed by President Nixon to use the granting of aid as leverage to obtain a cease-fire in Cambodia as well as a MIA accounting.[134] Shortly thereafter, a United States-D.R.V. joint communiqué issued on February 14, 1973, announced the formation of a Joint Economic Commission that would be responsible for developing economic relations between the D.R.V. and the United States. The commission began work on March 1, 1973, in Paris and was headed on the American side by Maurice J. Williams and on the Vietnamese side by Dang Viet Chau, the finance minister of the D.R.V.[135] The commission quickly arrived at the formulation of an "Agreement on the Principle, Functions, Organization and Working Procedures of the D.R.V.-U.S. Joint Economic Commission" that would be in charge of a five-year assistance program for the D.R.V. and financed by American contributions.[136] The text of the agreement was finalized on March 27, 1973, but remained secret. That same day, Williams sent a top secret telegram to Washington, reporting rapid progress and asking for instructions about the formal signing. However, the JEC broke off discussions early in April as D.R.V. troops and military supplies continued to move steadily down the Ho Chi Minh trail into the Mekong delta, and the Lon Nol regime was on the verge of collapse. Nixon began to threaten military retaliation against the D.R.V. Talks soon began anew between the two sides concerning the alleged breaches in the Paris Agreement.

The Nixon administration was bent on extracting from the D.R.V. information concerning the "points of entry for war materiel for the P.R.G. [Provisional Revolutionary Government]" along with the promise that it would implement a cease-fire in Cambodia, a promise that became the *sine qua non* of economic aid.[137] The demands were repeated throughout the six weeks of negotiations. Curiously, Defense Secretary Elliot L. Richardson declared in a March press conference that "he doubted that the United States had *explicitly* [emphasis added] cautioned Hanoi that these aid funds would not be forthcoming unless the North worked to produce a real cease-fire."[138] As for the Joint Economic Commission, the United States decided on April 19, 1973, to unilaterally cease all discussions, "charging that North Vietnam had violated the agreements."[139] It was only after the Tho-Kissinger Communiqué of June 13, 1973, was announced that the JEC meetings resumed. Williams "drove home that their [the D.R.V.'s] performance on Laos and Cambodia under Article 20 was essential before the work of the JEC could result in a fruitful conclusion."[140] Henceforth, the JEC's work progressed rapidly. In mid-July, a detailed proposal for the first-year plan for reconstruction aid was ready to be sent to Congress for approval.[141] The signing of the proposal was to take place on July 23. On that day, Williams sent a telegram to Secretary of State Rogers stating that in view of both the D.R.V.'s economic needs and America's political objectives, which were to provide "incentive and option for D.R.V. leadership to abandon [their] policy of war and austere war mobilization of their economy in favor of demobilization and opportunity [to] redirect economy to meeting long neglected civilian needs," he would recommend "a fairly high level of first-year assistance" to the amount of $600 million.[142] However, it became apparent that American demands for a cessation of combat and the withdrawal of foreign troops from Laos and Cambodia could not be satisfied by the D.R.V., which did not have complete control of Lao and Khmer revolutionary forces. Nixon then made good on one of his threats by announcing that the D.R.V. would not receive the promised aid—although his secret letter stated that there would not be any political conditions—since it had violated the Paris Agreement by infiltrating troops and weapons into the R.V.N., continuing combat in Laos and Cambodia, and not respecting Article 8(b).[143] In *The Illusion of Peace*, Tad Szulc argues that "there are reasons to believe that the president may have used the cease-fire problems as a handy justification for halting the economic negotiations in the knowledge that Congress would never approve help to the Communists."[144]

All discussions with the JEC were suspended on July 23, 1973, and the commission ceased to exist. A 1974 U.S. Congress Committee on Foreign Affairs survey on U.S. aid to Indochina indicated that the U.S. unwillingness to provide economic assistance to the D.R.V. had become "a factor in the refusal of the Government of North Vietnam to abide by provisions of the cease-fire in Indochina" and that it was also "a factor in the refusal of the Communists to permit the U.S. Joint Casualty Resolution Center to investigate the approximately 2,300 cases of U.S. personnel still unaccounted for throughout Indochina."[145] In the difficult months that followed the Paris Peace Agreement, the D.R.V. continued to raise the question of economic assistance, making all other issues contingent upon its delivery, for example, the functioning of the International Commission for Control and Supervision (ICCS), which was supposed to oversee the application and respect of the agreement by all parties concerned. In a letter to the ICCS chairman, the D.R.V. insisted that "when the U.S. Government is refusing to correctly implement many essential provisions of the Paris Agreement, on Vietnam, including Article 21 regarding the U.S. Government's obligation to contribute to the healing of the wounds of war in the D.R.V., the implementation of Article 18 of the Paris Agreement providing, inter-alia, for contributions to the expenditures of the I.C. will be also hampered."[146] As the author of the survey observed, the application of Article 18 was essential to an effective enforcement and monitoring of the cease-fire. Such continued insistence showed how desperate for economic assistance the D.R.V. must have been in the post–Paris Agreement years and how it was "much more important to the North Vietnamese than is generally recognized."[147]

American public opinion and the international community were ignorant of the existence of the presidential letters and of the fact that in the summer of 1973, the United States came close to concluding an economic agreement with the D.R.V. that would have contributed to the reconstruction of the war-torn country. From that point onward, the American policy concerning reconstruction aid to the D.R.V. came to a standstill. American policy acquired a hostile tone after the Communist victory in April 1975 as it rejected the D.R.V.'s demands for U.S. reparation aid made based on the then-undisclosed Nixon letter to Prime Minister Pham Van Dong of February 1973. The United States vetoed Vietnam's application for UN membership in November 1975 and initiated a trade embargo.

All hopes of diplomatic normalization between the two countries vanished in late spring 1977 as the MIA question resurfaced and the Socialist Republic of Vietnam (S.R.V.) continued to demand reparations. Congress had taken a hardened stand that was reflected in the matter of economic aid by the passing of the Foreign Assistance Appropriations Act of 1976, which stipulated that direct aid appropriations could not be used in providing "assistance to the Democratic Republic of Vietnam [*sic*], South Vietnam [*sic*], Cambodia, or Laos."[148] In 1977, the indirect aid loophole was also closed with passage of the Foreign Assistance Appropriations Act, which stipulated that no direct or indirect aid could be given to these countries. A hiatus of two decades followed during which there were no diplomatic relations between the United States and the S.R.V. It may be said in conclusion to this question that the Nixon-Kissinger promise of U.S. aid for reconstruction was at the same time pretext and stake: to demand of the D.R.V. a cease-fire in Cambodia and Laos in exchange for economic aid (while knowing full well that such aid would not be forthcoming without congressional approval, which was unlikely if not impossible); to use the D.R.V.'s cease-fire infringements as a pretext for not honoring the promises for unconditional economic aid.

The Asian Development Bank

In the 1950s and 1960s, American economic aid was essentially bilateral, organized and operated by U.S. AID. For instance, in 1968, its budget was 266 percent greater than the total U.S. contributions to multilateral lending institutions (MLIs).[149] During that time, U.S. subscription payments to the MLIs represented only 2 percent of the overall American economic aid. However, under increasing pressure from the U.S. Congress, which wanted to limit what it considered to be exorbitant aid spending, and from financial lobbies that demanded a wider American export market, as well as in conjunction with the world's economic evolution, developments in the Vietnam War, and presidential policy, the United States turned to the MLIs as one of its major aid channels. From 1968 to 1979, American subscriptions to MLIs far exceeded AID's bilateral aid budget and, by 1979, took up the largest share in the American aid budget.

On the other hand, by the 1970s, MLIs of the World Bank group had become such indispensable elements in economic planning by developing countries that the concerned governments had come to consider the U.S. attitude vis-à-vis the MLIs as an important indicator of its degree of support. Thus, while preaching greater self-reliance to its allies, the United States had to reassure them and only "a renewed U.S. commitment to multilateral development can give needed assurance to the world that the United States is not turning inward, and that it is prepared to help tangibly—that we will maintain a leading position in global affairs."[150]

The MLIs also helped safeguard U.S. economic and financial interests. During the 1960s, most MLI loans went to finance infrastructure projects (harbors, roads, electrification) in developing countries. From 1946 to 1962, more than 60 percent of the World Bank's loans went into transportation and electricity and later into industry and agriculture projects. The advantage of such a lending policy was that by building up the infrastructure, MLI-funded projects prepared the groundwork for foreign capital, in particular U.S. interests, to invest safely and profitably. Furthermore, these very low-interest, long-term soft loans were generally conditional upon the obligation of purchase of services and products from the main lending country. For instance, $1 million contributed by a lending nation to a soft-loan special fund corresponded to the value of $1 million of exports for the lender, which could thus broaden the market for its products. Secretary of the Treasury George P. Schultz, in his testimony to the House of Representatives Committee on Banking and Currency in November 1973, stated: "Our relations with developing countries are important to the United States economically and politically. The developing countries provided a $14.6 billion market in 1972 for US goods and services; . . . perhaps more important, they provide us with one-third of our raw material imports; . . . it makes good sense for us to utilize such proven vehicles such as the international development lending institutions, for aiding the growth of nations that are at the same time such important sources and markets for us."[151]

Under the Nixon administration then, along with regional anti-Communist alliances, the United States adopted a more multilateral approach to economic aid with a strong emphasis on multilateral institutions and regional development banks such as the Asian Development Bank. This regional institution in which the United States originally held 20 percent of the ordinary capital is dominated by Japan, a world economic power and loyal U.S. ally. It was through this institution that the Nixon administration, interested in promoting Indochinese regionalism, attempted to attract a large number of donor countries in the postwar reconstruction effort and in the strengthening of the economies of the Indochinese countries. Within this effort, notwithstanding budgetary constraints that were to curtail grandiose but expensive projects, and despite conditions that were more precarious than before, the ADB and the Mekong Project, closely linked in a complex process, became at the same time instruments and consequences of the Nixon policy in Southeast Asia. Both were ideal channels for the Nixon Doctrine's main tenets in Asia, which did not neglect the interests of American companies that invested in the region.

Under the Nixon administration, the ADB spearheaded its Asian regional economic policy by spreading the financial aid burden among the bank's main contributors, mostly U.S. allies such as Australia, Canada, Great Britain, the Netherlands, and Japan. Originally, the bank was foremost an institution that followed a traditional policy of loans for the financing of large-scale projects such as infrastructure construction in developing countries of Asia. In its first five years of operation (1968–1972), more than 60 percent of its hard loans were for power plant, harbor, or road construction projects. However, since a large number of Asian member nations could not meet the bank's stringent conditions because of their precarious economic situations, the ADB offered the possibility of soft loans from Special Funds.[152] For a while, Congress was hesitant about appropriating for Special Funds, one of which involved a three-year, $100 million contribution that was proposed first by Johnson and then by Nixon.

In his "Special Message to the Congress on Foreign Aid," May 28, 1969, Nixon explained that "the United States should join with other donor countries in establishing this Special Fund and strengthen the Bank so that it can better deal with Asia's current development problems and future needs."[153] This Special Fund was to be used not in the form of grants but as loans payable in dollars with concessionary repayment terms and for the procurement of American products and services. It was not until 1972 that Congress finally gave its approval, and the first appropriation of $50 million went into effect in 1974, with the second following in 1975. The $100 million with contributions from other members formed a multilateral Special Fund called the Asian Development Fund (ADF) managed by the ADB.[154] Since its inception in 1974, the ADF has been the bank's sole source of concessionary loans.[155] The House of Representatives Committee on Appropriations hearings on foreign aid helped shed some light on the use and true goals of American participation in the Asian Development Fund, and by extension in the ADB. The bank—as an instrument of stability and growth—played a vital part in U.S. foreign policy in Asia: "We are convinced that the Asian Development Bank effectively supports US interests in Asia. Through its lending programs, the Bank is contributing significantly to the economic development and well-being of many of our Asia friends and allies."[156]

As an instrument of stability, the bank helps the poorest country members reach a certain growth level through the financing of long-term programs that are essential to the country's long-term economic development but that do not have an immediate financial yield. Countries such as Laos, Cambodia, and Vietnam urgently needed capital for the financing of their infrastructure in order to develop a market economy. This kind of investment produces over the long term essential economic and social benefits, the cost of which cannot be judged according to strictly commercial criteria. Thus, the bank could be considered as helping the growth of developing countries of the region, and U.S. support to the bank could have a leverage effect of three times its actual contribution. The U.S. participation was perceived as a guarantee that could attract other donors' contributions to Asian countries that were of concern to the United States. Consequently, it was of utmost importance to Washington that the bank have at its disposal adequate resources and that it continue to do so: "The Bank will continue to operate in a manner fully compatible with U.S. interests, provided it has adequate resources at its disposal. Therefore, the need for further contributions is great and, in our opinion, crucial to the effectiveness of the Bank as an instrument for stability in the region."[157] American allies in the region such as Indonesia and the Philippines were well aware of how useful the bank was. Both Presidents Suharto and Marcos wrote to Nixon to express how important the ADB was for their countries.[158]

From the economic point of view, the U.S. presence in the bank and in other regional institutions helped generate confidence in international and regional financial systems at a time when the U.S. military withdrawal from Southeast Asia threatened to undermine financial networks, leading to the flight of funds from possible investors and aid donors. In order to prevent such a development, the United States had to clearly signal its intentions to continue participating in the development of Asian countries. A positive American attitude toward the bank was essential, on one hand, to incite other industrialized nations to join the United States in providing "concessionary" aid, supplemental contributions for Asia which had, until then, largely relied on American aid and presence. On the other hand, such clear signals could reinforce the bank's prestige and weight as a multilateral, regional institution capable of dealing with present and future problems.

Furthermore, from the commercial point of view, there was the important question of raw materials and markets to take into consideration, and "one thing these institutions do is help these countries develop the infrastructure needed to get at the raw materials. They finance port, rail, and power projects. The private business which . . . exploits these raw materials could not otherwise do it because it is not going to build a road, a dam, or a port project."[159] Any American contribution to an ADB Special Fund potentially opened up Asian markets to American businessmen and encouraged the development of U.S. commercial interests in Asia because it was a contribution conditional upon the obligation to purchase American goods and services. It allowed American companies the right to bid for all of ADB's projects that were financed by a Special Fund to which the United States had contributed and in countries that were politically vital such as Indonesia, the R.V.N., and Thailand. The U.S. government, mindful of the interests of American firms—thanks to their powerful lobbies—and the pressure of Congress, pushed to have a larger share of contracts granted to the companies in ADB's projects.[160] According to Nicholas W. Philip, former deputy to David E. Lilienthal as well as former director of operations for the Development & Resources Corporation, "fourteen of the largest U.S. construction companies held foreign contracts (with Mekong projects) totaling $3.5 billion in 1969."[161]

In 1969 the ADB further involved itself in the Indochinese countries as it made numerous loans, actively participated in the formulation of regional projects and national development plans, and sent numerous technical missions to Laos and Cambodia, countries with weak and unstable economies.[162] In fact, it was thanks to their memberships in the bank that the Indochinese countries, despite their minimal contributions and voting power, had been able to have access to advantageous loans.[163] To the R.V.N., the bank granted loans of US$ 11.3 million for agricultural and power projects; to Laos, it granted loans of US$ 4.34 million, also for agricultural and power projects; and to Cambodia, it granted a loan of US$ 1.67 million for the financing of a high-power line project for Phnom-Penh at favorable terms.[164] This granting of loans to war-ravaged economies was rather unusual, since the bank generally operated according to the strictest selection criteria, such as the country's healthy economic conditions and its capacity to serve a supplemental external debt. The Indochinese countries were thus exceptions to the bank's strict financial rules with the latter stating that it was its duty to be involved in the former by taking still a larger share of development responsibilities.[165] Naturally, the loans were made from the bank's Special Funds, and the Indochinese countries were not the only ones to benefit from such funds. Indonesia, the Philippines, and Nepal had been recipients of such loans but with the difference that their economies and societies had not suffered lengthy, destructive wars. One may wonder whether these loans were the result of pressure exerted by the United States with its enormous financial and political weight in international financial institutions such as the World Bank, IDA, and the IMF. One way for the United States to force the ADB to heed its advice was to stall its contributions to the bank's soft loans, leading to delays from other sources.[166] According to one study on the ADB, "the United States stands out as the one member that has systematically used voting against projects as an instrument of policy. . . . During the 1970s, U.S. policy in development banks was marked by a shift from reliance on behind-the-scenes pressure to abstention on or voting against loans on specific policy grounds."[167]

The ADB's role increased with the signing of the Paris Agreement in January 1973 because the United States put into effect the Indochina Postwar Reconstruction Program, which included two essential aspects: (1) the economic reconstruction, country by country, (2) and the overall regional economic development of the Indochinese countries. The bank's financial involvement fit the U.S. goals of broadening the range of financial sources contributing to the U.S. Indochina Postwar Reconstruction Program as stated by Secretary of State William P. Rogers in his "Report on U.S. Foreign Policy 1972" presented to the Congress in

April 1973: "The program will and should be one in which other nations—notably Japan and members of the European Community—also make an important contribution."[168]

The Indochina Postwar Reconstruction Program, under AID's responsibility, was to be a five-year plan aimed at helping the Indochinese countries to rebuild their war-ravaged economies. It involved four aspects: humanitarian aid to refugees; financing of essential products such as fertilizers, raw materials for industries, and oil and food products; reconstruction of infrastructures damaged by war; and long-term development programs.[169] The program resulted from the 1973 decision of Congress to drastically reduce American involvement in Indochina by the imposition of budgetary ceilings. The decision was made into law with the Foreign Assistance Act of 1974, which "called on the executive to begin planning for economic reconstruction and development of Indochina, using both bilateral and multilateral sources of international assistance."[170]

The reconstruction program was founded on the assumption that with the cession of hostilities and the return of stability, industrialized countries would not hesitate to increase their aid to Laos, Cambodia, and the Republic of Vietnam "to begin meeting from one-third to one-half of Indochina's economic assistance needs and as the countries of Indochina increase their ability to develop themselves."[171] The program would allow the United States to reduce its spending in this program and to compensate for the economic vacuum left by the withdrawal of American troops. In April 1973, at a meeting of the ADB's Board of Governors, France, which had often opposed the United States within the bank, as well as other Western European donors along with such traditional U.S. allies as Australia and New Zealand, advocated that the bank participate in the postwar reconstruction of Indochina, in particular, the Lao People's Democratic Republic, the D.R.V., and the R.V.N. and not solely the R.V.N.[172] To attract potential participants to the reconstruction program, Washington called on the World Bank president, Robert McNamara, who, along with the ADB, organized a meeting in October 1973 to mobilize possible contributors and to set up an international consulting group that would gather and coordinate multilateral aid. Canada, Germany, Australia, and Japan, as well as France, expressed their willingness to participate in the program.

From 1973, the ADB's loans from its Special Fund were granted to Laos and the Republic of Vietnam in response to American initiatives. Cambodia was the exception. Since 1970, it had received from the bank only one loan for a power project that did not materialize. In 1973—the year of the Paris Agreement—the R.V.N. received from the bank a US$ 3.93 million loan on ordinary capital resources—usually granted only to minimal-risk countries with a high GNP—for telecommunications and water conduit projects around Sai-gon.[173] As soon as the ADF—in which the United States was the second most important contributor—became operational in June 1974, the R.V.N. and Laos obtained substantial loans of US$ 20 million and US$ 6 million, respectively, although the military situation in both countries had reached a point of no return. However, apart from the

ADB's effort, which became a means for Washington to attract capital from multilateral sources to Indochinese countries, the flow of international aid actually granted was below expectations and needs. Even combined with the much reduced U.S. aid, overall assistance to these countries was too small to bring, in such a short lapse of time, an improvement in societies plagued with unemployment and poverty and faced with mass exodus and economic collapse. Already, since the Tet Offensive of 1972, foreign investments as well as bilateral loans had became scarcer and more difficult to obtain, with the exception of the oil sector. Since the Paris Peace Agreement of 1973 did not seem to have a moderating impact on the pace of the war in Vietnam, Laos, or Cambodia, potential contributors hesitated to fulfill their aid promises.

The intense activity deployed by the bank in each of the lower Mekong basin countries, Thailand included—loans for individual projects, technical missions, and cooperation with other MLIs and international organizations for the exchange of information about possible development projects and potential financing sources for these countries—paralleled its more conventional responsibilities as coordinator and executive agent for certain Mekong projects. The Nixon administration defined the role played by the bank with regard to the Mekong Project in the following manner:

The Bank may also be expected to cooperate with interested countries and international agencies in financing projects which may emerge over the years in the development of the Lower Mekong River Basin. The Bank's involvement in Mekong River development is expected to be through financial participation on a project by project basis, where such projects are of priority in the development programs of the riparian countries and appropriate for Special Fund financing.[174]

Since its establishment in December 1966, the bank had maintained a very close working relationship with the Mekong Committee, which customarily presented to the institution development projects for financing. In 1969, the Mekong Committee, with the agreement of the UNDP, conceived a vast program of agricultural pioneer projects for the riparian nations of the lower Mekong basin.[175] At a meeting in August 1971 between international aid agencies, MLIs, and the four riparian nations to discuss the plan of operation for such a program, of which the World Bank was initially the official executive agency, participants acknowledged the ADB's experience and influence in the riparian nations as well as the necessity of its participation. An agreement resulted between the UNDP, the World Bank, the Mekong Committee, and the ADB that recognized the ADB's "de facto role of executing agent by delegation from the World Bank" in the Agricultural Pioneer Project Program.[176] The ADB thereafter officially attended all meetings of the different organizations related to the development of the lower Mekong basin. Thanks to the contributions of the UN and of a number of countries (including the United States, Japan, the Netherlands, and the United Kingdom), a fund of US$ 2.04 million for the study of fifteen agricultural pioneer projects in Thailand, Laos, Cambodia, and the R.V.N. was set up. It was therefore as the executive agent that the bank oversaw agricultural pioneer projects in Prek Thnot (Cambodia), Go-cong (R.V.N.), Casier Sud (Laos), and Nong Wai (Thailand).[177]

Overall, ADB's participation in and support of the Mekong Project made possible its continuation. The bank played a major financial role by helping the Mekong Committee find funds to finance projects; by coordinating multilateral aid for Mekong projects; and by serving as the financial conduit among the riparian nations, the Mekong Committee, international aid organizations, and aid donors. The bank proved to be indispensable to the riparian members in contacting potential contributors, the more so with the World Bank's support as well as Washington's, a crucial facilitating factor in international loan or grant negotiations. As we shall see, the bank's pre-eminence would become all pervasive in the postwar era, when peace finally returned to the lower Mekong basin.

After almost two decades of involvement in the Mekong Committee and the Mekong Project and $46.4 million in contributions, the United States decided to end its commitment when the S.R.V. took over the Mekong membership from the defunct R.V.N. in 1975. Concurrently, the Second Indochina Conflict ended with the disengagement of the United States from the lower Mekong basin, and the phenomenon that it had fought so hard to contain, communism, swept over some of the riparian nations. Presidents Johnson (whose belief in New Deal achievements and material progress was strongly part of his Mekong policy) and Nixon (out of political convenience and a need for continuity) saw the usefulness of the Mekong Project to U.S. policy in Indochina. Each believed that, via massive U.S. involvement, either directly in Johnson's case, or indirectly through multilateral aid in Nixon's case, the project's potential was encompassing enough to entice the Communist enemy to envision a negotiated settlement and ultimately to allow the United States to carry out its containment goal through economic development and social progress. But as demonstrated time and again in differing contexts, when the fury of war overwhelmed all else, such "Water for Peace" proposals could not constitute a viable solution. No socioeconomic achievement is possible when such vast resources are consumed by war, when people's passions are so focused on conflict, and when the watered land is too arid for any peace to prosper.

NOTES

1. *The Pentagon Papers: The Defense Department History of U.S. Decision-Making on Vietnam: The Senator Gravel Edition*, 4 vols. (Boston: Beacon Press, 1971) [hereafter, *PP* Gravel], 2:517.

2. Lyndon B. Johnson, *The Vantage Point: Perspectives of the Presidency, 1963–1969* (New York: Holt, Rinehart and Winston, 1971), 347. Lloyd C. Gardner mentions that Rostow was the author of this "Johnson Doctrine" proposal. In March 1965, Rostow sent it to Rusk, who, in turn, took it up. Lloyd C. Gardner, *Pay Any Price: Lyndon Johnson and the Wars for Vietnam* (Chicago: Ivan R. Dee, 1995), 191.

3. Ibid., 348.

4. "Four Essentials for Peace in Asia," Address by President Johnson, *The Department of State Bulletin* [hereafter, *DSB*] (August 1, 1966): 158.

5. Ibid., 159–161.

6. "The Foreign Assistance Program, Remarks by President Johnson," White House Press Release dated February 1, 1966, *DSB* (February 28, 1966): 321.

7. Ibid.

8. "Foreign Aid, Message from President Johnson to the Congress," White House Press Release dated February 1, 1966, *DSB* (February 28, 1966): 324.

9. "The Foreign Assistance Program for 1967, Statement by Secretary Rusk," *DSB* (April 18, 1966): 631–632.

10. Johnson, *The Vantage Point*, 435.

11. Ibid., 358.

12. Rudy Abramson, *Spanning the Century: The Life of W. Averell Harriman, 1891–1986* (New York: William Morrow, 1992), 639.

13. Ibid., 641.

14. *PP* Gravel, 2:543.

15. Memo, 11/1/1968 [*sic;* date should read "1966"], "Presidential Decisions, The Seven-Nation Manila Conference and the President's Asian Trip, October 17–November 2, 1966," NSC History, NSF, Box 45, L.B.J. Library.

16. Gardner, *Pay Any Price*, 298.

17. Robert W. Komer, *Bureaucracy at War: U.S. Performance in the Vietnam Conflict* (Boulder, CO: Westview Press, 1986), 105.

18. Robert Komer, one of the architects of the pacification campaign of 1968–1971, criticized the lack of "adequate overall plans" and unified management of the conduct of the war, which, according to him, was one of the factors that explained America's "poor performance" in the R.V.N. Komer remarked that the United States should have absolutely tied its massive aid to the R.V.N. to demands for internal reforms and "required performance standards to optimize its effective use," even at the cost of being accused of colonialism. Komer, *Bureaucracy at War*, 37.

19. "For the President and the Secretary from Lodge," telegram sent October 21, 1965, in *PP* Gravel, 2:532.

20. Airgram, Embassy Saigon to Department of State, 6/28/1968, "Seventh MACV Package on VC/NVA Use of Cambodian Territory," Vietnam Country File, NSF, Boxes 92–94, L.B.J. Library.

21. William Colby, former CIA director, claims that it was he who, after Tet 1968, suggested that the Mekong delta be made the priority of the Accelerated Pacification Campaign "since it contained a disproportionate percentage of the people of the nation, especially the rural population . . . and was the rice basket for the whole country." William Colby with James McCargar, *Lost Victory: A Firsthand Account of America's Sixteen-Year Involvement in Vietnam* (Chicago: Contemporary Books, 1989), 256.

22. Kahin gives one of the most accurate analyses of the Buddhist rationale and political standing as well as Marshall Ky's motivations and machinations. George McT. Kahin, *Intervention: How America Became Involved in Vietnam* (New York: Knopf, 1986), 403–432.

23. "Declaration of Honolulu," *Saigon Post* [hereafter, *SP*], 2/10/66.

24. Memo, Meeting of the President with Thieu and Ky (Republic of Vietnam), 10/23/1966, Files of Walt W. Rostow, NSF, Box 8, L.B.J. Library.

25. Memo, Richard Moorsteen to Robert Komer, 8/17/1966, "Study of Postwar Reconstruction and Development in Vietnam," Komer-Leonhart File (1966–1968), NSF, Box 21, L.B.J. Library.

26. Ibid.

27. Ibid.

28. Ibid.

29. Memo, Richard Moorsteen to Komer and Leonhart, 9/26/1966, "Public Announcement of Postwar Planning Study," Komer-Leonhart File (1966–1968), NSF, Box 21, L.B.J. Library.

30. David Lilienthal was chairman of Development and Resources Corporation, a private company that advised developing countries on regional planning. Vu Quoc Thuc was chairman of the Postwar Planning Committee and minister in charge of reconstruction and development.

31. Lilienthal had met the president earlier in June 1964 when he came to the White House to report on his development work in Iran. In March 1967, as Johnson flew to Guam for another conference with Thieu and Ky, Johnson said: "I am taking along Dave Lilienthal to work on a sort of a TVA of the Mekong River. If we can get those things started, we'll really be getting someplace." Gardner, *Pay Any Price*, 123, 356.

32. "Economic Situation in Vietnam," Press briefing held at the White House on February 27, 1967, by President Johnson, David E. Lilienthal, and Robert W. Komer, Special Assistant to the President, *DSB* (March 20, 1967): 467.

33. Walt Whitman Rostow, *The Diffusion of Power: An Essay in Recent History* (New York: Macmillan, 1972), 510.

34. David E. Lilienthal, *The Journals of D. E. Lilienthal*, 7 vols. (New York: Harper and Row, 1976), 6:283.

35. *PP* Gravel, 2:557.

36. "What Should We Do Now? Five Experts Give Their Answer," *Look Magazine* (August 9, 1966): 7.

37. Albert P. Williams, Jr., *South Vietnam's Development Prospects in a Postwar Era: A Review of the Thuc-Lilienthal Report*, Rand Paper no. 4365 (Santa Monica, CA: Rand Corporation, 1971), 4.

38. This fascination with hydraulic projects, the potential of rivers, water, and its use for political purposes seemed, in many respects, to define the Johnson era. It can be found in his October 1965 speech announcing the Water for Peace Program that created the Water for Peace Bureau within the State Department in May 1967. Note the elaboration of water-related themes in a speech by Secretary of State Dean Rusk to the International Conference on Water for Peace held in Washington on May 31, 1967: "As President Johnson said so recently here, the field of water resource management is made for cooperation, . . . water is vital . . . [and] water tends basically to unify and not to divide. . . . We thus see how the laws of logic point toward cooperation in this field of water management: cooperation between nations, . . . between neighbors, . . . between institutions. . . . In turn, such cooperation can bring increasing understanding, mutual respect, and confidence . . . ; this will work in the direction of better international relations, of an improved international political climate." "Address by Secretary Rusk," *DSB* (June 19, 1967): 905–906.

39. Letter, Lilienthal to the President, 5/2/1968, Komer-Leonhart File (1966–1968), NSF, Box 13, L.B.J. Library. Johnson was so keen about the Mekong theme that he wanted "this grass roots story be portrayed on film, as we did the story of the Tennessee Valley." Ibid.

40. *New York Times* [hereafter, *NYT*], 10/29/67.

41. "Le Développement de la République du Vietnam après la guerre: Politique économique et programmes," *Revue Tiers-Monde* (April–September 1970): 438.

42. "Mr. Lilienthal Discusses Vietnam's Economic Development Program," *DSB* (December 25, 1967): 864.

43. "Economic Situation in Vietnam," 469.

44. Lilienthal, *The Journals*, 7:44.

45. There are two versions of the report. The original English version included two volumes listing the author as Joint Development Group and entitled *The Postwar Development of the Republic of Vietnam: Policies and Programs* (Saigon and New York: Development and Resources Corporation, 1969). The Vietnamese version, longer and more detailed, offered different suggestions: Nhom Nghien Cuu Ke Hoach Hau Chien (Postwar Planning Group), *Phuc Trinh ve Chinh Sach va Chuong Trinh Phat Trien Truong Ky cua Viet Nam Cong Hoa* (Report on the Postwar Development of the Republic of Vietnam, Policies and Programs), 3 vols. (Sai-gon: The Republic of Vietnam, 1969). The official English translation of the Vietnamese version is erroneous: *Phat Trien Truong Ky* should read "long-term development" rather than "postwar development."

46. U.S. Congress, House of Representatives, Committee on Appropriations, *Foreign Assistance and Related Agencies Appropriations for 1970*, 2 vols. (Washington, DC: U.S. Government Printing Office, 1969), 2:585.

47. Eugene R. Black, *Alternative in Southeast Asia* (London: Pall Mall Press, 1969), 124–125.

48. David E. Lilienthal, "Postwar Development in Vietnam," *Foreign Affairs* (January 1969): 326.

49. This mathematical model, relying on methodical observations of flood incursions in the delta in Cambodia and Vietnam, made possible the calculation of the impact of all fluctuations in the river flow when it enters the delta and of all dikes, drainage, or dams in the region. Paul Bourrières, "Les Grands Travaux du Mékong," *Revue Tiers-Monde* (April–September 1970): 556.

50. Development and Resources Corporation, *Mekong Delta Development Program, Preliminary Appraisal Report* (New York, December 1968), 45.

51. Ibid., 45–47.

52. Ibid., 48.

53. In the previous several decades, the question of navigation on the Mekong River and delimitation of borders had often pitted the two neighbors Cambodia and Vietnam against each other. During the First and especially the Second Indochina War, the Vietnamese Chau-doc province bordering Cambodia was a porous region through which moved weapons and ammunition via the Mekong River.

54. Lilienthal, *The Journals*, 7:8, 20.

55. *Foreign Assistance and Related Agencies Appropriations for 1970*, 2:595.

56. U.S. Engineer Agency for Resources Inventory, *Accelerated Development Plain of Reeds*, Sponsored by the Department of Defense, Advanced Research Projects Agency, ARPA order no. 1068, Prepared by Department of the Army (Washington, DC, July 1968), v.

57. Ibid., 231.

58. Ibid., ix.

59. Ibid., x.

60. By 1966–1967, the stated goal of U.S. aid in the R.V.N. was to control the rampant inflation. Douglas C. Dacy, *Foreign Aid, War, and Economic Development: South Vietnam, 1955–1975* (Cambridge: Cambridge University Press, 1986), 29.

61. Lilienthal, *The Journals*, 7:20.

62. George C. Herring argues that the Johnson administration seemed to be of two minds as to its organizing of public relations, reacting defensively in a "low key approach" rather than creatively and preventatively about the public opinion's perception of the war in the years 1966–1967. See George C. Herring, *"Cold Blood": LBJ's Conduct of Limited War in Vietnam* (Colorado Springs, CO: United States Air Force Academy, 1990), 16–22.

63. General William C. Westmoreland, "Progress Report on the War in Vietnam: An Address Made before the National Press Club, Washington, D.C., on Nov. 21," *DSB* (December 11, 1967): 788.

64. For an analysis of the events that led to the Tet Offensive of 1968, see Ronald H. Spector, *After Tet: The Bloodiest Year in Vietnam* (New York: The Free Press, 1993); of the U.S. failures to anticipate or prevent its happening, see James J. Wirtz, *The Tet Offensive: Intelligence Failure in War* (Ithaca, NY: Cornell University Press, 1991). For a brief view of the other side's preparation of the Tet Offensive, see Ronnie E. Ford, *Tet 1968: Understanding the Surprise* (London: Frank Cass, 1995).

65. U.S. Government, *Public Papers of the Presidents of the United States, Lyndon B. Johnson, 1968–1969*, 2 vols. (Washington, DC: U.S. Government Printing Office, 1970), 1:469–470.

66. Russell H. Fifield, *Americans in Southeast Asia: The Roots of Commitment* (New York: Thomas Y. Crowell, 1973), 316.

67. *Public Papers of the Presidents of the United States, L.B.J., 1968–1969*, 1:474.

68. Ibid., 1:589–590.

69. Ibid., 1:515.

70. For an analysis of the role played by Congress in Johnson's economic aid policy, see Burton I. Kaufman, "Foreign Aid and the Balance-of-Payments Problem: Vietnam and Johnson's Foreign Economic Policy," in Robert A. Divine, ed., *The Johnson Years*, Vol. 2: *Vietnam, the Environment, and Science* (Lawrence: University Press of Kansas, 1987), 79–109. Kaufman argues that Johnson's economic aid and balance-of-payments programs were handicapped by the Vietnam War and Congress's ensuing opposition.

71. P. Edward Haley, *Congress and the Fall of South Vietnam and Cambodia* (London: Associated University Presses, 1982), 206.

72. "Memorandum from Secretary of Defense Melvin Laird for the President, February 17, 1970," in Gareth Porter, ed., *Vietnam: The Definitive Documentation of Human Decisions*, 2 vols. (Stanfordville, NY: Earl M. Coleman Enterprises Publishers, 1979), 2:388.

73. U.S. President's Task Force on International Development, *U.S. Foreign Assistance in the 1970s: A New Approach, Report to the President from the Task Force on International Development* (Washington, DC: U.S. Government Printing Office, 1970), 2.

74. Ibid., 3.

75. Ibid., 22.

76. Stuart H. Van Dyke, "Foreign Aid: Bilateral and Multilateral," *Columbia Journal of World Business* (November–December 1970): 55.

77. See Richard M. Nixon, *RN: The Memoirs of Richard Nixon* (New York: Grosset and Dunlap, 1978), 119–137.

78. Richard M. Nixon, "Meeting the People of Asia," *DSB* (January 4, 1954): 12.

79. Richard M. Nixon, "Asia after Vietnam," *Foreign Affairs* (October 1967): 113.

80. Cecil V. Crabb, Jr., credited Senator Mike Mansfield's 1969 report on U.S. policy and the situation in Southeast Asia for playing a part in the Nixon Doctrine's formulation, particularly its emphasis on a shift from bilateral to multilateral aid. Cecil V. Crabb,

Jr., *The Doctrines of American Foreign Policy* (Baton Rouge: Louisiana State University Press, 1982), 302–303. See also Mike Mansfield, *Perspective on Asia: The New U.S. Doctrine and Southeast Asia* (Washington, DC: U.S. Government Printing Office, 1969).

81. *Public Papers of the Presidents of the United States, Richard Nixon, 1971* (Washington, DC: U.S. Government Printing Office, 1972), 272.

82. For an overview of "containment," see John L. Gaddis, *Strategies of Containment: A Critical Appraisal of Postwar American National Security Policy* (New York: Oxford University Press, 1982); and *We Now Know: Rethinking Cold War History* (New York: Oxford University Press, 1997). Duiker's study of the U.S. containment policy in Indochina disagrees with a number of works such as Kahin's *Intervention*, notably concerning the advisability of U.S. intervention. For instance, Kahin considers President Harry Truman's decision to grant assistance to French Indochina a fundamental mistake, whereas Duiker qualifies it as being "prudent and . . . based on a reasonable concern," given the circumstances, although aid was applied in ways that were, Duiker concedes, "sometimes shortsighted and unimaginative." William J. Duiker, *U.S. Containment Policy and the Conflict in Indochina* (Stanford, CA: Stanford University Press, 1994), 83.

83. For a discussion of the Johnson and Nixon Doctrines, see Crabb, *The Doctrines of American Foreign Policy.*

84. Richard M. Nixon, "Report on the Situation in Southeast Asia: Radio-Television Address by President Nixon, April 7, 1971," in Richard P. Stebbins and Elaine P. Adam, eds., *American Foreign Relations, 1971* (New York: New York University Press, 1976), 279–280.

85. As a number of historians have pointed out, the ideas of Nixon and Johnson were hardly original, harking back in many respects to notions prevalent since the cold war decades of the 1940s and 1950s. See, for instance, John W. Dower, "Asia and the Nixon Doctrine: The New Face of Empire," in Virginia Brodine and Mark Selden, *Open Secret: The Kissinger-Nixon Doctrine in Asia* (New York: Perennial Library, 1972), 137–218.

86. U.S. Congress, House of Representatives, Committee on Appropriations, *Foreign Assistance and Related Agencies Appropriations for 1968*, 2 vols. (Washington, DC: U.S. Government Printing Office, 1967), 2:783.

87. For an analysis of the Nixon Doctrine and its impact on U.S. foreign policy in the 1960s–1970s, see Earl C. Ravenal, *Large-Scale Foreign Policy Change: The Nixon Doctrine as History and Portent* (Berkeley, CA: Institute of International Studies, University of California, 1989); Franz Schurman, *The Foreign Politics of Richard Nixon: The Grand Design* (Berkeley, CA: Institute of International Studies, University of California, 1987); Robert S. Litvak, *Détente and the Nixon Doctrine: American Foreign Policy and the Pursuit of Stability, 1969–1976* (Cambridge: Cambridge University Press, 1984).

88. "Third Annual Report to the Congress on U.S. Foreign Policy, February 9, 1972," in *Public Papers of the Presidents of the United States, Richard Nixon, 1972* (Washington, DC: U.S. Government Printing Office, 1973), 256.

89. Congress's attitude was not very favorable to multilateral aid, and the part played by the United States in multilateral lending institutions such as the ADB was restricted to the point that its voting power dropped from "an initial 17.1 percent to a temporary low of 7.5 percent in 1974." Robert Wihtol, *The Asian Development Bank and Rural Development: Policy and Practice* (New York: St. Martin's Press, 1988), 44.

90. A 1974 study prepared by the Advanced Research Projects Agency of the Department of Defense on the Nixon Doctrine in Asia remarked that of the different kinds of regionalism (political, military, economic), the economic one "may over the long run prove the most important. . . . ECAFE, the Asian Development Bank, foreign aid pro-

grams, and a variety of other economic organizations are beginning to constitute an interlocking directorate in which the Japanese increasingly play the dominant role." William H. Overholt and Herman Kahn, *The United States and Pacific Asia in the Seventies*, 2 vols. (New York: Hudson Institute, 1973–1974), 1:178.

91. Black, *Alternative in Southeast Asia*, 121–151.

92. Ibid., 132.

93. Ibid., 133.

94. Ibid., 145.

95. Ibid., 125.

96. "First Annual Report to the Congress on U.S. Foreign Policy for the 1970s, February 18, 1970," in *Public Papers of the Presidents of the United States, Richard Nixon, 1970* (Washington, DC: U.S. Government Printing Office, 1971), 45. Nixon, traveling to Asia as a private citizen in 1963, recounted a conversation he had with Henry Cabot Lodge, then ambassador to the R.V.N., in which he, Nixon, expressed doubt about economic development as the solution to the Communist threat in Southeast Asia. Nixon, *The Memoirs*, 258.

97. "Second Annual Report to the Congress on U.S. Foreign Policy, February 25, 1971," in *Public Papers of the Presidents of the United States, Richard Nixon, 1971*, 274–275.

98. U.S. Congress, House of Representatives, Committee on Appropriations, *Foreign Assistance and Related Agencies Appropriations for 1975* (Washington, DC: U.S. Government Printing Office, 1974), 2:882.

99. *Foreign Assistance 1970*, 2:692.

100. U.S. Congress, House of Representatives, Committee on Appropriations, *Foreign Assistance and Related Agencies Appropriations for 1972* (Washington, DC: U.S. Government Printing Office, 1971), 2:274.

101. *Foreign Assistance 1975*, 2:882.

102. *Foreign Assistance 1970*, 2:844.

103. *Foreign Assistance 1975*, 2:883.

104. U.S. Congress, House of Representatives, Committee on Appropriations, *Foreign Assistance and Related Agencies Appropriations for 1974* (Washington, DC: U.S. Government Printing Office, 1973), 2:1498–1499.

105. Commission Economique et Sociale pour l'Asie et le Pacifique, *Rapport Annuel 7 avril 1974–7 mars 1975* (Bangkok: United Nations, 1975), Supplement no. 7:27. By 1975, the Nam Ngum Phase II's cost had jumped to US$ 39.095 million and the total of the Nam Ngum Fund to US$ 38.609 million. Committee for the Coordination of Investigations of the Lower Mekong Basin, *Annual Report 1975* (Bangkok: United Nations, 1975), 69.

106. Wihtol, *The Asian Development Bank*, 48.

107. See the U.S. Bureau of Reclamation's study that summarizes more than eight years of research carried out by the bureau on the Pa Mong Project: U.S. Bureau of Reclamation, *L'Aménagement de Pa Mong, Premier Stade, Phase II* (1973).

108. Joel M. Halpern, "Mekong River Development Schemes for Laos and Thailand: A Hope for the Future?" *Courrier de l'Extrême-Orient* 49 (1971): 154.

109. Ibid., 145.

110. Such achievements did not necessarily mean that it was not plagued by the perennial problem of corruption. In October 1969, the head of the resettlement project for the Nam Ngum Dam asked the Mekong Committee to provide a sum of US$ 300,000 supposedly for the resettlement of 3,000 refugees from the war as well as from the flooding of the valley. The sum was granted, but the refugees did not benefit from it. A

magnificent bowling alley, which reportedly cost US$ 300,000, was inaugurated instead. Fred Branfman, "Presidential War in Laos," in Nina S. Adams and Alfred W. McCoy, eds., *Laos: War and Revolution* (New York: Harper & Row, 1970), 227.

111. U.S. Congress, Senate, Subcommittee on U.S. Security Agreements and Commitments Abroad, *Thailand, Laos, and Cambodia, Jan. 1972* (Washington, DC: U.S. Government Printing Office, 1972), 12.

112. Within the framework of the U.S.-sponsored Accelerated Development Program in Thailand's Northeast, a number of roads were built to connect sensitive areas and especially to allow for the speedy transportation of troops. Their impact on villagers who lived along those roads were generally negative. Thak Chaloemtiarana, *Thailand: The Politics of Despotic Paternalism* (Bangkok: Thammasat University, 1979), 266–270.

113. Halpern, "Mekong River," 155.

114. Committee for the Coordination of Investigations of the Lower Mekong Basin, *Report on Indicative Basin Plan: A Proposed Framework for the Development of Water and Related Resources of the Lower Mekong Basin, 1970* (E/CN.11/WRD/MKG/L.340) (Bangkok: United Nations, 1970).

115. Ibid., 5:52–56.

116. Ibid., 5:59–75.

117. Ibid., 5:90.

118. Marjorie Niehaus, *A Chronology of Selected Statements by Administration Officials on the Subject of Postwar Reconstruction Aid to Indochina* (Washington, DC: Congressional Research Service, April 4, 1973), 6.

119. *Public Papers of the Presidents of the United States, Richard Nixon, 1972*, 279.

120. Niehaus, *A Chronology*, 8–9.

121. U.S. Congress, House of Representatives, Committee on International Relations, *US Aid to North Vietnam* (Washington, DC: U.S. Government Printing Office, 1979), Appendix 12:51.

122. However, economic aid and the POW-MIA question is barely discussed by Henry Kissinger in his memoir *White House Years* (Boston: Little, Brown, 1979).

123. U.S. Congress, Senate, *Report of the U.S. Senate Select Committee on POW/MIA Affairs*. 2 vols. (Washington, DC: The Committee, 1993), 1:90.

124. Memorandum of Conversation between Nixon and the Joint Leadership of Congress on the Status of Vietnam Negotiations, Jan. 24, 1973 in Porter, ed., *Vietnam: The Definitive Documentation*, 2:598–599.

125. Nixon, *The Memoirs*, 692.

126. *Report of the U.S. Senate Select Committee*, 1:92.

127. Ibid.

128. *U.S. Aid to North Vietnam*, Appendix 14:68.

129. Ibid.

130. Ibid., Appendix 12:52.

131. "The Vietnam Agreement and Protocols, Signed January 27, 1973: Agreement on Ending the War and Restoring Peace in Vietnam," in U.S. Congress, Senate, Committee on Foreign Relations, *Background Information Relating to Southeast Asia and Vietnam* (Washington, DC: U.S. Government Printing Office, 1975), 522.

132. Regarding the Paris Peace talks and related negotiations, see George C. Herring, *The Secret Diplomacy of the Vietnam War: The Negotiating Volumes of the Pentagon Papers* (Austin: University of Texas, 1983); and Gareth Porter, *A Peace Denied: The United States, Vietnam, and the Paris Agreement* (Bloomington: Indiana University Press, 1975), 236–237. Porter mentions that when the U.S. team went to Hai-phong harbor to start the process of demining, it observed that the Vietnamese generally took it to

be a foregone conclusion that the United States was to provide aid and normalize relations rapidly.

133. *U.S. Aid to North Vietnam*, Appendix 2:25. Mention has been made of a second Nixon letter that "allegedly specified the constitutional procedures that would be involved in any reconstruction aid program for North Vietnam." Ibid., Appendix 12:55. The questions about whether the U.S. government formally committed itself via the Nixon letter to provide economic aid to the D.R.V. and, if so, whether the United States remained bound by its terms given subsequent violations of the Paris Accords by both sides have generated a lengthy controversy and contributed to acrimonious normalization talks between the United States and the then-D.R.V. See Joseph J. Zasloff and MacAlister Brown, *Communist Indochina and U.S. Foreign Policy: Postwar Realities* (Boulder, CO: Westview Press, 1978).

134. Zasloff and Brown, *Communist Indochina*, 22.

135. Maurice J. Williams was the deputy for AID's head administrator, John A. Hannah, at the time of the JEC's discussions in 1973.

136. Porter, *Vietnam: The Definitive Documentation*, 2:623–624.

137. Ibid., 2:633; Zasloff and Brown, *Communist Indochina*, 22.

138. Niehaus, *A Chronology*, 16.

139. *U.S. Aid to North Vietnam*, Appendix 12:55.

140. Telegram from Chief of the U.S. Delegation to the Joint Economic Commission Maurice J. Williams to Rogers, June 18, 1973 in Porter, *Vietnam: The Definitive Documentation*, 2:638.

141. It included a list of goods that had to be purchased in the United States, including "materials and tools for shelter and building construction, agriculture and food processing." Zasloff and Brown, *Communist Indochina*, 21.

142. Telegram from U.S. Chief of Delegation Williams to Rogers, July 23, 1973 in Porter, *Vietnam: The Definitive Documentation*, 2:639.

143. Article 8(b) deals with the question of "information . . . location . . . and repatriation of the remains" of the MIAs. "The Vietnam Agreement and Protocols, Signed January 27, 1973," in *Background Information*, 518.

144. Tad Szulc, *The Illusion of Peace: Foreign Policy in the Nixon Years* (New York: The Viking Press, 1978), 680.

145. John J. Brady, *U.S. Aid to Indochina: Report of a Staff Survey Team to South Vietnam, Cambodia, and Laos* (Washington, DC: U.S. Government Printing Office, 1974), 18.

146. Ibid.

147. Ibid.

148. Zasloff and Brown, *Communist Indochina*, 26.

149. MLIs finance projects and development programs in developing countries and include such institutions as the International Bank for Reconstruction and Development (IBRD), the International Development Association (IDA), and the International Finance Corporation (IFC). U.S. Congress, Senate, Committee on Governmental Affairs, *U.S. Participation in the Multilateral Banks* (Washington, DC: U.S. Government Printing Office, 1979), 21. For a detailed analysis of MLIs' evolution from the post–Second World War period to the 1980s, see Anne O. Krueger, "The Role of Multilateral Lending Institutions in the Development Process," *Asian Development Review* 7 (1989): 1–20.

150. *Foreign Assistance 1975*, 1:651.

151. Ibid.

152. Loans from Special Fund Resources (SFR) are advantageous, since they "have a 10-year grace period, a maturity period of 40 years, and carry interest only in the form of a 1 per cent service charge." Wihtol, *The Asian Development Bank*, 17.

153. "Special Message to the Congress on Foreign Aid, May 28, 1969" in *Public Papers of the President of the United States, Richard Nixon, 1969* (Washington, DC: U.S. Government Printing Office, 1970), 414.

154. In fact, this Asian Development Fund was not the first American contribution to an ADB's Special Fund. In June 1967 and May 1969, the United States made two grants of technical aid of $250,000 and $1 million to the same fund. The latter grant was made "for carrying out the Regional Transport Survey," and both were conditional on "procurement of services from the United States." Asian Development Bank, *Annual Report 1971* (Manila: Asian Development Bank, 1972), 109.

155. Ibid., 19.

156. *Foreign Assistance 1975*, 1:651.

157. Ibid.

158. *Foreign Assistance 1974*, 1:776.

159. *Foreign Assistance 1975*, 1:649.

160. Ibid., 1:648–649.

161. Nicholas W. Philip, "Southeast Asia: Investment and Development," *Columbia Journal of World Business* (November–December 1970): 64–65.

162. According to the Senate Subcommittee on U.S. Security Agreements and Commitments Abroad, 50 percent of Laos's national budget was spent solely on the Lao army's salaries. Without foreign, particularly American aid, the Lao government would not have been able to take care of its refugees or to maintain its presence in the countryside, to say nothing of its essential functions. In 1971, for instance, "all [U.S.] military and economic assistance [to Laos] . . . was about ten times the Lao national budget." *Thailand, Laos, and Cambodia*, 24. Furthermore, thanks to the IMF, Laos and Cambodia each had an Exchange Support Fund to which U.S. allies contributed and which was used to finance "(a) commodities for which Cambodian reserves and earnings are insufficient, and (b) services and commodities required in connection with capital projects or technical assistance." *Foreign Assistance 1975*, 2:876.

163. Cambodia: 0.36 percent of the total, 0.89 percent of the voting right; Laos: 0.04 percent of the total, 0.64 percent of the voting right; South Vietnam: 1.22 percent of the total, 1.59 percent of the voting right; Thailand: 2.04 percent of the total, 2.24 percent of the voting right. U.S. Congress, House of Representatives, Committee on Banking and Currency, *To Authorize the United States to Participate in Increases in the Resources of the ADB, the IMF, the IBRD* (Washington, DC: U.S. Government Printing Office, 1970), 18.

164. Asian Development Bank, *Annual Report 1971* (Manila: Asian Development Bank, 1972), 94–95. It must be recalled that Cambodia under Sihanouk had not obtained a single ADB loan; yet two weeks after the Lon Nol coup in March 1970, the bank agreed to grant a loan of US$ 1.67 million. Richard de Camp, "The ADB: An Imperial Thrust into the Pacific," in Mark Selden, ed., *Remaking Asia: Essays on the American Uses of Power* (New York: Pantheon Books, 1974), 83.

165. Asian Development Bank, *Annual Report 1972* (Manila: Asian Development Bank, 1973), 11.

166. A. Rowley, "Ideology Before Need," *Far Eastern Economic Review* (February 14, 1985), 72.

167. Wihtol, *The Asian Development Bank*, 46.

168. "U.S. Foreign Policy 1972: A Report of the Secretary of State," *DSB* (May 7, 1973): 549.

169. *Foreign Assistance 1974*, 2:5.

170. Haley, *Congress*, 46.

171. "The U.S. Foreign Assistance Program and Current International Realities, Statement by Secretary Rogers Made before the Subcommittee on Foreign Operations of the Senate Committee on Appropriations on July 27, 1973," *DSB* (August 20, 1973): 293.

172. Wihtol, *The Asian Development Bank*, 54.

173. Ordinary capital loans have grace periods of two to seven years and maturity periods from ten to thirty years with interest rates varying from 6.87 percent in the 1960s to 10.5 percent in 1983. Wihtol, *The Asian Development Bank*, 17.

174. *To Authorize the United States*, 44.

175. Agricultural pioneer projects differ from experimental farms in the sense that the latter study farmers' reactions to new methods introduced by the experimental farms as well as the soil-plant-water balance. The pioneer projects are prototypes meant to solve problems related to irrigation and to the organization of human and physical resources in the lower Mekong basin. Comité pour la Coordination des Etudes sur le Bassin Inférieur du Mékong, *Projets pionniers agricoles: Etendue et objectifs* (Bangkok: United Nations, December 1970), Appendix 2. For a summary of the Pioneer Project Program, see IBRD, *Detailed Preparation of a Programme of Pioneer Agricultural Projects in the Lower Mekong Basin* (August 20, 1974).

176. Asian Development Bank, *Annual Report 1971*, 48.

177. Asian Development Bank, *Annual Report 1972*, 41.

PART III

And Peace

Commercial activities on the Mekong River

5

The Greater Mekong
Region

The Second Indochina War ended in April 1975. At last the sound of war had quieted. The United States had departed, vowing never to let itself be caught again in such a conflict, turning its back on a land that it had so profoundly embraced for decades. For peoples of the lower Mekong basin, the time for reconstruction had come, and all efforts were now to be dedicated to rebuilding peace. At last alone, apparently no more imposed upon by outside forces and superpowers, Thai, Lao, Cambodians, and Vietnamese found themselves under the same roof, living by the banks of the same river, the Mekong, that has coursed through and bound their territories together in times of war and now of peace. But again in 1978–1979, war (the Third Indochina Conflict) came thundering, turning brothers into enemies, riparians against riparians, wreaking further havoc to the land for another decade.[1] At the beginning of the 1990s, timid portents of normalcy began to emerge. Slowly, with many setbacks, peace seemed to have returned at last. Against this background, once again, the Mekong River and the Mekong Project became the bearers of hope for a bright future for the riparians who could now forge ahead and shape their own destinies. Or could they?

BROTHERS, ENEMIES, RIPARIANS

In the aftermath of 1975, the Ford, Carter, and Reagan administrations, backed by Congress or sometimes compelled by it, hardened the American position concerning Vietnam (Socialist Republic of Vietnam, S.R.V.), Laos (Lao People's Democratic Republic, L.P.D.R.), and Cambodia (Democratic Kampuchea, D.K.). This hardening of position took many forms, one of which was via economic assistance either directly or through international organizations.[2] Direct aid to the Indochinese countries was curtailed when Congress passed the Foreign Assistance Appropriations Act of 1976, section 108, which effectively prevented any direct aid funds to be used for the three countries of Indochina.

What remained was indirect aid contributions to international lending organizations: World Bank–related agencies such as IDA (International Development Association) or regional ones such as the ADB (Asian Development Bank). The United States followed a pattern of negative voting that consistently opposed the granting of loans (most of them related to agriculture and rural development) to the three socialist countries on the basis of human rights violations or non-respect thereof.[3] The U.S. administration after 1977 qualified its negative voting records on a number of ADB, IDA, or World Bank loan proposals to Laos, Cambodia, and Vietnam as being human-rights inspired and conditional on the S.R.V.'s cooperation in the search for American servicemen missing in action. It became more focused on the S.R.V. after the latter's invasion of Cambodia in 1978.[4] The World Bank and the ADB, which had attempted to resume their lending to the S.R.V. after 1975, reacted adversely to Vietnam's invasion by freezing all loans to it (a 1978 US$ 60 million IDA loan, for instance).[5] World Bank President Robert McNamara, in an unusual move and apparently on his own initiative, explained in a letter to Congress that "because of the conditions, the World Bank Group will not be providing loans to Vietnam."[6] The United States also moved to put pressure on allies such as Japan not to grant any aid whether official or private to Vietnam.[7]

This cutting of aid had enormous repercussions on the three socialist countries, pushing them to rely more on the Soviet bloc. Furthermore, during the 1980s through the beginning of the 1990s, all four nations continued to be inextricably entangled in the Gordian Knot of the Cambodian problem. Nevertheless, toward the end of the 1980s, the collapse of the USSR, which ushered in a post–cold war era in Southeast Asia, as well as positive political developments in the region, made possible the return of some precarious stability to the lower Mekong nations of Laos, Cambodia, Vietnam, and Thailand.[8] With the departure starting in September 1989 of Vietnamese troops from Cambodia after more than ten years of occupation, followed by the peace brokered in Paris in 1991 ("The Peace Agreement on the Comprehensive Political Settlement for Cambodia") between the different contending factions, Cambodia was able to hold nationwide elections in 1993. The ensuing lifting of the U.S. trade embargo (1994) followed by the establishment of diplomatic relations between the United States and Vietnam (July 1995) removed the last obstacle to a return to normalcy.[9] These different steps toward peace were powerful incentives for countries of the region to formulate plans for the future and for investors, private companies, and banking institutions, as well as international development organizations, to resume activities in Indochina. Such political developments have had enormous repercussions not only on the Mekong region but also inescapably on the Mekong Committee and the Mekong Project.

Whither the Mekong Committee and the Mekong Project?

The four countries of the lower Mekong basin, emerging from long conflicts and decades of distrust and misunderstanding, had no enduring heritage of peaceful neighborly relationships on which to build a postwar entente, a fact that was further complicated by the contrasting ideologies and systems adopted by Thailand, Laos, Cambodia, and Vietnam. Nor had they any long experience in economic exchanges, common infrastructure projects, or intergovernmental cooperation—except in one instance, their work together on the Mekong Committee. As Pachoom Chomchai, former assistant executive agent of the Mekong Committee, phrases it: "The Mekong Committee has been unique in that it represented the outcome of the first United Nations' direct involvement in a continuing program to plan and develop an international river basin on a scale not hitherto attempted anywhere else in the world."[10] But even the committee is not immune to the wider context of political instability, divisiveness, and rivalry that gripped the region in the past.

The Mekong Committee, which had weathered decades of war without any major disruption, saw its activities momentarily interrupted in the post–Vietnam War period. From 1957 to 1975, the Mekong Committee had met sixty-nine times in full plenary sessions, but the Communist takeover in 1975 in all three countries of Indochina, followed by the war between Cambodia and Vietnam in 1978–1979, brought on a long hiatus in the four-member meetings and activities. In April 1977, when Cambodia, under the control of the Khmer Rouge, withdrew from the Mekong Committee, the three remaining riparian nations—the Kingdom of Thailand, the L.P.D.R., and the S.R.V.—decided to meet again in Bangkok to discuss the situation.[11] In the absence of its fourth member, because of the necessity of consensus and unanimity, these countries decided that, instead of disbanding the institution, and to prevent the shrinkage in the Mekong Committee's activities and fundings, they should establish an interim committee aided by its secretariat that would carry on the work until such time as Cambodia would rejoin it. Hence, on January 5, 1978, "the Interim Committee for Co-ordination of Investigation of the Lower Mekong Basin (Interim Mekong Committee)" was established by representatives of the three nations.[12]

From its inception in 1957, the Mekong Committee formulated principles meant to guarantee that none of the four signatories would obstruct the mainstream discharge, navigability, or utilization of the river. The first two principles asserted were: "(1) the existing low water discharge of the Mekong would not be reduced in any way at any site; and (2) the supplies to be diverted for irrigation purposes would be met by some storage during high stages of the river."[13] These principles of nonobstruction were reaffirmed in 1967. Then again, at one of the last plenary sessions, held in 1975 in Vientiane, the four Mekong nations officially adopted the Joint Declaration of Principles for Utilization of the Waters of the Lower Mekong Basin. Two of the most important of its thirty-eight articles were Article X: "Mainstream waters are a resource of common interest not subject to major unilateral appropriation by any riparian State without prior approval by the other Basin States through the Committee"; and Article XI: "The sovereign jurisdiction of a riparian State over mainstream waters is subject to the equal rights of the other riparian States to use these waters."[14] These two articles meant, in effect, that no mainstream projects can be implemented without the unanimous approval of all four members. The 1978 document that instituted the Interim Committee, however, did not reiterate the 1975 unanimity of concern about the use of the Mekong River's resources. This weaker document signaled a retreat from a previous, stronger commitment to safeguard the rights of all parties concerned to the full usage of the river's resources.

As to the financing of the Mekong Committee, on the eve of the Vietnamese invasion in December 1978, pledges and commitments coming from a large number of countries and most of the UN agencies reached a total of US$ 377.7 million, 76 percent of which was in grants.[15] After the Vietnamese occupation of Cambodia in 1979, although the fundings by donors continued, they nevertheless suffered a sharp drop. The second most important donor (after Thailand) to the Mekong Committee, the United States, after contributing more than $46 million ($13.9 million of which was spent on Pa Mong surveys) in the past decades, ceased its aid altogether and withdrew from participation in the Mekong Project after 1975.[16] In its several decades of work on the Mekong Project, the United States had contributed more than just dollars. It was the leading impetus behind the Mekong drive during the Second Indochina Conflict, a reflection of its all-encompassing political and military involvement, greatly influencing the Mekong nations and the Mekong Project and Committee. It had contributed greatly toward a better knowledge of the Mekong River by being first to launch a reconnaissance study of the basin in the 1950s; in the ensuing years, it had helped found data-collecting stations, train specialists in hydrology and meteorology, prepare an atlas of the Mekong's physical resources, and assist in the study of river-borne diseases such as schistosomiasis.[17] The United States was heavily involved in the study of Pa Mong, one of the major mainstream projects that has caused a great amount of concern over the question of human and ecological impact. U.S. assistance also went to finance projects in individual countries such as the three Mekong tributary projects (Lam Takong, Lam Phra Plerng, and Lam Pao) in the Northeast of Thailand, the sum ($10.2 million) of which was not counted as part of the Mekong Project's financing but considered U.S. bilateral aid to Thailand.[18] As Chomchai notes, "While the total amount of funds committed to the Mekong cause has been modest, by careful selection of key areas for support, the United States has served usefully as a catalyst and the funds supplied have, in most cases, served as 'seed money' rather than anything else."[19] Once the United States disengaged itself from the whole process and lost interest, the Mekong Project and Committee suffered setbacks that had as much to do with the absence of the United States as with the nature of the relationships between the four lower Mekong basin nations. The dominant concern was and remains this: Can these nations forge ahead and realize many of the projects that have been envisioned, planned, and studied over the years and at what costs?

The Mekong Committee's goals, since its inception in 1957, have always been to aid the member nations to attain "through the development of the potential of the lower Mekong basin, self-sufficiency of food production, increased energy output resulting from hydro-power schemes in support of agriculture and industry, and the improvement of navigation as well as the transport system in the region," to be realized through the framework provided by its Indicative Basin Plan (1970–2000) published in 1971. By the 1980s, enough time had elapsed to render the information collected in the Basin Plan somewhat obsolete, and the unresolved situation in Cambodia prevented the progress of any mainstream plan. Consequently, the Interim Mekong Committee decided to revise its Basin Plan to take into account political events and new data.[20] None of the sixteen mainstream schemes that had always been accorded priority had reached fruition, and of the more than 180 proposed projects of the Indicative Basin Plan, sixteen had been completed by the 1970s (with an investment totaling US$ 300 million); almost all of them are located in the Northeast of Thailand (e.g., Nam Pong, Nam Pung, Lam Pao, Lam Pra Plerng, Lam Ta Kong, Nam Phrom, Nam Oon, and Lam Dom Noi), with two in Laos (Selabam and Nam Dong Dams).[21] The Nam Ngum (Phase I and II) was the only Mekong Committee–initiated, international (Thailand and Laos) project that, despite the wartime conditions of its construction, succeeded thanks to the U.S. patronage, as well as to regional and international cooperation, and met its goals of electricity production and sale to Thailand.

It was thus decided that while the long-term plan remains, a medium-term plan over a period of ten to fifteen years should be established to "ensure complementarity between national development programmes and the Committee's development activities."[22] Eventually, in 1987, the Mekong secretariat came up with a revised version of the 1970 Indicative Basin Plan, which did not include Cambodia, then still a nonmember, and published it in 1988 under the title *Perspectives for Mekong Development: Revised Indicative Plan (1987) for the Development of Land, Water and Related Resources of the Lower Mekong Basin*. The revised version was more nationally focused rather than regionally oriented and constituted a departure from the integrated water-resources development advocated since the beginning. Thus, these Mekong projects, which are factored into each nation's planning, are usually tributary-related, medium-scale, medium-term, and multipurpose. Desk studies identified possible multipurpose projects in the Northeast of Thailand, in the Huai Samran, Huai Khayung, and Huai Thap Than tributaries of the Nam Mun, and in the Vietnamese delta, in Cuu-long province, with the Tam-phuong project situated between the Co-chien and Ham-luong River branches. The Mekong delta project was also part of the Vietnamese government's Cuu-long project of building new sluices and restoring existing sluices and drainage systems. Its aim was "to supply fresh water through an irrigation network and to improve drainage conditions to prevent water logging."[23]

The 1987 revised plan took into consideration the protest raised against the 1970 Pa Mong project because of the number of people who would have to be resettled (480,000 if the project were built at an elevation of 260 meters and approximately 250,000 if it were built at 250 meters) and the vast expanse of agricultural land that would be flooded, as well as potentially serious ecological effects.[24] The revised plan presented a more modest version of the Pa Mong project with a 210-meter elevation and only 60,000 people to be resettled (renamed thus Low Pa Mong). It would necessitate an additional upstream dam in Chiang Khan (both situated astride Laos and Thailand) to compensate for the loss in height and volume. The proposed cascade of eight dams, despite its being "less powerful than the cascade of 1970," could cause salt water intrusion, for instance, in the Vietnamese rice-growing delta, a problem that the revised plan addressed by suggesting a better use of the land through shrimp aquaculture.[25] The 1987 plan accorded very little attention to the socioeconomic and environmental consequences of such a cascade. It left out intangible but powerful factors such as "equity, finance, and regional politics," the very factors that determine the human success or the realization or nonrealization of such schemes, which could be carried out only "if there was an authority with absolute power running the development of the Mekong subregion as a whole," which the Interim Committee was definitely not.[26]

While great proposals such as Pa Mong have generated much attention in the past, for several decades work has been conducted at a more modest level on ancillary activities, such as the establishment of hydrologic and meteorological stations basinwide to record flood and flow information, the study of the impact of dam building and new cultivation techniques, and the training of technicians. Hydropower production as a "purpose" has been emphasized, but it is not the sole purpose of the Mekong development. Irrigation, flood control, and salinity prevention are as important within the multipurpose framework. While hydropower production constitutes a priority for upstream nations such as Laos and Thailand, downstream nations such as Vietnam and Cambodia have priorities that are somewhat different and focus on irrigation and flood control. Yet, lately, the trend in Mekong Project milieus seems to emphasize dam construction and hydropower production as priority projects, relegating irrigation and flood control to lesser status as the 1994 Mekong Secretariat's *Mekong Mainstream Run-of-River Hydropower: Main Report* seemed to show. It presents yet again another cascade of hydropower mainstream dams, which are supposed to be less harmful than the previously proposed ones (1970 and 1987), but which have led to talk that the newly formed Mekong River Commission has "a dam building agenda."[27]

Since the late 1980s, there has been a flurry of activities at all levels directly related to the Interim Mekong Committee. In June 1991, as the political situation improved, Cambodia's Supreme National Council (SNC), the twelve-member governing body representing all the Khmer factions, requested its re-entrance as a member of the four-nation Mekong Committee. Two years of hard bargaining ensued and finally led to the signing in Ha-noi of a draft agreement entitled "Cooperation in the Sustainable Development of the Mekong River" on November 28, 1994, by the four riparian nations. They ratified on April 5, 1995, in Chiang

Rai, Thailand, the "Agreement on the Cooperation for the Sustainable Development of the Mekong River Basin," formally establishing the Mekong River Commission (MRC) to replace the 1957 Mekong Committee and the 1978 Interim Mekong Committee and its secretariat with a three-bodied entity.[28] According to the new agreement, each country is to be represented at the ministerial level in a "council for making policies and decisions and settling disputes," each country is to be represented on a committee in charge of executing the decisions reached by the council, and a secretariat is to provide "technical and administrative support."[29] Article 2 of the agreement mentions the need for a new Basin Development Plan (BDP), which the MRC promptly set out to prepare in June 1995 by organizing workshops and conferences.[30] The BDP has a geographic focus that is identical to previous ones, that is, the lower Mekong basin, with the same four riparian states. However, it also provides for the integration of the two upstream nations of China and Myanmar.[31] During the arduous negotiations for the Mekong River Commission, the four nations in acknowledgment of the changed reality had invited China and Myanmar to sit in the sessions, which they did as observers.[32]

The Mekong River Commission's agreement does not, however, contain any mutually binding clauses concerning the use of the river's resources, much to the chagrin of the downstream nations of Cambodia, and in particular, of Vietnam. It, in fact, effectively undid what the 1975 agreement had accomplished, which was the stipulation that all members inform one another of projects that they intended to carry out on the river as well as obtain the members' unanimous approval before implementation of any project.[33] All that they are required to do in this new agreement in the case of "intra-basin uses and inter-basin diversions" on the Mekong River's mainstream and tributaries is to notify and consult with the Joint Committee.[34] Basically, each member nation is free to carry out whatever plan or plans it has for its future. This "free-for-all" spirit has consistently been the position taken by Thailand concerning the exploitation of the Mekong River and has constituted a bone of contention. Ironically, it was at a time when the future seemed brightest that the Mekong Committee was the most threatened with fragmentation as the result of the opposing interests of Thailand and Vietnam. The former used Cambodia's request in June 1991 for reintegration into the Mekong Committee to impose its preconditions, which were that the committee should discard the 1957 founding statute and the 1975 agreement.[35] There were tugs-of-war between Thailand, eager to proceed with mainstream hydropower and irrigation schemes (in particular, its Mun-Chi project of diverting water from the Mekong to irrigate the dry Northeast), and Vietnam, anxious because of the potentially negative impacts of such projects on its delta. The Mekong spirit of cooperation seems to be at stake in the changed circumstances of the 1990s. There has even been talk of moving the Mekong Committee's headquarters from Bangkok, its home since 1957, to a location more central to the river such as Vientiane, the capital of Laos, which is at the epicenter of the other capitals and important cities of the Mekong countries.

As environmental awareness and pressures became more acute, the Mekong Secretariat responded with the *Mekong Mainstream Run-of-River Hydropower: Main Report* in 1994, which presented hydropower projects that purported to be less harmful for the environment. It recommended a "cascade" of thirty dams covering more than 600 kilometers of the 1,800 kilometers of river studied.[36] Of these, two stand out in terms of their overall extended impact. One is the Low Pa Mong project reprised from the 1987 plan. The former 1970 Pa Mong project, on the Mekong between Thailand's Northeast and Laos, was conceived as a 250-meter-high dam that would have produced 4,800 megawatts and irrigated 1.6 million hectares in Laos and Thailand but would have flooded an area of 3,700 square kilometers of forests and forced the resettlement of more than 250,000 people.[37] Given the extent of the resettlement, the project was scaled down in the 1987 revised plan, and now Low Pa Mong would be 210 meters high, flooding only 600 square kilometers while displacing the smaller number of 60,000 people in Laos and Thailand.[38]

The second major dam is the Nam Theun 2 in Laos, which is meant to produce only electricity. This is a project (reprised from the 1987 plan) that has elicited as much (if not more) criticism and opposition locally and internationally as has the Pa Mong because of its location and the extensive damage it could cause to the population and the environment. The Nam Theun River's drainage area is 14,650 square kilometers, and the project if built would have an installed capacity of 1,200 megawatts, producing around 4,650 gigawatt hours a year, at an estimated cost of US$ 615 million (revised later to US$ 1.4 billion). Its construction would take place in the midst of one of Laos's most pristine evergreen forests, the Nam Theun-Nakai National Biodiversity Conservation Area (NBCA), declared as such in 1993 by the Lao government. The 3,445-square kilometer NBCA "constitutes one of Southeast Asia's largest remaining areas of undisturbed rivers and forests," with a rich and rare wildlife biologically still unexplored. It has remained relatively safe from poachers and loggers (legal and illegal) for the moment because of its remoteness.[39] The number of people living in the Nakai area that will have to be resettled is somewhere near 4,000 (fourteen villages). Most of these people would thus lose not only their homes but also their means of subsistence, the land and forest that will be flooded as a result of the construction of the reservoir. The twenty-seven villages situated downstream will also be affected, although no one knows with certainty what will be their fate. There are other negative impacts that have not been carefully studied; for example, the construction of dams on so many tributaries will most certainly affect the Mekong mainstream flow and, hence, the livelihood of the downstream nations.

While the Mekong projects conceived during the wars in the 1960s and 1970s were multipurpose, aiming at the production of electricity, irrigation, flood control, navigation, salinity prevention, and so on, the revised versions of the 1990s apparently emphasize solely hydropower production to be marketed mostly to Thailand, the only nation advanced enough to need the power produced by these future dams and close enough to receive it. Sanguan Patamatamkul, head of the Water Resources and Environment Institute at Khon Kaen University, points out that "their impact on agriculture [will not be] as good as expected" because most of the revised versions do not include irrigation, which is one of the features most needed by farmers in the Northeast of Thailand, who grow only one crop a year, whereas their counterparts in the rest of the country commonly harvest two to three crops a year.[40] Furthermore, dam building on the mainstream has direct, immediate, and negative repercussions on the economic and social activities of the people downstream in Cambodia and Vietnam. Cambodian Vice-Premier Long Somol, in charge of economic development, expressed his concern about the impact of mainstream dams on the Tonle Sap in terms of fish spawning and rice harvests because any project would necessarily change the cycles of the river.[41] The Vietnamese fear that the big dams on the mainstream as far back upstream as China will diminish its flow, allowing salinity to spread farther inland, endangering the rice cultivation on which Vietnam is so dependent for its hard currency income. Hence, Vietnam and, to a lesser degree, Cambodia are at loggerheads with China and Thailand (and Laos), the upstream nations most eager to pursue the Mekong development.

The Riparians

The return of peace and stability has found the region and the lower Mekong basin nations in vastly different circumstances from when the Mekong Committee was first founded in 1957. Each riparian nation is fully bent on economic development, but not all nations are alike in their assets, capacities, needs, and prospects. Thailand, Laos, Cambodia, and Vietnam all have one common goal, which is economic growth, but each is at its own stage of development, with its own form of dependency on the Mekong River's resources and its own concerns and strategies that put it increasingly at odds with the others.

Thailand. Thailand, the most economically advanced of the four lower Mekong basin nations, showed itself the most eager to push for the construction of hydropower projects, particularly in neighboring Laos. Its energy-hungry economy made great strides in the past two decades. Nevertheless, the Northeast, the region of its territory that is part of the lower Mekong basin, despite decades of regional development planning and millions of dollars in economic aid (mostly U.S.), remains poor, arid, and underdeveloped.[42] The average income in the Northeast was only about half of the Thai national average. Its total arable land amounts to 8.5 million hectares, of which only 500,000 hectares can be irrigated because of the lack of water.[43] It suffers not only from droughts but also from the seasonal flash floods that submerge the banks of the Mekong tributaries. About 0.5 percent of the Northeast farmers used fertilizers as opposed to 13 percent of farmers in the Central Plain in 1970.[44] After the closure of U.S. bases, which had employed a massive Thai workforce, the Northeast no longer was a magnet of employment for workers from other regions of Thailand.[45] The population has actually declined in the Northeast over the years as impoverished farmers migrated to Bangkok and other cities in search of subsistence.[46] From the 1950s to the 1970s, irredentist insurrection simmered, leading to strong ties with the Thai Communist Party, which was actively involved in the region on the right bank of the Mekong River.[47] The Bangkok government, battling the problem for decades, has tried to open the Northeast economically through land reforms, irrigation, and hydropower projects.

However, the most determining factor in Thailand's aggressive push for the implementation of Mekong-related projects was its rapid industrialization. Its factories and cities, most of them situated in the southern Chao Phya basin, are heavy consumers of electricity, with demands jumping by 12–16 percent a year, from 9,730 megawatts in 1994 to a projected 88,000 megawatts by 2020.[48] Thailand's total hydropower potential was estimated at 10,626 megawatts; in 1994 its generating capacity was 2,416 megawatts.[49] As demonstrated by the composition of its GDP, Thailand's industry accounted for 40 percent and its service sector 49 percent, whereas agriculture constituted only 11 percent.[50] Clearly, of the four Mekong nations, Thailand has had the most developed and the fastest-growing economy, one that feeds on natural resources and has ever-increasing energy needs. It is estimated that in 1995, of the 16,500 megawatts in total power demand for the four countries, Thailand consumed 81 percent, Vietnam 17.6 percent, Laos and Cambodia barely 1.4 percent each. Power demand is expected to increase by 9 percent a year until 2000 and by 7 percent a year between 2001 and 2010.[51] Paradoxically, Laos and Cambodia contain 84 percent of the supply potential.[52]

Thailand is no stranger to river basin development as shown by its numerous schemes to tap its myriad rivers, the most ambitious of which was the Greater Chao Phya Project (GCPP) launched in 1952 thanks to a US$ 18 million World Bank loan.[53] Based on the construction of a series of large dams (one of which was the Yanhee, later renamed Bhumibol Dam, the seventh largest in the world) and extensive irrigation canals, it was considered "Asia's largest irrigation project."[54] Some of the dams also generated hydropower that serves Bangkok. Since the 1950s, Thailand had feverishly built hydropower dams, and among the most recently completed hydropower projects, there was the US$ 178 million Pak Mool Dam, completed—despite numerous delays—in 1993 by the French firm SOGREAH in the Northeast in part thanks to a US$ 22 million loan from the World Bank. This was one of the projects that sparked widespread protests, not only from the environmentalists, but also from local NGOs and the traditionally authority-fearing local villagers directly affected by the dam.[55] Protests were so vociferous that the bank sent fourteen of its twenty-two directors for a field visit and discussions with the local villagers. In fact, Electricity Generating Authority of Thailand (EGAT), the Thai governmental agency responsible for dam building, has been under fire in the past few years for its policy of building dams at all costs and of neglecting the question of resettlement of the people displaced by dam construction. Existing dams such as the Nam Pong/Ubolratana in Khon Kaen province or the older Bhumibol and Sirikit Dams have silted so rapidly as a result of the deforestation caused by the slash-and-burn activities of the reset-tled families that it has been necessary to dredge them frequently, and the elec-tricity and irrigation purposes for which they were built could not be met satisfac-torily.[56]

The World Bank and other international organizations, faced with mounting international and local outcry, prudently decided either to halt their funding while awaiting further environmental and social studies or to withdraw altogether as in the case of the 600-megawatt Nam Choan project in the Thung Yai Nare-suan Wildlife Sanctuary in the western province of Kanchanaburi, near the Bur-mese border, and the Kaeng Sua Ten project in one of Thailand's last teak for-ests in the north.[57] In fact, the Nam Choan project nearly provoked a political crisis in 1988 as it was furiously opposed by a wide spectrum of Thai public opinion from Kanchanaburi villagers to townspeople to students to the local mass media as well as more than forty international conservation groups. The project unavoidably attracted opposition because of its location within an earth-quake-prone region and within a unique wildlife sanctuary of "international eco-logical importance." The high-level governmental team appointed to investigate the matter, chaired by the deputy prime minister, made the unusual decision to halt the project while waiting for further studies.[58] EGAT, nevertheless, argued that Nam Choan provided one of the cheapest and cleanest power source poten-tials, pointing out that the upper Kwae Yai River on which the project was to be built was "the last major source in Thailand from which substantial hydroelectric power could be generated."[59]

Since it was running out of dam sites, with the few left situated in Thailand's last teak forests, and was faced with widespread opposition that could lead to political unrest, EGAT has been expanding into the lands and waters of neigh-bors with which it has brisk business ties: Thailand, the most important investor in Laos, accounts for 20 percent of investments in Myanmar and is the sixth largest in Yunnan.[60] Thailand showed its enterprising spirit by being the first to finance road, railway, and bridge construction in China (Yunnan), Myanmar, and Laos: for instance, financing the bridge across the Mekong from Chiang Khong to Ban Huey Xai on the planned road that would link Thailand to Yunnan, and extending a soft loan to Myanmar for the construction of the Chiang Rai (Thai-land)–Kengtung (Myanmar)–Kunming (China) Road.[61] It bought electricity from Malaysia (30 megawatts) and agreed to purchase US$ 400 million worth of natu-ral gas from Myanmar's Gulf of Mataban for electricity production in West Thailand.[62] It also had plans to acquire water from Myanmar's Salween River.[63] Thailand and Cambodia announced in April 1995 that an agreement had been concluded to divert water from the Stung Nam River in Cambodia to power plants in Thailand.[64] Its commercial ties with Laos are especially close: It buys from the latter electricity (146 megawatts annually), timber, and ores. In June 1996, Thailand signed another agreement with Laos to buy 3,000 megawatts by the year 2000. There were even talks of a Baht Zone in the Mekong region, since Thailand had the most prosperous economy with an apparently strong currency widely used in the area.[65] Yet, as it relies more and more on its neighbors, Thailand has come to be viewed as a nation that is attempting to export its problems of pollution, depletion of natural resources, and destruction of the environment.[66] As a result, Laos and Myanmar have been somewhat cautious in their responses to Thai offers of dam construction, timber concessions, and road building.

Laos. Laos emerged from the war one of the poorest countries, depending almost entirely for its survival on foreign assistance, especially that of the Communist bloc. The former Soviet Union's aid to Laos accounted for 3 percent of the latter's GDP, and before it ended in 1991, financed 80 percent of the Lao budget deficit.[67] The Soviet aid made up 57 percent of total aid to Laos in 1986 but shrank to 17 percent in 1990 before it stopped altogether. Such drastic reduction did not mean that Laos was totally helpless, because Western aid increased in importance after 1988,[68] and by the time of the USSR's collapse, Laos had already taken urgent measures to adapt. In 1986, Laos began to open up its economy, which became more market-oriented but was handicapped by a number of factors. Arable land in the narrow plains is very limited: Of approximately 800,000 hectares, barely 1 percent is irrigated, whereas 48 percent of the country's national income is generated by agriculture.[69] With an underdeveloped economy, a small population (4.5 million), a lack of infrastructure, a heavy, long-term reliance on foreign aid (15 to 20 percent of the GDP), serious trade imbalances (US$ 130 million to US$ 140 million a year) as well as war-related difficulties (provinces such as Xieng Khouang are still heavily mined), Laos had to find a source of income and exports.[70] Fortunately, Laos has abundant mineral resources (gold, gemstones, iron ore, huge reserves of coal, and possibly oil), forests, and rivers coursing down steep slopes that provide excellent sites for hydroelectric projects. In fact, it has the largest hydropower potential (37,000 megawatts) of the four countries but can consume very little of it for the moment, since 60 percent of its economy is taken up by agriculture; exporting hydroelectricity to its neighbors is one of its best opportunities to earn hard currency. Indeed, it is often referred to as "the Kuwait of Asia."

Kamphoui Keoboualapha, Laos's deputy prime minister and chairman of the State Committee for Planning and Cooperation, noted that Laos wanted "to build dams and hydroelectric power plants. . . . In this way, prosperity will come also to the countryside," with schools and hospitals, with electricity reaching villages that have never known it.[71] The Electricité du Laos (EDL) deputy director for corporate finance, Monekham Keonakhone, expressed the hope that privately built projects will earn Laos approximately US$ 150 million per year over a twenty-five-year period.[72] It has been exporting to Thailand more than 100 megawatts of electricity generated by the Nam Ngum and the Xeset Dams.[73] The Lao government listed sixty potential BOT-type (build-operate-transfer) hydropower projects to be built by the year 2020, most of them concentrated in the provinces of Attapeu, Bolikhamsai, and Vientiane, where Mekong tributary basins are located.[74] Among them, the Nam Theun 2 project, situated in the Bolovens province, elicited much criticism.

A large scheme (600 megawatts), the Nam Theun 2 Project Development Group was a joint venture involving Laos with a 25 percent share and the rest in foreign investment: Electricité de France (30 percent), the Transfield Corp. of Australia (10 percent), and a consortium of Thai firms, including Jasmine International, Italian-Thai Development, and Phatra Thanakit (35 percent).[75] The consortium thus formed was given the acronym of NTEC (Nam Theun 2 Electricity Consortium). Germany and Japan, as well as the UNDP, the World Bank, and the ADB, were approached but did not express any firm commitment to this project because of its negative environmental impact.[76] Approximately 700 square kilometers of forest would be flooded, while about 1,000 hectares of farmland were planned for irrigation. The *Wall Street Journal* mentioned the figure of US$ 40 million a year in revenue for twenty-five years, after which the BOT project would become the property of Laos, bringing a hypothetical revenue of US$ 100 million a year.[77] The developers—in an attempt to placate ecologists the world over—pledged to contribute US$ 1 million yearly for thirty years, to a fund that "would create a special conservation area to protect the dam's watershed from hunting, logging and other encroachment."[78] The World Bank became wary of the project's unfavorable ecological press (a state of affairs with which the bank is quite familiar because of the Narmada Dam in India and the Three Gorges Dam in China) and ordered a number of studies "on resettlement plans, watershed conservation, environmental effects . . . and alternatives to Nam Theun Two," while insisting that they "be conducted in 'an open, transparent, participatory process.'"[79] So far, NTEC appears to have fulfilled its promise of paying due consideration to the human and environmental factors, that is, the evacuees and their habitat, by spending millions in sustainable development studies and demonstration farms. This concern has led to the unavoidable question of whether these millions could have been better used for the good of larger segments of the population and for finding alternatives to development other than costly and uncertain hydropower projects.

Close by, there is the 210-megawatt, US$ 280 million Nam Theun-Hinboum project financed by the consortium formed by EDL, Nordic Hydropower, and a Thai real estate firm, MDX Public Company, to sell to EGAT the power produced (this being the second EGAT-EDL electricity sale agreement of its kind).[80] This project involved another set of players that usually do not call attention to themselves—the Nordic countries of Norway and Sweden, whose governments, along with companies such as Nordic Hydropower, over several decades have been faithful contributors to the Mekong Project through numerous studies. Unlike the Nam Theun 2, the Theun-Hinboum's construction began in November 1994 thanks to ADB's US$ 60 million loan and loans from Norway and Sweden. Ann Danaiya Usher, a former journalist with the Bangkok-based *The Nation*, who studied the question of dams in Laos, reported that it was a

Norwegian consultant firm, Norconsult, that carried out the environmental impact study (a typical case of "aid with strings") and "concluded that the project has significant *beneficial* environmental impacts" (italics in the text).[81] Unlike the Nam Theun 2 project, the Theun-Hinboum reservoir was conceived so as not to flood the thirteen villages in the valley. Since there would be no flooding, it was argued, then no compensation was deemed necessary. The conclusion was disputed by the environmental advocacy and other NGO groups that reviewed the document, leading its patron, the Norwegian Agency for Development Co-operation (NORAD), to reject Norconsult's findings.[82]

The Theun-Hinboum will be the first BOT-type dam for Laos that has to repay ADB an estimated US$ 60 million. Again, the concern for this type of dam where the financing was provided in large part by private companies is that the participating country, in this case Laos, may lose sovereignty over the project as it leases its natural resources out to private companies that are not under public mandate to assist in economic development. Hence, construction and environmental standards may be less rigorously enforced, and because of what the World Bank's energy economist, John Besant-Jones, terms "pervasive appraisal optimism," cost estimates may not be respected.[83] Naturally, one of the questions that arises when discussing BOT-dams is that no one can predict a dam's condition two or three decades hence. It may be silted or cracked beyond repair, or if repairs are necessary and feasible, they may not be affordable to a developing country.

Furthermore, there is the question of supply and demand to consider. Thailand will be Laos's sole buyer of hydropower for years to come and, thus, has been able to dictate kilowatt-hour rates.[84] In fact, *The Nation* noted that "Laos is getting a poor price for its exports . . . because it is selling to a monopsony: a market situation in which there is a single buyer," that is, EGAT.[85] The other neighboring Mekong countries all have their own hydropower schemes—from China with its Lancang Jiang/Mekong projects to Myanmar with a huge project on the Salween River—and are not in need of Laos's hydropower. Even Vietnam, with which Laos signed a Head of Agreement in September 1995 according to which it would sell to the former 1,500–2,010 megawatts of its hydropower by 1998–2010, has hydropower projects of its own on the Yali River, a Mekong tributary.[86]

The government of Laos was eager to proceed with the construction of the Mekong tributary dams, as the many public statements of its officials at conferences and workshops locally and internationally manifested. For example, Laos's Minister of Communications, Transport, Post and Construction Phao Bounnaphol's presentation at the 1996 ADB-supported Fifth Conference on the Greater Mekong Subregion stressed "the need for all of us to move toward implementation" of the priority projects in all sectors.[87] This eagerness is also clear in the many memoranda of understanding that Laos has signed with its neighbors (e.g., with China for a possible cooperation in the supply of electricity from Yunnan to the northern provinces of Laos, or with Cambodia to provide electricity to its border provinces).[88] Paradoxically, although Laos fully intends to develop its economy and find new sources of income, the government is somewhat wary of the "evils" that a too-rapid economic growth could bring to the country, such as prostitution, drug use, the spread of AIDS, and cultural losses. These effects can be seen wreaking their havoc on Laos's neighbor Thailand. Most of the dams (built or projected) in Laos are geared toward Thailand; hence, the "benefits" will be exported, whereas the social and environmental costs will be borne by the local people and their environment.[89] Amid the flurry of paperwork generated by the sixty projects envisioned and the twenty-three preliminary agreements signed with dam-building foreign companies, the emerging consensus was that very few of them will ever reach the feasibility study stage let alone be financed and implemented. However, the fact that these sites were under consideration led to premature and widespread logging, since the Lao government allows "salvage logging" in the areas where dam construction is supposed to take place.[90] There are many problematic aspects linked to the question of dam-building, but in the end, one has to consider the questions of who will benefit, what will be the cost, and who will pay that cost.

Cambodia. War went on the longest and the cruelest in Cambodia. In the postwar period, one of Cambodia's foremost tasks was to achieve food-sufficiency and, according to the vice-premier in charge of economy, Kong Somol, "to achieve that we need a good system of irrigation," since "less than 7 percent of Cambodia's rice fields are irrigated."[91] Because of this lack of a viable irrigation system, more than 85 percent of the agricultural production has to rely on irregular rainfall in a land that is generally arid except in the vicinity of the Tonle Sap.[92] Cambodia's forest cover, which used to extend over 13 million hectares in 1969, fell to 7.5 million hectares in the early 1980s as a result of long years of war, fuelwood use (the country's main energy source along with charcoal), and undiscerning and frantic exploitation by Japanese, Taiwanese, and Thai timber companies, to the monetary benefit of the rival Khmer political factions.[93] Cambodia's greatest resource is the bountiful Tonle Sap, where flooding and fish spawning are at risk. As a Mekong Committee report notes, "Fish, particularly young ones, that enter the inundated areas along with the flood waters thrive on the rich food that develops there, grow luxuriantly and contribute to the rich harvest from such areas. Thus any body of water in the basin, be it large or small, yields a natural crop of fish of some value."[94]

V. R. Pantulu, a former Mekong Committee fisheries expert, pointed out that "90 percent of the fish in the Mekong basin spawn not in the rivers themselves, but in the surrounding lakes, submerged fields and flooded forests . . . during the wet season."[95] Toward the end of the rainy season as the floodwater recedes, the fish that feed on the surrounding vegetation will return to the lake. This process allows thousands of fishermen to reap bountiful harvests of fish, such as the famous elephantfish (*Oxyeleotris marmoratus*) and the gigantic catfish (*Pangasianodon gigas*) that can reach several hundred kilograms.[96] Recently, however, the catch in the lake dropped to less than half of the 1960s-era levels, mainly because of siltation, which, in turn, is caused by the rapid deforestation that is taking place in Cambodia. The deforestation accelerated with the return of peace as Japanese and Thai timber companies carried out large-scale logging.[97] Fish is one of the major sources of protein for most Cambodians (and other riparians) and is getting scarcer and more difficult to catch as the environment suffers increasing degradation. In recognition of this situation, Cambodia presented at the Mekong River Commission's 1996 Annual Workshop a number of projects, including studies of the migration and spawning of Mekong fish species and inventories of Cambodia's wetlands.[98]

In terms of electricity, Cambodia relies totally on imported gas and oil; its (diesel) generating capacity is barely 90 megawatts, of which 90 percent can be found in the capital, Phnom Penh.[99] Yet, in terms of hydroelectricity and agricultural potential, the country offers plenty: hydroelectricity in the north thanks to its numerous falls and agriculture in the south in the plains surrounding the Tonle Sap. Under Khmer Rouge rule, in a gesture meant to revive the Angkor splendor but also to secure food self-sufficiency, a program of irrigation network construction was implemented on a national scale that enlisted the entire population. As one of the Khmer Rouge's slogans affirmed, "With water we'll have rice, and with rice we'll have everything."[100] Driven forward at the cost of hundreds of thousands of lives, a third of Cambodia reportedly was irrigated from 1975 to 1978. In a repetition of the Angkor-age exploits, Cambodia once again became a land dotted with dams, reservoirs, and irrigation canals at the province, district, and village level.[101] Yet, the reports that came out later on of that period concerning the irrigation works seem to indicate mixed results. Apparently, not much thought was given to topography, technology, and durability, and the irrigation did not yield the bountiful harvests of rice expected or last beyond the first monsoon.[102] For a time, however, in certain provinces such as Battambang, for instance, visitors reported double- and even triple-cropping.

At times shut off by or isolating itself from the international community, Cambodia saw relatively little of that Mekong aid manna in the 1960s–1970s, since most of the studies, field investigations, and data collections on the lower Mekong basin performed during the 1960s and 1970s focused on the other riparian states. With Cambodia rejoining the ranks of the Mekong Committee, attention focused on reviving the Prek Thnot project situated southwest of Phnom Penh. Started in 1968, its construction was interrupted in 1971, although the Khmer Rouge leaders asserted that it was completed in 1978 without any outside help.[103] If and when achieved, the project would not only provide Phnom Penh with eighteen megawatts of electricity but could also irrigate 70,000 hectares of arid land in one of Cambodia's poorest regions, which is comprised of Kompong Speu and three other provinces.[104] The Bovel irrigation project, in the Battambang province, one of the Mekong schemes, was presumably completed during the Khmer Rouge years thanks to French assistance. It was hoped that the combined mainstream multipurpose projects of Stung Treng, Sambor, and Tonle Sap would bring more hectares under irrigation as well as provide electricity for consumption and export to Vietnam, although given the country's enormous and more urgent needs in other sectors, it is most unlikely that these enormous projects will ever be developed.

Because Cambodia rejoined the Mekong Committee only in 1991, up-to-date studies are somewhat lacking on potential Mekong projects in Cambodia. At the 1996 ADB Conference on the Greater Mekong Subregion, Cambodian Minister of Planning Chea Chanta noted that "the major challenge facing Cambodia today is the restoration and management of its natural resources."[105] Electricité du Cambodge formulated a Power Development Plan that includes eight hydropower projects in the Elephant and Cardamom Mountains. However, given their remote location (southwestern Cambodia) and the continued political instability (the Hun Sen coup of summer 1997 that led to international aid reduction; the continuing Khmer Rouge presence), aid donors are not eager to finance even preliminary studies.

Vietnam. In Vietnam, the region that lies within the lower Mekong basin encompasses part of Dien-bien (with the Nam Ou River), the central highlands (with the Se San and Sre Pok Mekong tributaries), and the delta. Mekong-related projects for Vietnam include fisheries, flood and salinity control, and hydropower production. The central highlands are propitious for hydropower production, and plans were made to expand Drayling, a small dam built in the 1960s, with the addition of generators. There are hydropower projects for the Upper Se San and Upper Sre Pok Rivers, one of the major ones being the Yali Falls hydropower scheme in the Mekong tributary of the upper Se San River, which aims to provide cheap electricity to the cities of Kontum and Pleiku and irrigation to the Gia-lai-Kontum province.[106]

Because of its topography, the delta as such presents different constraints, which are reflected in projects that do not include power production but instead involve flood and salinity control through the construction of an entire network of canals and low-lift pumps. Irrigation was planned on a large scale (150,000 hectares) along with fisheries and agricultural stations. The Mekong delta, with a potential agricultural area of 3.9 million hectares, 2.4 million hectares currently cultivated, of which 2 million is in paddy, is one of the two "rice baskets" of the country (along with the Red River delta).[107] By providing half of the rice production, the Mekong delta contributes to Vietnam's position as the "world's third-largest rice exporter after Thailand and the United States," with 1.885 million tons of exported rice.[108] However, the delta suffers from saline intrusion (1.6 million hectares) and acid soils (1.5 million hectares) and needs a certain volume of water discharge to flush the salinity and acidity from the land. Yearly, between about 1.2 million and 1.4 million hectares are subject to Mekong floods for several months, which can wreak havoc on the economy.[109] The 1994 flood, though not the worst in memory, caused losses estimated at US$ 100 million. In addition, an estimated 300,000 homes were submerged, 250,000 acres of crops were damaged, and 407 people were killed.[110] The two ensuing years brought more floods in the delta. In February 1996, the government issued decree 99/TT implementing "the five-year plan (1996–2000) for the development of hydraulics, transportation, and rural construction in the Mekong delta."[111] The extensive measures aimed at protecting the delta against the seasonal floods, desalinizing regions such as Cà-mau, and providing farmers with rural credit. But since *doi moi* or "renovation" legitimized market incentives, Vietnamese farmers have sought more lucrative activities by cutting down coastal mangroves and *melaleuca* forests and turning them into foreign-currency-yielding shrimp farms that are extremely polluting and destructive.[112] In recognition of the urgency of the situation, the Mekong Delta Master Plan (based on an earlier version published in the 1960s) focused on the protection of mangrove and melaleuca forests as well as coastal afforestation.[113]

Of all of the Mekong basin's regions, the Cambodian Tonle Sap and the Vietnamese Mekong delta would be the most affected by the construction of dams upstream, by tributary projects, and by other water diversion schemes. As stated by Mikael Bahrke, a representative of the Swedish International Development Authority: "The whole river basin is a very fragile system. Any project can have consequences downstream. If you build a dam, environmentally you must be very careful, especially with the Mekong Delta."[114] The deputy secretary-general of the Vietnam National Mekong Committee expressed these concerns, noting that "due attention has to be given to various alternative measures for flood control and salinity prevention. With a sensitive aquatic living system and wetlands in the delta, any proposed project in the basin, especially a basin-wide project, needs to be, beside feasible in technology and economy, environmentally sound."[115]

PROSPECTS FOR THE NEW MILLENNIUM

The Outer Circles

Beyond the primordial circle of long-involved lower Mekong basin nations, there are wider, outer circles of nations and organizations that are equally interested in the development of the Mekong River and its region. Some of these are new players such as China and Myanmar; others have been in the game for decades such as Japan and the ADB. China and Myanmar, the two riparian states of the upper Mekong basin, expressed interest in joining and expanding the Mekong regional activities. The increased interest was manifested in a flurry of activities related to the Mekong region. Several joint projects were completed, including the Mitraphap/Friendship Bridge that joins Vientiane in Laos to Nongkhai in Thailand over the Mekong River thanks to an Australian loan of US$ 30 million; it was inaugurated in April 1994.[116] The Mekong is navigable only on a limited stretch of its stream, from the delta mouth to Phnom-Penh and with some difficulties over segments of it in Laos. It carries a limited number of tonnage and its importance to the four countries varies. For Vietnam, Cambodia, and Laos, especially, the river does serve a vital function as a means of transportation and a fluvial highway. But for Thailand, the center of its economic activities resides in the Central Plain and the Chao Phya, and the Mekong is seldom used as a means of transportation.

Numerous conferences and meetings at the ministerial level among the six riparian nations were organized to discuss opening up the region via improved or new communication links. For instance, the first Quadripartite Meeting on Transport Linkages involved Myanmar, Thailand, Laos, and China (Yunnan) and was held in 1993. After the meeting, the four nations called on the ADB "to provide a central secretariat which will extend technical, administrative and logistical support to the Ministerial-level Conference and to the forums and working groups."[117] The Golden Quadrangle nations, as they are sometimes called, were eager to open the region formed by the confluence of all four territories to trade and tourism. (The area also comprises the infamous Golden Triangle, known mostly for opium cultivation and drug trafficking.)[118] Other conferences such as the Subregional Transport Forum, the Subregional Electric Power Forum, and the Subregional Economic Co-operation Conference held in Ha-noi, in April 1994, all organized by ADB, revealed the Mekong nations' concern about the absence or insufficiency of transportation links such as roads, railways, airports, and navigable channels. Projects conceived would, for instance, link Bangkok, Phnom Penh, and Ho Chi Minh City via a road (R1) that would end in Vung-tau; another would run transversally from northeastern Thailand to southern Laos to northeastern Cambodia and reach central Vietnam (R9); or a railway line would connect Yunnan to Vietnam to Thailand.[119] These ideas led to the Japan- and UN-sponsored symposium held in December 1994 in Tokyo, to discuss "the issue of how to proceed with infrastructure construction while conducting development in the Mekong River basin."[120]

China has emerged as one of the dominant forces in the newly considered wider Mekong basin region. For centuries, China has been acutely plagued by flooding and droughts. In summer 1996, for instance, "floods ravaged about half of China's provinces and caused a record 220 billion yuan (US$ 26.5 billion) worth of damage, the worst of its kind in the last few years."[121] Some 48 percent of China's arable land is irrigated, producing "74 percent of the country's grain, 60 percent of cash crops and 80 percent of vegetables."[122] China has the world's greatest hydropower potential, estimated at 380,000 megawatts, of which only 10 percent is being exploited.[123]

In the post–cold war era, China has launched the most extensive dam-building program of all the Asian states; it accounts for half of the dams built in the world. It has launched the construction of a number of gigantic dams, the most colossal being the Three Gorges Dam, dubbed "the world's largest water conservancy project."[124] Located on the Yangzi River, between Sichuan and Hubei provinces, the dam, begun in 1994, is expected to take more than twenty years to complete, displacing more than 1 million people, at a cost estimated between US$ 11 billion and US$ 30 billion.[125] Its expected generating capacity of 17,680 megawatts would supply Shanghai as well as contribute to the industrialization of the upper Yangzi region around the city of Chongqing.[126]

Concurrently, China, without attracting significant publicity or opposition from the outside world, has built or is in the process of building dams on the Mekong, or Lancang Jiang as it is known in China. The Manwan Dam, located on the upperstream of the Mekong River in Yunnan province between Yunxian and Jingdong counties, with an installed capacity of 1,500 megawatts of electricity, is a hydropower dam that started functioning in mid-1994 to provide electricity not only to the provincial capital, Kunming, but also to the surrounding towns.[127] The Dachaoshan Dam farther downstream with a 1,300 megawatts installed capacity is also being built. There are five other projects (Gongguoqiao, Xiaowan, Nuozhadu, Jinghong, Mengsong) on the Lancang Jiang and nine tributary schemes that China intends to carry out with or without external assistance.[128] The Chinese Lancang/Mekong projects will have a total capacity of 15,400 megawatts that will feed the booming province of Yunnan.[129] All these projects are hydropower schemes and do not include any irrigation planning.

The Lancang Jiang basin has more than 10,000 species of flora and fauna, some of them quite rare, and comprises several different ecological zones, which led China to establish there a number of protected areas in the interest of attracting tourism. Unlike the lower Mekong basin, which has been studied for decades by regional institutions such as the Mekong Committee, it is only recently that the Chinese government has begun to launch long-term studies on China's own "Mekong Cascade" and its possible impact on the hydrology and ecology of the downstream region from the Yunnan-Lao border to the Vietnamese delta. According to E. C. Chapman and He Daming, authors of an article on China's Mekong project, the general impact of Manwan (completed and functioning), Dachaoshan (in construction), and Jinghong (in negotiations with Thailand for joint construction and power sharing) "will be negligible," whereas the Xiaowan and Nuozhadu projects "will have a major effect."[130] The authors argue that, given the location of the dams in "a steep-walled gorge," the construction of these high-walled dams is justified in the sense that "relatively few village households [will be] needing to be resettled," although "careful management as to volumes and timing, to optimize potential benefits downstream (e.g., in irrigation and power generation) and to minimize adverse effects such as the much-publicized potential losses in Lower Mekong fish population and in reduction of the inflow . . . to Tonle Sap" will be necessary.[131] In comparing the potential benefits with the cost, the authors put in the balance, on one hand, a larger volume of water for hydropower production in Laos, for irrigation of the arid north and northeast of Thailand, for domestic consumption in the basin, and for stemming salt intrusion in the delta of Vietnam, and on the other hand, the devastating impact on "fish populations, fish habitat and to the livelihood of fisherfolk," especially around the Tonle Sap, where environmental degradation is quite serious and advanced. Chapman and Daming posit a fundamental question, which is at the core of all developmental projects, especially concerning dam construction: "What matters most? . . . sustaining the fish population and greater bio-diversity, or providing a better life for the human population (now and in the future) in two of the world's poorest countries, Laos and Cambodia?"[132] This fundamental but slightly skewed question ignores the link between the two matters. It is not simply fish versus humans, since in the long run, the fisherfolk and beyond them, the populations of Laos and Cambodia, could have a better life only if the fish population is allowed to survive and thrive in an environment propitious for their multiplication. What, after all, are fisherfolk to do when the river runs dry of both water and fish?

Chinese Vice-Premier Jiang Chun-yun announced during a conference on waterworks in Beijing, October 1996, that in its ninth five-year plan (1996–2000), China would "speed up its construction of hydropower stations," which will "electrify 300 grain-growing counties."[133] The fact that China has forged ahead with its projects on the Lancang Jiang/Mekong River without consulting its downstream neighbors has caused concern among the latter for the same reasons that the lower Mekong riparians worry about mainstream dam construction: insufficient water flow during the dry season, salinity intrusion, impediment to navigation and fish spawning, siltation, and pollution.[134]

Among the upstream nations, China (especially Yunnan province) is eager to push for the implementation of projects that will make the upper Mekong usable not only for hydropower production but also for navigation. With its booming population of 30 million, an expanding economy eager for markets, yet lacking in a convenient means of transportation and ready access to its eastern coastal ports, Yunnan's provincial authorities have envisioned the Mekong as an accessible, cheap, and navigable—by dynamiting the rapids on the Myanmar-Laos stretch—road that will allow it to penetrate markets in Myanmar, Laos, and the lowerstream states. Ironically, this was the dream of nineteenth-century Western colonizers: to locate and penetrate the mythical China market with its millions of potential consumers. It was the French, in particular, who, when searching for such a road, stumbled inadvertently on the Mekong River first and then on the Red River, leading them to conquer Vietnam.[135]

China suggested the building of a bridge spanning the Mekong at Chiang Khong between Laos and Thailand, farther upstream of the Friendship Bridge and less than 200 kilometers from the Lao-Chinese border.[136] The booming Chinese economy is in need of markets and consumers, and the regions of Myanmar, Thailand, and Laos closest to the border with Yunnan are already swamped with Chinese consumer goods. Yunnan is part of China's Southwest (along with Guizhou and Sichuan), a booming region that is acquiring an increasing economic importance. As He Shengda, the deputy director of the Yunnan Institute of Southeast Asian Studies (Kunming), has remarked, the Southwest is joined to the Indochinese countries not only by land, mountains, and rivers but also by common nationalities that live straddled over both sides.[137] This then could form an economic sphere of its own that would be beneficial to all nations concerned, each contributing to the others based on their respective strengths (for example, the Southwest's industrial products in exchange for the agricultural goods of the lower Mekong basin's countries), and the whole sphere could be linked by land (a highway network that would connect Yunnan to Myanmar to Thailand) and by river transportation (the Lancang/Mekong, the Red River, and the Irrawaddy River lanes).[138] Yet, the emergence of a region linking China to the other Mekong nations would carry with it unavoidable disadvantages in the form of cross-border migration of illegal workers, the spread of AIDS and other sexually transmissible diseases brought on by prostitution, and the rise of crime and pollution, all phenomena that are already taking place in towns and cities in the border regions of Myanmar, Thailand, Laos, and China. [139]

China's rival for influence in the region is Japan, which is not new to the Mekong Project or the Mekong Committee. Indeed, the Japanese government and companies have long been involved in the lower Mekong basin through the financing and realization of studies on the Mekong tributaries and in Cambodia and Vietnam. Japanese aid, as economists have often remarked, "has been motivated largely by economic self-interest."[140] Ninety-eight percent of Japanese aid in the 1970s went to Asia, compared with 60 percent in the 1990s. Cambodia, Vietnam, and Laos, which used to rank first on the Japanese list of recipients, were replaced by Indonesia, China, the Philippines, and Thailand. It does not mean that Southeast Asia has decreased in importance in Japan's economic and foreign policy. On the contrary, as economist Ryokichi Hirono emphasizes, "the economic interdependence between Japan and East Asia [by which he means also Southeast Asia] . . . has deepened . . . whether in international trade, investment, or financial flows."[141] Japan, naturally, is present through multilateral banks, the most important one in the region being the ADB, in which its share, while equal to that of the United States, is less involved in political motivations. Its ADB financial contribution has increased "because it sees the Bank as a major vehicle for recycling its surpluses."[142] Over the years, Japan's assistance was funneled toward the financing of infrastructures such as transportation, communication, and power.[143] In the matter of the Mekong basin, Japan also took the lead by organizing the Forum for Comprehensive Development of Indochina to discuss the issues of the Mekong region's infrastructure and job creation. Japan wanted to be among the first to compete for the contracts on the planned construction of highways, airports, harbors, and railways that will link capitals and key urban centers of the region. There was also the Japanese-led AEM-MITI, which was a joint effort by the Japanese Ministry of Trade and Industry and the Ministries of Economy of ASEAN to assist socialist economies (Laos, Myanmar, Cambodia, Vietnam) in making the transition into market economies.[144]

In the midst of these activities, ASEAN (of which Vietnam became a member in July 1995) also launched its own Mekong Basin Development Cooperation initiative. Spearheaded by Malaysia and Singapore, the initiative invited "China, Japan and South Korea to join ASEAN in the development of the Mekong River basin."[145] On June 17, 1996, the ASEAN-Mekong Basin Development Cooperation was formally set up in Kuala Lumpur, involving the ASEAN member nations and Cambodia, China, Laos, and Myanmar. One of ASEAN's unofficial reasons for this initiative was to attempt to engage China in security matters to reduce the potential for conflicts, such as the dispute over the Spratly Islands in the South China Sea. So far, China has remained noncommittal, refusing to sign the Southeast Asia Nuclear Weapon–Free Zone Treaty at the December 1995 ASEAN Conference and declining to make any commitment concerning the Mekong River Commission and the river's usages. Further, ASEAN, viewing the Mekong region as a potential market, may not wish to be the last to profit from the manna, although questions about its redundancy and lack of experience in Mekong issues are germane.[146]

The Links

Connecting these different circles are the perennial international organizations that have been involved in the region for decades and are mentioned in the previous chapters: the UNDP, the World Bank, the IMF, and the ADB. Of them, the ADB was the most aggressive in terms of involvement. The bank organized a number of conferences to launch its idea of the so-called Greater Mekong Subregion or GMS, which includes the six nations of the Mekong: Myanmar, Laos, Thailand, China, Cambodia, and Vietnam. The GMS covers an area of approximately 2.3 million square kilometers with a population of 220 million (see Map 5.1).[147] The bank conducted field studies, organized conferences, and provided technical and financial assistance within the framework of its "Medium-Term Strategic Framework (1993–1996)."[148] It intended to promote economic cooperation in the GMS nations in which it sees a potential "regional market of 220 million people."[149] The bank has identified seventy-seven priority projects in the Greater Mekong Subregion in numerous sectors (transport, energy, trade, investment), the priority being given to the first two. Some of the projects were financed by the bank itself or jointly with private companies (for instance, the Nam Theun-Hinboum project in Laos jointly with Norwegian and Thai private groups); for others it called on bilateral and multilateral institutions (for instance, the Australian Agency for International Development and the Canadian International Development Agency) and the private sector.[150] This role of "third-party facilitator" has allowed the bank to bring governmental officials and international business executives, ministries, and private companies with their capital, technology, and experience together.[151] A number of these projects concern hydroelectricity in the Mekong basin (e.g., the Xe Kong and Se San Basin Hydropower Development in Cambodia, Laos, and Vietnam, with a power grid linking them to Thailand). In general, however, they go beyond the Mekong River's multiple resources development and pertain directly to the building of the region's infrastructure, such as the Bangkok-Phnom Penh-Ho Chi Minh City-Vung-tau Road Project, the Upstream Lancang/Mekong River Navigation Improvement Project, and the Cambodia Airports Improvement Project.[152] The cost is immeasurably great: The road construction cost alone is estimated by the bank

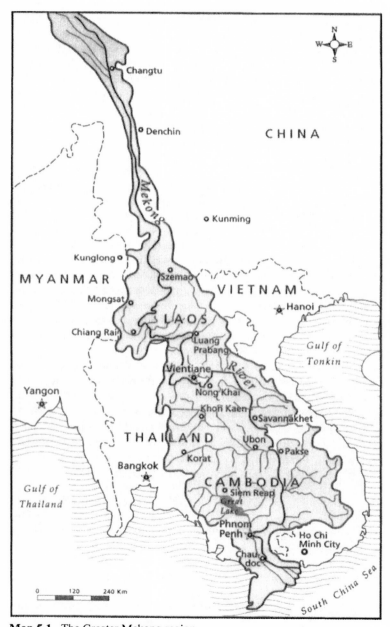

Map 5.1 The Greater Mekong region

to be US$ 1.5 billion. In all these cases, the ADB supplants the Mekong Committee in its role as coordinator, organizer, and planner, giving rise to the question of whether the latter or rather its latest reincarnation, the Mekong River Commission, may become redundant, obsolete, and useless and whether it has to surpass the roles traditionally ascribed to its previous avatars in order to survive.

Finally, there is also the perennial player, the United States, whose Asian trade reached $100 billion in 1995, during which year American companies invested approximately $60 billion and reaped in return $6 billion from the region.[153] While American businessmen were eager to go into the Mekong region after having lost their early advantage to competitors because of past U.S. trade embargoes, the U.S. government was slow to follow, coming up with statements and policies that were often contradictory. Through its long-term involvement in the region and in the Mekong Project, it has acquired decades of valuable knowledge and experience. The Bureau of Reclamation spent more than ten years studying Pa Mong. However, the bureau has since forsworn its previous policy of big dam building. As its head, Daniel Beard, announced in 1994: "The dam-building era in the United States is over."[154] American companies provided expertise and accumulated lucrative contracts throughout the Mekong Project's evolution during the Second Indochina War. Numerous U.S. private companies present during the Vietnam War were eager to be involved again as Vietnam, among other Mekong nations, was touted as the last "tiger," and the Mekong region seen as one of the last frontiers. One of the major U.S. companies dealing with Southeast Asia, Black and Veatch Corporation, specializes in "water infrastructure engineering and construction services." Its C.E.O., Jim Adam, stated to the House of Representatives that "nearly 70 percent of our 1995 sales in the power sector" was generated by exports to Southeast Asia and elsewhere.[155] Such companies were naturally eager to sign contracts for dam construction in the Mekong basin. However, in the brouhaha generated by the revival of interest in the Mekong Project and the Mekong region, the U.S. government was noticeably noncommittal concerning the Mekong development, without even an official observer at the ADB-sponsored Fifth Conference on Economic Cooperation in the Mekong region in June 1996, leaving the initiative to the countries of the region, and to regional institutions such as the ADB or ASEAN.

Like David against Goliath, overshadowed but not powerless, the environmental advocacy organizations, indigenous peoples' rights organizations, and other NGOs, have attempted to stem the Mekong nations' seemingly inexorable journey toward damming one of the last giant rivers by drawing the world's attention to the dangers and the destruction that such construction may bring to the environment and the people living in it. These groups often cite the Pa Mong as an example of potential threat. Its scaled-down version, the Low Pa Mong, presents advantages and disadvantages. It would increase hydropower production and, when combined with other mainstream projects such as the High Luang Prabang (Laos) and the Sambor (Cambodia), could help limit flooding by storing runoff and combat salinity by releasing the stored water during the dry season.[156]

Nevertheless, the Mekong has more fish species than even the Yangzi or the Ganges, and their spawning in the Tonle Sap's submerged woods could be blocked by the dam-regulated flow. This could lead to a depletion in the volume of more than 200,000 tons of freshwater fish caught yearly in Cambodia and the Vietnamese delta.[157] Furthermore, the regulated flow would cause serious disruption in the agricultural traditions of Vietnamese farmers that have for centuries adapted their cultivation to the flooding and salinity of the delta. The coastal ecosystems formed by the mangroves would also be profoundly affected by the changed flow of the Mekong River. Environmentalists point to the loss of the Mekong basin's forest cover (50 percent in the 1970s to a depleted 25 percent in the 1980s) and warn that major dams such as the Nam Theun 2 could aggravate deforestation, which could result in serious soil erosion and loss of retentive capacity in the basin.[158] This may partially explain the phenomenon of increased silting in most of Thailand's dams with their diminished storage capacity, electricity output, and halieutic volume, a situation that is equally true in Laos and Cambodia. In Laos, for instance, logging that resulted from dam construction has wrought havoc to the country's primary rainforests. Additionally, scientists have warned that climatic changes caused by global warming might affect the river in ways that are not well known.[159] One must also mention the spread of such water-related diseases as schistosomiasis and lung or liver flukes. The NGOs have been pressuring international organizations such as the World Bank, in some cases forcing them to revise their standards and to review loans that went into financing dams: for example, the Narmada project in India and the Arun Dam project in Nepal. Governmental aid agencies such as the Swedish International Development Agency (SIDA) have backed out in the financing of hydropower schemes in Laos; SIDA even reduced its contribution to the Mekong Committee from 1992 to 1994 out of concern for the possible environmental damage caused by dams.

Outside of the environmental concerns, many observers have remarked that in the changed circumstances of the post–cold war world, given the scarcity of public funding and the fact that international aid is drying up or getting smaller and more expensive, an increasing number of developing countries have resorted to the BOT solution approved by the World Bank in 1989. Private companies build a project on a site donated by the government and operate it long enough (five to ten years or longer) to make profits before transferring the dam to the government. In these cases, the state has very little control over the quality of the workmanship, nor can it provide any guarantee as to its positive social, economic, or environmental impact, making this solution a risky one. In other words, the BOT system in practice may mean that hydropower projects will escape governmental scrutiny, with projects determined by market considerations and imposed by international companies that will intervene in the economy of the participating country. Eventually, the latter may lose control of its precious national natural resources. As the author of a report for the Lao Protected Areas

Division points out, none of the private sector or development agencies has yet suggested that the Lao government consider the "social, ecological, and economic project cost of all projects in a balanced fashion before deciding which projects to pursue. In so doing, [the] Lao government would regain some of the control over project choice which now is largely with the private sector companies involved."[160] In contrast, the Lao government was able to retain full control of the Nam Ngum and Xeset Dams in Laos. Completed in the late 1970s with the financial assistance of the World Bank, the ADB, and a host of Western donors, in addition to the Lao government, the Nam Ngum has been owned and managed by Laos's electricity agency, the Electricité du Laos, from the beginning.[161] The Xeset, built in the 1980s and completed in 1991, with the help of the UNDP, the ADB, and the Swedish government, is also entirely the property of the Lao government.[162]

Given the enhanced awareness and increased protests worldwide concerning dam building and its environmental and social impact, institutions such as the ADB, the World Bank, and the UNDP are increasingly reluctant to finance projects "whose environmental and social impact has been inadequately assessed."[163] Furthermore, such pressures have forced these institutions to reform their lending rules, paying more attention to questions of resettlement and environment rather than just yield and productivity. The World Bank's financing of the 680-megawatt Nam Theun 2 project in Laos is a case in point. President James Wolfensohn vowed to remake the bank into "a more democratic, ecosensitive and entrepreneurial force."[164] The bank spent millions of dollars and forced the developers to do so as well on studies to assess the impact of the dam. On several occasions, however, international lenders such as the World Bank and the ADB, faced with pressure from NGOs and local and environmental groups, have delayed, withheld, or canceled altogether their loans and grants, leaving Third World nations alarmed at not being able to find financing for their development projects. Malaysia's prime minister, Mahathir Mohammed, voiced this concern to the UN: "We in the poor countries would like to have some cheap hydroelectric power. But all manner of campaigns are mounted against our proposals. . . . The World Bank will be used to deprive poor countries of cheap hydroelectric power. And all this after the rich have developed most of their hydro potentials."[165]

A Greater Mekong Region

The area that is currently considered the Mekong region is much greater than in the past, when only the lower basin and the four nations were regarded as part of it. It comprises now a land area of approximately 2.3 million square kilometers and has a population of 230 million that will increase by an estimated 100 million by the year 2000. It is a region with a combined GDP of approximately US$ 200 billion in 1995. Its potential is enormous but remains to be fully developed. Endowed with agricultural land, timber, minerals, oil, and natural gas, and with the Mekong River as the potential provider of cheap and abundant hydropower, the region has tremendous promise.[166]

Will these Mekong basin countries, given the centuries-old animosity between them, especially between Cambodia and Vietnam, further exacerbated during the Third Indochina Conflict, and given their fear of potential Chinese hegemony, be able to cooperate on regional development and to share the Mekong's resources in an equitable way? There have been talks about Thailand's own "geopolitics of resource development," whereby Thailand is viewed as the resource-hungry economy, expanding into Laos, Cambodia, and Myanmar by applying a strategy of "development and exploitation of neighboring countries' resources."[167] Thai hydropower and timber exploitation are two cases that illustrate this view. Would Laos then replicate, with respect to Thailand, the role that colonized countries have played in the past, becoming a source of raw materials and a market for Thai consumer products, by selling its timber and hydropower to Thailand and getting in return Thai baht and products? Would Cambodia, so weak and unstable in the midst of such strong neighbors, have the opportunity and the means to safeguard its natural resources, the two most precious ones being the Mekong and the Tonle Sap? Would Vietnam be adversely affected by Thailand's plans to divert water to its arid Northeast region, leaving the delta with an insufficient volume of water in the dry season? Or is the greater threat to Vietnam to come, as in the past, from China, this time by means of its construction of dams on the Lancang Jiang and the pollution of the river by its chemical plants? Hoang Trong Quang, the director of international cooperation in the Vietnamese Ministry of Water Resources, sees Thailand as "a security risk" for Vietnam because of Thailand's potential Mekong projects in the Northeast, raising the possibility that the Mekong's "low flow will cut off our main 'rice bowl' and starve Vietnam."[168] The estimation of the costs and benefits of Mekong projects is a complex and thorny issue complicated by elusive factors such as environmental costs, which are impossible to quantify. In the end, whether the Mekong development will be carried out piecemeal or comprehensively—and which projects will be implemented—depends less on economic or financial factors than on the political will of the leaders of the riparian nations.

CONCLUSION

The Mekong Project gave rise to high expectations during the 1960s, to dreams of an electrified countryside, bountiful harvests, abundant fish catches, a speedy riverine commerce sailing up and down the Mekong, and an end to flooding. Forty years later, most of it has not come to pass, but the long hiatus has made it possible for researchers to conduct studies that show that lurking behind these dreams are darker realities, particularly those involving environmental and social costs. Furthermore, we now have a better understanding of the problematic relationship between economic development, social stratification, and national power. As Nayan Chanda of the *Far Eastern Economic Review* points out, "Enduring peace can be achieved only if economic development plans help redress the deep socio-economic gap *within* Cambodia and the glaring economic imbalance between Cambodia and its neighbors, especially Vietnam."[169] Chanda's statement is valid for all six nations, though more germane for some than for others. At another level, economic cooperation between the Mekong states, if it succeeds in strengthening and stabilizing them, may counterbalance China's ever expanding and dominating presence in the region.

For the Mekong River itself, the difficulty will be to entice China to cooperate with its neighbors in developing the river's resources instead of carrying out its own schemes without any regard for the downstream nations. The military-security implication of linking the six nations is evident: As a potential superpower, China's increasing influence (with Myanmar and Laos) has rendered its neighbors extremely wary. Although there are economic advantages to a connecting infrastructure, none of China's southern neighbors is, for the moment, eager to see it materialize. In the past, the advantage of an underdeveloped "Northern Quadrangle" was that it served as a buffer zone for all concerned. However, there are rumors that China intends to extend its influence into Southeast Asia through its southern neighbors, especially Myanmar, to which China has been shipping weapons and other military equipment (to Myanmar's army, navy, and air force), as well as consumer goods.[170] Terms such as "the Chinese Monroe Doctrine in Asia" have been bandied about.[171] China's increasing influence in Laos—long tied to its powerful eastern neighbor, Vietnam—is reflected in the augmented volume of sales not only of Chinese consumer goods but also of military hardware and increased economic assistance.[172] This change in the balance of power is cause for concern for the Mekong nations and for the whole of Asia—and the rest of the world.

NOTES

1. David W. P. Elliott, ed., *The Third Indochina Conflict* (Boulder, CO: Westview Press, 1981).

2. For an analysis of U.S. post–Indochina War policy, see Frederick Z. Brown, *Second Chance: The United States and Indochina in the 1990s* (New York: Council on Foreign Relations Press, 1989).

3. Lars Schoultz, "Politics, Economics, and U.S. Participation in Multilateral Development Banks," *International Organization* 36 (Summer 1982): 565.

4. Ibid., 561–573.

5. Robert Wihtol, *The Asian Development Bank and Rural Development: Policy and Practice* (New York: St. Martin's Press, 1988), 46.

6. Jonathan E. Sanford, "Restrictions on U.S. Contributions to Multilateral Development Banks," *Journal of International Law and Economics* 15 (1981): 565.

7. Akikiko Tanaka and Yasuhiro Takeda, "Japan's Economic Policy toward China and Vietnam," in Kaoro Okuizumi, Kent E. Calder, and Gerritt W. Gong, eds., *The U.S.-Japan Economic Relationship in East and Southeast Asia: A Policy Framework for Asia-*

Pacific Economic Cooperation (Tokyo: Asia Pacific Association of Japan; Washington, DC: The Center for Strategic and International Studies, 1992), 222.

8. The end of the cold war and the fragmentation of the Soviet bloc had tremendous financial and economic repercussions on the three socialist countries of the lower Mekong basin, which had come to rely essentially on Soviet aid after the U.S. aid cession. They had also come to depend on the trade exchange within the Council for Mutual Economic Assistance (otherwise known as COMECON). Aid to Vietnam from the Soviet Union, for instance, went from US$ 1 billion in 1988 to US$ 322 million in 1990 and ended in 1991. Chia Siow Yue, "Means of Inter-Regional Economic Cooperation Between ASEAN and Indochina," in Osamu Yasuda, Chira Hongladarom, and Mya Than, eds., *Vietnam, Laos and Cambodia: The Path to Economic Development*, 2 vols. (Tokyo: The Sasakawa Peace Foundation, 1993), 2:104.

9. The U.S. economic embargo included Vietnam and Cambodia but was not imposed on Laos, with which diplomatic relations were reduced but not severed. Hence, Laos was able to continue receiving aid from the Soviet bloc and from Western countries. Yue, "Means of Inter-Regional Economic Cooperation," 104.

10. Pachoom Chomchai, *The United States, the Mekong Committee and Thailand: A Study of American Multilateral and Bilateral Assistance to North-East Thailand since the 1950s* (Bangkok: Institute of Asian Studies, Chulalongkorn University, 1994), 172.

11. Committee for the Coordination of Investigations of the Lower Mekong Basin, *Annual Report 1978* (Bangkok: United Nations, 1978), 2.

12. Ibid.

13. Chomchai, *The United States, the Mekong Committee and Thailand*, 176.

14. Committee for the Coordination of Investigations of the Lower Mekong Basin, *Report by the Ad-Hoc Working Group on the Draft Joint Declaration of Principles for Utilization of the Waters of the Lower Mekong Basin* (September 27, 1974, Mekong Secretariat) (Bangkok: United Nations), 8.

15. Peter Fish, "Money from the West," *Far Eastern Economic Review* [hereafter, *FEER*] (February 23, 1979): 86–87.

16. Committee for the Coordination of Investigations of the Lower Mekong Basin, *Annual Report 1975* (Bangkok: United Nations), 69.

17. Chomchai, *The United States, the Mekong Committee and Thailand*, 180.

18. Ibid., 186.

19. Ibid., 194.

20. Interim Committee for Coordination of Investigations of the Lower Mekong Basin, *Annual Report 1984* (Bangkok: United Nations), 4.

21. Ibid., 48.

22. Ibid., 6.

23. Ibid., 53.

24. University of Michigan Team for Pa Mong Research, *Pa Mong Resettlement: Final Report* (Ann Arbor: Department of Geography and Center for South and Southeast Asian Studies, University of Michigan, 1977), 1. The report remarks that the figure of 480,000 "involves four times the population displaced by any other dam project for which statistics are available." See also Interim Committee for Coordination of Investigations of the Lower Mekong Basin, *Perspectives for Mekong Development: Revised Indicative Plan (1987) for the Development of Land, Water and Related Resources of the Lower Mekong Basin* (Bangkok: The Committee, April 1988), xv.

25. *Perspectives for Mekong Development*, xv, 37.

26. Peter Hinton, "Is It Possible to 'Manage' a River? Reflections from the Mekong," in Bob Stensholt, ed., *Development Dilemmas in the Mekong Subregion* (Clayton, Vic.: Monash Asia Institute, Monash University, 1996), 53.

27. Ann Danaiya Usher, "The Race for Power in Laos: The Nordic Connections," in Michael J. G. Parnwell and Raymond L. Bryant, eds., *Environmental Change in South-East Asia: People, Politics, and Sustainable Development* (London: Routledge, 1996), 130.

28. Mekong River Commission Towards Sustainable Development, *Annual Report 1995* (Bangkok: Mekong River Secretariat, 1995), 5; Paul Handley, "Hostile Undercurrents," *FEER* (April 2, 1992): 16; Gráinne Ryder, "New Agreement on Mekong Could Hasten Damming," *World Rivers Review*, Special Mekong Issue, 9 (Fourth Quarter 1994): 1 and 19. Gráinne Ryder is a Canadian engineer who has worked on environmental issues for TERRA (Towards Ecological Recovery and Regional Alliance).

29. Ryder, "New Agreement on Mekong," 1. For an organizational chart, see also Samran Chooduangngern, "The Mekong Basin Development Plan," in Stensholt, ed., *Development Dilemmas in the Mekong Subregion,* 186. The founding in April 1995 of the Mekong River Commission in Chiang Rai led a number of Thai NGOs to stage a protest against the MRC, "opposing the 'influence of the dam-building industry' in the creation of the new Commission." Usher, "The Race for Power in Laos," 130.

30. "Agreement on the Cooperation for the Sustainable Development of the Mekong River Basin," Appendix 1, in Stensholt, ed., *Development Dilemmas in the Mekong Subregion,* 261.

31. Chooduangngern, "The Mekong Basin Development Plan," 187–189. The author's title is adviser, Policy and Planning Division of the MRC Secretariat.

32. "Initiative Overload," *The Economist* (September 7, 1996): 32.

33. Handley, "Hostile Undercurrents," 16.

34. "Agreement on the Cooperation," 262; Ryder, "New Agreement," 19.

35. One of the reasons for Thailand's push to discard the 1975 agreement was that one of its principles required that any Mekong nation that proposed to carry out a mainstream project must inform the other members of its intent and provide them with the project's studies and plans. Murray Hiebert, "Muddy Waters," *FEER* (February 21, 1991): 28.

36. Letter addressed to Mr. James Gustave Speth, Administrator, United Nations Development Program, by *International Rivers Network* (Berkeley, CA, April 17, 1995), 2.

37. Murray Hiebert, "The Common Stream," *FEER* (February 21, 1991): 25.

38. Ibid. Even the reduced number of 60,000 people to be resettled was considered too large and the potential devastation of fisheries essential to their livelihoods much too serious. It even led to a disagreement within the Mekong Committee, between its executive agent Chuck Lankester, eager to push for the Low Pa Mong's realization, and its Swedish worker, Eric Skoglund, warning of the serious losses that the project could cause. Usher, "The Race for Power in Laos," 129.

39. "Nam Theun 2 Hydroelectric Project in Lao PDR: An International Venture," Briefing compiled by TERRA (Vientiane, May 1995), 4. For a discussion of the biological richness of the region, see Motor Columbus Consulting Engineers, Inc., *Prefeasibility Study Report of a Future Major Hydroelectric Project: Nam Theun 2, Nam Ngum 2, Nam Ngum 3* (Baden, Switzerland, June 1987).

40. Hiebert, "The Common Stream," 26.

41. Ibid.

42. From the 1950s to the 1970s, U.S. economic aid to Thailand totaled $650 million, most of which was geared toward abating insurgency. John L. S. Girling, *Thailand, Society and Politics* (Ithaca, NY: Cornell University Press, 1981), 235. Bridge and road construction such as the Friendship Highway between Bangkok and Nongkhai was another U.S. economic assistance priority having to do more with strategic concerns than economic development. Thak Chaloemtiarana, *Thailand: The Politics of Despotic Paternalism* (Bangkok: Thammasat University, 1979), 259–260.

43. Hiebert, "The Common Stream," 24.

44. Chomchai, *The United States, The Mekong Committee and Thailand*, 259.

45. David Elliott, *Thailand: Origins of Military Rule* (London: Zed Press, 1978), 132.

46. Hiebert, "The Common Stream," 24.

47. Girling, *Thailand*, 268. In the post–Vietnam War era, the Communist Party of Thailand (CPT) suffered a setback when refugees from Laos and Cambodia fled the Communist takeover of their countries and settled in the Northeast of Thailand, revealing to the world the hardships they had endured under Communist regimes.

48. Hiebert, "The Common Stream," 24; Bertil Lintner, "Add Water," *FEER* (October 13, 1994): 70.

49. Steve Van Beek, *The Chao Phya: River in Transition* (Kuala Lumpur: Oxford University Press, 1995), 193.

50. Michael Vatikiotis, "Construction Ahead," *FEER* (December 1, 1994): 63.

51. Choung Phanrajsavong, "Hydropower Development in the Lower Mekong Basin," in Stensholt, ed., *Development Dilemmas in the Mekong Subregion,* 31.

52. Yue, "Means of Inter-Regional Economic Cooperation," 110.

53. Van Beek, *The Chao Phya*, 137.

54. Ibid., 138. The GCPP yielded mixed results. It was praised for raising Thailand's rice yield, making it one of the world's leading rice producers. But with success came a host of problems linked to water resources development such as water shortage, water-borne diseases, and pollution by pesticides and human waste.

55. In 1990 and 1991, thousands of Thai villagers marched to Bangkok to demand a dam-building moratorium in Thailand as well as to protest the construction of the Pak Mool Dam, occupying its site in an attempt to block its construction. Larry Lohmann, "Engineers Move In on the Mekong," *New Scientist* (July 13, 1991): 46. For an aperçu on local NGOs in the four countries of the Mekong basin, see Sunil Subhanrao Pednekar, "NGOs and Natural Resources Management in Mainland Southeast Asia," *Thailand Development Research Institute Quarterly Newsletter* 10 (September 1995).

56. See Jasper Ingersoll, *Human Dimensions of Mekong River Basin Development* (Washington, DC: Agency for International Development, 1968); Samuel H. Johnson III, "The Effects of Major Dam Construction: The Nam Pong Project in Thailand," in Colin MacAndrews and Chia In Sine, eds., *Too Rapid Rural Development: Perceptions and Perspectives from Southeast Asia* (Athens: Ohio University Press, 1982), 172–207. These studies show that in the matter of the Nam Pong—destined to be a forerunner to the Pa Mong project—EGAT failed to properly resettle the evacuees. This failure led to their economic and social distress, provoking further social alienation.

57. "Nam Theun 2: A Painful Lesson for Laos Government," *The Nation*, 3/26/1995.

58. Parasol Sricharatchanya, "Politics of Power," *FEER* (March 31 1988): 24.

59. Ibid.

60. Vatikiotis, "Construction Ahead," 63.

61. Medhi Krongkaew, "Thailand and the Development of the Greater Mekong Subregion (GMS)," in Stensholt, ed., *Development Dilemmas in the Mekong Subregion*, 100; Bertil Lintner, "Open for Business," *FEER* (February 9, 1995): 23.

62. Krongkaew, "Thailand and the Development of the Greater Mekong Subregion," 101.

63. Van Beek, *The Chao Phya*, 195–196.

64. *International Rivers Network* (Berkeley, CA, April 17, 1995), 1.

65. Krongkaew, "Thailand and the Development of the Greater Mekong Subregion," 102.

66. It seems that Thai companies are so well known for exploiting workers in the neighboring countries that some of them have to resort to going through third-party companies from Singapore. Ian McGovern, "Regional Development in the Mekong Basin," in Stensholt, ed., *Development Dilemmas in the Mekong Subregion*, 91.

67. Yue, "Means of Inter-Regional Economic Cooperation," 104.

68. Motoyoshi Suzuki, "Present Economic Conditions and Future Prospect for Laos and its Neighboring Countries: Trade, Aid and Foreign Direct Investment," in Yasuda et al., eds., *Vietnam, Laos and Cambodia*, 154.

69. Hiebert, "The Common Stream," 24; Sivixay Saysanavongphet, "Mekong Development Management: Views of the Lao People's Democratic Principle," in Stensholt, ed., *Development Dilemmas in the Mekong Subregion*, 195.

70. Lintner, "Add Water," 71.

71. "Economic Tsar," *FEER* (February 9, 1995): 22.

72. Maya Weber, "The Money of Power," *World Trade* (November 1996): 30.

73. "Laos Should Reconsider the Nam Theun II Dam," *The Nation*, 3/12/1995.

74. Klaus Berkmuller, *Hydropower Development and Protected Areas*, Forest Conservation/Protected Areas Division (Vientiane, April 1995), 2.

75. "Laos Should Reconsider the Nam Theun II Dam"; "Nam Theun 2: A Painful Lesson."

76. "Nam Theun 2 Hydroelectric Project in Lao PDR," 2.

77. Peter Waldman, "Dam Proposed for Laos Is of Immense Meaning to an Array of Interests," *Wall Street Journal*, 8/12/1997.

78. Ibid.

79. Ibid. The "participatory" character of these studies as demanded by the bank is a rather difficult problem, since Laos (or Vietnam or Cambodia, for that matter) with its one-party system and its authoritarian experience is not very adept at this sort of "participation."

80. Lintner, "Add Water," 71. For a discussion of the project and the role played by Norway and Sweden through their aid agencies and power companies, see Usher, "The Race for Power in Laos," 123–144.

81. Usher, "The Race for Power in Laos," 132.

82. Ibid., 125–126.

83. Ibid., 135.

84. For instance, for the Nam Theun-Hinboum and Nam Theun 2 projects, Laos accepted the rates imposed by EGAT of 4.3 cents and 4.5 cents, respectively, per kilowatt-hour. "Laos should reconsider."

85. Ibid.

86. Weber, "The Money of Power," 31; Presentation by H. E. Phao Bounnaphol, Minister of Communications, Transport, Post and Construction, to the ADB-sponsored Fifth Conference on Subregional Economic Cooperation, in *Economic Cooperation in the Greater Mekong Subregion: Facing the Challenges* (Manila: Asian Development Bank, June 1996), 47.

87. Presentation by H. E. Phao Bounnaphol, 47.

88. Ibid.

89. Usher, "The Race for Power in Laos," 133.

90. Berkmuller, *Hydropower Development*, 5. For an analysis on the exploitation of Laos's forestry resources, see Jonathan Rigg and Randi Jerndall, "Plenty in the Context of Scarcity: Forest Management in Laos," in Parnwell and Bryant, eds., *Environmental Change in South-East Asia*, 145–162.

91. Murray Hiebert, "Fertile Imagination," *FEER* (February 21, 1996): 26.

92. Nayan Chanda, "Indochina," in Anthony Lake et al., *After the Wars* (New Brunswick, NJ: Transaction Publishers, 1990), 90.

93. The environmental lobbying group Global Witness charged that the deforestation of Cambodia through logging had lately accelerated, seemingly with the government's collusion despite its official pronouncement against illegal logging. It led the International Monetary Fund to partially suspend a three-year, US$ 120 million loan to Cambodia. Seth Mydans, "To Control Cambodia, Rivals Are Stripping It Bare," *New York Times*, 12/22/1996.

94. Mekong Committee, *Annual Report 1984*, 54.

95. Lohmann, "Engineers Move In," 44.

96. Mok Mareth, Minister for the Environment, "Statement of the Kingdom of Cambodia," presented at the Sixth Annual U.S.-NGO Conference on Vietnam, Cambodia, and Laos, June 8–11, 1995, Washington, DC.

97. Clayton Jones, "Mekong Ecology Threatened by Siltation, Deforestation," *Christian Science Monitor* [hereafter, *CSM*], 1/12/1994, 12.

98. Mok Mareth, "Managing the Mekong: Cambodia Context," in Stensholt, ed., *Development Dilemmas in the Mekong Subregion*, 106–108.

99. Phanrajsavong, "Hydropower Development," 32.

100. Chanda, "Indochina," 85.

101. Charles H. Twining, "The Economy," in Karl D. Jackson, ed., *Cambodia 1975–1978* (Princeton, NJ: Princeton University Press, 1989), 145–146.

102. Ibid.

103. Mekong Committee, *Annual Report 1975* (Bangkok: United Nations, 1975), 75; Twining, "The Economy," 142.

104. Comité pour la Coordination des Etudes sur le Bassin Inférieur du Mékong, *Aménagement Du Prek Thnot, Affluent Du Mékong Au Cambodge, Première Phase* (Bangkok: United Nations, 1966). However, there have been concerns about Cambodia's capability to manage the project, since the Khmer Rouge years wrought havoc in the ranks of trained Khmer engineers and technicians who could have handled the day-to-day operation. Hiebert, "Fertile Imagination," 26.

105. Presentation by H. E. Chea Chanto in *Economic Cooperation in the Greater Mekong Subregion*, 38.

106. Mekong Committee, *Annual Report 1984*, 23.

107. Interim Committee for Coordination of Investigations of the Lower Mekong Basin, *Perspectives for Mekong Development: Revised Indicative Plan (1987) for the Development of Land, Water and Related Resources of the Lower Mekong Basin* (Bangkok: The Committee, April 1988), 32; Nguyen Cong Binh, ed., *Dong Bang Song Cuu Long: Nghien Cuu Phat Trien* (The Mekong Delta: Analysis of Development) (Ha-noi: Nha Xuat Ban Khoa Hoc Xa Hoi, 1995), 26.

108. Hiebert, "The Common Stream," 24; Cameron W. Barr, "Floods in Mekong River Delta Bog Down Vietnam's Economy," *CSM*, 11/8/1994.

109. *Perspectives for Mekong Development*, 32.

110. Barr, "Floods in Mekong River Delta," 6.

111. Nguyen Van Hung, "Dong Bang Song Cuu Long Truoc Mua Nuoc Noi," *Thanh Nien*, 8/17/1996.

112. Clayton Jones, "Mekong Ecology," *CSM*, 1/12/1994. For an aperçu on the problem of shrimp farming and its impacts on the environment in provinces such as Minh-hai, see Carole Beaulieu, *Going for Broke in the Mekong Delta: How the Next Southeast Asian War May Be Fought Over Water* (Hanover, NH: Institute of Current World Affairs, 1994). The author quotes a figure of 0.2 million hectares of dwindling mangroves and forests in the delta. Beaulieu, *Going for Broke*, 10.

113. Beaulieu, *Going for Broke*, 10.

114. Usher, "The Race for Power in Laos," 130.

115. Nguyen Nhan Quang, "The Mekong Basin Development: Vietnam's Concerns," in Stensholt, ed., *Development Dilemmas in the Mekong Subregion*, 124. The author was careful to state that these remarks are his own and do not "necessarily reflect or imply the position of Vietnam." Nguyen Nhan Quang, "The Mekong Basin Development," 120.

116. Although according to the *Far Eastern Economic Review*, the hoped-for increase in traffic and business that the bridge was meant to generate was rather slow to materialize, seemingly because of the red tape imposed by the Lao bureaucracy on the incoming commerce. Vatikiotis, "Construction Ahead," 63.

117. Ricardo M. Tan and George Abonyi, "Economic Co-operation in the Greater Mekong Subregion," in Kiichiro Fukasaku, ed., *Regional Co-operation and Integration in Asia* (Paris: Organization for Economic Co-operation and Development, 1995), 235.

118. "Watching the Mekong Flow," *The Economist* (September 7, 1996): 24–25. See also Mya Than, "Subregional Economic Cooperation: The Case of the Golden Quadrangle in the Mekong Subregion," in Stensholt, ed., *Development Dilemmas in the Mekong Subregion*, 111–117.

119. For a review of the priority projects concerning the development of the ADB's Greater Mekong Subregion, see Tan and Abonyi, *Economic Cooperation in the Greater Mekong Subregion*, 9–14.

120. Nikkan Kogyo Shimbun, 12/01/94.

121. Liang Chao, "Li Calls for Hydroprojects," *China Daily*, 10/26/1996.

122. Xi Mi, "Water Can Bring Bonanza or Disaster," *China Daily*, 10/29/1996.

123. Fred Pearce, "The Biggest Dam in the World," *New Scientist*, 1/28/1995, 26.

124. "Li Stresses Resettlement," *China Daily*, 10/22/1996.

125. The English-language *China Daily*, reporting on the ADB-China's sponsored Conference on Waterworks held in October 1996 in Beijing, mentions that China is calling on foreign investors to help it finance its vast water works program by accepting the practice of "build, operate, transfer," or BOT, whereby "projects are built by foreign private capital and then transferred to China after several years of operation." Liang Chao, "State to Use New Leasing Rules for Waterworks," *China Daily*, 10/24/1996.

126. Pearce, "The Biggest Dam," 25.

127. Hiebert, "The Common Stream," 26.

128. Wang Shui, "The Lancang Jiang Basin: Steps Towards the Realization of Sustainable Development," in Stensholt, ed., *Development Dilemmas in the Mekong Subregion*, 242.

129. "Dammed If You Don't," *The Economist* (November 18, 1996): 39.

130. E. C. Chapman and He Daming, "Downstream Implications of China's Dams on the Lancang Jiang (Upper Mekong) and their Potential Significance for Greater Regional Cooperation, Basin-Wide," in Stensholt, ed., *Development Dilemmas in the Mekong Sub-*

region, 19–20. Chapman's title is director, National Thai Studies Centre, Faculty of Asian Studies, The Australian National University; He Daming's title is director, Center for Environmental Evolution and Sustainable Development, Yunnan Institute of Geography (Kunming, China).

131. Ibid., 21.

132. Ibid., 23.

133. Liang Chao, "Anti-Flood Plans to be Accelerated," *China Daily*, 10/28/1996.

134. "Dammed If You Don't," 39. Curiously enough, there is a part of the Mekong basin that seems to be forgotten in all the activities concerning the Mekong River's development: the upper third of the river, situated in the Tibetan plateau, a region that administratively includes Tibet Autonomous Region (TAR) and the Chinese province of Qinghai. It would mean taking into account the Tibetan view concerning the development of river-related resources, which would likely generate (from China's point of view) considerable negative publicity. Yet the issue needs to be addressed, for what takes place in terms of deforestation or soil erosion in the Tibetan stretch of the river has an enormous impact on the downstream users. Gabriel Lafitte, "Upper Mekong: Ethnicity, Identity and Economy," in Stensholt, ed., *Development Dilemmas in the Mekong Subregion,* 64–69.

135. David Murray, "'From Battlefield to Market Place'—Regional Economic Cooperation in the Mekong Zone," *Geography* 79 (October 1994): 351; Clayton Jones, "A New Dawn Along the Mekong," *CSM*, 1/2/1994, 11.

136. Murray, "'From Battlefield to Market Place,'" 351.

137. He Shengda, "The Economic Cooperation Between Southwest China and Indochina in the 1990s," in Stensholt, ed., *Development Dilemmas in the Mekong Subregion,* 168.

138. Ibid., 171.

139. Mya Than, "Subregional Economic Cooperation,"116.

140. Joseph W. Sewell and W. Patrick Murphy, "The United States and Japan in Southeast Asia: Is a Shared Development Agenda Possible?" in Okuizumi et al., eds., *The U.S.-Japan Economic Relationship,* 125.

141. Ryokichi Hirono, "Japan and the United States in Development Cooperation with East Asian Countries," in Okuizumi et al., eds., *The U.S.-Japan Economic Relationship,* 162.

142. Sewell and Murphy, "The United States and Japan," 134.

143. Hirono, "Japan and the United States," 161.

144. "Initiative Overload," *The Economist*, 9/7/1996.

145. Michael Vatikiotis and Rodney Tasker, "Hang on Tight," *FEER* (December 28, 1995–January 4, 1996): 17.

146. See McGovern, "Regional Development in the Mekong Basin," 87.

147. Tan and Abonyi, "Economic Co-operation," 225.

148. Ibid., 235.

149. Vatikiotis, "Construction Ahead," 62.

150. Tan and Abonyi, "Economic Co-operation," 237.

151. Ibid., 233.

152. Ibid., 241–243.

153. Statement of Dr. Marcus Noland, Senior Fellow, Institute for International Economics, Johns Hopkins University, in U.S. Congress, House of Representatives, Committee on International Relations, *U.S. Interests in Southeast Asia* (Washington, DC: U.S. Government Printing Office, May 30 and June 19, 1997), 59.

154. D. Beard, "Keynote Address to the International Commission on Large Dams (ICOLD)," cited by Usher, "The Race for Power in Laos," 128. Nevertheless, large dam-building is in progress in developing countries, one reason being, as Beard recognizes, that "there is a substantial infrastructure that surrounds dam-building. There are people in the business to make money. They are spreading around the globe trying to encourage dam construction. They are less interested in the problems because promoting dams is their business." Ibid., 128–129.

155. Statement of Mr. Jim Adams, Chief Executive Officer, Black and Veatch Corporation in Ibid., 62.

156. Lohmann, "Engineers Move In," 46.

157. Ibid., 46–47.

158. Hiebert, "The Common Stream," 25.

159. See for instance, Jeffrey W. Jacobs, "International River Basin Development and Climatic Change: The Lower Mekong of Southeast Asia" (Ph.D. dissertation, University of Colorado at Boulder, 1992).

160. Berkmuller, *Hydropower Development,* 5.

161. Nam Ngum Dam in its Phase I was completed in 1971 at the cost of US$ 28.6 million thanks to grants by Western countries and the World Bank. Its Phase II, completed in 1978, was financed in large part by concessional loans and in small part (US$ 5 million out of US$ 49.7 million) by grants, all managed by the ADB. Peter Fish, "Money from the West," *FEER* (February 23, 1979): 87.

162. Lintner, "Add Water," 70.

163. Berkmuller, *Hydropower Development,* 6.

164. Waldman, "Dam Proposed for Laos."

165. Paul Handley, "Power Struggles," *FEER* (October 17, 1991): 98.

166. Filologo Pante, Jr., "Prospects of Economic Cooperation in the Greater Mekong Subregion," in Stensholt, ed., *Development Dilemmas in the Mekong Subregion,* 137.

167. Philip Hirsch, "Thailand and the New Geopolitics of Southeast Asia: Resource and Environmental Issues," in J. Rigg, ed., *Counting the Costs: Economic Growth and Environmental Change in Thailand* (Singapore: Institute of Southeast Asian Studies, 1995), 235–236.

168. Jones, "A New Dawn Along the Mekong," 12.

169. Chanda, "Indochina," 78.

170. Bertil Lintner, "Enter the Dragon," *FEER* (December 22, 1994): 23.

171. Ibid.

172. 1,600 tons of military hardware and a pledge of a US$ 9 million five-year credit. Bertil Lintner, "Ties That Bind," *FEER* (February 9, 1995): 19.

Epilogue

As it has for millennia, the Mekong River will continue to flow through land and peoples that, by contrast, have undergone tremendous changes over the past century. As it courses its way to the sea, the Mekong River affects societies and peoples who, in turn, have attempted to shape it, transforming in the process its environment, its flow, and soon, unavoidably, its course to fit their needs. In the time when it was known to the inhabitants of its banks as simply "the River" or "Mother River," it ran wild, untamed, unharnessed, feared for its floods, loved for its bounties of fish, roaring down cascades and falls, meandering through lush rain forests and swampy mangroves, forcing humans to bend to its seasonal will, carrying them from valleys to plains in a dangerous journey, too mighty a force for them to master. Then, with the rise of ever more powerful kingdoms, it became less of a physical obstacle separating enemies and began to witness movements of population from one bank to the other, as well as tumultuous battles, as invaders from one side crossed it to swoop down on riches on the other shore.

In modern times, new forces penetrated the Mekong region—capitalism, imperialism, modern science and technology—that modified the way the River was perceived. Now the tools were being forged that would allow humans to harness the River's potential, as they dreamed of riches that the Mekong could deposit at their feet. As imperialism broke down the old traditional boundaries to impose its own, it opened the conquered regions to global commerce and exchange, linking one area to another and reshaping the environment. New values were introduced that viewed the River in a different light; new dogmas were imposed that made the River a geopolitical pawn, the development of its resources a solution to perceived ideological threats.

In the nineteenth century, the imperial powers France and Britain divided the Mekong basin's territories according to their own interests. In the process, they also drew maps, imposing imagined borders where there had been none, determining the shape of modern-day nation-states such as Thailand, Laos, Cambodia, and Vietnam from vanquished kingdoms that long had fought each other, from neighbors that long had recognized each other in unequal suzerain-vassal tributes, political marriages, and commercial exchanges. Meanwhile, new methods and new technologies were used that changed the way the Mekong riparians interacted with the River and with each other. No longer content to live by it or on it or to travel with it, these inhabitants and their colonizers attempted to exploit the River efficiently as they cleared new land for cultivation. Canals were dug to bring large-scale irrigation for the cultivation and export of monocultures, and navigational channels were opened for the transport of these products to seaharbors where ships were waiting to carry them to the metropolis. Most regions of the world began to be integrated into a global capitalist economy as resource-extraction economies arose. Southeast Asia and the Mekong basin became part of the world market as suppliers of natural resources while larger and larger swathes of forest were cleared to open the way for cities, markets, and intensive agriculture. Yet these transformations were still too slight to alter fundamentally the natural rhythm of the River's yearly floods or impede its course.

It was only in the second half of the twentieth century that the pace picked up as the result of a confluence of forces. By then the cold war had spread its mantle over the world, forcing nation-states to choose one ideology over another, making them into pawns that had to be coaxed or coerced into aligning themselves in the name of communism or capitalism. Thus arose the decades-long, all-consuming wars in the lower Mekong basin that brought into the region more powerful players—the United States and a host of other politico-economic actors such as the UN, the World Bank, and the Asian Development Bank, served by that continuing agent of change, an ever-evolving science and technology. In the name of security and containment, on one hand, and of economic development, on the other, the River's harnessing truly began, not yet centrally, but increasingly on its tributaries.

The United States has always had two main concerns in its relationships with other nations: security and trade, which are truly the driving forces of all American concerns. Depending on the values of the moment (the Monroe Doctrine or anticommunism, for instance) and how strong their grips were on American society, the United States has been at times willing to go to war; at other times, as in the 1990s under the influence of the "Vietnam syndrome," the country has been more reticent. Because of these tendencies, it has contributed tremendously to (as it has destroyed greatly) the spawning of new forces such as regionalism and multilateralism in the second half of the century. It has exported to the region its credo of a more efficient, market-based, productive economic development based on industrialization (ideas and systems that had been already introduced by the French and British colonial powers) that requires, among other things, an enormous volume of electricity, thermal, nuclear, or hydraulic. The United States brought its know-how on dam-building; its several decades of TVA experience, of harnessing river systems for the production of electricity, irrigation, and flood-control. These became the models the rest of the world and particularly developing nations with river systems were to follow. The Mekong River happens to be a system flowing through several nations that, in the past, passively accepted its presence, not yet acknowledging their common bonds through this river and not knowing that their future would be partially defined by how they would interact with it from source to sea.

It was a "river man" from Texas, a politician who had ambitions of bringing a Great Society to his own people and yet was himself trapped in a historical time in which there was seemingly no other possibility but war, who brought the world's attention to the unbound richness and untapped potentiality of the Mekong River. President Johnson saw the Mekong as the Tennessee of Asia, the Mekong Project as an Asian TVA. The development of this area would bring electricity to Vietnamese farmers and put food on their tables, showing them that Americans do not just leave cigars (or land mines, for that matter) in their wake. He and the forces he unleashed propelled the Mekong Project forward. For a brief moment, his billion-dollar Mekong proposal created the illusion that peace was within reach if only enough money, food, and electricity were proffered to lure the enemy away from the battlefield, to put down its weapons, and negotiate an end to the conflict. Because of the weight of the United States on the international scene and its all-pervasive influence, the Mekong Project truly began to gain momentum despite the war. Still, the River's course, like that of the war, was not yet permanently altered. The "carrot and stick" policy failed militarily and economically. Once the lure was demonstrated to be ineffective, the United States turned its attention away from the Mekong Project to more urgent military and political matters. It proved impossible to reap immediate social and political benefits from economic development conceived and executed for political expediency. Johnson's Mekong Enterprise did not prove to be the panacea that it was projected to be. At the time, no thought was truly paid to the impact that the proposed development of the Mekong via damming might have on the regional societies and environment and not enough knowledge was available—nor did such a consciousness exist. It was only after the return of peace that the awareness of the impact and the dear price already paid for such development in industrialized countries began to emerge. Meanwhile, regional institutions and organizations such as the ADB and ASEAN grew stronger as nations of the region came into their own, becoming more active players on the international scene and taking the lead in decisions that concern their future.

In the post–Third Indochina War era—in a time of peace, paradoxically—more is at stake than in times of war. Globally, forests are increasingly disappearing, rivers are polluted, as are the oceans, and the world's climate is becoming warmer as the result of human actions. Yet the poorest populations of the world, the teeming masses of Asia and Africa, are pushing farther and farther into the last corners of land yet unopened. These populations demand to be fed and clothed and allowed to pursue their dreams of prosperity in the image of developed countries of the West. Southeast Asia in general, and the Mekong basin in particular, happen to be regions where land, rivers, forests, and other resources are still abundant. But for how long, and for whom?

In the first half of the twentieth century, the all-encompassing concern of nation-states was the potential for a nuclear holocaust resulting from a war between two superpowers of opposing ideologies. By the second half of the twentieth century, the safeguarding of security lies more in the possession of or access to ever-scarcer natural resources, one of the most important of which is water, without which no life is possible. In the Mekong basin, although Thailand's resounding rallying cry of "battlefield to market place" has been eagerly heard throughout the region, opposing interests, usages, and understandings of riparian rights may well lead to more wars between or among riparian nations that now have the means to fight large-scale, destructive conflicts. Centuries-old historical antagonisms (e.g., China versus Vietnam, Cambodia versus Vietnam, Thailand versus Laos and Cambodia) are further exacerbated because of the competition for the access to and use of resources such as oil, minerals, or water (witness the fight for the possession of the Spratly Islands or the Mischief Reef). Concurrently, human awareness of the fragility of local and global ecosystems has led to the formulation of new concepts such as "sustainable development" as well as to the rise of movements for the defense of such concepts. They have become the stakes of geopolitics in the second half of the twentieth century and surely will be in the twenty-first century. The players are much the same, but their positions and capacities have changed politically, economically, and socially.

The harnessing of rivers is a millennial struggle that is the result of the interaction of people with nature and of their endless desire to tame the rivers' forceful manifestations. Carried out partially, it can leave rivers and the riverine environment relatively intact. With modern science and technology, the harnessing can become thorough and effect permanent damage to both humans and nature. The ideology of development through exploitation of river resources and dam building (and the accompanying apparatus of dam-building firms, consultancy companies, and assistance agencies) is a powerful one that is exerting a strong fascination on the minds of the region's governmental officials, economists, and planners—people whose business is to develop and who speak in the name of national interests and survival. Lao, Cambodian, Vietnamese, and Thai governments have expressed their views that the prosperity of their lands and peoples is inseparable from water development. Joining the chorus are the voices of China and Myanmar, forging ahead as their multitudes increase, their survival into the next millennium hanging in the balance. Who can blame them, for what they demand is what the Western world already has. Unfortunately, lost in the drive for development, for highways, electricity, and irrigation, are the peoples that have interacted the most closely with their environment, the so-called indigenous peoples, those often-despised minorities who happen to live on the last available patches of forest and rivers, their cultures and societies determined by their environment. Their existence and mode of living conflict with the higher national interests that demand that the forests and rivers that have nurtured their ancestors and themselves be cleared or submerged. For the greater good of the nation and for their own good as well, "backward peoples still living in the Stone Age" must be taught the modern way of civilized society.

The Mekong River and the course chosen by its riparians epitomize the future that awaits us all. The lessons that can be learned here must be applied to other regions and countries of the world that are awakening not only to the potential but also to the problems presented by the development of their own rivers. The Nile River—that quintessential presence that gave rise to the millennial civilization of Egypt, whose floods fertilized the fields of wheat and cotton portrayed on the pyramids—is facing a host of new problems and choices not very different from those now confronting the Mekong riparians. In the past, the Egyptians never had to share their resources with any riparian nation as the Nile flowed from source to sea. But now Ethiopia and Sudan, upstream from Egypt and emerging from decades of warfare and revolution, are attempting to follow in Egypt's path by building dams that may one day rival the mighty Aswan. The Nile, the Jordan, the Euphrates, the Mekong—will they be known to future generations as rivers of peace or as rivers of war?

The success of the riparian nations of the Mekong basin in agreeing on rights of usage or tenancy will depend very much on a number of factors, tangible and intangible, including China's willingness to enter into the discussions, Thailand's and Laos's acceptance of a more cautious approach to the development of water resources, Cambodia's capacity to stand on its own to defend its water rights, and Vietnam's patience and cooperation. The rivers of peace have the potential for being rivers of war as water becomes scarcer while populations increase and natural resources are over-exploited. Water politics can be as deadly as any other kind of politics.

Selected Bibliography

Abramson, Rudy. *Spanning the Century: The Life of W. Averell Harriman, 1891–1986.* New York: William Morrow, 1992.

Adams, Nina S., and Alfred W. McCoy, eds. *Laos: War and Revolution.* New York: Harper and Row, 1970.

Asian Development Bank. *Annual Report.* Manila: Asian Development Bank. Various issues.

———. *Economic Cooperation in the Greater Mekong Subregion: Facing the Challenges.* Manila: Asian Development Bank, 1996.

Berman, Larry. *Planning a Tragedy: The Americanization of the War in Vietnam.* New York: W. W. Norton, 1982.

Berval, René de, ed. *Kingdom of Laos.* Limoges, France: A. Bontemps Co., 1959.

Black, Eugene R. *Alternative in Southeast Asia.* London: Pall Mall Press, 1969.

Bray, Francesca. *The Rice Economies: Technology and Development in Asian Societies.* Berkeley and Los Angeles: University of California Press, 1994.

Brocheux, Pierre. *The Mekong Delta: Ecology, Economy, and Revolution, 1860–1960.* Madison: University of Wisconsin–Madison, 1995.

Brocheux, Pierre, and Daniel Hémery. *Indochine, la colonisation ambiguë (1858–1954).* Paris: Editions La Découverte, 1995.

Centre d'Etudes et de Recherches Marxistes, ed. *Sur le mode de production asiatique.* Paris: Editions Sociales, 1974.

Chaloemtiarana, Thak. *Thailand: The Politics of Despotic Paternalism.* Bangkok: Thammasat University, 1979.

Chandler, David P. *A History of Cambodia.* Boulder, CO: Westview Press, 1992.

Coedès, Georges. *Les États hindouisés d'Indochine et d'Indonésie.* Paris: Editions de Boccard, 1964.

———. *The Making of Southeast Asia.* Berkeley and Los Angeles: University of California Press, 1972.

Comité pour la Coordination des Etudes sur le Bassin Inférieur du Mékong (Comité du Mékong). *Rapport Annuel.* Bangkok: United Nations. Various issues.

Committee for the Coordination of Investigations of the Lower Mekong Basin (Mekong Committee). *Annual Report*. Bangkok: United Nations. Various issues.

―――. *Atlas of Physical, Economic, and Social Resources of the Lower Mekong Basin*. New York: Engineer Agency for Resources Inventories, 1968.

―――. *Report on Indicative Basin Plan: A Proposed Framework for the Development of Water and Related Resources of the Lower Mekong Basin, 1970*. Bangkok: United Nations, 1972.

Crabb, Cecil V., Jr. *The Doctrines of American Foreign Policy*. Baton Rouge: Louisiana State University Press, 1982.

Dauphin-Meunier, Achille. *Histoire du Cambodge*. Paris: Presses Universitaires de France, 1968.

Economic Commission for Asia and the Far East (ECAFE). *Annual Report*. New York: United Nations. Various issues.

Fifield, Russell H. *Americans in Southeast Asia: The Roots of Commitments*. New York: Thomas Y. Crowell, 1973.

Finlayson, George. *The Mission to Siam and Hue, the Capital of Cochinchina, in the Years 1821–1822*. London: Albemarle-Street, 1826.

Forest, Alain. *Le Cambodge et la colonisation française: Histoire d'une colonisation sans heurts (1897–1920)*. Paris: Editions L'Harmattan, 1980.

Fukasaku, Kiichiro, ed. *Regional Co-operation and Integration in Asia*. Paris: Organization for Economic Co-Operation and Development, 1995.

Gaiduk, Ilya V. *The Soviet Union and the Vietnam War*. Chicago: Ivan R. Dee, 1996.

Gardner, Lloyd C. *Pay Any Price: Lyndon Johnson and the Wars for Vietnam*. Chicago: Ivan R. Dee, 1995.

Garnier, Francis. *Voyage d'exploration en Indochine*. Paris: Editions La Découverte, 1985.

Girling, John L. S. *Thailand: Society and Politics*. Ithaca, NY: Cornell University Press, 1981.

Glos, George Ernest. *International Rivers: A Policy-Oriented Perspective*. Singapore: University of Malaya, 1961.

Gomane, Jean-Pierre. *L'Exploration du Mékong: La Mission Ernest Doudart de Lagrée-Francis Garnier (1866–1868)*. Paris: L'Harmattan, 1994.

Groslier, Bernard Philippe. *Angkor et le Cambodge au XVIème siècle, d'après les sources portugaises et espagnoles*. Paris: Presses Universitaires de France, 1958.

Haley, P. Edward. *Congress and the Fall of South Vietnam and Cambodia*. London: Associated University Presses, 1982.

Hanna, Willard A. *The Mekong Project*. Southeast Asia series. New York: American Universities Field Staff Studies, 1968.

Hayes, Samuel P. *The Beginning of American Aid to Southeast Asia: The Griffin Mission of 1950*. Lexington, MA: Heath Lexington Books, 1971.

Huang, Po-Wen, Jr. *The Asian Development Bank: Diplomacy and Development in Asia*. New York: Vantage Press, 1975.

Huddle, Franklin P. *The Mekong Project: Opportunities and Problems of Regionalism*. Washington, DC: U.S. Government Printing Office, 1972.

Huynh Lua, ed. *Lich Su Khai Pha Vung Dat Nam Bo*. Thanh Pho Ho Chi Minh: Nha Xuat Ban Thanh Pho Ho Chi Minh, 1987.

Isoart, Paul. *Le Phénomène national vietnamien*. Paris: R. Pichon et R. Durand-Augias, 1961.

Jackson, Karl D. *Cambodia, 1975–1978*. Princeton, NJ: Princeton University Press, 1989.

Johnson, Lyndon B. *The Vantage Point: Perspectives of the Presidency, 1963–1969.* New York: Holt, Rinehart and Winston, 1971.

Kahin, George McT. *Intervention: How America Became Involved in Vietnam.* New York: Knopf, 1986.

Kearns, Doris. *Lyndon Johnson and the American Dream.* New York: Harper and Row, 1976.

Le Boulanger, Paul. *Histoire du Laos français: Essai d'une étude chronologique des principautés laotiennes.* Paris: Librairie Plon, 1931.

Lejosne, Jean-Claude. *Le Journal de voyage de Gerrit van Wuysthoff et de ses assistants au Laos (1641–1642).* Metz, France: Centre de documentation et d'information sur le Laos, 1993.

Lilienthal, David E. *The Journals of D. E. Lilienthal.* 7 vols. New York: Harper and Row, 1976.

MacAndrews, Colin, and Chia In Sine, eds. *Too Rapid Rural Development: Perceptions and Perspectives from Southeast Asia.* Athens: Ohio University Press, 1982.

McLeod, Mark W. *The Vietnamese Response to French Intervention, 1862–1874.* New York: Praeger, 1991.

Migot, André. *Les Khmers: Des origines d'Angkor au Cambodge d'aujourd'hui.* Paris: Le Livre Contemporain, 1960.

Mouhot, Henri. *Travels in Siam, Cambodia and Laos, 1858–1860.* 2 vols. Singapore: Oxford University Press, 1989.

Moura, J. *Le Royaume du Cambodge.* 2 vols. Paris: Ernest Leroux, 1883.

Muscat, Robert J. *Thailand and the United States: Development, Security, and Foreign Aid.* New York: Columbia University Press, 1990.

Nguyen Cong Binh, ed. *Dong Bang Song Cuu Long: Nghien Cuu Phat Trien.* Ha-noi: Nha Xuat Ban Khoa Hoc Xa Hoi, 1995.

Nhom Nghien Cuu Ke Hoach Hau Chien. *Phuc Trinh ve Chinh Sach va Chuong Trinh Phat Trien Truong Ky cua Viet Nam Cong Hoa.* 3 vols. Saigon: The Republic of Vietnam, 1969.

Nuechterlein, Donald E. *Thailand and the Struggle for Southeast Asia.* Ithaca, NY: Cornell University Press, 1965.

Osborne, Milton. *River Road to China: The Mekong River Expedition, 1866–1873.* New York: Liveright, 1975.

Parnwell, Michael J. G., and Raymond L. Bryant, eds. *Environmental Change in South-East Asia: People, Politics, and Sustainable Development.* London: Routledge, 1996.

The Pentagon Papers: The Defense Department History of U.S. Decision-Making on Vietnam: The Senator Gravel Edition. 4 vols. Boston: Beacon Press, 1971.

Porter, Gareth, ed. *A Peace Denied: The United States, Vietnam, and the Paris Agreement.* Bloomington: Indiana University Press, 1975.

———. *Vietnam: The Definitive Documentation of Human Decisions.* 2 vols. Stanfordville, NY: Earl M. Coleman Enterprises Publishers, 1979.

Pouyanne, A. A. *Les Travaux publics de l'Indochine.* Hanoi: Imprimerie d'Extrême-Orient, 1926.

Pradhan, P. C. *Foreign Policy of Kampuchea.* New Delhi: Radiant Publishers, 1985.

Robequain, Charles. *L'Évolution économique de l'Indochine française.* Paris: Paul Hartmann, 1939.

Rostow, Walt Whitman. *The Diffusion of Power: An Essay in Recent History.* New York: Macmillan, 1972.

Schaaf, C. Hart, and Russel H. Fifield. *The Lower Mekong: Challenge to Cooperation in Southeast Asia.* Princeton, NJ: Van Nostrand, 1963.

Singh, Lalita Prasad. *The Politics of Economic Cooperation in Asia: A Study of Asian International Organizations*. Columbia: University of Missouri Press, 1966.

Smith, R. B., and W. Watson, eds. *Early South East Asia: Essays in Archaeology, History and Historical Geography*. New York: Oxford University Press, 1979.

Stargardt, Janice. *The Ancient Pyu of Burma*. Singapore: The Institute of Southeast Asian Studies, 1990.

Stuart-Fox, Martin. *Laos: Politics, Economics and Society*. London: Frances Pinter Publishers, 1986.

Szulc, Tad. *The Illusion of Peace: Foreign Policy in the Nixon Years*. New York: The Viking Press, 1978.

Taboulet, Georges. *La Geste française en Indochine*. 2 vols. Paris: Adrien-Maisonneuve, 1956.

Tana, Li, and Anthony Reid, eds. *Southern Vietnam under the Nguyen: Documents on the Economic History of Cochinchina (Dang Trong), 1602–1777*. Singapore: Institute of Southeast Asian Studies, 1993.

Tarling, Nicholas, ed. *The Cambridge History of Southeast Asia*. 2 vols. Singapore: Cambridge University Press, 1992.

Teston Eugène, and Maurice Percheron. *L'Indochine moderne: Encyclopédie administrative, touristique, artistique et économique*. Paris: Librairie de France, 1932.

Thies, Wallace J. *When Governments Collide: Coercion and Diplomacy in the Vietnam Conflict, 1964–1968*. Berkeley and Los Angeles: University of California Press, 1980.

Tichit, L. *L'Agriculture au Cambodge*. Paris: Agence de Coopération Culturelle et Technique, 1981.

Tran Van Giau, ed. *Dia Chi Van Hoa Thanh Pho Ho Chi Minh*. 2 vols. Thanh Pho Ho Chi Minh: Nha Xuat Ban Thanh Pho Ho Chi Minh, 1987.

Trinh Hoai Duc. *Gia Dinh Thanh Thong Chi*. Translated by Nguyen Tao. 3 vols. Saigon: Nha Van Hoa Phu Quoc Vu Khanh Dac Trach Van Hoa, 1972.

U.S. Congress, House of Representatives, Committee on Appropriations. *Foreign Assistance and Related Agencies Appropriations*. Washington, DC: U.S. Government Printing Office. Various years.

U.S. Engineer Agency for Resources Inventories. *Accelerated Development Plain of Reeds*. Sponsored by the Department of Defense. Advanced Research Projects Agency, ARPA order no. 1068. Prepared by Department of the Army. Washington, DC, July 1968.

———. *Atlas of Physical, Economic, and Social Resources of the Lower Mekong Basin*. New York: United Nations, 1968.

U.S. Government. *Public Papers of the Presidents of the United States: Lyndon B. Johnson, 1968–1969*. Washington, DC: U.S. Government Printing Office, 1970.

———. *Public Papers of the Presidents of the United States: Richard Nixon, 1972*. Washington, DC: U.S. Government Printing Office, 1973.

———. *United States-Vietnam Relations, 1945–1967*. Study Prepared by the Department of Defense. 12 vols. Washington, DC: U.S. Government Printing Office, 1971.

Van Beek, Steve. *The Chao Phya: River in Transition*. Kuala Lumpur: Oxford University Press, 1995.

Wightman, David. *Toward Economic Cooperation in Asia*. New Haven, CT: Yale University Press, 1963.

Wihtol, Robert. *The Asian Development Bank and Rural Development: Policy and Practice*. New York: St. Martin's Press, 1988.

Wolf, Charles, Jr. *Foreign Aid: Theory and Practice in Southern Asia*. Princeton, NJ: Princeton University Press, 1960.

Yang Dao. *Les Hmong du Laos face au développement*. Vientiane: Edition Siaosawath, 1975.

Zasloff, Joseph J., and MacAlister Brown. *Communist Indochina and U.S. Foreign Policy: Postwar Realities*. Boulder, CO: Westview Press, 1978.

Index

A

Accelerated Development of the Plain of Reeds, 156

Accelerated Pacification Campaign, 187n.21

Accelerated Rural Development (ARD) program, 137, 146n.182, 193n.112

Acheson, Dean, 70–72

Act for International Development, 73

Agricultural Development Organization (ADO), 125

Agricultural Pioneer Projects Program, 168, 185–186, 196n.175

Agricultural programs, postwar Mekong Project proposals for, 168

AID. *See* U.S. Agency for International Development (USAID)

Akahata, 113

Al-Akhbar newspaper, 114–115

Alliance for Progress, 107

Alternative in Southeast Asia, 165–167

"Angkorean floods," 15

Angkor empire, hydraulic technology in, xiv, 10, 13–17, 39nn.54, 56, 60, 129. *See also* Cambodia; Khmer empire

Annam, empire of, 20–21

Annamitic chain, Mekong River geography and, 6–8

ANZUS Pact, 72

Army of the Republic of Vietnam (ARVN), 98, 131, 158

Asahi newspaper, 133

Asia Foundation: Mekong Committee and, 57; Mekong Project support by, 59

Asian and Pacific Council (ASPAC), 149

Asian Development Bank (ADB): environmental issues, and concern over, 225; Greater Mekong Subregion (GMS) and, 221–227; Japanese influence in, 220–221; Johnson administration support for, 118–119, 137; Mekong Project of 1970s and, 167, 175–176; Mekong Project support from, 113, 119–123, 142n.103, 159, 200, 238–241; Nixon's postwar proposals and, 179–186; outer circle Mekong development projects and, 217–221; Special Funds of, 143n.120, 154, 181–186, 195n.152

Asian Development Fund (ADF), 181–186, 195n.154

Asian Development Task Force (ADTF), 136

Asian Highway proposal, 104, 123

Associated State of Vietnam, 75, 77, 92n.92

Associated States of Indochina, 35, 72–74

Association of Southeast Asian Nations (ASEAN), 103, 150, 220–221, 239

Australia: Asian Development Bank and, 121, 181, 184; Colombo Plan support from, 65–66; Johnson's Southeast Asian policies and, 116; Mekong Project aid from, 74–75, 77, 83–88, 100, 117; Mitraphap/Friendship Bridge project and, 216; Nam Ngum Dam project and, 126; postwar ECAFE projects and, 50, 52–54; Prek Thnot project support by, 132, 134; U.S. security agreements with, 72

Australian Agency for International Development, 221

Ayuthaya kingdom, 10–12, 15

B

Bangkok-Nakhon Ratchasima-Udorn Thani railway, 95n.126

Bank of Malaysia, 117

Bank of Thailand, 116–117

Barr, Joseph W., 142n.108

Basin Development Plan (BDP), 205

Bassac tributary, Mekong River, 6

Battambang project, 61

Beard, Daniel, 223, 235n.154

Belgrade Conference, 106

Bhumibol Dam, 208

Black, Eugene R.: Asian Development Bank (ADB) and, 119, 122, 143n.113; Mekong Project and, 109, 111, 116, 118, 135–136, 140n.57, 141n.65, 153, 165–167; Nam Ngum Dam project and, 126

Bonard, Louis A. (Admiral), 24–25, 42n.109

BOT (build, operate, transfer) projects: in China, 233n.125; Greater Mekong Subregion (GMS) and, 224–227

Bovel irrigation project, 214–215

Bray, Francesca, 16, 40n.78

bridges, Chinese construction of, on Mekong River, 219–221

Buddhists, protests in Vietnam by, 147, 151, 187n.22

Bundy, McGeorge, 98, 103–104, 117–118, 150

Bundy, William P., 98

Bureau of Flood Control and Water Resources Development, 52

Bureau of Reclamation (U.S.), 79, 85–86, 88n.12, 94n.111, 118; Pa Mong Falls development project, 127–129, 176, 192n.107, 223

Burma. *See* Myanmar

C

Ca-mau peninsula: canal development and, 31; Mekong River geography and, 5

Cambodia: Asian Development Bank aid to, 121–122, 181–186, 195nn.162–164; Colombo Plan membership of, 65; Communist troops used by, 133, 145n.164; ECAFE water management projects and, 50–51, 53–55; economic development projects in, 213–215; end to war in, 200; French colonialism and, 27–28; Greater Mekong Subregion (GMS), inclusion in, 221; Indicative Basin Plan and, 203; Japanese relations with, 220; Johnson administration's Southeast Asian policy and, 124; Mekong as commercial route for, 31, 33; Mekong Committee membership of, 55; Mekong Project and, xv, 54–55, 60, 84–85, 129–138; Mekong River Commission and, 205–207; Mekong River geography in, 5; Nam Ngum Dam project and, 123–124, 126; Nixon administration and, 169–172, 178–179; Pa Mong Falls development project and, 128–129; postwar ECAFE projects and, 54; postwar Mekong delta development and, 156, 201–207; pre-colonial water management in (*see* Angkor empire); Shimla Conference, participation in, 78; spread of war to, 147; Supreme National Council, 204–205; Thai expansion and, 226; Thailand's economic ties with, 82, 95n.125, 209–210; U.S. policies in, 117, 199–200; Vietnam's relations with, 226; water management and control in, 12–17, 35

Canada: Asian Development Bank and, 121, 181; Colombo Plan support by, 65–66; Nam Ngum Dam project and, 126; opposition to Vietnam War in, 99; Prek Thnot project support from, 132, 134

Canadian International Development Agency, 221

canals: colonial construction of, 29–36, 44n.150, 238; pre-colonial construction of, 11–17; Vietnamese construction of, 19–20

"Carrot and the Stick" memo, 102–103, 106–107, 239

Cater, Douglass, 103

Central Intelligence Agency (CIA): anti–Pathet Lao forces financed by, 124, 144n.127; reports on coups in Vietnam by, 98; Udorn Thani air bases and, 171

Champassak: dissolution of Lan Xang and, 12; Vietnamese/Siamese rivalry over, 20–21

Chao Anu rebellion, 41n.97

Charner, Leonard V. (Vice-Admiral), 23, 42n.109

Chasseloup-Laubat, 24–25

Chea Chanta, 215

Chen La empire, Mekong water management and, 7–8, 13, 37n.21

Chiang Kai-shek, 79

Chi basin, 11

China: colonial exploitation of Mekong as route to, 21–22; Greater Mekong Subregion (GMS), inclusion in, 221; Japanese relations with, 220; Laotian development projects and, 212–213; Mekong River Commission and,

205–207; Mekong River development and, 216–227, 233n.125; political influence of, 7–8, 37n.21; postwar flood control projects and, 52, 88n.9; Qinghai province in, 234n.134; Thai investment in, 209; water management and control techniques, 7–8; Yangzi River development proposal and, 79, 94n.112. *See also* People's Republic of China (P.R.C.)

China Area Aid Act, 73

China Daily, 233n.125

Chou Ta-kuan, 14

Chulalongkorn (Rama V), 12

Cleveland, Harlan, 105

Clifford, Clark, 158

Cluster Villages concept, 125

Cochinchina: canal development in, 31–33, 44n.157; development of, 29–36; French colonization of, 23–24, 42n.109; Mekong Delta and, xiv, 40n.78

Cochinchinese Shipping Company, 33

Coedès, George, 21

Colby, William, 151, 187n.21

cold war: Mekong River and, xv, 49; U.S. Southeast Asian policy and, 200, 228n.8

Colombo Plan, Mekong Project and, 58, 62, 65–69

colonialism: Mekong River and, xiv, 21–28, 237–238; water management of Mekong River and, 28–36

Commodity Import Program, 168

communism: advent of Chinese, 69; ECAFE membership negotiations and, 50–55; postwar Mekong Project and, 201–207; Thailand's internal disputes and, 80–83

Congress (U.S.): Asian Development Bank (ADB) and, 180–186; military spending in Asia ended by, 161–165, 177–179, 190n.70, 191n.89

Consultative Committee (CC), 121

containment policy, Johnson and Nixon
    Doctrines and, 164–165, 191n.82
Cooper, Chester, 104, 110
Council for Mutual Economic Assistance
    (COMECON), 228n.8
Crabb, Cecil V. Jr., 190n.80

D

Dachaoshan Dam, 218
Da Couto, Diego, 14
Da Cruz, Gaspar (Father), 22
Dai Nam Thuc Luc, 18
Dams: Chinese construction of, 217–221;
    environmental impact of, 224; Indica-
    tive Basin Plan proposals for, 203–
    207; in Laos, 210–213; Mekong
    Project proposals for, 60; pre-modern
    construction of, on Mekong, 7–8; in
    Thailand, 207–210; U.S. support for
    construction of, 223, 235n.154; in
    Vietnam's Mekong delta, 215–216
Dang Viet Chau, 177
Dauphin-Meunier, Achille, 14
Defense Department (U.S.): postwar Me-
    kong delta development and, 156;
    Southeast Asian policies and, 70
"defensive perimeter" concept, 72
de Gaulle, Charles (French president),
    101, 112, 150
"Delta Plan," 150
de Marini (Father), 10
Democratic Kampuchea, 199. *See also*
    Cambodia
Democratic Republic of Vietnam
    (D.R.V.): Asian Development Bank
    aid for, 184; exclusion of, from
    ECAFE discussions, 111; founding
    and recognition of, 50, 69–70; four-
    point proposal of, 114–115, 141n.84;
    Johnson administration policies to-
    ward, 98–100, 103–108, 111–115,
    124, 135, 141n.84, 157; Nixon ad-
    ministration and, 174–179; peace ne-
    gotiations with, 159; Soviet support
    of, 113, 141n.78; U.S. bombing of,
    151–152; victory over France, 85–86

Denmark, Nam Ngum Dam project and,
    126
Development and Resources Corpora-
    tion, 154–155, 189n.45
Don dien policy in Vietnam, 18
Drayling dam project, 215
Duiker, William J., 91n.67, 191n.82
Dulles, John Foster, 77–78

E

Economic Commission for Asia and the
    Far East (ECAFE): Asian Develop-
    ment Bank and, 119–123; Cambo-
    dian hydraulic projects and, 133–
    134; Johnson administration's
    policies and, 111, 116, 118; Mekong
    Committee and, 55–58; Mekong
    Project and, 123; Nam Ngum Dam
    project and, 126; regionalism and
    postwar Mekong Project and, 49–55,
    86–88
Economic development in Southeast
    Asia: Cambodia, 213–215; Chi-
    nese influence on, 217–221; John-
    son administration proposals for,
    108–138; Laos, 210–213; Me-
    kong Project proposals for, 61;
    Thailand, 207–210; Vietnam, 215–
    216
Edison Electricity Institute, 117
Eisenhower, Dwight D. (President):
    Colombo Plan and, 66; Presidential
    Fund for Asian Economic Develop-
    ment, 140n.49; Southeast Asian
    policies of, 75–78, 84–88, 124,
    143n.124; "Water for Peace" plan,
    97
Electricité de France, 211
Electricité du Cambodge, 215
Electricité Générale du Laos, 170, 210,
    225
Electricity Generating Authority of
    Thailand (EGAT), 208–210,
    230n.56
Emergency Fund for Southeast Asia,
    169–70

Environmental issues: Chinese hydroelectric projects and, 218–21; economic development in Southeast Asia and, 210–14, 216, 232n.90, 233n.112, 239–40; Greater Mekong Subregion projects and, 224–27

F

Fa Ngum, 9, 11
Finer, Herman, 93n.107
First Indochina War, 80–83
Fisheries: Cambodian exploitation of, 213–214; Chinese hydroelectric projects, impact on, 218–219; Greater Mekong Subregion (GMS) and, 224–227
Flaming Dart initiative, 99
Flood Control Bureau (ECAFE), 52
Flood control projects: China and Mekong River dam-building, 217–221; ECAFE negotiations concerning, 52–55; Mekong Committee proposals for, 60; pre-colonial, 7–8, 12–17; U.N.-sponsored studies of, 96n.136
Food Aid program, 168
Food and Agriculture Organization (FAO), Mekong Project support from, 59, 61
Ford Foundation: Mekong Committee and, 57, 61; Mekong Project support from, 59, 101
Foreign Assistance Act (1974), 184
Foreign Assistance Appropriations Act (1976), 179, 200
Foreign Economic Assistance Act (1950), 73
Forests, exploitation of: in Cambodia, 213–214, 232n.93; Greater Mekong Subregion projects and, 224–227; in Laos, 211–213, 232n.90; in Thailand, 208–209; in Vietnam, 216
Forum for Comprehensive Development of Indochina, 220
Fourth Solution, to Vietnam War, 101–106

France: Asian Development Bank and, 121, 143n.113, 184; colonization of Mekong by, 21–28, 237–238; D.R.V. victory over, 85–86; ECAFE and, 50, 54–55; First Indochina War and, 80; Lao kingdoms and, 41n.100; Mekong Project supported by, 54–55, 58, 61, 67; Mekong River and, xiv; opposition to Vietnam War in, 99; Prek Thnot project and, 131–132; rivalry with U.S. over Indochina, 54–55; U.S. Southeast Asian policies and, 74, 112; water management of Mekong by, 28–36
Franco-Siamese International Convention of 1926, 34, 44n.161
Franco-Siamese Treaty of 1893, 27
"Free Thai" organization, 81
Friendship, Commerce and Navigation Treaty, 34
Friendship Highway project (Thailand), 230n.42
Fulbright, J. William (Senator), 101, 133, 163
Funan Empire, Mekong water management and, 7–8, 13, 37n.21, 38n.49
Fund for the Economic Development of Asia, 122

G

Gaiduk, Ilya V., 141n.78
Gardner, Lloyd C., 104, 139n.24, 140n.44, 186n.2
Garnier, Francis, 22, 25–26, 42n.121
Gayet, G., 36
Geneva Agreements of 1954, 51, 76–77, 86, 113–114
Geneva Conference of 1962, 101
Gia Dinh Thanh Thong Chi, 18, 41n.92
Gia-long, 18–19
Global warming, Mekong River development and, 224
Global Witness, 232n.93
Go-cong project, 186
Goldberg, Arthur, 132, 150

Golden Quadrangle nations, Mekong
River development and, 217–221
Goldschmidt, Arthur, 86
Goodwin, Richard, 140n.44
Gray Report, 72
Great Britain: Asian Development Bank
and, 121, 181, 185; Colombo Plan
support from, 65–66; Mekong Project
support from, 61; Mekong River
colonialization and, xiv, 21–36, 237–
238; opposition to Vietnam War in,
99; Prek Thnot project support from,
134
Greater Chao Phya Project (GCPP), 208–
210, 230n.54
Greater Mekong Subregion (GMS), es-
tablishment of, 221–227
Great Lake. *See* Tonle Sap
"Great Rivers for Peace" concept, 166
Green, Marshall, 102–103, 139n.25
Greenstein, Fred I., 143n.124
Griffin, Robert Allen, 72–73
Groslier, Bernard Philippe, 14–15

H

Halpern, Joel, 170–71
Hammarsjkold, Dag (UN Secretary-
General), 55
Hannah, John A., 174
Harriman, W. Averell, 107, 120, 150
Harza Engineering, 59
He Daming, 218–219
He Shengda, 219–220
Hess, Gary R., 91n.62
High Permanent Franco-Siamese Com-
mission, 34–35
Ho Chi Minh, 50, 70; on Johnson's peace
initiatives, 150; reaction by, to John-
son's Johns Hopkins speech, 113–
155; U Thant's talks with, 100
Hoc Tap newspaper, 114
Honolulu Conference of 1966, 151–152
Huddle, Franklin P., 86, 136
Humanitarian Aid to Refugees, 168
Humphrey, Hubert H., 150
Hun Sen, 215

hydraulic technology. *See* water management and control
hydroelectric projects: in Cambodia,
214–215; in China, 217–221;
Greater Mekong Subregion (GMS)
and, 221–227; Indicative Basin Plan
proposals for, 203–207; in Laos,
210–213; postwar ECAFE initiatives
for, 53–55; in Thailand, 207–210; by
U.S. Bureau of Reclamation,
94n.111; in Vietnam, 215–216

I

Illusion of Peace, The, 178
Immerman, Richard H., 143n.124
India: Mekong Project and, 55, 67; opposition to Vietnam War in, 100;
political and cultural influence of, 7–
8, 11, 37n.22, 39n.60; Prek Thnot
project support from, 134; Shimla
Conference and, 77–78; tensions
with Pakistan, 52
Indicative Basin Plan, 171–172, 203–
204
Indochina: Allied decision-making con-
cerning, 91n.57; colonial water man-
agement and control in, 33–36;
French colonialism and, 25–28;
U.S.-French rivalry concerning, 54–
55; U.S. policy toward, 71, 73–78,
80–88, 91n.67, 92n.85, 147
Indochina Postwar Reconstruction Pro-
gram, 168, 183–184
Indonesia, 116, 182–183; Japanese rela-
tions with, 220
Indus Basin Development Fund, 66
Indus River Project, 62
Infrastructure projects, Greater Mekong
Subregion (GMS) and, 221–227
Interim Mekong Committee, 201, 203–
207
International Bank for Reconstruction
and Development (IBRD). *See*
World Bank
International Commission for Control
and Supervision (ICCS), 178–179

International Cooperation Administration (ICA), 57, 63, 85, 89n.13. *See also* U.S. Agency for International Development (USAID)

International Development Agency (IDA), Mekong Project support from, 59, 175, 183, 200

International Monetary Fund (IMF): Exchange Support Funds and, 183, 195n.162; loans to Cambodia by, 232n.93

International Rice Research Institute, 168

Iran, Mekong Project support from, 67

Irrawaddy River, British colonization of, 21–22

irrigation practices on Mekong River: Cambodian economic development and, 213–215; ethnic group differences and, 8–9, 11–12; Khmer empire and, 14–17; Mekong Committee proposals for, 60; postwar ECAFE proposals, 52–55

Isan ethnic groups, 10, 80–81, 94nn.114, 116

Israel, 130

Italian-Thai Development, 211

J

Japan: Asian Development Bank (ADB) and, 105, 121–122, 142nn.103, 180–181, 185; Colombo Plan support by, 65–66; economic development of Southeast Asia and, 220–221; Mekong Project and, 55, 58–59, 61, 66–67; Nam Ngum Dam project and, 126–127; outer circle Mekong River development and, 216–217; perceived Communist threat to, 76; Prek Thnot project and, 130–132, 134; U.S. Southeast Asian policies and, 71–72, 78, 116

Jasmine International, 211

Jayavarman VII, 14

Jayavarman IX, 15

Jessup, Philip, 72, 74

Jiang Chun-yun, 219

Johns Hopkins University, Johnson's speech at, 105–119, 127–129, 131, 134–135, 140nn.44–45, 157, 159–161

Johnson, Harold K. (General), 105–106

Johnson, Lyndon B. (President): Asian Development Bank and, 119–123, 142n.108; Cambodian hydraulic projects and, 129–138; escalation of Vietnam War under, 98–100, 138n.9; Johns Hopkins University speech by, 105–119, 127–129, 131, 134–135, 140nn.44–45; Johnson Doctrine for Asia, 147–150; Mekong Project and, xv–xvi, 86–87, 97–138, 159–161, 186, 239; Nam Ngum Dam project and, 124–127; "other war" of, 150–153; Pa Mong Falls development project and, 127–129; postwar development proposals for Vietnam by, 39, 154–161, 188n.31; Southeast Asian economic aid proposals by, 107–108, 117–119, 136–138; Tet Offensive and, 158–159; troop increases in Vietnam ordered by, 147; War on Poverty and Vietnam War linked by, 139n.24; and Water for Peace, 188n.38

Johnson Doctrine for Asia, 85, 147–150, 153, 164–165, 186n.2, 191nn.83, 85

Johnston, Eric, 79

Joint Chiefs of Staff Memorandum on Indochina, 75–76, 93n.97

Joint Development Group, 154–155, 189n.45

Joint Economic Commission, 177–178, 194n.141

Jordan River Valley Project, 79, 93n.108, 97

K

Kahin, George McT., 100, 187n.22, 191n.82

Kearns, Doris, 86, 137

Kennedy, John F. (President), 86, 107, 124, 143n.124
Kennedy, Robert F., 87, 154
Khemmarat Falls, 5, 54–55
Khmer empire: hydraulic technology of, xiv, 9, 12–17, 38nn.51, 54; invasions and floods in, 15; Vietnamese relations with, 17–18, 41n.92. *See also* Angkor empire; Cambodia
Khmer Republic, Commodity Import Program, 168. *See also* Cambodia
Khmer Rouge, 201, 214–215, 232n.104
Khone Falls, 5, 54–55, 129–130
Khorat plateau: ethnic groups in, 10–11; Mekong River drainage in, 5–6; separatist movements in, 80–81, 94n.116
Kiang Cheng State (Muong Sing), 27, 43n.133
Kissinger, Henry R., 172, 174–179
Kittikachorn, Thanom (Prime Minister), 160
Komer, Robert W., 150–152, 187n.18
Korean War, 69, 72–74, 143n.125

L
Lagrée, Doudart de, 23, 25–26
Laird, Melvin, 159, 162
Lancang Jiang River, 218–219. *See also* Mekong River
Lansdale, Edward (Major General), 151
Lan Xang kingdom: Ayuthaya kingdom and, 11; dissolution of, 12; water management and control in, 9–10
Lao Dong newspaper, 114
Lao ethnic groups, 8
Lao kingdoms, Vietnamese/Siamese rivalry over, 20, 41n.97
Lao People's Democratic Republic (L.D.P.R.), 184, 199; postwar Mekong Project proposals and, 201–207. *See also* Laos
Laos: Asian Development Bank aid to, 181–186, 195nn.162–163; Cambodian hydraulic projects and, 131, 135; China's relations with, 219–221, 227, 235n.172; Colombo Plan membership

of, 65; concept of nationhood in, 21, 41n.100; Congressional legislation concerning, 162; D.R.V. encroachment in, 113; ECAFE membership for, 50–51, 130; economic development projects in, 210–213, 225; First Indochina War and, 81–82; French colonial ambitions in, 24–27; geography of, 8; Greater Mekong Subregion (GMS), inclusion in, 221; Japanese relations with, 220; Johnson's Southeast Asian policies and, 116–117, 137, 143n.125, 144n.127; Mekong as commercial route for, 31, 33; Mekong Committee membership of, 55; Mekong Project and, xv, 54–55, 60, 68, 87; Mitraphap/Friendship Bridge project and, 216–217, 233n.116; Nam Ngum Dam project and, 124–127; Nixon administration and, 169–172, 178–179; Pa Mong Falls development project and, 127–129; postwar Mekong delta development and, 156, 169, 201–207, 210–213; spread of war into, 147; Thai expansion and, 226; Thai investment in, 209, 212–213; U.S. peacetime policies in, 199–200; water management projects and, 10–12, 35
La Tabula Geographica Imperii Annamitici, 23
Le Duc Tho, 174, 176–178
Le Sangkum periodical, 133
Lévy, Paul, 41n.100
Lilienthal, David, 94n.110, 138n.16, 153–161, 183, 188nn.30–31
Lodge, Henry Cabot, 151, 192n.96
Lokanathan, P. S., 89n.13
Lon Nol (Prime Minister), 177, 195n.164
Lower Mekong Basin: development of, as solution to Vietnam War, 101–106; United States and, 69–78
Low Pa Mong project, 206, 223–224, 229n.38

Luang Prabang: dissolution of Lan Xang and, 12; First Indochina War and, 80; postwar ECAFE irrigation proposals and, 52; Vietnamese/Siamese rivalry over, 20–21; water management and control in, 10

M

Mahathir Mohammed, 225
Malaysia, 220, 225
Malleret, Louis, 16–17
Manila Treaty, 77
Mansfield, Mike (Senator), 133, 176, 190n.80
Manwan Dam, 218
Marshall Plan, 51, 105
McMaster, H. R., 138n.9
McNamara, Robert, 98–100, 138n.4, 158, 175, 184, 200
Mekong Basin Development Cooperation initiative, 220–221
Mekong Committee, 35; Advisory Board, 55–56; Asian Development Bank and, 123, 185–186, 223; Cambodian hydraulic projects and, 129–138, 214–215; D.R.V. exclusion from, 115; Executive Agent Bureau of, 55–56; financial aid policies of, 62–64; formation of, 55–58, 87; General Assembly of, 55; Indicative Basin Plan, 171–172; Johnson administration support for, 118, 123; multilateral approach of, 67; Pa Mong Falls development project and, 128–129, 144n.143; peacetime prospects for, 201–207; postwar Mekong Project proposals and, 155–156, 169; Prek Thnot project and, 131–132; priorities of, 59–60
"Mekong Consultative Committee," 35
Mekong delta: colonial exploitation of, 30–36; ethnic groups in, 17–18; geography of, 5–6; Johnson's development policies for, 108–112; postwar proposals for, 150–161; Vietnamese economic development and, 215–216, 233n.112

Mekong Delta Development Authority, 156
Mekong Delta Development Program, Preliminary Appraisal Report, 155
Mekong delta Mathematical Model, 155, 189n.49
Mekong Mainstream Run-of-River Hydropower: Main Report, 204, 206
Mekong Project, xv–xvi; Asian Development Bank support for, 119–123, 180–186; Cambodia and, 129–138; Colombo Plan support for, 66–69; D.R.V. rejection of, 115; early years of, 58–69; ECAFE negotiations concerning, 51–55; financing for, 62–69; history of, xv–xvi; Johns Hopkins speech by Johnson and, 107–108, 123; Johnson administration and, 86–87, 97–138, 154, 159–161; Johnson Doctrine for Asia and, 148–150; Nixon administration and, 161–186; Paris Peace talks and, 175–176; peacetime prospects for, 201–207; Postwar Reconstruction Program and, 168–179; proposals for 1970s, 167–172; as solution to Vietnam War, 101–106; stages of, 64; U.S. interest in, 58–60, 63–64, 66–69, 78–88. *See also specific sites,* e.g., Nam Ngum Dam project
Mekong River: branches of, 5–6; climatic influences of, 6; early history of, xii–xiv; etymology of, 36n.1; French and British colonialism and, 21–28; future prospects for development of, 237–241; geography of, 3–6, 36n.3, xiii; as military transport route, 151; modern exploitation of, 28–36; postwar ECAFE management projects and, 50–55; pre-colonial history of, 3–21; research resurgence on, 42n.103; territorial disputes concerning, 20–21
Mekong River Commission (MRC), 205–207, 229n.29; Greater Mekong Subregion (GMS) and, 223–227

"Mekong Spirit" of cooperation, 115, 130

Mien Tây (Trans-Bassac), French exploitation of, 29–36

Mitraphap/Friendship Bridge, 216, 233n.116

moats: Cambodian construction of, 13; pre-modern construction of, on Mekong, 7–8

Mon civilization, hydraulic technology of, 39n.62

Mouhot, Henri, 22–23

multilateral aid programs, Nixon Doctrine for Asia and, 163–165, 191n.89

multilateral lending institutions (MLIs), postwar Mekong projects and, 179–186, 194n.149

Mun basin, 11

Muscat, Robert J., 82–83, 92n.91

Mutual Security Program, 66

Myanmar (Burma): Asian Development Bank and, 121–122; China's relations with, 219–221, 227; colonialization by British and French and, 25–27; Greater Mekong Subregion (GMS), inclusion in, 221; Lan Xang kingdom invaded by, 12; Mekong River Commission and, 205–207; Mekong River development and, 216–225; postwar flood control projects and, 52; Thai expansion and, 226; Thai investment in, 209; water management and control practices in, 8, 39n.60

N

Nam Choan project, 209

Nam Ngum Dam project: first phase of, 61, 116, 120, 123–127, 137, 141n.65; Laotian control of, 225, 235n.161; second phase of, 110, 161, 169–172, 192n.105, 203, 210–213

Nam Ngum Development Fund Agreement, 126–127

Nam Pong tributary project, 61, 63, 68, 129, 209–210, 230n.56

Nam Pung tributary project, 61, 129

Nam Theun 2 Electricity Consortium (NTEC), 211

Nam Theun-Hinboum project, 211, 231n.84

Nam Theun-Nakai National Biodiversity Conservation Area (NBCA), 206

Nam Theun project, 176, 207, 211, 224, 231n.84

Nam Tien policy, 18

Narasimhan, C. V., 58, 66, 111

Nation, The, 211–212

National Liberation Front (NLF), 99–100, 112, 114–115, 151

National Security Council (NSC): Johnson's Vietnam policies and, 103, 105–106; Southeast Asian policies and, 70–72, 76, 84–88

Navigation projects: Chinese, on Mekong River, 219–221; Mekong Committee proposals for, 61

Netherlands: Asian Development Bank (ADB) and, 181, 185; Nam Ngum Dam project and, 126; Prek Thnot project support, 134

Neutralism, Johnson's opposition to, 100–101

New York Times, 109–110

New Zealand: Asian Development Bank and, 184; Colombo Plan support from, 65–66; Mekong Project support from, 58, 61, 66; Nam Ngum Dam project and, 126; U.S. security agreements with, 72

Ngo Dinh Diem, 77

Nguyen Anh. *See* Gia-long

Nguyen Cao Ky (Vice-Marshal), 147, 151–152, 187n.22

Nguyen Duy Trinh, 175

Nguyen dynasty, Vietnam and, 17–20, 40n.83, 41n.85

Nguyen Van Thieu, 147

Nhan Dan newspaper, 113–114

Nippon Electric, Mekong Committee and, 57

Nixon, Richard M. (President): Mekong Project and, xv–xvi, 161–186; multilateral lending institutions (MLIs) and, 180–186; Paris Peace Agreement and, 174–179, 194n.133; postwar reconstruction and Mekong Project and, 172–179; Southeast Asian policies of, 163–165, 190n.80, 192n.96; Vietnamization policy of, 159
Nixon Doctrine for Asia, 85, 90, 162–165, 180–186, 190n.80, 191nn.85, 87
nongovernmental organizations (NGOs): Greater Mekong Subregion (GMS) and, 223–224; hydroelectric dam construction and, 209–210, 230n.55; Mekong Committee and, 56–57; Mekong River Commission and, 229n.29
Nordic countries, involvement by, in Thai development projects, 211–212, 231n.80
Nordic Hydropower, 211
North Vietnam. See Democratic Republic of Vietnam (D.R.V.)
Norwegian Agency for Development Cooperation (NORAD), 212

O
Oc-Eo civilization, 16–17
Operation Rice Bowl, 150
Operation Rolling Thunder, 99
Ortiz-Tinoco, Cesar, 86

P
Pacification concept, Vietnam War and, 150–151, 187n.18
Pakistan, 52, 134; Mekong Project support from, 67–68
Pak Mool Dam, 208–209, 230n.55
Pa Mong Falls development, 54–55, 59–60, 64, 67, 223–224; Indicative Basin Plan and, 202–204, 228n.24; Johnson's proposals for, 104–105, 118, 137, 155, 161; Mekong Project development of, 127–129; Nixon administration and, 169–172, 176, 192n.107
Pantulu, V. R., 213–214

Paris Convention, 35
Paris Peace Agreement, 172, 174–179, 183, 185, 193n.132, 194n.133
Pathet Lao movement, 81–82, 100, 124, 144n.127; Nixon administration and, 170–172
Pavie, Auguste, 26–26, 43n.129
"Peace Offensive" of the United States, 117
Pearson, Lester (Prime Minister), 99–100, 150
Pentagon Papers, 109
People's Army of Vietnam (PAVN), 151
People's Republic of China (P.R.C.): founding of, 69; influence over D.R.V., 112, 115; Johnson administration Southeast Asian policies and, 98–100, 107–108, 112–113, 140n.52; Thailand's separatist movements and, 81–82. See also China
Peterson, Rudolph A., 162
Peterson Report, 162–163
Pham Van Dong (Prime Minister), 114–115, 141n.84, 176–177, 179, 193n.122
Phan Huy Quat, 116
Philip, Nicholas W., 183
Philippines: Asian Development Bank aid to, 183; Japanese relations with, 220; Mekong Project support from, 67–68; Prek Thnot project support from, 134; U.S. Southeast Asian policies and, 71–72, 149, 182
Phnom Penh, Mekong as commercial route for, 31, 33
Plain of Reeds: Mekong River geography and, 5; postwar Mekong delta development and, 156–157
Poats, Rutherford, 103
Point IV Program, 72, 92n.78
Porter, William J., 174, 193n.132
Position of the United States with Respect to Asia, The, 70

POW-MIA problem, 174–175, 178–179,
    193n.122
Prea Cheychesda, 17, 40n.83
Preah Vihar temple, 131, 145n.153
Prek-Thnot project, 61, 64, 130–135,
    186, 214–215
Presidential Fund for Asian Economic
    Development, 140n.49
Price Waterhouse, Mekong Project sup-
    port from, 59
private sector, Mekong regional devel-
    opment and, 221
*Program of Studies and Investigations
    for Comprehensive Development
    Lower Mekong Basin* (Wheeler Re-
    port), 57
Provisional Mekong Committee, 35
Provisional Revolutionary Government
    (P.R.G.), 177

Q

Quadripartite Meeting on Transport
    Linkages, 217

R

Radio Liberation, 114
Radio Moscow, 113
Rainfall, Mekong River and, 6–7
Reagan, Ronald (President), Southeast
    Asian policies of, 199
*Reconnaissance Report—Lower Mekong
    Basin,* 85
Red River, 17, 26, 142n.91
regionalism: Johnson Doctrine for Asia
    and, 149–150; in Johnson's Vietnam
    policies, 108–110, 140n.45; Mekong
    River development and, 49–55; Nixon
    Doctrine for Asia and, 162–186; U.S.
    interest in Mekong Project and, 78–
    88, 134–135
Regional Technical Conference on Flood
    Control, 52
Republic of Vietnam (R.V.N.): Asian
    Development Bank aid to, 181–186,
    195n.163; blockade of Mekong by,
    95n.125; Cambodian hydraulic proj-
    ects and, 131, 135; Colombo Plan

membership of, 65; Commodity Im-
    port Program and, 168; flood control
    projects in, 53; Johnson administra-
    tion policies toward, 98, 100, 115–
    119, 137, 150–153, 187n.18;
    Mekong Committee membership of,
    55, 130; Mekong Project and, 58, 68;
    Nam Ngum Dam project and, 126;
    Nixon administration and, 169–172;
    postwar development projects for,
    153–161
reservoirs, Khmer construction of, 12–
    17
Resources for the Future, Inc.: Mekong
    Committee and, 57; Mekong Project
    support from, 59
rice cultivation, postwar Mekong Project
    proposals for, 168, 215–216
Rockefeller Report, 72
Rogers, William P. (Secretary of State),
    174–175, 178, 183–184
Roosevelt, Franklin D. (President), 75
Rostow, Walt W., 103, 132–133,
    140n.45, 153, 186n.2
Rotter, Andrew J., 91n.62
Royal Lao Government (R.L.G.): Com-
    modity Import Program and, 168;
    Nixon administration and, 171–172;
    U.S. support of, 100, 124–125,
    144n.127
rural development proposals for Me-
    kong delta, 150–151
Rusk, Dean (Secretary of State), 100,
    106, 119, 135, 148–149, 186n.2,
    188n.38

S

Sai-gonese Navigation and Transporta-
    tion Company, 33
Sambor Falls, 5, 55, 60; Mekong Project
    dam proposal and, 129–130, 161,
    214–215
Sarit Thanarat, 87
Satha (King), 16
Satingpra, hydraulic technology of,
    39n.62
Sat Lao concept, 41n.100

Sato Eisaku (Prime Minister), 116, 119
Savang Vatthana, 171
Schaaf, C. Hart, 56, 123
Schlesinger, Arthur, Jr., 154
Schultz, George P., 180
Second Indochina War, 80, 199, 223;
    Kennedy's Southeast Asian policies
    and, 124, 143n.124; Mekong Project
    and, xv–xvi, 186, 189n.53; Nixon ad-
    ministration and, 169
Second Mekong Committee, 35
Second Nam Ngum Development Fund,
    170, 192n.105
Shell Oil: Mekong Committee and, 57;
    Mekong Project support from, 59
Shimla Conference, 77–78, 93n.104
shrimp farming, environmental impact of,
    233n.112
Siam: emergence of, 12, 38n.48; French
    relations with, 24–28, 33; Indochina
    and, 34–35; Mekong territory domi-
    nance and, 20–21, 41n.97. See also
    Thailand
Sihanouk, Norodom, 53, 129, 131, 133,
    147
Sipson Chu Tai region, 27, 43n.129
slash-and-burn cultivation, in early irri-
    gation societies, 8
Smith, Roger M., 131, 135
Snowy Mountains Hydro-Electric
    Authority, 60
Socialist Republic of Vietnam (S.R.V.),
    179, 186, 199–200; postwar Mekong
    Project proposals and, 201–207. See
    also Vietnam
Société Nationale des Grands Barrages du
    Cambodge, 134
socioeconomic concerns, economic
    growth in Southeast Asia and, 213,
    220
SOGREAH firm, 208
Souligna Vongsa, 9, 20
Southeast Asia, postwar political up-
    heaval in, 69–78, 91n.62
"Southeast Asia Development Associa-
    tion" concept, 103
Southeast Asia Development Fund, 122

Southeast Asian Development Associa-
    tion (SEADA), 103–104
Southeast Asian Ministers of Education
    Council, 149
Southeast Asia Nuclear Weapon-Free
    Zone Treaty, 221
Southeast Asia Treaty Organization
    (SEATO), 53, 76–77, 109, 116, 150
South Korea, 149, 220–221
South Vietnam. See Republic of Viet-
    nam (R.V.N.)
South Vietnamese Liberation Front,
    116. See also National Liberation
    Front (NLF)
Souvanna Phouma (Prince), 87, 116
Soviet Union: Asian Development Bank
    and, 121; Cambodian economic aid
    from, 129; D.R.V. supported by,
    112–113, 141n.78; Laos aided by,
    210; Mekong Project support from,
    58; U.S. Southeast Asian policies
    and, 70–71, 98–99, 107–108, 115,
    200, 228n.8
Special Fund Resources (SRF),
    195n.152
Special Programs for Technical and
    Economic Aid, 73–75
Spratly Islands dispute, 221, 240
Stargardt, Janice, 8, 37n.19, 39n.62
State Department (U.S.), Southeast
    Asian policies and, 70
State of Vietnam (S.O.V.), founding and
    recognition of, 50–51
Stevenson, Adlai, 111
Stung Treng project, 130, 155, 161, 215
subregional cooperation, Mekong River
    development and, 216–221
Subregional Economic Co-operation
    Conference, 217
Subregional Electric Power Forum, 217
Subregional Transport Forum, 217
Suharto (President), 182
Sukhotai kingdom, 10–11
Sun Yat-sen, 79
Supporting Assistance Funds, 169–170
sustained reprisal strategy of U.S. in
    Vietnam, 99–100

Swedish International Development
     Authority, 216, 224
Szulc, Tad, 178

T

Taberd, Monsignor, 23
Tai ethnic groups, water management
     practices of, 8–9
Tai-Lao ethnic groups, differences in, 8–
     9, 37n.26
Taiwan, Mekong Project support from,
     67–68
Takeushi Ryuji, 135
Task Force on Economic and Social De-
     velopment for Southeast Asia, 117–
     118
Task Force on International Develop-
     ment, 162
Taylor, Keith W., 41n.85
Tay-son rebels, 18
Technical Assistance Administration
     (TAA) (UN), 52–55, 58–59
Teheran Conference, 75
Tennessee Valley Authority (TVA): Me-
     kong Project compared with, xvi, 78–
     80, 86–87, 93n.107, 94n.110, 104,
     239; as postwar Mekong water man-
     agement model, 52–53, 153
Tet Offensive, 154–155, 158, 185
Thai Communist Party, 208, 230n.47
Thailand: Asian Development Bank and,
     182–183, 185, 195n.163; Cambodia
     and, 131, 135, 145n.153; China's re-
     lations with, 219–221; Chinese mi-
     nority in, 81, 95n.118; Colombo Plan
     membership by, 65; Communist in-
     surgency in, 147; Congressional leg-
     islation concerning, 162; economic
     development projects in Mekong Ba-
     sin in, 207–210, 231n.66; geopolitics
     in, 226; Greater Mekong Subregion
     (GMS), inclusion in, 221; Japanese
     relations with, 220; Johnson's South-
     east Asian policies and, 116–117,
     124, 137, 149; Kanchanaburi prov-
     ince in, 209; Mekong Committee
     membership of, 55, 130; Mekong

Project and, xv, 58, 60; Mekong
     River Commission and, 35, 205–
     207, 229n.29; Mitraphap/Friendship
     Bridge project and, 216–217; Nam
     Ngum Dam project and, 126–127;
     Nixon administration and, 169–172,
     178–179; Pa Mong Falls develop-
     ment project and, 127–129; postwar
     Mekong delta development and,
     156, 167, 201–207; separatist
     movements in, 80–83; socioeco-
     nomic costs of development in, 213.
     See also Siam
Third Indochina War: greater Mekong
     region and, 226; Mekong Project
     and, xvi, 239; outbreak of, 199
Thoai Ha canal, establishment of, 19–
     20
Thoai Ngoc Hau, 19
Thompson, Robert (Sir), 150
Three Gorges Dam project, 94n.112,
     217–218
Thuc-Lilienthal plan, 157. *See also*
     Lilienthal, David; Vu Quoc Thuc
Thung Yai Naresuan Wildlife Sanc-
     tuary, 209
Tibet Autonomous Region (TAR),
     234n.134
"Tonkin Affair," 26
Tonle Sap: Angkor site at, 15–16; Chi-
     nese hydroelectric projects, impact
     on, 218–219; environmental exploi-
     tation of, 213, 216; Greater Mekong
     Subregion projects and, 224; Indica-
     tive Basin Plan and, 172; Mekong
     Project and, 54–55, 60, 129–30, 161,
     214–215; Mekong River geography
     and, 5
Tour du Monde, 23, 43n.121
trade embargoes in Southeast Asia, 200,
     228n.9
Transfield Corp. of Australia, 211
transportation links: Greater Mekong
     Subregion (GMS) projects, 221–227;
     outer circle Mekong River projects,
     217–221
Tran Van Do, 116

Trinh dynasty, 17–18
Truman, Harry S (President), 70–74, 191n.82

U

Udhayatiya-Varman II, 14
Udong kingdom, 17
Udorn Thani air bases, 171, 193n.112
Unger, Leonard, 117
Union Indochinoise, Mekong River and, xiv
United Kingdom. *See* Great Britain
United Nations: Johnson's Southeast Asian policies and, 109, 118–119; Mekong Committee and, 55–58; Mekong Project support from, 58, 79; Mekong River policies and, 49, 238–241; Nam Ngum Dam project and, 126; postwar Mekong Project proposals by, 52–55, 202–207
United Nations Development Program (UNDP), 167, 185, 196n.175, 225
United Nations Economic and Social Council (ECOSOC), postwar regional construction policies of, 49–50
United Nations Security Council, First Indochina War and, 82
United Nations Special Fund, Mekong Project support from, 59, 61, 126
United States: Cambodian hydraulic projects and, 130–138; Colombo Plan support from, 65–66; economic aid programs to Southeast Asia, 72–78, 83–88; economic aid to Laos, 230n.42; economic aid to Thailand, 82–83, 95n.126; First Indochina War and, 82–83; Greater Mekong Subregion (GMS) and, 223–227; Lower Mekong Basin and, 69–78; Mekong Project support from, 58–60, 63–64, 66–69, 78–88, 167–172; Mekong River and, xv, 238–241; Nam Ngum Dam project and, 125–127; Pa Mong Falls development project and, 127–129; postwar ECAFE water management projects and, 51–55, 88nn.11–12, 89n.13; postwar Mekong Project aid, 202–207; Southeast Asian policy and Mekong project, 97–138, 200
U.S. Agency for International Development (USAID): Indochina Postwar Reconstruction Program, 184; Johnson administration and, 117, 125–128, 137, 154, 156, 159–161, 164; Mekong River development and, 63, 83, 103–104; and Nixon administration's Mekong Project proposals, 167–172, 179–180
U.S. Operations Mission (USOM), 85
U Nyun, 86, 103, 125
Usher, Ann Danaiya, 211
U Thant (UN Secretary-General), 100, 103, 105; Cambodian hydraulic projects and, 133–134; Johnson and, 109–112, 118; Mekong Project and, 123; Nam Ngum Dam project and, 123–125

V

Valenti, Jack, 104
Van DeMark Brian, 138n.9, 140n.52
Vang Pao (General), 124
Van Liere, W. J., 11, 13, 37n.56
van Wuysthoff, Gerrit, 22
Vientiane: dissolution of Lan Xang and, 12; postwar ECAFE irrigation proposals and, 52; Vietnamese/Siamese rivalry over, 20
Vientiane Plain farm project, 63
Viet Cong, Cambodia's use of, 133, 145n.164
Viet Minh: First Indochina War and, 80–82; U.S. Southeast Asian policies and, 76–77
Vietnam: Cambodian relations with, 226; ECAFE membership negotiations with, 50; economic development projects in, 215–216; Greater Mekong Subregion (GMS), inclusion in, 221, 224–227; Japanese relations with, 220; Mekong delta and, xiv; Mekong Project and, xv, 60–61; Mekong water management and

control in, 17–20, 35; Shimla Conference and, 78; Siamese rivalry with,
20–21; U.S. Southeast Asian policy
and, 76–78. *See also* Democratic Republic of Vietnam (D.R.V.); Republic
of Vietnam (R.V.N.); Socialist Republic of Vietnam (S.R.V.)
"Vietnamization" of Vietnam War, 159–
161
Vietnam National Mekong Committee,
216, 233n.115
"Vietnam syndrome" in.U.S. foreign
policy, 238–241
Vietnam War: Asian Development Bank
and, 120; Johnson's Mekong policies
and, 98–138; Mekong delta development and, 157–161; neutralization
policy considered, 100–101; pacification campaigns escalation of, 150–
153, 187n.18; publicity campaigns surrounding, 158, 190n.62; "Vietnamization" of, 159–161
Vinh-te canal, establishment of, 19–20
Voyage d'exploration en Indochine,
42n.121
Vu quoc Thuc, 153, 155, 188n.30

W

Wachirawut, King, 95n.118
Watanabe Takeshi, 159
Water for Peace Program, 186, 188n.38
water management and control: ECAFE
negotiations concerning, 51–55; future prospects for, 240–241; Greater
Mekong Subregion (GMS) and, 223–
227; Indicative Basin Plan proposals
for, 202–207; Mekong River history
and, 7–20; modern colonial exploitation and, 28–36; as political issue,
xiii; postwar Mekong delta proposals
for, 155–161, 189n.53
West Germany, 121; Prek Thnot project
support from, 132, 134
Westmoreland, William C. (General), 99,
158

Wheeler, Earl G. (General), 99, 158
Wheeler, Raymond A. (Lieutenant-
General), 57–58, 89n.28
White, Gilbert F., 61, 101–102
White, John, 19
Williams, Maurice J., 177–178
Wilson, Harold (British prime minister),
111–112, 150
World Bank: Asian Development Bank
(ADB) and, 119, 121–122, 183–186;
BOT (build, operate, transfer) proj-
ects and, 224–225; environmental is-
sues and Southeast Asian develop-
ment and, 211, 224–225; McNamara
as president of, 158; Mekong Project
support from, 59, 116, 167–168,
175–176, 200; multilateral lending
institutions (MLIs) and, 180; Nam
Ngum Dam project and, 126–127,
170; postwar Mekong water management projects and, 88n.11, 238–
241; Prek Thnot project and, 134;
Thailand's hydroelectric projects
and, 209–210
World Health Organization (WHO),
Mekong Project research supported
by, 61
World Meteorological Organization
(WMO), Mekong Project support
from, 59
Wyatt, David K., 20

X

Xeset Dam, 210–211, 225
Xieng Khouang, 20; dissolution of Lan
Xang and, 12

Y

Yaçovarman I, 13
Yangzi River, development proposals
for, 79, 94n.112, 217–218
Young, Kenneth T., 102
Yugoslavia, 121, 129
Yunnan Institute of Southeast Asian
Studies, 219–220

About the Author

NGUYEN THI DIEU is Associate Professor of History at Temple University. An expert in Southeast Asian history, she has published in the *Journal of World History*, *Études Indochinoises*, and *Afrique-Asie*.

ISBN 0-275-96137-0

90000>

EAN

9 780275 961374

HARDCOVER BAR CODE